The Courtiers

by the same author

CAVALIER

The Courtiers

*Splendor and Intrigue
in the Georgian Court
at Kensington Palace*

Lucy Worsley

Walker & Co.
New York

Library of Congress Cataloging-in-Publication Data has been applied for.

ISBN: 978-0-8027-1987-4 (hardcover)

First published in Great Britain by Faber and Faber Limited in 2010 as *Courtiers*
First published in the United States by Walker & Company in 2010

1 3 5 7 9 10 8 6 4 2

Typeset by Faber and Faber Limited
Printed in the United States of America by Worldcolor Fairfield

'Those who have a curiosity to see courts and courtiers dissected must bear with the dirt they find.'[1]
JOHN HERVEY

Contents

Illustrations

George II and Queen Caroline.

Frederick, Prince of Wales and his sisters.

William Hogarth's painting of a theatrical performance, with
Lady Deloraine in the audience.

John Hervey, holding his ceremonial purse of office as Lord
Privy Seal.

John Hervey's letter book, with certain pages mysteriously
missing.

The iron collar worn by Peter the Wild Boy.

Queen Caroline.

Henrietta Howard at the age of thirty-five.

George II in old age.

TEXT ILLUSTRATIONS

Map

Hanover was one of many small German states. Its ruler, or Elector,
helped 'elect' the states' overlord, the Holy Roman Emperor

Family Trees

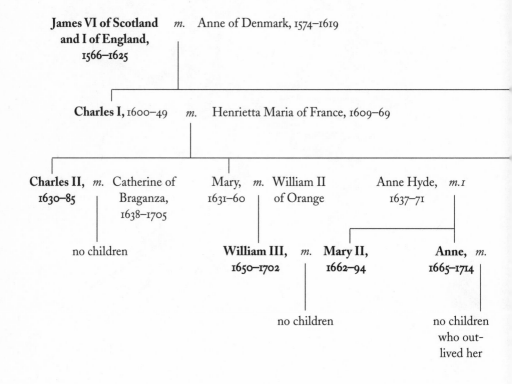

James VI of Scotland and I of England, 1566–1625 *m.* Anne of Denmark, 1574–1619

Charles I, 1600–49 *m.* Henrietta Maria of France, 1609–69

Charles II, 1630–85 *m.* Catherine of Braganza, 1638–1705

Mary, 1631–60 *m.* William II of Orange

Anne Hyde, 1637–71 *m.1*

no children

William III, 1650–1702 *m.* **Mary II,** 1662–94

Anne, *m.* 1665–1714

no children

no children who out-lived her

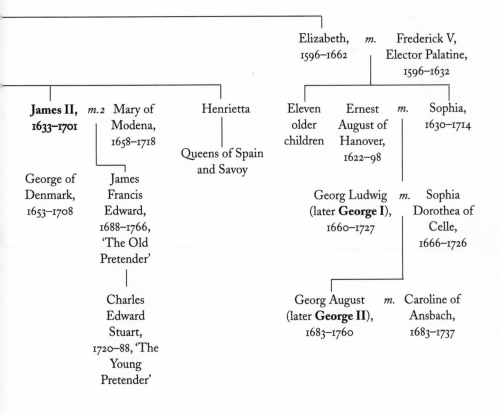

Elizabeth,   *m.*   Frederick V,
1596–1662   Elector Palatine,
                     1596–1632

James II, *m.2* Mary of   Henrietta   Eleven   Ernest   *m.*   Sophia,
1633–1701   Modena,   older   August of   1630–1714
                    1658–1718   children   Hanover,
                                    Queens of Spain   1622–98
George of   James   and Savoy
Denmark,   Francis   Georg Ludwig   *m.*   Sophia
1653–1708   Edward,   (later **George I**),   Dorothea of
               1688–1766,   1660–1727   Celle,
               'The Old   1666–1726
               Pretender'
                                                     Georg August   *m.* Caroline of
Charles   (later **George II**),   Ansbach,
Edward   1683–1760   1683–1737
Stuart,
1720–88, 'The
Young
Pretender'

THE HANOVERIANS

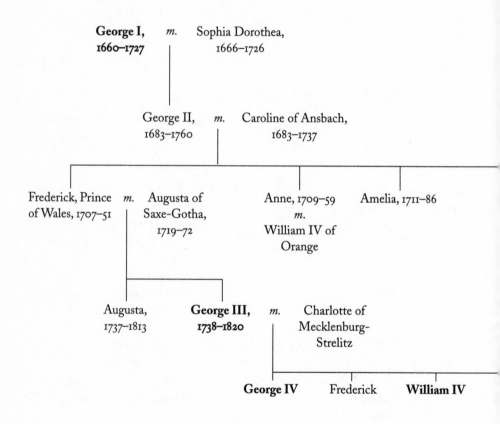

George I, *m.* Sophia Dorothea,
1660–1727   1666–1726

George II, *m.* Caroline of Ansbach,
1683–1760   1683–1737

Frederick, Prince *m.* Augusta of   Anne, 1709–59   Amelia, 1711–86
of Wales, 1707–51   Saxe-Gotha,   *m.*
                         1719–72   William IV of
                                            Orange

Augusta,   George III, *m.* Charlotte of
1737–1813   1738–1820   Mecklenburg-
                                      Strelitz

George IV   Frederick   William IV

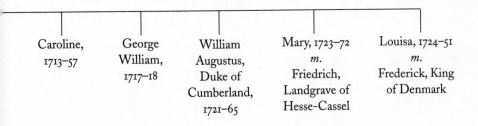

| Caroline, 1713–57 | George William, 1717–18 | William Augustus, Duke of Cumberland, 1721–65 | Mary, 1723–72 *m.* Friedrich, Landgrave of Hesse-Cassel | Louisa, 1724–51 *m.* Frederick, King of Denmark |

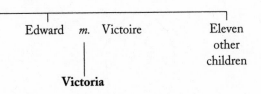

Edward   *m.*   Victoire   Eleven other children

Victoria

Cast List

George I, the king

George Augustus, the Prince of Wales

Caroline, the Princess of Wales

Frederick, the foolish heir to the throne

Amelia, a prickly princess

Molly Lepell, a Maid of Honour

CAST LIST

Henrietta Howard, a Woman
of the Bedchamber

John Hervey, the Vice-Chamberlain

Peter the Wild Boy, a court pet

William Kent, a pushy painter

Elizabeth Butler, an actress,
Kent's mistress

Mohammed True-to-the-King,
keeper of the king's closet

Mustapha, a Turkish valet

Dr Arbuthnot, a physician and satirist

John Gay, a penniless poet

Ulrich Jorry, a dwarf entertainer
from Poland

Preface

'I will send you a general map of Courts; a
region yet unexplored . . . all the paths are
slippery, and every slip is dangerous.'
(Lord Chesterfield, 1749)

The Great Drawing Room, crammed full of courtiers, lay at the heart of the Georgian royal palace. Here the king mingled most evenings with his guests, signalling welcome with a nod and displeasure with a blank stare or, worse, a turned back.

The winners and the losers of the Georgian age could calculate precisely how high they'd climbed – or how far they'd fallen – by the warmth of their reception at court. High-heeled and elegant shoes crushed into the floorboards of the drawing room the reputations of those who'd dropped out of favour, while those whose status was on the rise stood firmly in possession of their few square inches of space.

In the eighteenth century, the palace's most elegant assembly room was in fact a bloody battlefield. This was a world of skulduggery, politicking, wigs and beauty spots, where fans whistled open like flick knives. Intrigue hissed through the crowd, and court factions were also known as 'fuctions'.[2]

Beneath their powder and perfume, the courtiers stank of sweat, insecurity and glittering ambition.

The ambitious visitors crowding into the drawing room were usually unaware that they were under constant observation from behind the scenes. The palace servants – overlooked but ever-present – knew of every move made at court. That's why, in this book, we'll meet kings and queens, but also many of the people who worked to meet their most intimate needs.

The Georgian royal household was staggeringly vast and complicated. The highest ranking of its members, the courtiers proper, were the ladies- and gentlemen-in-waiting. These noblemen and women were glad to serve the king and queen in even quite menial ways because of the honour involved.

Beneath them in status were about 950 other royal servants, organised into a byzantine web of departments ranging from hairdressing to rat-catching, and extending right down to the four 'necessary women' who cleaned the palace and emptied the 'necessaries' or chamber pots.[3]

If you want to know what these people looked like, you need only visit Kensington Palace. There, in the 1720s, the artist William Kent painted portraits of forty-five royal servants that look down upon palace visitors from the walls and ceiling of the King's Grand Staircase.

Kensington Palace itself had existed long before the Hanoverian dynasty arrived in Britain to replace the Stuarts in 1714, yet it was also the one royal home that George I and his son really transformed and made their own. The servants there witnessed romance and violence, intrigue and infighting, and almost unimaginable acts of hatred and cruelty between members of the same family.

I often find myself climbing the King's Grand Staircase during the course of my working day, and the faces of the people populating it have always fascinated me. I've spent many hours studying them, wondering who they all were, and curiosity finally compelled me to try to find out.

When I first began investigating their identities, I was surprised to discover that some of the names traditionally attached to the characters were wrong, while other obvious connections had been overlooked. My efforts to unearth each sitter's true story led me on a much longer and more exciting journey than I'd expected, through caches of court papers in London, Windsor, Oxford and Suffolk. I found myself examining paintings at Buckingham Palace, gardens in Germany, and hitching lifts from kind strangers in rural Hertfordshire. My adventures both in and outside the archives led eventually to this book.

Those picked to sit for the staircase paintings were the most appealing, exotic and memorable among the lower servants. Some of them possessed something rarer than rubies: the influence that came with access to the royal ear. Their colleagues included some of the oddest characters of the Georgian age: a dwarf comedian; a feral boy; a rapacious royal mistress; a mysterious turbaned Turk; bored if beautiful Maids of Honour. I've selected the stories of just seven of them to illuminate the strange phenomenon of the Georgian court and to give a new perspective upon the lives of the kings, queens and princes inhabiting the rarefied court stratosphere above their heads.

While the monarchy was slowly sinking in status throughout the eighteenth century, the glamour of the court still attracted the pretty, the witty, the pushy and the powerful.

But although Kensington Palace teemed with ambitious and clever people in search of fame and fashion, it was also a lonely place, and courtiers and servants alike often found themselves weary and heart-sore. Success in their world demanded a level head and a cold heart; secrets were never safe. A courtier had to keep up appearances in the face of gambling debts, loss of office or even unwanted pregnancy.

Thousands longed to be part of the court, but John Hervey, one of our seven, knew all too well that danger lay hidden behind the palace walls.

'I do not know any people in the world', he wrote to a courtier colleague, 'so much to be pitied as that gay young company with which you and I stand every day in the drawing-room.'[4]

ONE

To the Palace

'Really, it must be confessed that a court is a fine thing.
It is the cause of so much show and splendour that
people are kept gay and spirited.'
(James Boswell, 1763)

Prince George Augustus had bulging, bright-blue eyes

On 25 April 1720, a special sense of anticipation was building in the fashionable parts of London. The party planned at St James's Palace that night was the most hotly anticipated court occasion for many years.

Nowhere was the excitement greater than in the rambling old mansion called Leicester House. This building, dominating the north side of Leicester Fields, was the home of the king's son and daughter-in-law, the Prince and Princess of Wales, George Augustus (1683–1760) and Caroline (1683–1737). While the prince and princess were losing their looks and fast approaching middle age, they remained a jovial, lively and friendly couple.

Tonight's entertainment, though, would sorely strain their good spirits. They were going to have to pay a reluctant visit to the court of King George I (1660–1727).

The late afternoon saw Prince George Augustus berating a clumsy servant as he struggled into an outfit of peacock splendour. He aimed to be 'always richly dressed, being fond of fine clothes'.[2]

Bad-tempered, full of bluster, fond of music and of fighting, this prince would become best known as George II, the last British king to lead troops in person upon the battlefield. He struts through Britain's history books like a kind of tin-pot dictator: brusque, pompous and a little bit ludicrous. Despite his tantrums, though, he deserves at least a pinch of sympathy. Like all courtiers, he spent his days performing a part upon a stage.

Unfortunately, for a man of his gaudy tastes, he was considerably shorter than average.[3] He had bulging china-blue eyes and his prominent nose was rather Roman.[4] He also had an imperious temper: 'vehement, and irritable', 'hot, passionate, haughty'.[5] But his anger could cool as quickly as it came. He had the great redeeming feature of being passionately in love with his wife, the fat, funny and adorable Princess Caroline. He would rely upon her for the strength and steadiness to face the difficult evening that lay ahead.

She, meanwhile, was growing flustered as the Women of her Bedchamber tried to lace up her stiff stays.

Plump, yet pin-sharp, Princess Caroline had a sweet smile, and blossomed into beauty when her face and mouth were in motion. Wilhelmine Karoline of Ansbach, as she was born, had been celebrated in her youth as the 'most agreeable Princess in Germany'.[6] Her arms were admired for their 'whiteness and elegance'; she had 'a penetrating eye' and an 'expressive countenance'. Princess Caroline could split sides with her amusing impressions, loved a quick-fire duel of wit and spoke English 'uncommonly well for one born outside England'.[7] Friend of the philosophers Gottfried Leibniz and Isaac Newton, she would in due course become the cleverest queen consort ever to sit upon the throne of England.

Princess Caroline: fat, funny and adorable

With her greater intellectual skills, humour and sense of style, Princess Caroline would have made a far more successful heir to the crown than her husband, but the odds for opportunity were always stacked against eighteenth-century women. Caroline kept her husband subtly but firmly under her thumb, and always contrived 'that her opinion should appear as if it had been his own'.[8]

In spite of Princess Caroline's infectious laughter and her cleverness, and despite Prince George Augustus's visibly lavish love for his wife, he inflicted a regular humiliation upon her: he was carrying on an affair with one of Caroline's servants, and future conflict was inevitable.

At the time of his birth in 1683, the possibility that George Augustus would become Prince of Wales had seemed almost preposterously small. Both he and Caroline came from dinky little principalities that now form part of modern Germany. They'd only immigrated to Britain in 1714, when George Augustus's father, later King George I, had unexpectedly inherited the British throne because of the accidental failure of the Stuart line of monarchs.

Britain's previous queen, Anne, had endured seventeen

pregnancies in a desperate but ultimately futile attempt to squeeze out an heir. Her failure to produce a healthy child brought the Stuart line to a stuttering stop, with the exception of her Catholic half-brother. Anne's elder sister, Mary, had deposed their father James II in 1688 because of his despotic and Catholic regime. This was the so-called 'Glorious Revolution'.

The choice faced at Anne's death, then, was either to recall James II's Catholic offspring or to look back up the trunk of the Stuart family tree to identify a Protestant branch.

The Act of Settlement of 1701 tidied up the problem. It specified that the small, Protestant house of Hanover should provide Anne's successors. This was to be at the expense of the exclusion of fifty nearer relatives, who were regrettably but unacceptably Catholic.

Upon Anne's death in 1714, the Hanoverian succession unfold - ed surprisingly smoothly, and the small, provincial court of Hanover crossed the Channel to London. The Electoral Prince, Georg Ludwig of Hanover, became King George I of Great Britain, while his son and daughter-in-law became Prince and Princess of Wales.

But the great transformation in their fortunes in 1714 was the beginning, not the end, of this family's troubles.

All across London, the Prince and Princess of Wales's courtiers and supporters were likewise preening and squeezing themselves into their court clothes. As the sun sank, each of the ladies was reaching the end of a toilette that had taken two hours or more. 'Lud! Will you never have done fumbling?' grumbled many a modern lady to her maid.[9]

Once her figure had been transformed into the right shape by tight stays and a hooped petticoat, a female courtier was required to put on her court uniform. The 'mantua', as it was known, was an archaic, uncomfortable but supremely elegant form of dress. Pale forearms descended from wing-cuff sleeves with the requisite three rows of ruffles ('I am so incommoded with these nasty ruffles!'[10]). Long trains spilt at the back from tightly seamed waists. The mantua's skirts were spread out sideways over immensely wide hoops, too broad to pass through a door. 'Have you got the whalebone petticoats among you yet?' Jonathan Swift wrote from court. 'A woman here may hide a moderate gallant under them.'[11]

Any female courtier would be altogether unrecognisable without her warpaint, 'pale, dead, old and yellow'.[12] So maids were busily painting their mistresses with 'rosy cheeks, snowy foreheads and bosoms, jet eyebrows and scarlet lips', and puffing powder over piled coiffures. Once trussed up and coloured, the female courtiers resembled the beauties in Mrs Salmon's famous London gallery of waxworks, and had carefully to avoid the fire for fear 'of melting'.[13]

Meanwhile, the male courtiers were donning coat, waistcoat and breeches encrusted with embroidery. Their shoe buckles were jewelled, and each would rest a hand upon the hilt of a sword. On their heads, the itchy and sweaty full-bottomed periwig was still in fashion. Between each gentleman's left elbow and his side was clenched his *chapeau-bras*: a flat, unwearable parody of a hat, for the head was never covered in the presence of the king.

'Dress is a very foolish thing,' declared the arch-courtier Lord Chesterfield, and yet, at the same time, 'it is a very foolish thing for a man not to be well dressed'.[14]

Two junior members of Princess Caroline's household at Leicester Fields were preparing with particular care, because they and their colleagues would be the subject of intense and critical scrutiny on this special evening.

Mrs Henrietta Howard was one of the six Women of Princess Caroline's Bedchamber. The Princess's most senior servants were the Ladies of the Bedchamber, peeresses one and all. The Women of the Bedchamber, slightly lower down the social scale but still well-born, did the real work of dressing and undressing, watching and waiting. But Henrietta had both an official and an unofficial job. As well as being Princess Caroline's servant, she was also the

Henrietta Howard. She had a 'romantick turn of mind', an
'air of sadness' – and an alcoholic bully for a husband

recognised mistress of Caroline's husband. Neither role brought
her much pleasure.

Now in her thirty-first year, Henrietta was not an astounding
beauty. Yet her build was slim, she had 'the finest light brown hair'
and she was 'always well dressed with taste and simplicity'.[15] (This
'beautiful head of hair' had played a small but significant role in
her life story so far.[16]) Unlike many royal mistresses, she had not
exploited her position to amass influence and riches. She was of a
'romantick turn of mind', thoughtful, gentle, but 'close as a cork'd
bottle'.[17] Her friend, the poet Alexander Pope, accused her of 'not
loving herself so well as she does her friends', and he also
described a grievous 'air of sadness about her'.[18]

No wonder, for her life had been difficult. She was now living
apart from her brutal, heavy-drinking husband. Orphaned at a
young age and looking for security, marriage had looked like a safe
option. But marrying Charles Howard had turned out to be a terrible mistake.

And she had very little hold on the affections of the other problematic partner in her life, her royal lover. Prince George Augustus

rather reluctantly felt that it would be beneath his princely dignity to remain faithful to his wife, and he had a mistress only out of a sense that he ought to. So he was often cruel and abrupt with Henrietta.

She, too, was dreading the palace drawing room. Despite her privileged position as royal mistress, for her it held the risk of an unpleasant encounter with the husband who'd given her nothing but unhappiness, bruises and destitution.

By sharp contrast, Henrietta's junior colleague in the royal household, Molly Lepell, was dancing round her dressing room in delight. She was one of the merry Maids of Honour, a good-looking and audacious gang of girls whose job was to decorate and animate Prince George Augustus and Princess Caroline's court.

Born in the very first year of the eighteenth century, the now nineteen-year-old Molly was nicknamed 'The *Schatz*', German for 'treasure'. Part of her charm was her bottomless fund of jokes. She even mockingly (and wrongly) disparaged her own looks. 'I am little,' she said, but at least 'there are many less'. 'I am strait, the shoulders low . . . the neck long, the throat frightful, the head too large, the face flat . . . as to my hair it has nothing to make it tolerable, it grows badly, not thick, and of a pale and ugly brown'.[19]

In fact, she had big grey eyes, lustrous skin and an elegant, waif-like figure; she was the darling of the celebrity-obsessed London crowds.

Molly's father had bequeathed her the curse of breeding without the money to flaunt it. He'd fraudulently entered his baby girl upon the payroll of his army regiment, so that she got a salary unearned.[20] But the scam could not last, and Molly was sent out to earn her living as a palace good-time girl at a very young age. She certainly had all the easy graces of the courtier, having been 'bred all her life at courts'. She also understood Latin perfectly well, though wisely she concealed her skill.[21] (A lady's 'being learned' was 'commonly looked upon as a great fault'.[22])

Uniquely among her frivolous friends, her fellow Maids of

Honour, Molly was a good keeper of secrets. She was astonishingly composed and inscrutable for someone so young. Some people inevitably found her polished professional social manner insincere: she seemed to be 'of the same mind with every person she talked to'.[23] Others found her playful wit cutting rather than amusing, and her jokes 'extreme forward and pert'.[24]

But this smooth surface disguised a young woman who was 'very passionate' underneath. 'I find it beneath me not to be able to disguise it,' Molly explained, and she hid the essence of herself behind her endless jokes.[25] 'I look upon felicity in this world not to be a natural state, and consequently what cannot subsist,' she wrote in a rare unguarded moment.[26] Depression was her great secret enemy.

Tonight, for once, pleasure and excitement held it at bay. Unlike the other occupants of Leicester House, Molly could not wait for the evening to begin. The other Maids of Honour had no inkling that she'd recently thrown herself headlong into a mad, bad affair of the heart. The night would bring her once more into the company of her beloved.

At about 7 o'clock, sedan chairs carrying those lucky enough to be going to court began their swaying journeys across London. It would be foolish to walk: the jeers of hostile passers-by, rain and mud were all to be avoided, and the streets of the St James's district ought certainly 'to be better paved'.[27]

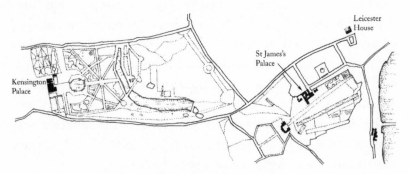

London's royal residences in the 1720s

A bristling bevy of red-clad Yeomen of the Guard preceded the sedan chairs of the Prince and Princess of Wales as they led the procession of their servants and supporters out of Leicester Fields. Ladies in court dress had to be literally crushed into sedan chairs, 'their immense hoops' folded 'like wings, pointing forward on each side'. To accommodate their 'preposterous high' headdresses, they had to tilt their necks backwards and keep motionless throughout the journey.[28]

Their destination, the old palace of St James's, was not particularly impressive. It had been a poorly designed, makeshift mansion for the monarchy since the great palace of Whitehall burned down in 1698. An eighteenth-century guidebook called it 'the contempt of foreign nations, and the disgrace of our own'; a visiting German confirmed that it was 'crazy, smoky, and dirty'.[29]

Although cramped and unsuitable, St James's Palace still provided the stage upon which the Georgian court's most important rituals were performed. To the courtiers its atmosphere was heady, dangerous but absolutely irresistible: 'full of politicks, anger, friendship, love, fucking and foppery'.[30]

Many of the people who weren't invited to palace parties would have claimed the court was no longer the beating heart of the nation that it had once indisputably been. There was Parliament, now, as an alternative arena for politics. Kings and queens no longer ruled by divine right. Monarchy was on the decline.

And yet, while all this was true, the early years of the eighteenth century were to see a last great gasp of court life and a late flowering of that strange, complex, alluring but destructive organism called the royal household.

The personal was still political at the early Georgian court. The king's mood, even his bowel movements, could determine the fate of many, as even now he was called upon to make real decisions about the running of the country. His opinion still mattered, and, as contemporaries showed by packing themselves into its drawing room or by begging for jobs as servants, the palace was still a seat of power.

[17]

*

As they approached the palace's lofty red-brick gatehouse, the sedan chairmen carrying Henrietta and Molly in Princess Caroline's wake had to force a passage through a raucous, torch-lit crowd. Hundreds of people had gathered expectantly to catch a glimpse of the blazing 'beauties' arriving in their jewels.[31]

Molly Lepell, along with her friend Mary Bellenden, another Maid of Honour, received the loudest sigh of admiration. Although they were not yet twenty, these two were the toast of their generation, and each was as lively and as pretty as the other. Then, as now, society beauties provided the shot of style and celebrity that the masses craved. One popular London ballad promised to expose

> What pranks are played behind the scenes,
> And who at Court the belle –
> Some swear it is the Bellenden,
> And others say Lepell.[32]

The arrival of the matchless Mary and Molly elicited the kind of greedy, semi-salacious gasp that still runs up and down red carpets today when the stars appear.

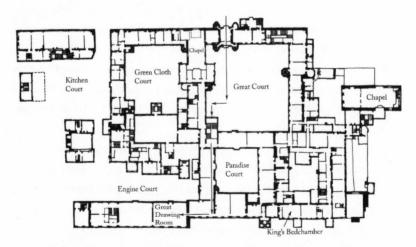

St James's Palace: 'crazy, smoky, and dirty'. The courtiers' route to the drawing room is marked

Through the palace gatehouse lay the Great Court, where soldiers kept guard. It was also called the 'Whalebone Court' after the whale's skeleton, 20 feet long, that was clamped to one wall.[33] Here a sea of servants and stationary sedan chairs jostled to drop people off before the fine columned portico sheltering the entrance to the royal apartments. The palace authorities complained constantly about all this traffic blocking the courtyards and passages.[34]

Emerging gingerly from their chairs, Molly, Mary and their colleagues were now faced with a wide and grand staircase. Here the scarlet-costumed Yeomen of the Guard acted as security staff and bouncers, refusing entry to the humbly or unsuitably dressed.

There was no official protocol involving invitations. To gain admission you simply had to look the part, so it was vital to swagger and to pretend to be 'mightily acquainted and accustomed at Court'.[35] One would-be gatecrasher, an enterprising young law student, was turned away at the bottom of the stairs. He went to a nearby coffee house for half an hour, returned refreshed, and discovered that a shilling pressed into the guard's hand was the key to getting through.[36]

The ladies of Princess Caroline's household were much more readily admitted. They pushed upwards and onwards, taking the tiny, geisha-like steps permitted by their hoops, their gait giving the impression of wheeled motion. They glided through the first-floor guard room, then the adjoining 'presence' and 'privy' chambers. Their destination was the large new drawing room built by Queen Anne overlooking the park and hung with 'beautiful old tapestries'.[37]

This was the 'Great Drawing-Room', where, four nights a week, 'the nobility, the ministers &c.' were accustomed to meet, 'and where all strangers, above the inferior rank, may see the King'.[38]

Here, at last, is the Georgian court en masse. There is scarcely room to breathe, the air is 'excessive hot', and the crush has prevented many of the nobility even from entering. Chairs are completely absent from the room so that nobody can make the mistake of sitting down in the royal presence.

The courtiers' colours are pale and sparkling. The penniless poet John Gay, hopeful of a royal patron, arrays himself in silver and blue as he asks himself, 'How much money will do?'[39] Knights of the Garter wear blue sashes; senior courtiers' staffs of office are white. The court's young bloods sport pale-blue silk coats, while their older colleagues have 'blue noses, pale faces, gauze heads and toupets'.[40] A glittering gown is spotted 'with great roses not unlike large silver soup plates'.[41]

The silver is relieved with touches of crimson: a red sash for a Knight of the Bath; a gentleman in a 'prodigiously effeminate' rose-coloured waistcoat; the stout Princess Caroline in pink, 'superior to her waiting nymphs/ as lobster to attendant shrimps'.[42]

Princess Caroline, Prince George Augustus and their party become the centre of attention immediately upon entering. All the most ambitious young courtiers behaved dutifully to the king when he was present, but preferred to pay their court to the younger, bolder, more promising heir to the throne. Peter Wentworth, a junior official, observed that on drawing-room nights, many people were 'backward in speaking to the King, tho' they are ready enough to speak to the Prince'.[43]

While the king's party had the greater power, the prince's had the greater glamour.

The younger courtiers now fought to fawn over Prince George Augustus, and drawing-room behaviour was often surprisingly ugly. In the crush people would 'jostle and squeeze by one another', shouting 'pardon' over their shoulders; it was simply 'impossible to hold a conversation'.[44] Everyone laughed when Lord Onslow tumbled 'backward among all the crowd' and lay sprawling, while another gentleman, 'drunk and saucy', had to be ejected for throwing a punch.[45]

In his sector of the drawing room, George Augustus spoke one by one to those courtiers desperately trying to catch his attention. He turned his backside to those he did not wish to acknowledge, a technique known as 'rumping'. The 'rumped' or spurned could console themselves with having earned membership of the exclusive 'Rumpsteak Club'.

This was boorish behaviour, and Prince George Augustus was not the handsome, charming prince of a fairy tale. His peppery personality and 'the fire of his temper' appeared 'in every look and gesture'.[46] He would let off steam rather comically by kicking his hat, and sometimes even his wig, around the room.[47] A sufferer from high blood pressure, he was subject to 'constant palpitations about the region of the heart, especially after dinner'.[48]

This prince, then, had passion. He made an excellent soldier when his courtiers' concerns for his safety allowed him to take the field. At the decisive European battle of Oudenarde in 1708, he'd led a celebrated cavalry charge against the enemy, 'and had his horse shot under him'; military trivia remained his greatest interest.[49]

In the drawing room on this particular evening, he faced a challenge that demanded rather more subtlety than a cavalry charge, though it was equally daunting for him to face.

He was about to have to be polite to the father he loathed.

After a long and painful period of gossiping, jostling and waiting, a whisper ran like wildfire around the room. A door from an inner chamber opened, and the king appeared.

The buzzing swarm of courtiers immediately clustered round him in a tight circle, and animated chatter in French and German, as well as English, broke out. This was not an ancient, staid and orderly court; it was mercurial as well as international. Many of the people here were German immigrants who had travelled from Hanover with George I in 1714.

Meanwhile, Prince George Augustus, Princess Caroline and their household remained huddled together at the lower end of the room, almost braced against the approach of the king. There were no warm greetings; the king merely gave his son a wintry nod.

A palace drawing room could be full of deception beneath its bonhomie: 'lying smiles, forced compliments, careful brows, and made laughs', a place in which 'people talk of nothing but foreign peace, and think of nothing but domestic war'.[50] The antagonism flickering between the two courts now made 'the whole thing look like two armies drawn up in battle array'.[51]

The two royal households, the king's and the prince's, had not shared the same room for more than two years. This evening's party was supposed to mark their official reconciliation after a terrible quarrel, but nothing could mask the genuine hostility that still burned between them.

The bad feeling had reached fever pitch, and it had been a long time in the building. To understand the roots of the resentment between father and son, we need to go back decades into the past.

TWO

The Petulant Prince

'Ungodly papers every week
Poor simple souls persuade
That courtiers good for nothing are
Or but for mischief made.'
(Lady Mary Wortley Montagu)

Some people pointed to 1705 as the date of the first disagreement between the king and the prince, and indeed Prince George Augustus had complained vociferously about his father's stingy wedding present upon his marriage to Caroline that year.[2] But it was after their move to London in 1714 that relations between father and son became positively and publicly bitter.

In 1715, it was said that 'the Prince is on very bad terms with his father, and that they won't speak to one another'.[3] They seemed more interested in provoking one another than in defeating the major rebellion led by the rejected Catholic claimants to the throne which threatened their new kingdom that year.

The following year saw George I planning to return to his native Hanover for a much-needed summer holiday. He refused to make his son regent of Britain in his place as precedent suggested. Now the sniping within the royal family began to be a grave threat to the nation's well-being. 'The Princess is all in a flame, the Prince in an agony,' wrote Princess Caroline's servant Mary Cowper. 'They are all mad, and for their own private ends will destroy all.'[4]

Juicy reports about the latest twists and turns of the royal family's persistently poor relationships constantly circulated around London. 'Have you not observed', asks Lord Chesterfield, 'how quickly a piece of news spreads itself all over the town?'[5] Londoners' appetite for gossip had helped to fan the flames of antagonism that burned between the king and his son: 'the more ridiculous the scandal is, the more greedily they will swallow it'.[6]

Yet there were also good political reasons behind the rift in the royal family. With his father out of the way in Hanover in 1716,

Prince George Augustus suddenly became very keen on politics, 'very intent upon holding the Parliament, very inquisitive about the revenue'. He asked 'daily for papers' and seemed 'to be preparing to keep an interest of his own in Parliament independent of the King's'.[7]

This was an early instance of what would become known as 'the reversionary problem'. A 'reversion' was the promise of an office or job in the event of a future vacancy. ('Everyone comes to Court to get,' remarks John Hervey, 'and if there is nothing to be got in present, it is natural to look for reversions.'[8]) A prince possessed the greatest reversion of all, and could expect the greatest achievement of his life – becoming king – only when his father died. His friends and supporters would also grow impatient for power. So the pattern of eighteenth-century British politics, where a king and his heir would lead rival factions in Parliament, began to form.

The reversionary problem was created in 1688, when the Stuart princesses (and future queens) Mary and Anne won a battle but lost a war. They'd accepted the support of the Whig aristocracy in removing their father James II from the throne, but in doing so they also accepted that a monarch *could* in fact be sacked. They therefore sacrificed a great deal of the mystical authority that had sustained their predecessors.

The loose coalition of aristocrats known as the Whigs, meanwhile, had acquired an addictive taste for power. Not yet a formal political party, the Whigs were keener on the innovative culture of credit recently created by the Bank of England than their landowning opponents, the Tories. Slightly warmer towards religious Dissenters than the Tories, the Whigs were also hotly opposed to tyrannical and absolutist rule. That said, like all politicians in the period, they belonged to society's upper echelons and were keen to defend the social hierarchy.

When Anne died childless, royal power was eroded even further. The Whig-dominated Parliament that invited George I to become king took the opportunity to place various restrictions upon his scope for action. Some were more onerous than others. On the one hand, he still had the power to appoint the ministers of his government, so he had the ultimate say, that of 'men rather than measures'. As first minister Sir Robert Walpole put it in 1716, 'nobody can carry on the King's business if he is not supported at Court'.[9] On the other hand, the Act of Settlement of 1701 had ring-fenced royal power. George I could not award peerages to his fellow Germans; he could not declare war or leave the country without Parliament's consent; he could not change his religion.

However, despite Parliament becoming more and more important as the arbiter of affairs, the Georgian kings would fight a skilful and determined rearguard action throughout the eighteenth century. But they would all experience problems with their heirs. 'Great divisions arose in the court,' it was said, 'some devoting themselves to the wearer of the crown, and others to the expectant.'[10] In Parliament, ambitious members continually used the heir as a focus for stirring up trouble. His ministers moaned 'to the King that the Prince's friends were like a battalion that broke through all their measures'.[11] There were clearly sound political reasons for father and son to be at war.

In addition to all this, their personalities were poles apart.

Prince George Augustus's father could not speak fluent English, but then he was not born to be a British king.

Hanover, their joint birthplace, was a conservative and sleepy little city on the River Leine between the north German plain and the mountains of Lower Saxony. George I inherited his claim to Britain through his mother Sophia, a granddaughter of James I of England who had married Hanover's Elector. The state's rulers were called 'Electors' because they belonged to a consortium of nine minor princes who 'elected' their overlord, the Holy Roman Emperor. Their territory included much of modern Germany and its neighbouring countries.

George I inherited Hanover when his father died in 1698. Meanwhile, back in Britain, Queen Anne was reluctant to face the

George I: an 'honest dull German gentleman'?

implications of her inevitable death and her childlessness, and neglected to invite her Hanoverian heirs to visit Britain during her lifetime. The mere suggestion that they should come over to familiarise themselves with their future inheritance was taken as 'a great piece of rudeness' and 'no better than presenting the Sovereign with a death's head'.[12]

During the Hanoverians' enforced absence, the supporters of their main rival were very vocal. These were the Jacobites, followers of the 'Pretender', the exiled Catholic son of James II (his more optimistic friends called him 'King James III'). Many Tory politicians held dangerous, treasonous Jacobite opinions. If a gentleman heard even his cook-maids and footmen shouting, wrote Daniel Defoe, he'd be wrong to assume that they were arguing about the pudding or the washing-up. Servants' feuds were just as likely to be about the 'mighty affairs of the government, and who is for the Protestant Succession, and who for the Pretender'.[13] It was quite remarkable, in the event, that George I became king without bloodshed in 1714, and in 1715 he easily defeated a Jacobite rebellion.

Five years later, by 1720, he was very nearly sixty. One eyewitness described how 'his cheeks are pendent, and his eyes are
too big . . . he is fond of pleasures'.[14] Lord Chesterfield claimed
that George I favoured fat women, and that those who aspired to
become his mistresses had to 'strain and swell' themselves to put
on weight ('Some succeeded, and others burst').[15] In his drawing
room the king was noticeably eager to kiss visiting ladies 'on the
lips', and was observed to take the 'most pleasure in kissing the
prettiest'.[16]

The king himself was short, 'very corpulent' and sadly lacking
in kingly charisma: 'his countenance was benign, but without
much expression'.[17] Most unfortunately, given his job, he was 'not
fond of attracting notice'. He hated crowds and 'the splendour of
majesty'.[18]

A certain snide, sophisticated, cynical category of British
courtier would give George I an enduring reputation as an uninterested, uneducated boor: an 'honest dull German gentleman',
as the snooty Chesterfield put it, 'as unfit as unwilling to act the
part of a King'.[19]

In actual fact, the passionate love he had for his homeland of
Hanover was misread as this supposed distaste for his adopted
country of Britain. His reputation as a perverted sexual athlete
was also completely undeserved. In reality, he liked to spend his
evenings quietly with his skinny and aging mistress and the three
dreary daughters she had given him.

So the crowded palace drawing room was rather like George I's
idea of hell. His glacial behaviour there meant many of his
courtiers believed him to be utterly heartless. On one occasion
Lady Nithsdale, whose husband was in the Tower awaiting execution, tried to hand the reluctant king a petition for mercy. She
caught hold of his coat in a desperate plea for attention, keeping
'such strong hold that he dragged' her to the very door. The petition for her husband's life 'fell down in the scuffle' and Lady
Nithsdale 'almost fainted through grief and disappointment'.[20]

But certainly the king was not, as many courtiers thought,

entirely 'so cold that he freezes everything into ice'.[21] With a small group of close friends he could throw off his protective carapace and act naturally, timidly allowing the people he loved to see his human side. If George I had friends in the sense of intimates who knew his every mood, they certainly included his servants. Above all, his two confidential Turkish valets, Georg Ludwig Maximilian Mohammed von Königstreu and Ernst August Mustapha, were among the few with whom he could relax.

The more acid members of George I's court thought him nothing but 'an honest blockhead', and that becoming king 'added nothing to his happiness, only prejudiced his honesty and shortened his days'.[22] Kinder friends feared that he would 'find more worry and trouble than pleasure in his regal condition', and guessed that he would 'often say to himself, "If only I were still Elector, and in Hanover."'[23]

He probably did indeed repeat the words to himself every drawing-room night.

The 'reconciliation' that was supposed to take place in the St

A bird's-eye view of St James's Palace. The Tudor gatehouse lies to the left, while the Great Drawing Room overlooks the formal gardens to the right

James's Palace drawing room on 25 April 1720 was intended to draw a line beneath an argument that had really begun to heat up late in 1717. The whole sorry affair would become known as 'the christening quarrel'.

On 3 November 1717, a courtier had written to a friend about the 'difference running as high between the two courts as ever'. He was altogether unaware that the tension between king and prince was about to turn a twist tighter.

Prince George Augustus and Princess Caroline already had a boy and three girls, and Caroline had spent most of 1717 pregnant once again. The same letter reported that she'd finally given birth, 'last night at six o'clock', to a young prince.[24] This baby boy became the innocent cause of an almighty but slightly ridiculous row.

The delivery took place in Caroline's apartment in St James's Palace. A venerable, if unfashionable, building, the palace had originally been a hospital founded to house 'fourteen leprous females'.[25] It still had red-brick ranges dating from the time of Henry VIII and remained the best address in London. Caroline had lived there with her husband since their arrival from Germany in 1714.

Soon after her baby was born, George I visited Caroline in her apartment. He wanted to meet his latest grandson. But even though he 'went up to the nursery and saw the child suck', everyone noticed that he 'did not at all speak to the Prince'.[26]

The baby needed to be christened and godparents chosen. George Augustus and Caroline had already given some thought to the important matter of a godfather to this second son. Now the king intervened. He insisted that they should stand down their previous choice and that the scratchy Duke of Newcastle, the Lord Chamberlain and his own highest court officer, should be invited to do the job instead. The prince and princess were infuriated by this interference in what they saw as their own business.

Henrietta Howard was an eyewitness to the actual christening ceremony, which took place in Princess Caroline's bedchamber.

On one side of the bed were all of Caroline's ladies; on the other stood the unwelcome figure of the Duke of Newcastle, the un-invited participant who was only there at the king's insistence.[27]

When the ceremony was complete, feelings boiled over. Prince George Augustus and the Duke of Newcastle had an unseemly and embarrassing verbal spat, and the duke somehow came away with the impression that he'd been challenged by the prince to a duel. In fact, it was a simple matter of a word mispronounced and misunderstood, a result of the Hanoverian habit of mangling the English language.

Language problems intensified the prejudice and xenophobia that thrived between the German and English factions at court. When the new royal family arrived in London, they'd inevitably brought with them a great number of German courtiers and servants. Not least among them were George I's German cooks, as he couldn't stomach English food.

A German countess caused immense offence by announcing that 'English women did not look like women of quality' because 'they hold their heads down, and look always in a fright, whereas those that are foreigners hold up their heads and hold out their breasts, and make themselves look as great and stately as they can'.

Lady Deloraine, whose husband served in the Prince of Wales's household, made a tart reply on behalf of the English: 'We show our quality by our birth and titles, Madam, and not by sticking out our bosoms.'[28]

The English constantly complained that the German inner circle surrounding the king created 'a court within a court', with concerns 'opposite to the true interest of England'.[29] While the Germans discreetly pretended to have nothing to do with English affairs, Peter Wentworth the equerry noticed that in reality they were the ones with the power of patronage. 'From the top to the bottom they have a great stroak,' he said.[30]

Behind closed doors, George I did in fact read English newspapers, receive English guests and take a studious interest in governing his new country. He even learnt to speak halting English, although he made typically German errors in grammar ('What did they go away for? It was their own *faults*.'[31]) But many people chose to ignore this. 'The King of England', ran wildly inaccurate reports, 'has no predilection for the English nation, and never receives in private any English of either sex.'[32]

So Prince George Augustus and Princess Caroline had learnt to needle the king by loudly and publicly praising the English and their customs. The prince declared that the English were 'the handsomest, the best shaped, the best natured, and lovingest people in the world, and that if anybody would make their court to him, it must be by telling him he was like an Englishman'.[33] He announced that he had not 'one drop of blood in his veins but what [was] English, and at the service of his new subjects'.[34] This was widely welcomed, though in fact his blood was a mixture of German, Scottish and French.

Yet his claim to be a thorough Englishman was undermined whenever he opened his mouth. Although his English was better than his father's, it was still far from perfect. He compensated for any mistakes by speaking very loudly, but he'd failed to eliminate his 'bluff Westphalian accent'.[35]

The day following the christening, the king sent messengers to ask his son if there was any truth in the outrageous reports he'd received about the christening and the subsequent quarrel in Princess Caroline's bedchamber. Was it the case, he asked, that Prince George Augustus 'had said to the Duke of Newcastle these words: You Rascal I will fight you?'[36]

In actual fact there'd been a straightforward linguistic slip. George Augustus didn't deny that he'd called the duke a rascal, but he answered angrily that he'd said, 'You Rascal I will *find* you.' He had wanted to *find*, not *fight*, the Duke of Newcastle, he explained, in order to give him a proper tongue-lashing. The duke's attendance at the christening had been the last straw in a succession of slights. 'He has often failed in his respect to me', the prince ranted to the king's envoys, 'particularly on this late occasion, by insisting on standing godfather to my son.'[37]

Although this was a silly misunderstanding, the prince would not apologise, and the king would not forgive. After the duke's continued complaints, George I ordered his son and daughter-in-law to vacate their apartments at St James's. He was expelling them from the family home.

Now the friends and servants of Prince George Augustus and Princess Caroline found the palace doors literally closed against them. When Henrietta Howard tried to go to work, the Yeomen of the Guard thrust forward their weapons to bar her route.

'What was my astonishment,' she recollected afterwards. 'I urged, that it was my duty to attend the Princess,' but 'they said, No matter; I must not pass that way'.[38]

But there was very much worse to come. When George I gave the order for his son and daughter-in-law to be evicted from St James's Palace, he excluded from it his grandchildren. The Prince and Princess of Wales's children, their three young daughters Anne, Amelia and little Caroline, and their new baby boy, were all to stay behind.

At first George Augustus and Caroline could not believe what they were hearing. But they were astonished and dismayed to discover that under English law a king could indeed demand their children. Unluckily for them, legal precedents were produced to show that a monarch had a perfect right to take control of his heirs.[39]

So, at 9 o'clock at night on 2 December 1717, Princess Caroline and Prince George Augustus left St James's Palace for good. They were forced to forsake their children, who would remain behind at St James's under the supervision of governesses. Poor Caroline 'went into one faint after another when her weeping little Princesses said goodbye'.[40]

Likewise, the prince could never conceal any emotional distress:

'so little master of Himself, is our Great Master!'[41] He and his wife 'retired to Lord Grantham's in Dover Street, in the utmost grief and disorder, the Prince cried for two hours, and the Princess swooned several times'.[42] Prince George Augustus's customary guard of yeomen was withdrawn, and his trips about town would henceforth be unprotected and undignified.

Outside the palace gates, Londoners observed these events with horror. At the same time, though, they relished the farcical note which had been struck. Newsletter writers gleefully speculated that their services would be much required to elucidate the absurd 'difference betwixt his Majesty and the Prince of *Wales*, which so much distracts us at present'.[43]

'An Excellent New Ballad' (to be sung to the tune of 'Chevy Chase') quickly appeared, describing events at the palace as amusingly shambolic:

> God prosper long our noble King
> His Turks and Germans all
> A woeful christ'ning late there did
> In James's house befall.

The balladeer took great pleasure from all 'this silly pother', visualising the royal family at their most ridiculous: George I writing to his son with a grey goose quill dipped in gall for ink; Princess Caroline calling out 'Oh! don't forget the close-stool' (or toilet) to her Women of the Bedchamber as they packed to leave.

Only Caroline's Maid of Honour Mary Bellenden took events in her stride. On the way out of St James's Palace, it was said, she jumped merrily down the stairs singing 'Over the Hills and Far Away'.[44] This was a Jacobite song, and by singing it she hinted that the king was falling significantly short of the mark as heir to the Stuarts.

The prince and princess's residence at Lord Grantham's was only brief, and they found a new home for themselves at Leicester House in Leicester Fields. A spacious seventeenth-century mansion, it was protected from the street by a courtyard and overlooked what would in due course become known as Leicester Square. It was here that Elizabeth of Bohemia, the daughter of King James I, had died, and here that Peter the Great of Russia had stayed during his recent visit to England.

It was a fine house, admittedly, but it did sit rather close to a row of shops. It was clearly not a palace, and it represented a sad blow to Prince George Augustus's self-esteem.

Following the catastrophic christening and the expulsion of his son from the palace, the king insisted that no one could serve both households. The courtiers now had to decide where their allegiance lay. 'All persons who should go to see the prince and princess of Wales', ran the royal proclamation, 'should forbear coming into his majesty's presence.'[45]

This new twist turned the quarrel into something like a popularity contest. How many of the courtiers would support the king, and how many the prince?

Consternation ensued: 'our courtiers . . . look so amaz'd, so thunder-struck, and knew so little how to behave themselves . . . that they betray'd the mercenary principles upon which they acted'. Those on the prince's side kept quiet because they feared the king, while the king's supporters were equally 'backward to declare themselves' as one day the prince would have his revenge.[46]

Luckily for her husband, Princess Caroline understood the art of cultivating public opinion – or the science of spin – unusually well. She had the good sense to see that the transplanted Hanoverians needed to cultivate their popularity as if it were a tender shoot in constant danger of dying, so she began to pay court to her potential supporters, buttering up the grandest courtiers and radiating kindness to the meanest.[47] She made her drawing room warm and welcoming almost to a fault, so that her guests departed 'wonderfully pleas'd' with her 'easy deportment and affability'.[48] Meanwhile, when George I tried to hold an assembly at St James's, Caroline was heard to say that 'no honest woman would appear at it'.[49]

Caroline even made clandestine arrangements to see valued friends on the other side of the divide who felt they could no longer afford to be publicly associated with her. One of her ladies-in-waiting told a nervous would-be visitor to come secretly to the summerhouse in Princess Caroline's garden 'by nine a clock in the morning . . . that nobody may see you'.[50]

But Caroline and George Augustus really needed their supporters to express an open commitment by crowding the drawing room at Leicester House. The poet and occasional courtier Lady Mary Wortley Montagu did not shirk her duty and turned up to support the plucky younger generation of rebellious royals. 'We old beauties', she wrote, 'are force'd to come out on show days to keep the [prince's] Court in countenance.'[51] Indeed, people began to say that 'the Prince's *levées* and court increase much' because 'we are very fond in this country of forbidden fruit'.[52]

While Princess Caroline loyally churned out the hours of endless chit-chat that were required to keep her drawing room happy and humming, it was rather a waste of her talents. Her private apartment was much more like the common room of a university. Behind the scenes, her 'ardent love of learning' still drove her to gulp down intellectual conversation during any spare moments in her day. Her private parties were

> a strange picture of the motley character and manners of a queen and a learned woman . . . learned men and divines were intermixed with courtiers and ladies of the household: the conversation turned upon metaphysical subjects, blended with repartees, sallies of mirth, and the tittle-tattle of a drawing-room.[53]

Prince George Augustus, meanwhile, had no time for his wife's interests and often used to brag about 'the contempt he had for books and letters' and 'to say how much he hated all that stuff from his infancy'.[54]

While their drawing room at Leicester House remained comfortably full, the prince and princess nevertheless found themselves paying a terribly high price for their principled stand. It was difficult and sometimes impossible for them to see their daughters and baby son left behind at St James's.

Once, when the princesses' governess refused to allow George Augustus access to his little girls, he 'flew into such a rage that he would literally have kicked her out of the room if the Princess had not thrown herself between them'.[55] Sadly the children's own interests were sacrificed in this quarrel between their elders. 'We've such a good father and such a good mother,' one of them said, 'and yet we are orphans.' Asked if her grandfather the king often visited them, she replied, 'Oh no, he doesn't love us enough.'[56]

Gossip about these events could not be contained and began to spill out across all the courts of Europe. 'The King of England is really cruel to the Princess of Wales,' wrote the Duchess of Orléans. 'Although she has done nothing, he has taken her children away from her.'[57]

In emotional terms, Prince George Augustus and Princess Caroline paid dearly for taking their stubborn stand against the king. They were robbed of their daughters' childhoods, and they would feel the pain of this for the rest of their lives.

Worse was soon to come. Early in 1718, George I planned his court's summer move to Kensington Palace. Set in fields and gardens beyond the edge of London, the palace was rather tumbledown, 'superior to St James's, but prodigiously beneath any idea we might form of a royal palace'.[58] Nevertheless, it was a more relaxed, attractive and healthy place than the main urban royal residence.

The king sent ahead the little baby boy George William, whose christening had ignited the argument. Once he was at Kensington Palace, though, the baby developed a cough and 'straitness of breathing'. After a short illness, he 'fell into convulsions' and died.[59]

Orders were placed for a pitiful amount of black velvet, just 'sufficient to cover the coffin' of a baby.[60] His funeral cortège left Kensington Palace at 10 p.m. on 12 February 1718.[61]

Given the circumstances, the cause of the child's death and his post-mortem were of enormous importance. A large team of doctors was drafted in to observe it, including Princess Caroline's own physician, Sir David Hamilton.[62] A draft of the team's report, written at Kensington Palace, reveals their discussions. It records that upon opening the baby prince's body, they found 'a large quantity of water' inside the head, inflamed viscera and a little heart containing a great 'polype', or cyst.

In the original document at the British Library, the nuanced, considered medical discourse is concluded by another, more politically aware hand. Protecting the king and his medical staff from any accusation of malpractice, it finishes firmly: 'it appears above all that it was impossible that this young prince could live'.[63]

Princess Caroline was nevertheless utterly distraught. Perhaps if she had swallowed her pride and ended the quarrel, her infant son would still be alive, or would at least have died in her care.

'My God!' wrote Prince George Augustus's great-aunt in Paris:

How I pity the poor dear Princess of Wales! She saw him [her son] at Kensington Palace just before the end. I wish she hadn't seen him, for it will be even more painful for her now. God grant that this Prince's death may extinguish all the flames kindled at his christening! But alas, there is no sign of that yet. God forgive me, but I think the King of England doesn't believe that the Prince of Wales is his son, because if he did he couldn't possibly treat him as he does.[64]

Parting a mother from her tiny baby appears to be outrageously callous, a ridiculously exaggerated retribution for the king to exact for a petty breach of etiquette. But in fact the 'christening quarrel' took place against a much more profound psychological background. Deep in the murky forest of possible motives for the hatred between king and prince there lies the mysterious matter of the missing queen.

During the drawing-room parties of the 1710s and 1720s, there was a conspicuous gap by George I's side. His wife, Prince George Augustus's mother, was completely absent from the court scene at

St James's. She was still alive, and perfectly well, but had long been imprisoned in a remote German castle. Her sad story was bound to have affected the emotions of both her husband and son.

During George Augustus's early years in Hanover, his mother Sophia had embarked upon a prolonged, flagrant and ultimately doomed affair with Philip von Königsmarck, a Swedish count then serving in the Hanoverian army. Some of his passionate letters to Sophia survive. On 19 July 1693, he described his memory of 'dying' (or having an orgasm, '*la petite mort*') in her eyes, and of her calling out to him, 'My dear König, let's do it together!'[65] By one dubious means or another, these letters would in due course come to be revealed to the drawing rooms of Europe.

Their grand passion came to a dark and horrible end. One night in 1694, Königsmarck was making his way towards Sophia's room through the shadowy corridors of the riverside Leine Palace at the heart of the old city of Hanover. Suddenly he was ambushed, set upon and strangled. An Italian assassin, assisted by three members of the court, did the dirty deed.[66] They disposed of his body by throwing it into the river.

The whole of the Hanoverian court was grimly united in its silence on the matter, especially when increasingly far-fetched and lurid rumours began to circulate, such as the story that the remains of a skeleton wearing Königsmarck's ring had been discovered during building work at the palace.[67]

Because she had been indiscreet with her lover, Sophia's affair was a matter of state interest, and her trial swiftly followed. While she was relieved to be divorced from her hated husband, she was less happy when he had her placed under house arrest at the distant castle of Ahlden. She was also denied access to her son, Prince George Augustus. He had only been eleven when his mother disappeared, but we know that her fate still darkened his thoughts.

The ancient scandal was constantly raked up around the courts of Europe. In 1716, Princess Caroline received a petition asking her to consider, just and God-fearing as she is known to be, that the only rightful heir to the kingdom is the one known as the Pretender, as he was King James II's son as surely as her husband was Count Königsmarck's.

'How unspeakably insolent, if this really was said to the Princess!' commented the Duchess of Orléans as she gleefully passed on the gossip. 'England is a mad country,' she concluded.[68]

At the point when Sophia had fallen in love with Count Königsmarck, she had long endured rampant infidelity from her husband. When he appeared in the drawing room at St James's Palace in London, George I was usually accompanied by two women assumed by everyone to be his long-term German mistresses.

First there was Ehrengard Melusina von der Schulenberg, usually known as Melusine, a tall thin lady known by the disapproving English as 'the May Pole'. Next to her stood Sophia Charlotte von Kielmansegg, a short fat female disparagingly called 'The Elephant'.

When George I had arrived in London in 1714, his companions Melusine and Sophia Charlotte came in for endless criticism. The low life of London were 'highly diverted' by the new king's seraglio.[69] The two ladies were just 'ugly old whores', the newspapers claimed, and would have found few clients even in the brothels of Drury Lane.[70]

The skeletal Melusine was said to be 'duller than the King and consequently did not find that he was so', while the obese Sophia Charlotte had 'fierce black eyes, large and rolling . . . two acres of cheeks spread with crimson, an ocean of neck that overflowed'.[71] Lord Chesterfield, one of the king's cruellest critics, claimed that no woman came amiss to George I 'if she was but very willing, very fat, and had great breasts'.[72] Indeed, a confectioner in the royal household had to be dismissed for using 'indecent expressions concerning the King & Madam Kielmansegg'.[73]

But Sophia Charlotte and Melusine were thoroughly and

deliberately misunderstood and misrepresented by the British, who did not – or would not – attempt to like foreigners. Truth at the Georgian court was even stranger than fiction, for Sophia Charlotte von Kielmansegg, 'The Elephant', was actually the king's half-sister. The princes of Europe usually maintained both wives and mistresses, creating a tangled jungle of official and unofficial children. George I's father had enjoyed an affair with his chief minister's wife; Sophia Charlotte was its result.

Despite all the talk, there is no evidence that George I and Sophia Charlotte had an incestuous relationship, and indeed an ambitious courtier in search of power thought himself on 'a fine road to it by furnishing Madame Kielmansegg both with money and a lover' of her own.[74]

George I remained silent upon the subject of his estranged wife, her lover and the murder. The shy king had a will of iron and an iron-clad ability to hold a grievance for years.

So there were unhealed wounds deep down in his relationship with his son. They allowed the ridiculous quarrel over the choice of a godfather to become the visible expression of an antagonism much more entrenched and damaging.

By 1720, everyone was sick of the inconvenience and unhappiness caused by the 'christening quarrel'. They all hoped that the St James's Palace drawing room would be the setting for a happy resolution.

As early as February 1718, Princess Caroline had been using the rules of polite social engagement to force the king to acknowledge her presence and to speak to her. A journalist congratulated his country upon 'the near prospect there is of a reconciliation between his Majesty and his Royal Highness. The Princess of Wales's appearance at court can forebode no less.'[75]

This, however, was only a lull in a two-year war of attrition. The submission or apology that the king required of his son remained unforthcoming. In May of the next year, when George I went to Hanover for the summer, he set up a Council of Regency from which Prince George Augustus was again pointedly excluded. He forbade his son and daughter-in-law from using St James's Palace in his absence, and announced that court gatherings would be hosted by his three grandchildren, the little princesses.

It was a turning of the political tide that eventually pressured the royal family into making more serious attempts at appeasement. Forces more potent than themselves were in motion. The turn-around was forced by the involvement of Sir Robert Walpole, the man who hoped to become all-powerful among the politicians.

Walpole, whom 'nothing terrifies, nothing astonishes', was something like the country's first 'Prime Minister'.[76] He certainly acted as if he were, though the title was not yet formalised. At this stage in his career he was still working closely with his brother-in-law, Charles Townshend (who'd later become known as 'Turnip Townshend' for his agricultural innovations).

These two were both Whigs, to be sure, but they were locked in close combat with other Whig factions, such as the one led by their nemeses, the Earls of Stanhope and Sunderland. Walpole once had to be restrained from throwing a candlestick at Stanhope during a Cabinet meeting.[77] The enfeebled Tories, meanwhile, remained in disarray, and Walpole and the Whigs ran rings around them.

As his struggle against his fellow Whigs Stanhope and Sunder - land intensified, Walpole began to need new allies. He sought an alliance with the king's Hanoverian ministers, and he also began to think that a united royal family could provide him with much-needed support. To secure a royal reunion would signal Walpole as the most powerful politician on the scene.

Though fat and often coarse, Sir Robert had a magnificently magnetic personality. A good speech by him in the House of Commons had 'as much of natural eloquence and of genius in it as had been heard by any of the audience within those walls', and 'whatever he proposes seldom fails of being pass'd'.[78] His elo-quence persuaded George I that reconciliation with his son was worth what was promised in return: £600,000, to be paid against the debt on the Civil List.

Walpole managed to convince the House of Commons to agree, and all he now needed was to win over Prince George Augustus and Princess Caroline. This too he achieved. Socially, emotionally, politically and financially, they couldn't afford to hold out against the king any longer.

But their submission would not be made without heartache. 'Half frighted, half persuaded' by Walpole to do his bidding, Princess Caroline in particular did so with many scruples. Weeping, she told her ladies that she considered herself to have been betrayed and her husband bribed.

All the pieces were eventually put into place and all the players prepared for Prince George Augustus's formal apology on St George's Day, 23 April 1720. He reluctantly wrote the letter of submission that the king required; or, at least, he copied it out from Sir Robert Walpole's draft. (Walpole had vetted 'everything beforehand, and it must be as he says'.[79])

When the letter was delivered to St James's Palace, the king's secretary came 'back with a message to the Prince to say that the King would see him'. He 'at once took his chair and went to St James's'.

So Prince George Augustus finally plodded back, with a heavy heart, to the palace from which he had been excluded for two years. Up the back-stairs and into the king's private closet he went. There he told his father that

> it had been a great grief to him to have been in his displeasure so long; that he was infinitely obliged to His Majesty for this permission of waiting upon him, and that he hoped the rest of his life would be such as the king would never have cause to complain of.

Then came the painful moment when George I also had to lay aside his anger.

> The King was much dismayed, pale, and could not speak to be heard but by broken sentences, and said several times, '*Votre conduite, votre conduite* [Your conduct, your conduct]', but the Prince said he could

not hear distinctly anything but those words. The prince went after he had stayed about five minutes in the closet.[80]

Five short minutes, but they were enough to make a powerful symbolic statement: father and son were on speaking terms once again.

In this moment, though, George Augustus was caught in a trap. A fiery man fuelled with an honest rage, he had gone to meet his father in good faith, hoping to be met halfway on the question of right and wrong. Even George I admitted that his son, though bad-tempered and blustery, was at heart simple and straight-forward. 'He is not a liar. He is mad, but he is a trustworthy man,' the king begrudgingly said.[81]

George Augustus expected and deserved a warmer reconcilia-tion than that provided by his father's muttered complaints.

From this point on, from this cold and half-hearted reception, he could no longer complain that he was suffering undeservedly from royal displeasure. Father and son were officially reunited. But an emotional resolution was still very far distant. The prince's grievance remained, and would now begin to fester. He finally understood that there was to be no apology from his father and no reparation for the stolen children.

The king still considered that the danger represented by the reversionary interest was just too strong to risk a real compromise with his son, and it is impossible to know what either of them really thought about the unspoken matter of the prince's mother. And reconciliation between the king and his daughter-in-law remained a step too far: 'The king could not be brought to see the Princess that night, and said, when he was pressed to it several times, "*L'occasion se trouvera!* [The time will come!]"'

Yet at this news of an official reconciliation within the royal family, there were the sort of celebrations usually seen after the winning of a battle or the lifting of a siege: 'The Prince came back, with the Beefeaters round his chair, and hallooing and all marks of joy which could be shown by the multitude.' To those in the know,

it seemed that Prince George Augustus did not share his supporters' high spirits: 'he looked grave, and his eyes were red and
swelled, as one has seen him on other occasions when he is mightily ruffled. He immediately dismissed all the company.'

His courtiers were nevertheless ordered to return to Leicester
House to report for duty at five that afternoon.

'At five I went', courtier Mary Cowper later recorded in her diary,
'and found the guards before the door, and the square full of
coaches; the rooms full of company, everything gay and laughing;
nothing but kissing and wishing of joy.'

Noisy celebrations took place at the news that the prince's court
was once more to be welcomed back from the wilderness. Mary
Cowper, though, was not alone in feeling unable to forget the
hatred and hostility of the last two years. There'd been a complete
and in some ways unconvincing volte-face: 'nobody could con-
ceive that so much joy should be had after so many resolutions
never to come to this'. Despite their sense that the reconciliation
was an empty charade, the courtiers who had thrown in their lot
with the prince and princess tried to act as if everything was right
with the world.

Now it came home to Prince George Augustus and Princess
Caroline that there was an awful price to be paid for their royal
status: they had to pretend to be happy.

The prince in particular, with his open and forthright character,
would find this terribly hard. Mary recorded a telling little inter-
change between herself and her employers on this supposedly celebratory evening. Her memory of the conversation shows how
George Augustus and Caroline could exert an almost magnetic
power, winning sincere affection and loyalty from their staff. 'I
wished the Prince joy,' she recollected, 'he embraced and kissed
me five or six times, and with his usual heartiness when he means
sincerely . . . The Princess burst out in a loud laugh, and said, "So!
I think you two always kiss upon great occasions."'[82]

The mixture of physical affection, jovial teasing and heartfelt words reveal the Prince and Princess of Wales at their best. It's possible to imagine the courtiers devoting their time, their health, their prospects to these people. And the couple won admirers in the most unlikely places. Even the grumpy old Duchess of Marlborough claimed that 'whatever may be deficient in the late reconcilement', Prince George Augustus and Princess Caroline would 'never want a full court of the best sort of people that this country affords'.[83]

The English courtiers were particularly proud of the fact that on this occasion they were better informed than their German counterparts: one of the Germans asked if the 'peace' being feted was the conclusion of a minor war that had been taking place in the Baltic.[84]

That night the festival mood rippled out from Leicester House: 'all the town' was 'feignedly or unfeignedly, transported'.[85] Down in Dorset, the gentleman who led the local militia lined up his men and began making toasts to each member of the royal family, commanding his troop to fire 'a volley of shot' after each one. An appalled neighbour described how they got through a bowl of punch, a barrel of ale and an unspecified quantity of wine before throwing their glasses over their heads. The next morning, the generous gentleman was observed to be 'a little disordered with that night's work'.[86]

It was on that next day, a Sunday, that the reconciliation between George I and his daughter-in-law did finally take place. The location was St James's Palace, and Princess Caroline was allowed to visit her daughters. King and princess 'went into a little closet' to talk, and remained there for more than an hour. The king's Turk, Mohammed, had to entertain Caroline's waiting servants with a horrible story of a suspected death by poison.[87]

All the actors were now ready for the reconciliation to be performed in public, before the world. Hence the spectacular drawing-room party planned for the next night, Monday 25 April.

Yet they all knew that it was more a matter of form than substance.[88] Mary Cowper acknowledged that the royal family were mere pawns in the hands of the politicians: 'I verily believe

Townshend and Walpole have agreed for themselves only,' while 'the Prince and Princess get nothing in reality by this agreement, but leave to come sometimes to Court; and for that they give up their children, suffer their friends to betray and quit them'.[89]

The king, too, was displeased with the terms agreed, berating Walpole for failing to bring his son fully under control. News of this came to the prince's camp 'by very good hands' of a trusted intermediary, 'Mohammed the Turk'.[90] And despite his marvellous powers of persuasion, Walpole had failed to arrange for the return of the prince's children. Behind the scenes, Princess Caroline wept bitterly.

'Mr Walpole,' she snarled, 'this will be no jesting matter for me; you will hear of me and my complaints every day and hour, in every place, if I have not my children again.'[91]

So, as Princess Caroline, Prince George Augustus and their court lined up in the king's drawing room on the evening of 25 April 1720, they were all angry. Caroline's powerful grievance made it

The crowded drawing room at St James's Palace, with ladies tottering under the weight of their highly patterned metallic mantuas

nearly impossible for her to force her famous smile. This was the fate of princesses. As her predecessor Mary II had said, 'I must grin when my heart is ready to break, and talk when my heart is so oppress'd I can scarce breathe.'[92]

Luckily Princess Caroline was surrounded on all sides by her ladies, and she relied even more than usual upon their physical and moral support. They were more than equal to the task. Jobs serving the princess, in what was normally such 'a very gay court', were in high demand and short supply.[93] The most senior were the Ladies of her Bedchamber, whose salaries were a generous £500 a year.[94] They included the diarist Mary Cowper, who brilliantly skewered many a drawing-room skirmish upon the nib of her pen, and the Countess of Bristol, who was unfortunately addicted to gambling. (She was miraculously transformed whenever she managed to get up from the card table: 'being resolv'd to make up for time misspent, she has 2 lovers at a time'.[95])

Their duties, though, had recently become more ceremonial than practical, and the actual work was now done by the next rank down, the six Women of the Bedchamber (on salaries of £300 a year). They included Charlotte Clayton, a staunch friend to everyone who thought the church too wealthy and powerful, and the emotional and imaginative Charlotte Amelia Titchborne.

'Mrs Clayton' and 'Mrs Titchborne' were really at the heart of Princess Caroline's supportive inner set. Because the Ladies of the Bedchamber had become too grand to do real work, they spent less time with the princess. As a result, the Women of the Bedchamber, while technically inferior, began to wield the greater influence. Everyone knew that their shared apartment was 'the fashionable evening rendezvous of the most distinguished wits and beauties', and Charlotte Clayton was bombarded with letters from petitioners seeking her 'clever way' of putting suggestions to Princess Caroline at a well-chosen moment.[96]

Henrietta Howard had a place in this charmed circle. Even Caroline could see that Henrietta took no pleasure in her role as Prince George Augustus's mistress and that she was also a hard-working, valuable and sympathetic servant. The princess probably felt more than a little sorry for her rival.

They had met seven years ago, when Henrietta had scraped together the last of her money and fled to Hanover in order to escape her husband's creditors. Like many others, she'd hoped to become intimate with Hanover's ruling family in the expectation that they would one day inherit the English throne.

The gamble had paid off. In Hanover, Henrietta did indeed meet and suit Princess Caroline, who offered her a job. Soon afterwards, Prince George Augustus indicated that he too would like a share of her services. Although she never discussed it, Caroline seemed on the surface to accept Henrietta's additional role as royal mistress. She rightly feared that a woman less sensible than Henrietta would be more likely to cause trouble.

Nor did the court as a whole see much cause for scandal: the prince's grandmother thought Henrietta would at the very least improve his English.

When the Hanoverians came to London, Henrietta's husband, Charles Howard, also managed to get a job at court. His position, though, was in the rival household of the king. Although it had been Henrietta's foresight and initiative that had improved their material circumstances so vastly, her greedy husband had continued to think up new ways to exploit his wife.

In fact, by 1720 Henrietta had plucked up the courage to leave him, an act much riskier and more shameful then than now. She remained under constant, grinding pressure to go back to him. Threats had been made, blackmail used and letters had even been written by the Archbishop of Canterbury commanding her to return to her lawful spouse.

Another, even worse aspect of her situation perhaps aroused Princess Caroline's particular pity, allowing her to tolerate rather than despise her rival. Henrietta, too, had had a son stolen. Eighteenth-century law and custom always favoured the father when couples separated, and her only child was in her husband's custody.

While Henrietta failed to enjoy life in the household of the Prince and Princess of Wales, she was at least protected there from Charles Howard's violent, alcohol-fuelled rages. She feared nothing more than being near him, and for her the antipathy they all felt towards the king's household was intensely strong.

On the evening of 25 April 1725, she scanned the drawing room nervously, looking out for trouble. But even Mr Howard dared not make any move upon his wife in such a crowd.

For now Henrietta remained safe. Yet her bizarre position at court, poised to please both prince and princess, involved endless effort. It would only take one moment's inattention for it all to come crashing down.

Last among Princess Caroline's wing women came the unruly Maids of Honour. These well-born, unmarried young ladies, earning £200 a year, were unlikely to remain single for long. Among the current crop, Mary Meadows was the steadiest, and Sophy Howe the flightiest. Then there was the elegant Molly Lepell, of course, and the broad-minded Mary Bellenden.

The Maids of Honour were all well known to the bawdy balladeers and gossip columnists of London. When the king had ordered them all to leave St James's Palace, the characteristic reactions of the individual maids were trumpeted abroad:

> Up leapt Lepell and frisk'd away
> As though she ran on wheels;
> Miss Meadows made a woeful face,
> Miss Howe be-pissed her heels.[97]

The poet John Gay placed Molly Lepell and Mary Bellenden at the very acme of desirability among the maids. Unsuccessfully touting for a sinecure at court, he offered flattery around the royal household as if it were snuff. 'So well I'm known at Court', he joked,

> None asks where *Cupid* dwells;
> But readily resort
> To *Bellenden*'s or *Lepell*'s.[98]

On the night of the reconciliation, many eyes followed the wand-like Molly Lepell, including those of the old king himself. Despite the presence of his long-time mistress Melusine, his faithful May Pole, and the provocation of having to receive his son, he was enthralled by Molly's effervescence.

Molly, though, was searching the room for the man to whom she was secretly married.

Molly's cloak-and-dagger wedding, altogether unsuspected by the courtiers, had taken place a mere four days previously. Despite the tension and confusion of the christening quarrel, a covert romance had bloomed at Leicester House. Her love was none other than the life and soul of the chic clique at court, the droll, amusing young butterfly John Hervey.

Hervey was a real court insider. His elder brother, Carr, was a Gentleman of the Bedchamber to Prince George Augustus, while the card-fanatic Lady Bristol was his mother. 'I came very early into the world', he told a friend, 'and had a satiating swing in the showish part of its pleasures.' Besieged by socialites and suitors on all sides, living in the very 'midst of a crowded court', he nevertheless felt that he spent 'many, many hours alone'.[99] He was ripe for a relationship more meaningful than the usual courtly intrigues.

Recently, having spied out Molly's hidden streak of vulnerability, he felt he had surely found the companion he sought. Together they could laugh at the world. He'd come to rely upon her and to love her in a manner most surprising at court: 'above himself'.[100]

Yet his mother's gambling had put the Hervey family's finances into a very sorry state. For the moment at least Molly could not admit to her marriage, because to do so would mean sacrificing her job and salary as a Maid of Honour. She and her clandestine husband had nothing else upon which to live.

By risking her career for a love match, Molly had shown herself to be deeply unconventional among the courtiers. More surprises would surely follow from this mysterious Maid of Honour who was secretly a maid no more.

*

On 25 April 1720, it became clear that the particular battle between the two courts sparked off by the 'christening quarrel' had reached a stalemate. Each protagonist was bruised but not broken, and Henrietta Howard and Molly Lepell (or Hervey) had yet to find out if they had chosen wisely in hitching their fortunes to the party of the passionate but petulant prince.

George I, meanwhile, had triumphed in the matter of the apology. He still retained the little princesses in his possession, and he'd saved face by having his son once again publicly compliant. He was now resolved to beat his son and daughter-in-law at their own game of popularity. He'd lost much ground with his recent bullying tactics, so he decided instead to use the splendour of his own court as a weapon to win back public favour.

He needed to build a new battlefield: a new and more splendid palace in which to carry forward the campaign.

THREE

The Pushy Painter

'Courts are the best keys to characters: there every
passion is busy, every art exerted.'
(Lord Chesterfield)

If you climb the King's Grand Staircase at Kensington Palace today, you'll see painted figures looking down upon you from the walls. There are valets, porters, maids, pages, guards, musicians, babies and lapdogs. They whisper, glance, fan themselves, climb upon the balustrade . . . everyone is in motion, and everyone is watching you.

This masterpiece of mural art was commissioned by George I in a concerted effort to transform his run-down palace at Kensington and to make his court more splendid and welcoming than that of his gregarious son and daughter-in-law. The smiling faces watching and welcoming you are portraits of real servants of the king, drafted in to do the duty of making the palace buzz and bustle.

It's a remarkable collection of portraits, celebrating a rank in society from which individuals are rarely remembered. But it was nearly never painted at all. It took luck as well as a liberal dash of talent for an outsider, William Kent, to win the job of populating the king's staircase with characters from his court.

In 1722, the twists and turns of this particular artistic commission coalesced into a cut-throat, all-out battle that divided artistic London.

William Kent was a rumbustious, gluttonous, outrageous character. Throughout the royal family's quarrel he had been studying painting in Italy. When he returned to London at the end of 1719, just before the royal reconciliation at St James's, he found only a rainy English winter and a chilly welcome. The days were so short, he complained, and so 'cold to an Italian constitution' that

William Kent, 'very hot, & very fat', at work with his pen

he kept to his 'little room'. He consoled himself by going twice a week to the opera, where he was 'highly entertain'd' and able to imagine himself 'out of this Gothick country'.[2]

Because of his adopted Italian ways, Kent's numerous friends called him 'The Signior'. His bosom buddy and patron, Richard Boyle, third Earl of Burlington and fourth Earl of Cork (1695–1753), addressed him, affectionately, as 'Kentino' ('little Kent').

The 'little room' that Kent used as his London bolthole was in Burlington's grand Piccadilly home. The two had first met in Italy in 1716, and Kent's fiery personality was the perfect foil to Burlington's considered coolness. Kent was given unique licence to tease: in one of his sketches of the earl, a dog urinates upon the aristocratic ankle. The odd couple nevertheless had many common interests, particularly as Burlington was enormously enthusiastic about architecture and design. Indeed, some people

considered that he took his interests far too seriously for an aristocrat, and 'lessened himself' by getting too technical.[3]

So the scientific Burlington and the artistic Kent lived on the
most amicable terms, together pouring scorn upon Kent's rival
artists with 'mortification – and mirth'.[4] Kent wrote in one letter
to his patron of their 'living and loving together, as you and I do',
and concluded another with 'a hundred more wild things that cannot be write'.[5]

Kent needed wildness, wine and sunshine to be happy. His
friends teased him for his dictatorial manner about the best way to
cook a steak; for entertaining himself 'with syllabubs and damsels';
for being in love with malt liquor; for being 'very hot, & very fat'.[6]
At one select party held in his little room, fourteen bottles of wine
were drunk 'in one sitting'.[7] Always volatile, Kent could be touchy
and 'very umbrageous in his drink'.[8]

Yet he also possessed the talent and immense self-confidence
that could catapult him into court circles.

As an extrovert, disingenuous character, Kent would find the
court a complicated and confusing place to work. Court politics
spilt over into all parts of palace life, including the remoter reaches
of the Office of the King's Works. It was only through a remarkable fluke that the unkempt Kent found himself in possession of a
plum royal commission, and his enemies would do their best to
take it from him.

The battle of the painters had begun long before Kent's return
from Italy. The opening salvo had been fired not by the king, but
by Prince George Augustus and Princess Caroline, with the help
of their chosen artist, Sir James Thornhill.[9]

In 1716, Caroline had redecorated her apartment at Hampton
Court Palace. Like Kensington, Hampton Court was another of
the summer residences to which the Hanoverian royal family had
become entitled in 1714. (Caroline, with her German accent, pronounced it 'Hamthancour'.[10]) When the king went off to Hanover
for the summer, Princess Caroline and Prince George Augustus

took advantage of his absence to host a series of sparkling parties at the palace. Caroline's suite there provided a particularly magnificent setting, for it had been decorated by Britain's greatest baroque painter, Sir James Thornhill.

Thornhill was becoming the definitive artist of the early eighteenth century. His work on Princess Caroline's apartment at Hampton Court was preceded by the Painted Hall at the Royal Naval Hospital, Greenwich, and would be followed by the decoration of the dome of St Paul's Cathedral. He'd faced stiff competition for the job at Hampton Court from Italian painters such as Sebastiano Ricci, and indeed continental artists had been snapping up most of the best recent commissions in England. Thornhill himself had studied under the partially sighted Italian Antonio Verrio. When he'd worked at Hampton Court previously, for Queen Anne, it had been as Verrio's assistant.

His compatriots were proud when Thornhill won the commission for Princess Caroline's bedchamber. Lord Halifax, first Lord of the Treasury, gushed generously that 'Mr Thornhill our countryman has strove against all oppositions & difficulties & now has got near the very top of the mountain'.[II]

Thornhill now demonstrated that the English could indeed do 'history painting' – showing mythical events on a dramatically grand scale – just as well as the Italians. On his ceiling for Princess Caroline, a Babylonian princess attempts to stop Apollo from driving his golden sun-chariot out of the sea so as not to disturb the sleepers (or lovers) below. Round the edge Thornhill placed portraits of Princess Caroline and Prince George Augustus themselves. When the couple lay together in Caroline's brand-new crimson damask bed, they could look up and admire their own faces.

James Thornhill had undoubtedly climbed to the summit of his profession, but he'd always been a bit too pleased with himself to be a truly likeable character. He was a man fond of his own dignity, jowly and fleshy, with beetling eyebrows. In a self-portrait, he's being slowly strangled by his own tight cravat as he glances rather glumly from his canvas. When he was honoured with a knighthood in 1720, he bought back his family's lost ancestral estate of Thornhill in Dorset. There he painted another self-portrait upon his drawing-room ceiling so that he, too, could easily gaze with satisfaction at his own smug countenance.[12]

Thornhill's work for Princess Caroline was much admired. When it was complete, she and her husband held a memorable season for the junior court in this romantic palace down by the river. Everybody had fun at their amusing crowded balls and masquerades, so much so that 'some virgins conceived'.[13] Meanwhile, George I's lacklustre court was constantly criticised in the newspapers, and his mistress and half-sister written off as '*whores*, nay, what is more *vexatious, ugly old whores!*'[14]

The king had much to achieve before his own court could outclass his son's in splendour and popularity.

In June 1716, while Prince George Augustus and Princess Caroline were living the high life at Hampton Court, a survey revealed the desperately poor condition of Kensington Palace. The king's summer residence there was veering towards the dangerous.

The rural royal retreat at Kensington was an old-fashioned mansion created in the 1690s by the Dutch King William III and his English wife Mary II. Kensington's great advantage lay in its air. Clean and dry by comparison with the damp old palace of St James's, it was said to 'cure without medicines'.[15] Its healthy properties had driven the asthmatic King William III to select Kensington as one of his principal homes. There:

> while the Town in damps and darkness lies,
> They breathe in sun-shine and see azure skies.[16]

So the wheezing William and his wife had purchased an old seventeenth-century villa there, and set their architect, Sir Christopher Wren, to work upon expanding it. He added a pavilion to each of its four corners and created a pair of new long galleries for king and queen respectively.

These alterations became Mary's pet project, and she drove work forward with such passion and speed that an imperfect mortar mix was overlooked and a workman killed. William and Mary's court followed their king and queen to this newly fashionable suburb, and within fifteen years Kensington village had grown to three times the size of Chelsea and was 'fill'd with persons of honour and distinction'.[17]

It was only six years after becoming queen, though, that Mary received the equivalent of a death sentence. Waking up at Kensington Palace on the morning of 21 December 1694, she discovered upon her arm the red rash preceding smallpox. The young queen, only thirty-two and radiantly beautiful, was 'suddenly become a frightful spectacle', and the country was devastated when the 'putrid smallpox' claimed her life at Kensington a week later.[18]

The palace she left behind was pleasant enough and beautifully situated among parks and gardens. But it had been built too quickly, and the poor quality of the workmanship meant it was already half falling down. By the time of George I's accession, it had been for some years 'much crack't and out of repair'.[19]

Yet at first George I seemed quite satisfied with his inheritance. Before the outbreak of the 'christening quarrel', he'd done his best to minimise his public appearances. 'The King locks himself up', the courtiers complained, 'and is never seen.'[20] It was only when the quarrel erupted in 1717 that it became necessary for him to wage a war of hospitality in order to win back the supporters who were slipping away to the prince's court.

The unfortunate death of his grandson at Kensington in 1718 was quickly followed by one of the busiest royal social seasons ever seen. A gentleman visiting from Virginia found 'a great crowd' at Kensington Palace dancing in the gardens, with fireworks to celebrate the king's birthday in May.[21] That summer, the king entertained fifty or sixty guests to dinner every night and held a ball twice a week.[22]

Also in 1718, at the very height of the quarrel, George I

embarked upon a grand plan to rebuild and redecorate the state apartments at Kensington. He intended to breathe new life into both his palace and his court.

All the craftsmen of London fervently hoped to become involved in this bold scheme to turn the crumbling Stuart house at Kensington into a magnificent and modern 'Roman' palace. To work in a royal palace would be the best commission of all.

Repairs and improvements to the royal palaces were the responsibility of the Office of the King's Works. This department received its income from the Treasury and spent it on all manner of building and decorating projects. But inevitably the factions and spats of the drawing room affected its decision-making.

The activities of the Office of the King's Works were overseen by a board of five: the Surveyor-General, the Comptroller, the Master Mason, the Master Carpenter and one other. They met for weekly progress checks in their office at Scotland Yard, Westminster, crowded with 'closets, presses &c for repositing the books, drawings & designs belonging to the several palaces'.[23] Each month they received a report upon the man-hours and materials expended, and every year they enjoyed a celebratory dinner together. So far, so good, but politics complicated all their doings.

The board's decisions were recorded in minute detail in its heavy, leathery and voluminous volumes of minutes and warrants, all dutifully kept up to date by its clerks. These books – some of them works of calligraphic art – stolidly track the protracted negotiations that preceded work on site. Everything moved very slowly through an undergrowth of respectful verbiage. 'His Majesty has commanded me to signify his pleasure to your Lordships, that you give orders for the following alterations to be made in the Duchess of Kendal's lodgings at St James's,' runs a typical letter.[24] This is a stately machine, slowly masticating upon its duty.

Sometimes, though, the machinery breaks down. Just

occasionally, a desperate flash of jealousy emerges from behind the ponderous prose and the sparks ignited by a power struggle still glimmer on the page.

On 19 June 1718, the king gave his 'orders for erecting a new building at Kensington'.[25] The accompanying plan showed the proposed reconstruction of the palace's chief chambers: the Privy Chamber, Cupola and Drawing Rooms. These were the three main spaces through which visitors invited to the court's evening 'drawing room' would pass. Soon the demolition of the seventeenth-century structure at the heart of the palace began, and the guts of the building were ripped out.[26]

In 1719, there was change at the Office of the King's Works: Sir Thomas Hewett was appointed as the new Surveyor-General. He was an odd, cantankerous fellow, but had the qualifications of being a good strong Whig and of having toured the continent to learn about foreign architecture. (From this trip he was said to have brought back 'a wife, atheism and many eccentricities'.[27]) He had dreams of building a great royal palace during his tenure as Surveyor.

Hewett now found himself placed under considerable pressure because the king wanted the alterations at Kensington Palace to be completed 'with all speed'.[28] Despite the demolition work continuing throughout 1719, the palace remained packed with a horde of locust-like guests taking full advantage of the king's music and free drinks. That summer was extraordinarily hot, with the result that London experienced a plague of 'damnable bedbugs'.[29]

The next year, 1720, London was convulsed by the South Sea Bubble, a frenzy of speculation in a company intending to trade with the islands of the Pacific Ocean. Fortunes were made in weeks, but the bursting of the Bubble was inevitable. Among those affected in the royal households was Peter Wentworth, the lowly equerry, whose permanent financial plight was made even more pitiful by unwise speculation.[30]

At the end of July 1720, just after the South Sea stock reached

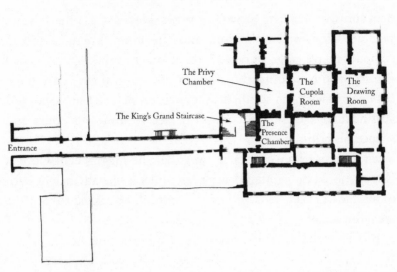

The main rooms rebuilt in the 1720s were the Privy, Cupola and Drawing Rooms,
with William Kent's King's Grand Staircase providing a prologue

its peak price, the courtiers began their first proper summer in the
rebuilt Kensington Palace now emerging from its chrysalis of scaffolding. The three little princesses, George I's granddaughters,
came into residence, and an excited inhabitant of Kensington village wrote in August that 'the Court is now in our neighbour-
hood; they say the King is extremely well pleased with his
apartment'.[31]

In 1721, a year in which smallpox went forth in London 'like a
destroying angel', the shell of the new rooms was finally completed.[32] There was an immense new Drawing Room overlooking
the gardens to the east, and an even more splendid reception room
called the 'Cupola' or 'Cube Room' in the centre of the palace.
Providing a fitting prologue to the whole was a vastly improved
King's Grand Staircase leading up from the courtyard. The great
carver Grinling Gibbons performed some of his last work here
before his death in 1721, and Sir James Thornhill's men were
employed to paint the woodwork.

Early in 1722, quotations were sought for the decorating of the
state apartments, beginning with the Cupola Room. This was to

be a summer of strife as well as miserable weather: there was a Jacobite plot for a rebellion, and the king's enemies spread rumours that 'a cargo of new German ladies of the largest size are coming, and Mohammed . . . is to be chief over them'.[33] Although his quarrel with his son had by now been patched up, George I still needed a freshly decorated palace to unite his court and silence his critics.

Sir Thomas Hewett's fancy was that the magnificent Cupola Room should be painted deceptively to look like an ancient bath of marble. As expected, Sir James Thornhill was asked to turn the idea into reality.

But Thornhill was about to suffer a 'mighty mortification'.[34]

The job had begun well for Thornhill. He'd sketched a range of proposals; the king had selected his favourite, and then ordered his Vice-Chamberlain to negotiate 'for the price'.[35] Everybody was happy; everything seemed agreed – but for the matter of the money.

Now Thornhill made his fatal mistake. His recent successes encouraged him to demand an outrageously high figure – £800 – for decorating the room. The court's Vice-Chamberlain, Thomas Coke, thought it simply 'too extravagant'. So, 'without more ado', he invited 'Mr Kent to Kensington & ask'd him what he would have for the same painting to be done'.[36]

William Kent, little known, low paid, ten years younger than Thornhill, had risen fast from provincial obscurity and had picked up many friends along the way. Born at Bridlington in Yorkshire, he had changed his name to 'Kent' from the less auspicious 'Cant' used by his father. Kent had begun an apprenticeship with a coach painter, but by the age of twenty he'd abandoned his master 'without leave' and run away to London.[37] He was soon attracting the kind of rich patrons who might pay for him to travel to Italy. It was a Lincolnshire gentleman, Burrell Massingberd, who eventually subsidised Kent's studies in Rome.

Massingberd often complained of his protégé's failure to correspond, but the dyslexic Kent suggested that he 'had as leave make a drawing as write a letter'.[38] Indeed, he took remarkably poor care of his patrons, rightly assuming that any he lost would soon be replaced by newer, richer, grander ones.

Back in London, Kent's uncanny knack of possessing the right contacts proved at least as important as his vigorous but rather crude talent as a painter in winning the job at Kensington Palace. To Sir Thomas Hewett, at least, he was an old friend from Italy. Hewett had actually visited Kent in his studio in Rome in 1717; the penny-pinching Vice-Chamberlain Thomas Coke also had contacts among 'Mr Kent's friends' in Italy.[39]

And Hewett was not at all reluctant to follow Coke's suggestion to drop Thornhill, because he had reasons of his own for being annoyed with Sir James.

As well as being the story of the decoration of a ceiling, this episode was something of a skirmish in a wider artistic struggle. Thornhill's brutal ejection was part of a pattern. The old guard, who still worked in the conservative, late-seventeenth-century style, were reluctantly giving way to a new wave of designers being championed by Lord Burlington.

Kent himself said he hated the 'dam'd gusto' that had dominated the last sixty years of British art.[40] The new 'gusto', or style, on the point of breaking through was Palladianism, named after the sixteenth-century Italian designer Andrea Palladio. It had long been favoured by the Electors of Hanover and their court, where even George I's servant Mohammed had been among the subscribers to a new edition of Palladio's work.[41]

Now poised to transform English architecture, Palladianism seemed to provide the right look for the modern, Hanoverian Britain. In contrast to the melodramatic art of the previous Stuart age, Palladianism depended upon a careful, controlled use of proportion to create its harmonious effect. While the enthusiasts for Palladio all wanted change, though, they couldn't agree upon exactly what it should look like. Burlington, Hewett and Kent had slightly different ideas, but they could concur that Thornhill's day was over.

Kent made his own quotation for decorating the Cupola Room ceiling in February 1722. The painting was to be done with the greatest of diligence, he promised, following the previously approved design and for the price of only £300.[42] Cleverly, Kent offered a slightly classier alternative: for an extra £50, he would use expensive ultramarine pigment instead of the cheaper Prussian blue. This proved a cunning ruse to prevent the king from looking cheap, and the ultramarine proposal for £350 was accepted.

However, the officials of the Office of the King's Works agreed to take particular care to check that Kent's painting was properly executed before he was paid. They felt that they were taking a risk in using this untried young artist.

In 1722, then, William Kent had quickly and easily ascended to the 'top of the mountain'. His previous acquaintance with Hewett weighed in his favour, and so did the powerful influence of his patron Lord Burlington, who promoted Kent 'on all occasions to everything in his power, to the King, to the Court Works, & Courtiers'.[43] But perhaps most vital of all to Kent's success was the fact that Thornhill's overconfidence had incensed a lot of important people.[44]

Sir James Thornhill had recently begun to think that his talents equipped him for a bigger role than that of a mere painter. He was heard to declare that 'he would practice as an architect', and not unreasonably so, as he 'certainly had skill and knowledge enough in that branch'. Yet there was an instant uproar at his presumption. 'What a clamour' rose up from the existing architects of London, 'what outcries of Invasion!'[45]

Thornhill made a grave tactical mistake in promoting himself as an architectural expert. What was worse, he'd been heard upbraiding the Office of the King's Works for their supposed 'ignorances' in the art of building, giving the impression that he 'would set himself up against them'. Hewett found this kind of hubris understandably offensive, so he and his board had 'played [Thornhill] this trick' over the Cupola Room commission.

The mighty man did manage to swallow enough of his pride to make one last attempt at winning back the job at Kensington. He returned to Vice-Chamberlain Coke with a new, lower quotation, writing a sad little letter saying that he 'would do it, for what any other would do it'. But it was too late. Kent was chosen, and Thornhill was categorically 'rejected'.[46]

Yet Thornhill did not lack friends and supporters of his own, including William Hogarth and the architect James Gibbs, vigorous opponents of Lord Burlington's Palladianising vision. This gang weren't willing to give up gracefully. William Kent may have been the surprise winner of the battle for the Cupola Room commission, but his enemies would now do their best to bring him down again.

In the words of another of Kent's friends, the poet John Gay, the king's new pet artist could expect a hostile reception from London's artistic community:

> But oh, consider, e'er thy works appear
> Canst thou unhurt the tongue of envy hear?[47]

Sir Thomas Hewett and his board were charged by the Treasury with ensuring that Kent's work was performed 'in the best manner'. They decided it would be wise to appoint an advisory committee of more experienced artists to keep Kent in line. By May 1722, the ceiling of the Cupola Room was more than half finished. An advisory committee of three – John Van der Vaart, Alexander Nesbitt, Jacob Rambour – was sent to inspect it, and to report on 'the true condition of the works, and if there should be any faults or mistakes'.[48]

So it was that three of London's most prominent painters came to see the bizarrely splendid and half-finished Cupola Room. High above them, William Kent was slowly transforming the plain plaster into a marvellously deceptive montage of marble and golden chrysanthemums, his tricks with perspective turning the room into a space seemingly twice as tall.

Kent and his assistants worked from a tall wooden scaffold tower, and also had a smaller, movable 'framed' scaffold that could run from place to place upon wheels. Kent was quite comfortable at heights up to forty precarious feet above the ground.[49]

His equipment included his brushes (hog's bristle and camel hair), his scraping or pallet knives, the earthen pots holding his colours, and cans of oil for thinning. His assistants Robert Clerece and Franciscus de Valentia were busy with the pestle and the heavy square grinding stone, working the pigments into the favoured medium of nut oil. Ready-mixed paint was not yet widely available for sale.

Kent had to paint each patch over and over again because oil-based paint rarely produces an even hue.[50] He was creating a design – roughly inspired by Thornhill's earlier scheme – of *trompe l'oeil* recessed octagons, each one painted complete with shadows. The backdrop was a luxuriantly veined imitation marble. In the centre was a great star of the Order of the Garter; at each corner were bushels of the flowing feathers of the Prince of Wales, a nod from George I to his son.

Although Kent's scheme was based on Thornhill's original proposal, this was certainly not the kind of baroque, figure-based painting at which Sir James excelled. At his glorious Painted Hall in Greenwich, princes and princesses are treated like deities, seated amidst angels, clouds and a cornucopia of gold. At Kensington Palace, Kent was using paint to emulate architecture, and to create the spectacular but solid effect of a Roman palace. There was no complicated iconographic message to puzzle out here. At this moment, wall art was becoming less of a lesson about people or ideas, and the concept of the 'interior decorator' as opposed to the artist was being born.

But this would not happen without birth pangs.

On 22 May, the painters on the inspection committee made their report, and they were not impressed. 'The perspective is not just,' they complained, and the 'ornaments . . . not done as such a place requires'. Mr Nesbitt thought he'd seen 'very few worse' pieces of work; Mr Rambour thought it 'not so much as tolerably well performed'.

Worse still for Kent was an accusation that he'd defrauded the king by using substandard materials. Mr Van der Vaart and Mr Rambour thought he hadn't used 'true ultramarine' because 'it does not look fine enough'. And Alexander Nesbitt condemned unequivocally: in his opinion Kent had used 'nothing but [inexpensive] Prussian Blue'.[51]

While other blue paints came from cornflowers, copper or glass, Kent, of course, was contractually obliged to use ultra - marine, the expensive blue made from lapis lazuli. For centuries it had been the most highly prized pigment of all, azure in hue, rich, deep, long-lasting and made from precious stone transported thousands of miles from the mines of Afghanistan. The painter Edward Norgate (d.1650) gives directions for the protracted process of preparing ultramarine. First you grind the mineral and mix it into a paste. Then you

> knead it and work it between your hands so long that you may see it sweat out drops of clear water of a blue colour . . . let this water stand and settle 24 hours, and then powder it off and let the grounds dry, and when it is thoroughly dried, wipe it out of the pan with a feather upon a paper and so put it up.[52]

The skill of the paint-maker was akin to that of the druggist or the cook, requiring exotic ingredients such as East Indian yellow or indigo from the West Indies. Crushed cochineal beetles went into carmine red, and pieces of ancient Egyptian mummies were a prized ingredient for brown.[53]

Even the cheap Prussian blue – proposed but rejected for the Cupola Room – was a peculiar product only available since 1710. It had been discovered by accident when an alchemist from Berlin threw away some waste potash (a compound containing potassium produced from wood ashes). A colleague mixed it accidentally with some alkali, thereby producing a new, robust, deep blue: less expensive than ultramarine, but not quite as good.[54]

The advisory committee's negative report destroyed Surveyor-General Sir Thomas Hewett's peace of mind. He thought that Kent's work had been 'perfectly well executed' and guessed that jealousy had fired up all the 'quacks', 'knaves' and 'fools' of the artistic world. He was deeply discouraged, and thought it 'impossible to have anything good' with such wrong-headed mules for colleagues.[55]

And the king, in his turn, was rumoured to be 'not a bit content' with Sir Thomas Hewett.

Surely, with these rumours of royal displeasure, Kent would now get his comeuppance for stealing the commission from Thornhill? With reports like these being bandied about, he must have been aware that he was in danger of getting the sack.

But whether it was due to inertia, disagreement or string-pulling by Kent's friends, there was no official response to the inspection committee's report. So he continued painting. By July, the king was said to be 'much pleased with Kensington, and the easy way of living he is fallen into there'.[56] Now officially, if not emotionally, reconciled with his son, the king and little princesses received stiff and sticky Sunday visits from Prince George Augustus and Princess Caroline.[57]

By August, Kent had finished the Cupola Room, and began to feel anxious and 'uneasy for want of his money'.[58] In response to his prodding for payment, he discovered nothing but further dispute at the Office of the King's Works. So he began to kick up a fuss about the officials' procrastination. On 22 August 1722, he invaded the board's actual meeting to make a scene 'in relation to his money'.[59] And he had friends working on his behalf elsewhere. After that particular meeting was adjourned without a decision, a letter arrived from the Treasury, commanding the Board of Works that Kent must be paid 'immediately without any further exceptions or delays whatsoever'.[60]

Happy-go-lucky and haphazard as he was, Kent was clearly 'sailing thro' the ways of life well befriended'.[61] He was beginning to prove the truth of a later judgement of his character: that he was 'bold and opinionative enough to dare to dictate, and born with a genius'.[62]

He would also prove to be vindicated in the matter of materials. Conservation work to the Cupola Room ceiling in the twentieth century established that Kent really had used the expensive ultramarine, not the cheaper Prussian blue.

Paid at last, Kent continued gaily to work through the other rooms at Kensington. In 1724, he began the Presence Chamber and Council Chamber. The king's Gallery and Great and Little Closets were soon under way.

Yet the finished Cupola Room continued to displease London's

William Kent's sketch for the drawing-room ceiling, Kensington Palace. In the oval are Jupiter and Semele, the human lover Jupiter accidentally killed with his Olympian thunder-flashes

cognoscenti. They found it 'a terrible glaring show, & truly gothic'. The connoisseur George Vertue thought its poor quality could be explained by the endless 'private piques' and quarrels among the members of the Board of Works.[63]

Undeterred by all the criticism, though, the king seemed to be serenely happy with progress on his palace. In addition to the decoration indoors, a tiger was acquired for the palace menagerie, an 'iron den' constructed for its accommodation, the 'snailery, and a place for breeding tortoises' were completed and the palace's kitchens were rebuilt.[64] Kensington was nearly ready for its golden days as the Hanoverian kings' beloved summer residence. George I now declared that he liked Kensington 'mightily' and was 'more at ease and tranquillity than ever before in England'.[65]

Among the artists of London, however, the quarrel ground on, and Thornhill refused to accept any commission for less than 'the

Hogarth calls Kent by the shortest word for the female genitalia. The statue of Kent, standing over the entrance to the 'Academy of Arts', is labelled 'KNT'

same price each picture as Mr Kent had'.[66] The engraver William Hogarth struck back on behalf of Thornhill and the old guard. He ridiculed Kent's pretensions in a series of caricatures. The most offensive of them showed the statue of a painter carved with the letters 'KNT', combining a reference to Kent himself with the shortest word for the female genitalia.

Despite his lucrative work at Kensington and his continued royal favour, these rude caricatures 'touch't Mr Kent and diverted the town'.[67] The quarrel seemed set to run and run, and it remained to be seen whether Kent could pay Hogarth back for his teasing.

In 1725, setting aside his irritation, Kent had begun the greatest and most successful of his works at the palace. In July, he was 'so busy about the staircase' at Kensington that he had no time for any other commissions.[68] This time he was creating an undoubted masterpiece: the mural masquerade in which the servants would show their faces to the world.

One by one, individuals from the lower ranks of the royal household were taking their painted places within a magnificent architectural setting, created in oils upon canvas covering the staircase walls.

The idea of painted people looking through painted windows, or of a painted sky glimpsed over fictitious rooftops, wasn't new. Kent's most likely source of inspiration was the Sala dei Corazzieri at the Quirinal Palace in Rome, from the early seventeenth century. There an exotically dressed crowd of people look between painted pillars down into the room below.[69] Kent's innovation was to make it all more realistic. His Kensington arcade was inhabited by genuine court servants, at a reasonable scale and in their normal clothes.

The lower walls and landing of Kent's staircase are decorated with monumental and sombre suits of armour, trophies, statues, seahorses, an impassive head of Britannia and a blank-eyed Roman warrior, all painted in shades of grey and gloom.

(Additionally, it would be many years before the 'lanterns on the great staircase' were finally 'fixed in a proper manner'.[70])

As you ascend the stairs you gradually come level, and enter into eye contact, with the portraits of the servants. The perspective begins to work as you rise to the proper vantage point on the upper landing. The figure of Diana, painted on this landing, was copied from a real antique statue.[71]

The people boldly eyeing you as you climb are not courtiers of the highest rank. Lord Chesterfield understood that those below stairs wielded great power, and that a history of the court should concentrate on the servants as well as the great:

> there is, at all Courts, a chain, which connects the Prince, or the Minister, with the Page of the back-stairs, or the Chambermaid. The King's Wife, or Mistress, has an influence over him; a Lover has an influence over her; the Chambermaid, or the Valet de Chambre, has an influence over both; and so *ad infinitum*.[72]

Kent's staircase put this philosophy into painted form.

There was no shortage of potential sitters. The royal household contained a Decipherer, a Secretary for translating into Latin, an Embellisher of Letters to Foreign Princes and forty-eight Chaplains, who attended in shifts of four. Then there was the Master of the Revels, the Surveyor of the Waterworks and the Keeper of the Lions in the Tower.[73] Not least were the Clerk of the Spicery, the Yeomen of the Salt-Stores and the three 'confectionaries' who made the king's cakes.[74]

In the end Kent selected forty-five sitters for his staircase. They were real servants with real jobs, some of them with considerable power and many of them living their whole lives at court rather than serving in rotation like the more senior courtiers. Chosen for their odd appearance or their close connection with the king, these figures must have been instantly recognisable to the denizens of Kensington Palace. Each must have sat for Kent or an assistant, willingly or unwillingly, for long enough to be painted

Ulrich Jorry, the loud-mouthed dwarf, a lively court
character who sometimes got into trouble

accurately enough to add to the masque-like effect. Most of them must have been filled with pride and pleasure at being asked to take part in this elaborate court joke.

And Kent must have been delighted by his new-won power as he, the intruder, stage-managed the court to fulfil his vision.

One of the great unsolved mysteries at Kensington Palace is the true identity of the forty-five different people shown on the staircase. And the first chapter of the mystery concerns Ulrich Jorry, the Polish dwarf.

A visitor to Kensington Palace writing in 1741 claimed the figures on the staircase included 'Mr. *Ulrick*, commonly called the Young *Turk*, in his *Polonese* dress, as he waited on the late King *George*'.[75]

Christian Ulrich Jorry was a member of the long and proud parade of jesters/truthsayers close to England's kings. His predecessors included, in the sixteenth century, King Henry VIII's Will Somers and, in the seventeenth century, Queen Henrietta Maria's Jeffery Hudson. Ulrich, like many a dwarf before him, was presented to George I as a gift, by the Duke of Saxe Gotha in this case, whose envoy was given a present of £330 in return.[76] (Jeffrey Hudson had also been a gift, and had made his entrance by jumping out of a pie served at Henrietta Maria's birthday party.)

Despite his small stature, Ulrich had an immensely loud, foundation-shaking voice, almost deafening enough to 'endanger the Royal Palace' at full volume.[77] Sometimes he wore Turkish dress, sometimes a fur-trimmed Polish cap.[78] Ulrich also benefited from English and painting lessons at the king's expense, and had his own servants.

Notwithstanding the claims of the 1741 guidebook, though, there is no figure present on the staircase with a close resemblance to Ulrich. We know exactly what he looks like from another picture of George I's court depicting a hunting expedition (it hangs today over a photocopier in an office at Buckingham Palace). Ulrich, clearly labelled, is excitedly beating his horse, a determined expression on his chubby round face.[79] Although tall enough to ride a pony, he is obviously a person of restricted growth, and his likeness cannot be spotted in the staircase mural.

However, two more exotic servants, Mohammed and Mustapha, do indeed appear, without doubt, at the upper turn in the staircase. They flank an unknown but seductive lady.

The power and strangeness of the two Turks made them targets of suspicion and envy among the English. Gossip reported that the king 'keeps two Turks for abominable uses', and the British were full of 'base reflections . . . that a TURK should be employed so near the *Throne*'.[80]

They were paid privately out of George I's Privy Purse and did all the work of washing and dressing him. These menial jobs, including activities such as warming a king's shirt by the fire, handing it to him or – best of all – attending him in what he called 'our Secret or Privy Room, when we go to ease ourself', had long been hotly contested.[81] Since the time of Henry VIII, the Groom of the Stool had the dubious honour of accompanying the king when 'he goeth to make water' and of handing him the flannel 'to wipe the nether end'.[82] These positions of intimacy with the king

Left: Mohammed, not a royal sex toy, but a discreet, trusted and
loyal servant. Right: Mustapha, who was snatched from his Turkish
home and family in his youth but retained his Turkish dress.
Turkish servants were a status symbol in the West

were traditionally the most powerful in a court of the *ancien
régime*, and in the past had been performed by noblemen.

When George I became king, though, he'd made no appointment to the post of Groom of the Stool, and broke with custom by
insisting that he would dress in private. Much to the annoyance of
the senior British courtiers, they were kept out of the bedchamber.
There the Turks ruled supreme.

On the staircase Mohammed is boldly dressed in a blue cape
with much gold braid, his head cropped, his eyebrow supercili-
ously curved. His colleague Mustapha, on the other hand, loiters
in the background, worried, older, white-bearded and turbaned.
He presents a more exotic appearance, and indeed his waistcoat
bears a Turkish crescent moon over his heart.

The pair had many royal secrets to keep. In August 1717, George
I showed the symptoms of haemorrhoids, or swellings in his anal
arteries. The horrific dangers of surgical removal – being 'cut for
the piles' – were well known. The whole matter was kept secret
from the English courtiers. Only the trusted Mohammed was able

to persuade the king to undergo a medical examination, and all proved well, although George I had to avoid sitting upon a saddle.[83] In gratitude the king nominated Mohammed for a special title to be awarded by the Holy Roman Emperor. His devoted servant chose the appropriate troponym 'von Königstreu', or 'True to the King'.

The two Turks had made a long journey to reach their current privileged position. Mohammed's father had been a pasha, sent by his superiors within the Ottoman hierarchy to govern part of Peloponnesian Greece.[84] The Muslim Ottoman and the Christian Hapsburg Empires clashed frequently in the late seventeenth century, and George I himself had campaigned in Hungary against the Turks, helping to lift the Ottoman siege of Vienna in 1683. At some early but unknown point in his life, the young Mohammed was captured by a Hanoverian officer and brought to Germany, where he made a conversion to Christianity and a marriage to the daughter of a wealthy brewer.

Entering George I's service and following the king to England, Mohammed worked his way up from 'bodyservant' (*Leibdiener*) to the much grander 'Keeper of the King's Closet'.[85] Mustapha, his junior colleague, made a similar journey. He arrived in Hanover after a period in the service of the Swedish army officer who had captured him.

Mohammed, controller of access to the king, was such a favoured servant that he was painted several times during his lifetime. He was effectively (if not officially) Master of the Robes and Keeper of the Privy Purse to the king, both important jobs.[86] Government ministers often paid him court. He had his own servant, who helped him wash the king's clothes, and he slept in a grand four-poster bed upholstered in scarlet and trimmed with lace.[87] Mustapha was also rich enough to employ a private tutor for his sons.[88]

Mohammed's even greater responsibilities and pay were earned through his discretion and his solid, reliable character. 'Never did he burden the ear of his Royal Master, with complaints,' it was said, nor did he 'ever presume to ask a favour'. Like Mustapha, he was a family man. Of his 'dear wife', Maria Hedewig Mohammed, a wealthy woman of Hanover, he declared: 'I love her most heartily.'[89] They had a daughter and two sons, and it's no surprise to find that their names – Sophia Caroline, Johann Ludewig and George Ludewig – were borrowed from the family Mohammed had served for nearly forty years.

However, William Kent did not choose just the most colourfully dressed members of the court to decorate his staircase. He could also be attracted by a pretty face. When he first met Mrs Elizabeth Tempest, Princess Caroline's milliner, he was 'so struck with her appearance, as to beg her to sit for her picture'.[90] To judge from her lovely visage, and her hyper-fashionable black hood, Mrs Tempest is probably the lady in the group near the window.[91]

Kent also included a number of scarlet-clad Yeomen of the Guard. The one hundred Yeomen of the Guard by now formed a great British institution, providing the king with a bodyguard whenever he left the palace.[92] Created shortly after the Battle of Bosworth Field in 1485 to protect the first Tudor monarch, Henry VII, this royal bodyguard has remained in continuous existence ever since.[93] Since the reign of Henry VIII, the Yeomen had worn 'scarlet, with braidings and laces of gold'. Their right hands grasped a ceremonial partisan, or bladed staff.[94] An Italian visitor to London in 1669 provided the first mention of their alternative, informal name: 'They are called "Beefeaters", that is, eaters of beef, of which a considerable portion is allowed them daily by the Court.'[95]

It's harder to know the identity of the other figures: the ladies, the children, the gigantic Scotsman and the gentleman commonly known as 'The Mysterious Quaker'. William Pyne, writing a history of the royal residences in 1819, when George I's court was only just out of living memory, made a series of further identifications which sound reasonable but can't be proved.[96] He claimed that the young page hanging precariously on the drop side of the balcony worked for Henrietta Howard. If that is indeed Henrietta's page, then maybe the little dog looking between the balusters is Fop, her spoiled and crabby lapdog, to whom Alexander Pope's dog Bounce wrote this poem:

> We Country Dogs love nobler sport,
> And scorn the pranks of Dogs at Court.
> Fye, naughty Fop! where e'er you come
> To fart and piss about the room,
> To lay your head in every lap,
> And, when they think not of you – snap![97]

Many of the ladies upon the staircase, probably colleagues of Mrs Tempest such as dressers, seamstresses and laundresses, are holding fans, and the fan could sometimes speak. The secret and allusive language in which messages were conveyed by a fan's position in the hands would not become formalised and codified until much later in the century. But it seems more than a curious accident that according to its conventions, all these women are speaking along the same lines. The lady in green tells the Scottish gentleman 'your flattery annoys me'. The lady next to Mohammed taps her left cheek, signifying 'no'. The lady with the dog says, 'I am not in love with you.'

Either this is a coincidence or else the language of fans existed earlier than historians think, and William Kent was enjoying the irony of portraying all these cruelly virtuous females with their languishing looks and emphatic denials.

Finally, on the staircase's ceiling, Kent added in four more personal portraits. He included himself – the cherubic, rosy-cheeked Signior, 'fat and hot' – and the two assistants, Robert and Franciscus, who helped him with the work. Kent's self-portrait provides a complete contrast to the rather stiff, uptight approach chosen by Sir James Thornhill in the painting mentioned earlier. Both wear a plain brown coat, but Thornhill's cravat is knotted tightly while Kent's is loose. Thornhill wears a formal wig; Kent wears a relaxed turban. Thornhill's hand is carefully poised, his

Elizabeth Butler: was she married to William Kent or not?
The two were certainly on-and-off partners for nearly a lifetime

brush loaded, while Kent nonchalantly brandishes his palette while being diverted by conversation. Thornhill is solitary; Kent is the focus of admiring attention. Indeed, lit from below, the cheeks of Kent and his assistants glow and their eyes sparkle as if they are actors upon a stage. There is no doubt that this is the coming man.

Whispering into Kent's left ear as she nonchalantly taps her fan on the balustrade is a real actress: the lady presumed to be his lover, the formidable Elizabeth Butler.[98] With perhaps more romance than truth, it was claimed that Elizabeth was 'an illegitimate daughter of a noble duke'.[99] Kent lived 'in particular friendship' with her and had begun to spend his free time, when he was not required by Lord Burlington, at her home in Leicester Fields.[100] At the date of the painting she was still early on in her career. She would later become renowned for playing frightening females: a fierce Lady Macbeth and a brutal Gertrude.[101]

In 1726, a year that began with heavy snow, the murals on the Grand Staircase were nearly finished. George I would shortly pronounce that the staircase pleased him 'very much' and that he approved 'of everything'. Like clients everywhere, though, he was impatient for completion, wanting to know 'how long it would be before Mr Kent would have done'.[102]

But Kent was adding one last figure into his painting. This was a boy with strange curly hair, whose even stranger story had been the talk of London since his arrival upon the drawing-room scene in April of 1726. Shortly after his first court appearance, it was reported that he 'hath begun to sit for his picture'.[103]

This enigmatic boy is our next courtier.

FOUR

The Wild Boy

'The best Court-talent in the world is Silence.'[1]
(Lord Berkeley of Stratton, 1760)

On the evening of 7 April 1726, the king and courtiers were gathered as usual in the Great Drawing Room at St James's Palace. The room was alive with their chatter, 'a sort of chit-chat, or *small talk*', which was unutterably trivial in its topics: the uniforms of the armies of foreign princes; the minor relations of important people; balls and masquerades.[2] As usual the crowd was alive to any breath of scandal, and anyone remotely notorious endured the customary ordeal of 'ogling', 'whispering' and 'glancing'.[3] Everything seemed just as normal.

But a sensational event would make this drawing room the most memorable in a long while. The doors suddenly burst open to a blur of bodies, arms and legs. In came a brace of footmen, bearing between them a curly-headed boy. He was perhaps twelve years old.

He had a friendly grin, but there was something decidedly odd about this youth. In the first place, he seemed not the least 'embarrassed at finding himself in the midst of such a fashionable assembly'.[4] Once lowered to the drawing-room floor, he crouched down and scuttled about using his arms, like a chimp. And instead of bowing and scraping to the Lord Chamberlain and taking his place in the circle, the young man boldly scampered straight up to the king.

The courtiers were scandalised by his audacious lack of ceremony.

This was their first encounter with Peter, the curious 'Wild Boy' of the woods, a feral child. Peter was a captivating character, green-eyed and with a peculiarly bushy brush of dark brown hair; he had 'very good strong teeth' and was prone to bouts of

A toy boy for the ladies of the court? Poor Peter, the
wild child found in the woods

irrepressible laughter.[5] In stark contrast to the fops of the drawing
room, Peter preferred to go about naked, had no table manners
and did not understand the use of a bed.[6] Strangest of all, he could
speak neither English nor German. In fact, the Wild Boy had
absolutely no language at all.

Now, showing great indulgence, the old king began to play
with his new toy. He relished Peter's refreshing lack of familiarity with the drawing-room world. The courtiers watched, fascinated, as Peter first encountered the fabric of their everyday
lives. Princess Caroline encouraged him to try on her glove, and
then let him examine 'the sparkling gems' on her black velvet
gown. Everyone shared Peter's delight when he discovered her
'gold watch that struck the hours', which 'was held to strike at his
ear'.[7]

Peter was about as far removed from the other courtiers – in
background, in behaviour – as could be possible. He provided
amusement for everybody with his comical ways. But his presence
also sparked off engrossing philosophical debates, the kind of
clever conversations that all courtiers enjoyed from time to time.

The occasional intellectual dispute signalled that the British court was sophisticated and superior, a heavyweight contender among the courts of Enlightenment Europe.

Peter's very existence raised the fascinating question of what it really meant to be human.

For Peter, the drawing room at St James's Palace marked the end of a strange odyssey that had begun in a German forest.

At George I's insistence, his court decamped to his birthplace in Hanover every other year for a few carefree weeks of vacation. He summered in the palace of Herrenhausen outside the city, surrounded by its gardens, canals and orange trees. Here, after years of endeavour, the king's engineers had finally persuaded Europe's tallest fountain to play. It spurted a joyous thirty-six metres into the air. Here, too, his gardeners in 1726 were planting the arrow-straight avenue that linked the palace to the city of Hanover with a staggering 1,219 new lime trees.

The king was so proud of his gardens at Herrenhausen that he even let tourists enjoy them too in his absence, just as long as they didn't disturb the nightingales or throw things at the swans.[8]

Peter the Wild Boy also grew up near Hanover, but his childhood was spent deep in the adjacent wild wood of Hertswold.[9] His family and early years remain muffled in mystery, and people speculated that he'd been suckled by a she-wolf. One day in 1725, local forest folk found Peter wandering all alone among the trees. A newspaper described how they'd discovered 'a creature of a real human kind and species, naked and wild'. It seemed that Peter had had no human contact since his infancy, and only his height suggested that he was 'about 12 or 13 years of age'.[10] And he had no words to tell his own story: it was 'not yet known by what strange fate he came into the wood, because he cannot speak'.[11]

There was a general assumption that the Wild Boy had been 'rescued' from the wilderness, but the more detailed accounts of his capture reveal that he was actually hunted down like a wild beast. 'When he was first discovered,' claimed one of many newspaper articles, he was 'so wild and savage, as to shun all human kind', and he could 'climb up the trees with an agility scarce to be considered'.[12] One report described him 'walking on all fours, running up trees like a squirrel, and feeding upon grass and moss'.[13] Perhaps, as another excited journalist claimed, he was first spotted 'sitting in the hollow of a tree cracking nuts and eating acorns'.[14] (As we shall see, acorns would retain a special significance for Peter.)

He did not leave his freedom readily. As his hunters closed in, Peter tried to hide at the top of a tree, and it had to be felled before he could be captured.[15] Once ensnared, Peter was taken to the town of Celle, where he was thrust with the vagabonds and criminals into the 'House of Correction'.[16]

News of Peter and his bizarre, speechless condition rippled out in ever wider circles, and in time reached Herrenhausen and the ears of George I. The king ordered Peter to be brought from the prison to the palace. He took a fancy to the Wild Boy, and decided to make him a member of his household. The king already had Turkish valets, a Polish dwarf entertainer and a menagerie full of rare beasts. This savage half-human from Hanover would strike a further pleasingly exotic note.

As the royal household began its long journey back across the German states to return to London, it would have been hard to imagine a greater transformation in Peter's lifestyle. People thought that the Wild Boy was 'more of the Ouran Outang species than of the human'.[17] Many of the other rare creatures previously obtained for the British royal menagerie had died from well-intentioned but misguided treatment: an elephant perished from drinking a gallon of wine a day, and ostriches were fed nails under the mistaken idea that they could digest iron.

How would the puckish Peter adapt to a new life in captivity?

Back in the drawing room, the courtiers tried to coach and coax Peter into producing a few halting words. 'What is your name?' they asked. He could be drilled into saying 'Pe–ter' in reply, but he would always pronounce the two syllables of his name with a short interval between them. 'Who is your father?' they asked, and the answer they expected was 'King George'.[18]

At first glance, Peter looked like any other boy, although his hair grew 'lower on his forehead than is common'.[19] Although he went about on his hands and knees, his body was 'strait and upright, & not hairy'. The most observant noticed that the middle and fourth fingers of his left hand bore the traces of a poorly healed wound, being 'web'd together like a duck's foot'. This was a souvenir from his solitary struggle for survival in the woods. People were particularly struck by his demeanour, which wasn't solemn and stately like the other courtiers: he had 'a roving look' in his eyes, and 'a merry disposition'.[20]

Although the courtiers found Peter endlessly fascinating, it was not planned that he should linger long at the king's court. Princess Caroline 'loved to see odd persons', and she had taken a great and instant fancy to the Wild Boy. Now, to please her, the king generously told her that he would present her with Peter as a gift.[21]

But it seems that George I was reluctant to keep his promise. Peter's transfer to Princess Caroline's household was several times delayed because 'the King and court were so entertained with him' and could not bear to give him up.[22]

A polite tug of war now began, with the Wild Boy at its centre. On one level he was just a damaged child. On another, he had become a commodity: as a subject for speculation and brainy showing-off, he was a valuable and status-enhancing curiosity. Both George I and Princess Caroline wanted Peter, and he became yet another symbol of the rivalry between the two courts.

The king's household, headed by a reserved but kindly master, seemed at first to be no bad place for Peter to remain. We have a glimpse of George I as he now was, in old age, through the eyes of another child. The ten-year-old Horace Walpole, Sir Robert's son, was taken by his mother to see the king. He recollected George I as 'an elderly man, rather pale, and exactly like his pictures and coins; not tall'. He wore 'a plain coat, waistcoat and breeches of snuff-coloured cloth, with stockings of the same colour, and a blue riband over all'.[23] Horace also passed juvenile judgement upon the king's mistress Melusine: she was 'a very tall, lean, ill-favoured old lady'.[24]

Even at the age of sixty-five, George I's hair was still a rich dark brown and only lightly peppered with white. (This same year, 1726, he gave a lock of hair to a courtier-in-waiting at Kensington Palace: wrapped up in a piece of paper, it remains today in the Manuscripts Room of the British Library.[25]) But his health was declining. Three years ago he had suffered a stroke, collapsing to the floor, where he 'remained senseless for a full hour', 'his wig on one side, and his hat on the other'.[26] He made what appeared to be a full recovery afterwards.

The king had absorbed many more of the customs and attitudes of his British subjects during the twelve years he had now spent on the throne, and his language skills had improved. Even so, a well-worn joke circulated that Sir Robert Walpole, weak in George I's preferred German or French, had brushed up on the Roman classics in order to converse with the king.

Walpole was surely exaggerating when he claimed to have 'governed the kingdom by the means of bad Latin', but he did indeed have an interpreter present during his meetings with the king, and George I's linguistic limitations remained very trying to his household.[27]

It was considered essential that the Lutheran-born king should support the Anglican Church, but he found the weekly services a particular trial. One story goes that he'd developed a habit of chatting with the German-speaking Dr Younger, Dean of Salisbury, during the sermons in the Chapel Royal, which were incomprehensible and boring to him. This was thought 'indecorous' and 'excited much offence'. The solution hit upon was to ban the dean from the palace and to inform the king that he'd been killed by an accidental kick from a horse. George I was deeply affected by the news. Many years later, to his amazement, he encountered Dr Younger still alive and well and living in Salisbury.[28]

Despite his continued image problems, George I had nevertheless begun to win some quiet appreciation for his consistent and solid work as sovereign. His hard graft at the business side of kingship, if not at its showmanship, had gained him respect if not popularity.[29] The chattering classes generally accepted that his abilities were not brilliant, but 'no man will presume to say they were contemptible'.[30] People were beginning to learn that his reserve stemmed not from pride, but from 'modesty, caution and deliberation'. And while he may have been reserved in company, Mustapha and Mohammed knew that there was nobody 'more free among his nearest servants'.[31]

Injured pride, though, or perhaps a legitimate fear about the threat to his authority still prevented the king from genuinely warming to his son.

The refurbishment of the state apartments at Kensington was very nearly complete by 1726. That year brought change at the Office of the King's Works. Just two days after Peter the Wild Boy's first appearance in the drawing room in April came the death of the curmudgeonly Sir Thomas Hewett, former chief of the Office. He died a disappointed man at his Nottinghamshire home, his dreams of a new classical architecture unfulfilled.

William Kent's numerous friends now used 'great endeavours' to get him into the office of Comptroller in the subsequent staff changes, but for once they were unsuccessful. He was made Master Carpenter instead.[32] Nevertheless, this was a significant coup. In a remarkable U-turn in his fortunes since he was investigated by the committee of enquiry, the young pretender had become an Office of Works insider.

Only a few days after Peter the Wild Boy's first appearance at St James's, he was taken over to Kensington to sit for Kent's staircase. Kent decided to hide the boy's injured left hand, and in his right painted the sprig of oak and acorns that served as a reminder of Peter's former forest life.

*

Outside this microcosm of the world defined by the palace walls, a mania for the Wild Boy had taken off. Londoners now hailed him as 'the most wonderful wonder' and 'one of the greatest curiosities of the world since the time of Adam'.[33]

Throughout the centuries, feral children like Peter have aroused feelings of pity, sometimes fear, and a sense of strangeness. Romulus and Remus, wolf-children, monkey-boys or the children imprisoned in kennels or cellars by twisted parents all give us a shudder of 'the other'.

Peter could not fail to fascinate the intellectuals then exploring the questions raised by the great revolutionary upheaval in thought generally known as 'The Enlightenment'. Philosophers were beginning to assert the primacy of reason over superstition, and to challenge the authority of the established church and nobility. They even debated the very definition of a human being, and whether or not people had souls. Peter proved to be a stimulating test case. If he possessed no speech, did he therefore possess no soul? Was he really just an animal? Or was he an admirable and 'noble savage' who'd lived a life untainted by society? Jonathan Swift remarked that the subject of the Wild Boy had been 'half our talk this fortnight', and Daniel Defoe thought he was the most interesting thing in the world.[34]

As a result of his wildfire celebrity, Peter the Wild Boy won the accolade of appearing as a waxwork in Mrs Salmon's celebrated gallery. Her collection of 140 figures was to be found at the sign of the Golden Salmon in the Strand.[35] Mrs Salmon was 'famed throughout England for her skilful wax modelling', and visitors could assess her accuracy by comparing her with her own waxwork of herself.[36]

Mocking the court and courtiers was already something of an obsession with certain parts of the London media, and the Wild Boy also became wonderful fodder for the city's satirists. The capital had a vigorous and apparently unchecked popular press, within which both court and Opposition factions had their own

One of many newspaper cuttings showing the 'Wild Youth'.
To the right he climbs a tree like a monkey

publications. The *London Gazette* reported respectfully on royal activities. In the course of the decade following Peter's arrival in London, Sir Robert Walpole would spend £50,000 from Secret Service funds in supporting Whig-friendly newspapers.[37] Meanwhile, *The Craftsman* was full of anonymous rants by Opposition politicians, and there were many other occasional publications and pamphlets devoted to jokes, politics and barbed comment of all kinds. Another twenty-five newspapers flourished outside London.[38]

The Wild Boy craze caused a new deluge of newspapers and pamphlets to pour off the presses. Few of them were accurate: 'some inconsistent with themselves, some with possibility, and most of them with fact'.[39] The minuscule number of accurate details about Peter's life were soon distorted or lost.

While they were ostensibly all about Peter, the real intention behind these publications was to mock the court, the courtiers and even the whole silly race of men.[40] The Wild Boy's lack of worldly knowledge exposed the shallow foundations upon which fashionable society was built. London's satirists ingeniously invented more and more ludicrous transgressions that Peter was said to have committed: he'd tried to kiss Sir Robert Walpole's wife; he licked people's hands in greeting; he wore a hat in the king's presence; he'd stolen the Lord Chamberlain's staff.

This was also the year of the publication of Daniel Defoe's *Mere*

NATURE Delineated: OR, A BODY without a SOUL. BEING OBSERVATIONS UPON THE Young FORESTER Lately brought to Town from GERMANY. Published on 23 July, this was a wild cadenza of speculation about Peter's life, situation and encounters with the courtiers. It would be a terrible indictment of the present age, Defoe argued, if the Wild Boy had actively chosen his previous way of life, to 'converse with the quadrupeds of the forest, and retire from human society'. He was really suggesting that Peter was in fact the only truly sensible person alive.

And Defoe was sensitive, where the others were not, to the fact that he was using a real and defenceless person, not just a freak, as fodder for his journalism. If he took liberties, he wrote, it was at the expense of 'our modern men of mode'. Unlike the other journalists, who amused themselves and their readers at Peter's expense, Defoe showed some humanity towards the boy.

Peter himself 'is certainly an object of great compassion', he acknowledged, 'and so I treat him all along'.[41]

So what were the court ceremonies and absurdities of which Peter was so blissfully unaware?

All new courtiers were expected to learn the rules. John Hervey had to endure a 'lecture of instructions, as to bows, steps, attitudes, &c.' before taking up the post of Vice-Chamberlain.[42] Lord Chesterfield (once again) describes the uncouth gait of those unfamiliar with court etiquette and accoutrements: 'when an awkward fellow first comes into a room, it is highly probable, that his sword gets between his legs, and throws him down'. Then he

How to bow, an art you learnt from your dancing master

drops his hat – twice, probably – and spends a quarter of an hour getting himself back in order again.[43]

Peter was supposed to learn to mock idiots such as the 'country boor' who did not know what to do with his *chapeau-bras*: 'sometimes he has it in his hand, sometimes in his mouth, and often betrayed a great inclination to put it on his head, concluding that it was a damned troublesome, useless thing'.[44]

The Wild Boy also had a shocking tendency simply to sit down when he felt like it, 'before any one, without distinction of persons'.[45] As we know, the drawing room was carefully kept seat-free, 'there being no chairs in the room lest anyone should be guilty of seating themselves', and courtier Mary Cowper found a week in waiting made her 'ill from standing so long upon [her] feet'.[46]

It was necessary to bow three times, 'according to ancient custom', when passing the vacant royal throne, and at night it was turned to face the wall in order to neutralise its power.[47] When the king himself appeared, the whole court sank into 'a profound reverence or bow', which he'd acknowledge with a slight nod.[48] To leave the king's presence was a particular challenge to a lady. She could not depart without making three curtseys, and then had to reverse out of the door – all quite a feat in her wide-skirted court mantua and heels. A newly appointed Maid of Honour had to take lessons with a dancing master just to learn how to 'stand still without tottering'.[49] Maids of Honour were punished if they turned their backs upon their mistress, and even more so if they committed the horrible crime of crossing their arms.[50]

And it was not possible to leave the royal presence without permission. One lady-in-waiting with a bursting bladder was forced to urinate on the floor, producing a humiliating puddle as big as a dining table which threatened the shoes of bystanders.[51]

What on earth was the point of such trivia? The surprising truth is that etiquette could be used to make a court career, or to break it. It was a clear indicator of status. Being treated with ceremonious respect could raise one's credit immeasurably, while an absence of ceremony could be terribly wounding. The modern historian Bob Bucholz calls court etiquette 'a weapon in the arsenal of the monarchy, as potent as any polemic or art; more flexible and subtle than any army or navy'.[52]

And so it was only when alone that the courtiers could whistle, loosen their garters or loll in an easy chair. Any of these things when done in company Lord Chesterfield thought 'injurious to superiors, shocking and offensive to equals, brutal and insulting to inferiors'.[53] Chesterfield definitively summed up the sterile and inhuman side of court life when he condemned even 'frequent and loud laughter' as being fit only for the London mob.

He was full of smug self-satisfaction when he claimed – so pitifully – that nobody had ever heard him laugh.[54]

Peter the Wild Boy, of course, ignored this curious nonsense. He seemed to settle down in this strange new world without a care, meeting its probing gaze with his own roving eyes and laughter. His gusts of giggles rang through the palace, as did his equine neighs and his merry, if wordless, songs.

As time went on, though, the Wild Boy was gradually forced into new and unnatural behaviours, and began to show signs of distress. The first time Peter saw someone undressing, he was 'in great pain', thinking the man was peeling the very skin off his leg when he removed his stockings.[55] He hated clothes, but the courtiers made him wear one of his two new suits – one blue, the other green – with red stockings.[56] His dressers had enormous trouble in getting Peter's suits on and off, and they seemed 'extremely uneasy to him'. As well as the daily struggle over his clothes, Peter could not be made 'to lie down on a bed, but sits and sleeps in a corner of the room'.[57] Nor did he understand the use of a chamber pot and 'foul'd himself, without offering to do otherwise'.[58]

It was like trying to dress a dog, frustrating to both parties. But these poignant details of a little boy bewildered really pierce the heart.

Peter's new suits were like straitjackets to him, and gradually his clothes changed his very posture. His tight court coat, cut much more restrictively than a modern jacket, meant that 'crawling or scrambling about, would now be more troublesome to him, than walking upright'.[59] Eighteenth-century court garments were designed to make the wearer stand up straight – shoulders lowered, chest puffed out, toes turned out – and they began to do their work upon the Wild Boy.

In time Peter grew fond of his fine clothes. He'd always liked the gleam of gold, and if a courtier was wearing 'anything smooth or shining in his dress', he would spot it at once and 'shew his attention by stroaking it'.[60] He also learnt to pick pockets, from the most innocent of motives: 'if he finds nuts or fruits, he is very glad of them'.[61] Jonathan Swift's pamphlet about Peter concluded with a spoof advert 'to warn all ladies and gentlemen who intend to visit this Wild Man' not to carry anything 'indecent' in their pockets, as he'd inevitably whip it out and embarrass them.[62]

This was charming and amusing. But when Peter stepped over the invisible line that defined acceptable behaviour, he was beaten on the legs with a 'broad leather strap to keep him in awe'.[63] His shock and confusion can only be imagined. Everyone was fascinated by the idea of the Wild Boy, but it seemed that no one really cared for the human child.

He began to pine for a return to the woods.

Eventually, a turning point came during a dinner at the king's table. George I invited Peter to taste any of the many dishes upon the table, but the Wild Boy threw his food about and refused to touch meat. He'd only eat 'asparagus, or other garden-things'.[64] Exasperated, the king ordered that Peter should be given the food he preferred, but also commanded that the Wild Boy should embark upon a course of 'instruction as may best fit him for human society'.[65]

Now Peter the Wild Boy was fortunate enough to find a friend. He was 'committed to the care of Dr Arbuthnot', one of the king's

The brilliant Dr John Arbuthnot. 'Inattentive in
company', his 'imagination was always at work'

physicians, in order to be taught to speak and be 'made a sociable
creature'.[66] According to the rationalists at court, a little application would bring certain success, and Peter would become fully
human at last.

Dr John Arbuthnot is yet another of the figures depicted in
William Kent's staircase at Kensington Palace. He's the elderly
man in a plain brown coat standing just behind Peter. (This portrait was usually known as the 'Mysterious Quaker' before his real
identity was deduced.) Dr Arbuthnot would now prove himself to
be a credit to his profession: gentle, caring and humane.

Born in Scotland in 1667, he'd trained at the Marischal College
in Aberdeen before heading south, studying mathematics and
becoming Queen Anne's physician in 1709. As well as being an
eminent scientist, he was also a member of the witty and icono-
clastic society of writers called the Scriblerus Club. His friends
Jonathan Swift and Alexander Pope were also members.

In Dr Arbuthnot's best-known satirical book, *The History of
John Bull*, the grumpy Everyman character John Bull personifies
the English people: red-faced, beer-drinking, plain-speaking,

Frenchman-hating. Yet Dr Arbuthnot's jokes were gentle rather than savage, 'like flaps of the face given in jest . . . no blackness will appear after the blows'.[67] Despite his talent and appetite for satire, he always managed to avoid giving offence. Unusually, he managed to remain 'in great esteem with the whole court' as a philosopher, a mathematician and a 'character of uncommon virtue and probity'.[68]

It's a relief to find that Dr Arbuthnot did have at least one imperfection of character: he was hopelessly addicted to cards. Despite all the hours of practice he put in, he remained a dreadful player. On one renowned occasion, which gave much amusement to his friends, he played two games of quadrille against a dog and was still 'most shamefully beaten'.[69]

And he also had some kind of physical problem with his legs. One friend joked that Dr Arbuthnot was 'a man that can do everything but walk', which he did with 'a sort of slouch'.[70] Indeed, on the King's Grand Staircase, William Kent painted the doctor leaning upon his indispensable stout stick.

The Scottish doctor was given 'an apartment joining' onto Peter's at the palace, and together they began the process of civilisation.[71] The Wild Boy had daily lessons in language and manners. His progress was slow and painful, as he had 'a natural tendency to get away if not held by his coat'.[72]

Yet it doesn't sound as if Dr Arbuthnot was capable of a sustained campaign of terror. 'Inattentive in company', his 'imagination was always at work' and his mind frequently wandered off the topic at hand.[73] Even the satirists allowed that he had shown 'care, skill and tenderness' in trying to tame the Wild Boy.[74]

Opinion was divided about whether Dr Arbuthnot was successful or not. Peter did indeed learn how to 'pronounce and utter after his tutor words of one syllable' and, like a performing dog, he learnt a few social graces: he could kiss his fingers and bow.[75]

Yet others thought that Dr Arbuthnot had failed, despite all his efforts, and that Peter still retained 'the natural wildness in all his actions and behaviour'.[76] And Peter would never really engage with other people through language, thereby disappointing all the earnest supporters who wished him well. Even with the advantage of hindsight, it's not exactly clear what Peter's condition was. It is likely that he was autistic, but medical opinion cannot agree upon whether he was born with his condition and abandoned in the woods by a mother who thought him defective, or whether he became the way he was because of an early family tragedy which left him completely alone and without social stimulus.

Unlike many others, Dr Arbuthnot remained absolutely convinced that Peter the Wild Boy did indeed have a soul. Despite the slow ebbing of the court's confidence that Peter would ever learn to speak, Dr Arbuthnot kept faith with his pupil. He arranged for Peter to be baptised at his own home in Cork Street.[77]

Peter the Wild Boy made his first appearance in George I's drawing room on 7 April, and he'd been promised to Princess Caroline soon afterwards. We left Caroline waiting in vain for the arrival of her new servant, for the king and court were reluctant to let Peter go. And the king showed no great generosity towards the princess, who had stood so firmly by her husband during the quarrel of recent years. He treated her respectfully, but 'he never cordially loved her'.[78]

Now aged forty-three, Caroline had become a meaty mountain of a woman. The fame of her prodigious bosom was so great that some people were actually disappointed by its reality. 'The Princess is really a good fine woman,' one visitor to the court wrote to a country neighbour, but 'her breasts they make such a wonder at I don't think exceed Mrs Abell's in size'.[79]

It was 16 April 1726 before Jonathan Swift could report that he had been to Princess Caroline's house in Leicester Square and had found Peter in residence there at last. (Swift sourly joked that he'd only received his own invitation to Leicester House because Princess Caroline, obsessed with the 'wild Boy from Germany', also 'had a curiosity to see a wild Dean from Ireland'.[80])

Caroline's genuine curiosity about odd people and strange

things stemmed from both her background and character. She'd been born in the sleepy German principality of Ansbach, orphaned early and adopted by the court of Prussia. While her formal education was very poor, she did at least in her youth make friends with the rationalist philosopher Gottfried Leibniz. He introduced her to the world of ideas (and would develop his celebrated calculating machine while librarian to the Hanoverian court).

Although Caroline lacked a dowry, she was placed upon the European marriage market for princesses, and the Catholic courts of Europe were baffled when she dithered about accepting a flattering matrimonial offer from the future king of Spain.

Leibniz went against the trend in noting that 'every one predicts the Spanish crown for her, but she deserves something surer than that'.[81] In fact, Princess Caroline was deeply reluctant to make the conversion to Catholicism necessary for the Spanish match. People reported that 'First the Princess of Ansbach says "Yes" and then "No". First she says we Protestants have no valid priests, then that Catholics are idolatrous and accursed.' There were reports that the Jesuit tasked with converting her frequently argued Caroline into tears.[82]

Eventually, the Spanish match was off. Princess Caroline won much respect for her resolute Protestantism, and people praised her for having 'scorn'd an empire for religion's sake', as John Gay put it.[83] She would remain a lifelong religious radical, more intrigued by the twists and turns of religious doctrine than by stolid service to the established church.

A little later she was wooed again, this time by Prince George Augustus (then of Hanover). He began his campaign of courtship incognito before declaring his hand and being accepted. The court of Hanover was delighted with his choice, and there were 'many healths drunk' to the engaged couple in 1705.[84]

Caroline had always been 'a most entertaining companion', an autodidact fonder of speaking than writing.[85] Her effusive but illegible letters, written in French, are terribly difficult to decipher, and her husband complained that she wrote 'like a cat'.[86] Always in too much of a hurry, Caroline would scribble '*asteur*' when she meant '*à cette heure*'; 'Harriet Campbell' became 'hariet cambel', and 'Isabella Finch' became 'belle fintzche'.[87] Her friends agreed that she spelt very badly, 'but then she taught herself to write, so it's no wonder'.[88]

Palace parties were often tedious and depressing to this princess who liked to talk philosophy. She was a stalwart supporter of Sir Isaac Newton, despite his epic row with her other pet philosopher Leibniz about which of them had discovered calculus. She admired Newton tremendously and told 'the whole circle' in the drawing room that she was honoured to have lived in the same age as such a great man.[89]

The less-than-charitable thought Princess Caroline's philo-sophical fancies were pretentious, and they scoffed at her for 'pre-tending to understand the metaphysicks of Leibniz'.[90] But her critics didn't understand that she was successfully following a German rather than a British pattern for royal females. By taking culture seriously, Caroline was admirably fulfilling the job descrip-tion of an eighteenth-century queen as it existed in the German states. There it was expected that the female half of a royal couple would lead the social life of a court, welcome guests and sparkle in erudite conversation, and Princess Caroline came from a grand tradition of clever, lively women who had ignited the courts of Germany.[91]

The dying words of Sophie Charlotte, Queen of Prussia, George I's sister, summed up their intellectualism and what can best be described as their tolerance rather than enjoyment of con-ventional court life: 'Do not pity me. I am at last going to satisfy my curiosity about the origin of things, which even Leibniz could never explain to me. As for the King, my husband,' she noncha-lantly added, 'well, I shall afford him the opportunity of giving me a magnificent funeral, and displaying all the pomp he loves so much.'[92]

These were the role models that Princess Caroline followed,

steeper, braver paths to climb than those conventionally chosen by English princesses.

And as well as clucking over the intellectuals who congregated in her drawing room, she was also a good mistress to her servants: wise, witty and maternal.

So the Wild Boy eventually found himself part of the prince and princess's household in Leicester Fields, discovering a snug place under Caroline's wing. Dr Arbuthnot continued to visit his pupil and would also drop in on his friend Henrietta Howard. (She thought he didn't come often enough, and when he tried to make an exit he would find himself 'prettily chid for leaving'.[93]) Leicester House remained a magnet for everyone and anyone talented or droll. The reversionary interest still ensured that the 'most promising of the young lords and gentlemen' and the 'prettiest and liveliest of the young ladies' were to be found there.[94]

As we already know, gaiety and glamour were brought to Princess Caroline's household by the Maids of Honour. A previous, promiscuous generation of Maids had liberally bestowed their favours 'to the right and to the left and not the least notice taken of their conduct'.[95] At the very creation of Princess Caroline's household in 1714, equerry Peter Wentworth noted that the town had 'named four beauties for Maids to her Highness', rightly predicting that the princess's husband would be 'very sociable' among them and that there'd be trouble if Caroline herself had 'any spice of jealousy'.[96]

The older, colder members of the court constantly complained about the Maids of Honour's 'little levities': an obsession with the new dresses to be worn on the king's birthday, with novels and romances, and with infuriating 'merry pranks' played late at night.[97] 'People who are of such very hot constitutions as to want to be refresh'd by night-walking', ran one complaint, 'need not disturb others who are not altogether so warm as they are.'[98]

Princess Caroline's Maids of Honour included the flighty and selfish Sophy Howe. Naughty and saucy Sophy was quick to exploit – and indeed to abuse – the relaxed atmosphere of the junior court. When told off for giggling in chapel by the Duchess of St Albans and being informed that 'she could not do a worse thing', Sophy pertly (but truthfully) answered, 'I beg your Grace's pardon, I can do a great many worse things.'[99]

One of these 'worse things' took place on the evening when Sophy and the Duchess of Marlborough had too much to drink at dinner. '"Lady Duchess, let us do something odd," Sophy suggested, "let us make – in the stone passage," and so they did before all the footmen.'[100] The dash is tantalising. We don't know if they made love or water or simply a spectacle of themselves.

In Sophy's letters the Maids of Honour sound like pupils at a riotous girls' boarding school. Updates addressed to her friend Henrietta Howard are full of news about potential partners: during one country visit she wrote that Henrietta would be wrong to assume that there was no flirtation to be had among the provincial gentlemen. But an absence from London meant an absence from the most desirable male matches and made her 'more sensible than ever' of her happiness in being a Maid of Honour.[101] She was also cruel to her mother and dangerously addicted to the dizzy, giddy side of life at court.

So the charmed circle of the Maids of Honour generally found their lives cheerful and comfortable. One of their number, belonging to the household of Princess Caroline's daughter Anne, extolled the conveniences of life in a royal household:

> We have people found us that clean our rooms and wash for us, so there is no expense of that kind; sheets and towels are also found, silver candlesticks, and china, (tea-things, I mean,) and sugar. The Ladies of the Bedchamber and Maids of Honour dine together . . . we have by much the best table; no allowance of wine, but may call for what quantity and what sort we please: we have two men to wait.[102]

This was not a bad life, if you could bear the rules and lack of privacy.

*

'And who would not go to the Devil, for the sake
of dear Molly Lepell?' (court ballad)

In defence of the Maids' philosophy of relentless fun, the former
Maid Molly Hervey (neé Lepell) explained that she personally
hated 'to look on the dark side of life' and would 'always be thank-
ful to those who turn[ed] the bright side of the lantern' towards
her.[103]

Molly had by now left Princess Caroline's household, having
been eventually forced to admit the marriage to John Hervey that
disqualified her from her post. Her husband's elder brother Carr
had died in 1723, so John himself was now in line to inherit his
family's titles. Molly remained much at court with her new name
of Lady Hervey, but some of her former friends found her less
sympathetic than before. Her husband, arch and critical, had
begun to taint her with his own bleak cynicism.

Alexander Pope, an admirer of the old Molly Lepell, was hurt
when the news of her marriage finally came out. Previously he and
she had been happy talking and walking together 'three or 4 hours,
by moonlight' in the palace gardens.[104] But Pope began to turn
against her as she became contaminated by her husband's affected
manners. 'Let me tell you, I don't like your style,' he wrote plainly

in answer to a letter of Molly's. 'Methinks I have lost the Mrs L. I formerly knew, who writ and talk'd like other people (and sometimes better).'[105] ('Mrs L' was Molly before her marriage, when like all unmarried ladies she was addressed as 'Mistress' Lepell.)

Lady Mary Wortley Montagu was another who had preferred the lovers separately rather than as a pair: she quickly grew 'weary of those Birds of Paradise'. She also thought that Molly had acquired new and exaggerated airs and graces: she'd become 'the top figure in town', condescending to show herself 'twice a-week at the drawing room and twice more at the opera for the entertainment of the public'.[106]

Perhaps inevitably, by 1726 the stylish, stylised Hervey couple were gradually growing apart. Maybe it was John's neglect that encouraged Molly to treat her six-year-old marriage a little less seriously, or perhaps it was the depressing realisation that she and her husband were still spending their way towards insolvency.

Her father-in-law, the Earl of Bristol, could not have been fonder of Molly herself, but he wished his son had married someone with more money. He castigated John for having even entertained the thought of 'marrying any woman without a considerable fortune'.[107] On the other hand, Molly's mother-in-law, Lady of the Bedchamber Lady Bristol, had never liked her, and they were well known for quarrelling together like the fishwives of Billingsgate Market.[108]

Now, perhaps feeling a little empty inside, Molly began to mirror the caricature of herself as the brittle court lady – 'the finely-polished, highly-bred, genuine woman of fashion' – by entering into an intrigue that did her reputation no good.[109]

Molly had long been a practised flirt, collecting admirers as others collected snuff boxes. Even Voltaire, when he visited England, was soon writing to her about the 'passion' she had kindled within him.[110] Despite the elderly king's supposed preference for fat women, he too was smitten by the ethereal Molly's 'soft and sprightly' grey eyes, which she used to open 'a little wider than ordinary'.[111] And he was also captivated by the spiky, sparky personality that comes through in Molly's derisive catalogue of her own considerable charms ('I had forgot my eyebrows. Observe that they are not very handsome, but well enough').[112]

In 1725, the year before Peter the Wild Boy came to court, rumours swirled around that Molly had finally solved her financial problems. The gossips had it that she'd deliberately gone 'to the Drawing-Room every night, and publicly attracted his Majesty in a most vehement manner' which was 'the diversion of the town'.[113] It was said that Melusine had paid Molly £4,000 to break off her increasingly flagrant relationship with the king.

Yet the rumours were just rumours, and Molly was equally criticised for *not* having had a royal affair. 'Lady Hervey, by aiming too high, has fallen very low,' commented Lady Mary Wortley Montagu. She 'is reduc'd to trying to persuade folks she has an intrigue, and gets nobody to believe her'.[114]

Even the shameless flattery penned by the poets about their former favourite, Molly Lepell, was not quite straightforward. It began to contain a mocking, spiteful note, typical of an age when wit had a cutting edge, but hurtful nonetheless. Lord Chesterfield and William Pulteney wrote a poem about Molly that would have soured upon her as she discerned its double meaning:

> So powerful her charms, and so moving
> They would warm an old Monk in his cell,
> Should the Pope himself ever go roaming,
> He would follow dear Molly Le[pel]l.
>
> Or were I the King of Great Britain
> To chuse a Minister well,
> And support the Throne that I sit on,
> I'd have under me Molly Le[pel]l.[115]

Molly herself was 'in a little sort of miff' about this ballad, which flashed around the court in an instant, and asked for the double entendres to be deleted. But her friend Dr Arbuthnot thought her philosophical: 'not displeas'd I believe with the ballad, but only with being bit'.[116]

At the time of Peter the Wild Boy's arrival, Princess Caroline had just lost the services of yet another Maid of Honour, Mary Howard. She'd had to resign because of her marriage, on 14 March 1726, to Henry Scott, first Earl of Deloraine, one of the Gentle - men of the Bedchamber to Prince George Augustus.[117] Soon to be widowed, though, Lady Deloraine would later return to become a court figure of great consequence.

Princess Caroline, the Maids of Honour and the Women of the Bedchamber were all fascinated by Peter. Petted and cosseted by the ladies of Leicester House, he settled down as well as could be expected. Yet he gave back very little, showing no affection and demanding inexhaustible patience. The female courtiers began to treat him as a joke, spreading it about that his sturdy body and his lack of speech would make him a fine, discreet toy boy.

Only the endlessly protective Princess Caroline and Dr Arbuthnot stood between Peter and a life as a character in a freak show.

The Wild Boy's overnight social success had been achieved at great cost to his high spirits and love of freedom. In Daniel Defoe's words, he'd made an extraordinary 'leap from the woods to the court; from the forest among beasts . . . to the society of all the wits and beaus of the age'. But despite the care that was lavished upon him, Peter was simply a creature in captivity. It was clear that really he longed 'to run wild again in the woods' and 'to live as he did before'.[118]

And he was not the only courtier to find the palace more like a prison.

FIVE

The Neglected Equerry

'An unfortunate man as I am is glad to catch at
any glimpse of happiness."
(Peter Wentworth, 1718)

The Wild Boy was a thrilling novelty at court. He brought a breath of fresh air into its stale confines, and to imagine seeing it through his eyes is to see something of its strangeness. But the court already contained another, very different, royal servant called Peter. This second Peter had arrived by a much more conventional route.

Peter Wentworth was an equerry. It was his job to accompany the king if he walked abroad from his private rooms, and to ride alongside whenever the royal coach left the palace. Wentworth was an insider, an old hand, and a witness to decades of changing court fortunes. To him the court was the world: familiar, fatiguing, of fundamental importance in his life. While he had the dedication of a true courtier, he also suffered from a sense of gnawing and growing frustration.

The Wentworths were a worthy, respectable, upright family. Peter's older brother Thomas, Earl of Strafford, was Britain's ambassador to Berlin. His own court career had begun long ago, as an equerry to George, Prince of Denmark, Queen Anne's rather tedious husband. ('I have tried him drunk', Charles II said of Prince George, 'and tried him sober and there's nothing in him.') At Prince George's death, Peter transferred to Queen Anne's own household.

While Peter Wentworth spent his undemanding days opening doors and standing to attention in the drawing room, he had a secret skill unsuspected by his courtier colleagues: he was a natural and gifted writer. He penned frequent and gossipy letters to his brother, first in Berlin and then later in rural retirement in England. As a long-time, if lowly, cog in the court machine, he vividly recorded the high dramas and low tricks of court life. His is one of the best accounts, for example, of the dramatic deathbed scene in 1714, when the dying Queen Anne averted the danger of the Stuart succession by handing the symbolic staff of the Treasurer's office to the Hanoverian-inclined Duke of Shrewsbury.[2]

Wentworth's letters were always deliciously full of court gossip, mercilessly exposing pretence, artifice and greed. His keen eyes and flapping ears missed nothing. Hopelessly indiscreet, he forwarded the scurrilous ballads the courtiers loved, accompanied by half-hearted injunctions to secrecy. He typically signed off with: 'I think here's a pretty deal of scandal for one letter.'

Wentworth had embarked upon his court career in high hope of winning high office. But he suffered from asthma, his progress had stalled, and by the 1720s he stood in sore need of a lucky break. 'I married young', he explained in his own defence, '& set out in the world with a smaller fortune than I ought.' He righteously claimed never to have 'lost any money at play, nor laid out any money upon whores'.[3] And yet his money simply seemed to disappear. As well as a wife and numerous children, he also had to support a small country estate in Dorset. It had been a foolish purchase, for the land was 'miserably worn out by bad tenants'.[4] Juliana, his wife, left back in Dorset with their brood, must have had constant call upon the 'patience and resignation to the will of God' for which she was celebrated by her friends.[5]

The year 1714, and the change of regime, brought with it new opportunities. At the very moment of George I's landing at Greenwich, Wentworth pushed others aside to welcome the new king. He proudly told his brother that he'd reached out to George I 'to help him out of the barge, the Duke of Shrewsbury presented me to kiss the King's hand'.[6] This was a valuable coup in Wentworth's world of constant, cut-throat competition, where success was expressed through the tiniest of details.

Wentworth thought he ought to be made a Groom of the Bedchamber, the next rank up from his own. 'I wou'd not be a Querry [equerry] all my life time,' he chuffed in frustration.[7] On 6

John Gay, the former silk mercer's apprentice who had
a secret soft spot for duchesses

August 1714, he appealed to his powerful brother the earl: 'this day
I have taken the oath of office to King George, but I hope to God
you'll get me something better'.[8]

His was a typical ambition, and many, many others likewise nearly
broke their hearts during the great mad quest for promotion at
court. The struggle for employment, explained Lady Mary
Wortley Montagu, was almost a physical one: 'there's a little door
to get in and a great crowd without, shoving and thrusting who
shall be the foremost'.[9]

The jobless and impecunious poet John Gay was even lower on
the ladder than Peter Wentworth. A former silk mercer's apprentice, he haunted the court of the Prince and Princess of Wales at
Leicester House in pursuit of a paid post. Their mutual friends
joked that the inept gambler Dr Arbuthnot and John Gay both
had unfortunate vices: 'The Dr. goes to cards, Gay to court; one
loses money, one loses his time.'[10]

Gay wrote a poem about the monotonous evenings devoted to
chasing the remote hope of a court job. He always found it hard

to get up from his writing desk in good time, and had to dress in high haste before pressing 'through the crowd of needy courtiers':

> Pensive each night, from room to room I walk'd,
> To one I bow'd, and with another talk'd;
> Enquir'd what news, or such a lady's name,
> And did the next day, and the next, the same.
> Places, I found, were daily given away,
> And yet no friendly Gazette mention'd *Gay*.
> I ask'd a friend what method to pursue;
> He cry'd, I want a place as well as you.[11]

Gay planned to better himself by dedicating a new book (his celebrated *Fables*) to Princess Caroline's son; by dining 'daily with the Maids of Honour'; by promiscuously sucking up to more important people.[12] 'Mr Gay was your servant yesterday,' wrote Alexander Pope to a female friend; 'I believe to-day he may be Mrs Lepell's.'[13]

Gay received some insightful advice from a court insider, his friend Henrietta Howard. She fondly chided him for his futile search for office and told him to exercise his true talents as a writer, rather than following his snobbish dreams. 'Your head is your best friend,' she told him. 'It wou'd clothe, lodge and wash you but you neglect it, and follow that false friend your heart.'[14]

Back in 1714, Peter Wentworth, likewise dangerously seduced by the glamour of the court, found himself in stomach-churning suspense about the appointment of the Grooms of the Bedchamber. But despite his acute analysis of the characters of everyone around him, Wentworth's colleagues tended to sideline someone with so little visible self-confidence. 'A modest merit, with a large share of impudence' was more certain of success at court than 'the greatest qualification without it'.[15] Not surprisingly, Wentworth found himself overlooked once again when the new Grooms of the Bedchamber were announced.

Making a resolution at last to act more positively, he selected Baron Görtz, George I's Hanoverian treasurer, as his counsellor.

Wentworth proposed the cheaper and slightly humiliating expedient of being made 'Groom Extraordinary' while retaining his lower salary as an equerry.[16]

Baron Görtz now assured Wentworth that if there were to be a 'Groom Extraordinary', the job would indeed be his, but that there were no plans for appointing one at present. Wentworth just had to wait.

Peter Wentworth's contemporary, Thomas Burnet, had an even more gruelling tale of desire and delay. He spent a whole tedious half-decade at court without employment, seeking a job simply by hanging round in the drawing room every single day. If a man 'can hold out five years', Burnet calculated, 'tis morally impossible he should not come into play'.

These five years were costly, both financially and emotionally. Burnet complained constantly about 'this cursed Court attendance'. 'I confess I am pretty heartily tired of it,' he groaned.[17] If he failed to get a job, he thought, he would have wasted 'half of the very flower of his life' standing waiting outside a door.[18]

Still, Thomas Burnet was eventually rewarded with 'much a better thing' than he'd ever hoped for: the offer of the position of British consul in Lisbon.[19]

And John Gay, too, was finally offered a job. Princess Caroline had by now given birth to seven surviving children. While her three elder daughters remained with her father-in-law, the king, the youngest three children lived with her at Leicester House. The proffered post was in the tiny fledgling household of the very youngest daughter, and even Gay was affronted by its insignificance. He decided that this most obscure backwater of the court was beneath his notice. Despite its salary of £200 a year, he eventually declined the office of Gentleman Usher to the baby Princess Louisa.

His friends worried about his rashness in refusing, saying that he had just as little foresight of age, sickness, poverty or the loss of his admirers as a girl of fifteen.[20] Yet this eventual curdling of his court hopes did Gay a world of good. He was forced to stop loitering about the palace and to seek theatrical success in the city outside.

But Peter Wentworth's wait was not to have such a happy ending. He subsequently found out that Baron Görtz had betrayed him. Despite the baron's reassurances, the post of 'Groom Extraordinary' did indeed exist, but it had been offered to and accepted by someone else ten days earlier. The treacherous Görtz was no friend, and Wentworth should have known 'he that holds a courtier by the hand, has a wet eel by the tail'.[21]

In his letters to his brother, Wentworth's bewildered pain leaps from the page. 'I have an innate horrid quality of an unaccountable foolish bashfulness,' Wentworth sighed in low moments.[22] He lacked the knack of making friends, as well as that of making money. By 1726, he was growing old in his search for a better job.

And he was becoming ever more dangerously devoted to the cure for his 'foolish bashfulness', a cure that came in a bottle.

Peter Wentworth had the kind of in-between status that allowed him to roam at will throughout Kensington Palace, both in the state apartments at the top of the stairs and in the extensive ser-

Courtiers enjoying themselves by the Round Pond
to the east of Kensington Palace in 1736

vants' quarters at the bottom. He happened to be on duty as equerry during George I's first-ever visit to Kensington and 'walked all over the gardens with him, and after all over the lodgings, both which he lik't very well'.[23]

Despite his setbacks, Wentworth was obviously still very close to the king on a regular basis, which gave him daily the chance to shine and, maybe, to rise. 'I'll rouse up my drowsy spirits,' he promised himself, 'double my diligence, & by the Grace of God am willing & ready to bustle thro' this bad world.'[24]

And while his position may have been lowly, Wentworth had one huge advantage over the absent Prince George Augustus and Princess Caroline: close contact with the couple's captive daughters.

At Kensington Palace, he would often have encountered these girls, the king's granddaughters, coming from a lesson in their 'learning room' or going out to ride.[25] After the 'christening quarrel', these three girls were never returned by George I to their parents' care.

The eldest, Princess Anne, now aged seventeen, was 'very pale, and would be good-looking were she not marked by small-pox'.[26] The disease had struck in April 1720, at the very height of the 'christening quarrel'. At the time, the king had informed Princess Caroline through Mohammed that she could visit her daughter, but that she was not to bring a doctor as he'd made his own medical arrangements.[27] Whatever these arrangements were, Anne survived but was severely scarred.

Anne was born in Hanover. Like the rest of the courtiers she'd become multilingual, speaking 'German and French to perfection'. She also knew 'a great deal of history and geography', spoke English 'very prettily' and danced 'very well'.[28] Conscious of a girl's inferior position, she was overheard wishing that she had no brothers and claiming that 'I would die tomorrow to be queen to-day!'[29]

Next in line after Anne came Amelia, aged fifteen in 1726. When Amelia too fell ill, Princess Caroline was desperate with worry about her daughter's treatment and furious with the king's medical staff. She complained that Dr Bussier had wanted 'to give

[Amelia] a vomit of Hypococyana. I tremble at that . . . My fears & the opposition I meet with are endless,' she wrote, 'these animals have propos'd a flannel shift to make her sweat.' And of the physician who suggested it: 'I believe I could . . . have pull'd out his eyes.'[30]

Amelia was 'a handsome blonde with charming features', and possessed 'much the prettiest person' of the whole family.[31] But she also had rather more acidity and intelligence than was quite appropriate in a Georgian princess, and suffered for it. She developed a reputation for being gruff and outspoken, for being overfond of music, for scandalously attending chapel 'in riding clothes with a dog under her arm'.[32]

Amelia's sharp tongue could be devastating, and one courtier complained that she told people just as many 'shocking things to their faces' as 'disagreeable ones behind their backs'.[33] However, her friends thought that Amelia (or 'Emily') had a character improved by her bluntness: one of the 'oddest princesses ever known', she had 'her ears shut to flattery, and her heart open to honesty'.[34]

The third daughter, Caroline, named for her mother, was at thirteen a placid and prematurely maternal character, 'very tall and stout, and looks like a woman', with 'very dark hair'.[35] She was the quietest and most conscientious member of the family. During the frequent fiery rows between her sisters, people would call for an intermission: 'stay, send for Caroline, and then we shall know the truth'.[36]

Anne, Amelia and Caroline's brother Frederick still remained in Hanover as the family's representative in the German part of their dominions. Their three younger siblings – William Augustus, five, Mary, two, and Louisa, eighteen months – remained with their mother at Leicester House. Through daily contact these younger children won a warm place in their parents' hearts, hearts that the absent children would never quite recapture.

For centuries royal children had been parted from their parents for their education and their health. Yet the eighteenth century saw the rise of a new, more compact, more affectionate family unit; parents and children were starting to spend more time together. This rise of bourgeois family values applied even to royalty, and kings all over Europe began to think of themselves as the figureheads of close-knit families as well as of nations.[37] Prince George Augustus and Princess Caroline actively wanted to be parents to their elder children, as their concerned letters show, but they were thwarted at every turn. They wanted a family life according to modern, more loving, notions, but it was beyond their reach.

Despite the care that their grandfather the king took of them, the three older girls also suffered badly from their enforced separation from their parents. On one occasion 'the poor little things' sent a basket of cherries to their father, 'with a message that though they were not allowed to go to him, their hearts, souls and thoughts were with their dear parents always'.[38]

They were allowed to see the prince and princess only once a week, and not surprisingly they were often rude to their governess, Lady Portland. Amelia wrote of a certain 'ugly *gouvernante* who hastes you always to come away, from people that love your company'.[39] Once, the girls were to be moved from Kensington to Windsor Castle, but as usual there was 'a sort of bustle about it'. When Lady Portland asked Princess Anne to tell her parents about the plan, she flatly refused on the grounds that 'if she was in their places she should not like to have her child carried about without her consent'.[40] So Lady Portland had to break the unwelcome news herself.

Amelia pined for her parents even more than her sisters. Precocious, intelligent but lacking guidance, she claimed to be 'mightily tir'd of [her] self', and was becoming spiky and difficult in a way that would harm her chances of marriage.[41]

The girls' daily timetable as semi-prisoners in their grandfather's palace at Kensington was monotonous: they rose at seven, prayed, dressed and breakfasted. They walked between eight and nine beneath the noses of the 'guards & sentinels' placed around the palace gardens.[42] They read to themselves between nine and ten, read aloud between ten and eleven, and then it was time to 'learn by heart' until twelve. An hour of prayer was followed by an hour for dinner, and then an hour playing shuttlecocks, an hour of needlework and an hour practising the clavichord or performing with their music teacher, George Frederic Handel.[43] Handel also taught the king's three illegitimate daughters. They too lived at Kensington Palace with their mother, Melusine.

But the princesses' lives at Kensington were not entirely unpleasant. They had balls, with 'all the garden illuminated and music in it and dancing in the Green House and the long Gallery'.[44] And they clearly enjoyed their grandfather's annual birthday celebrations: fine fireworks were fired at ten, and 'the little Princesses danced till 11'.[45]

The girls were certainly not kept short of clothes either. An account by their mother's Mistress of the Robes records that every winter they each had:

> Two coats embroider'd
> [1] trim'd or rich stuff
> 1 velvet or rich silk without.
> 3 coats brocaded or damask
> A damask night gown
> Two silk under petticoats trim'd with gold or silver.

Their summer clothes, issued annually, consisted of:

> 3 flower'd coats one of them with silver.
> 3 plain or stripped [lustrous silk dresses]
> 1 night gown   four silk hoops[46]

In addition to their clothes, the girls had a new pair of shoes *every week*, sixteen dozen pairs of gloves a year and plentiful supplies of 'powder, patches, combs, pins, May dew, quilted caps, band boxes, wax, pens and paper'. Their other expenses included the tuning of their harpsichord and food for their birds. Each princess had a personal staff of five, including a Page of Honour, a

Gentleman Usher, a Dresser, a Chambermaid and a Page of the Back-stairs. There was only one thing lacking from all this luxury: they had 'no certain allowance for ribbons or artificial flowers'.[47]

Lady Portland can't have had an easy time of it, looking after three hostile princesses and thereby earning the lasting enmity of their parents. The Prince and Princess of Wales nursed 'a most irreconcilable hatred' towards the woman who saw their daughters more than they did.[48]

At Kensington Palace the little princesses lived around an old courtyard recently rebuilt and renamed 'Princesses' Court' for its new occupants. From it a 'colonnade of communication' led to Melusine's lodgings, and it must often have been used by the king making his frequent visits to his own, strange, self-selected and entirely female family: his legitimate granddaughters, his illegitimate daughters and his mistress.[49]

Melusine von der Schulenberg had by now been rewarded for her services as the king's mistress with the titles of Duchess of Kendal and of Munster. She had a three-storey apartment overlooking the gardens, and George I would visit her there 'every afternoon from five till eight'.[50] Melusine enjoyed a special allowance of yellow wax candles to light the stairs leading to the room in her apartment where 'his Majesty sups'.[51]

Ambassadors guessed that during these evening visits she attempted 'to penetrate the sentiments of his Britannic Majesty' at Sir Robert Walpole's request. But Melusine was not tied to Walpole, and her influence with the king could be bought for money by the highest bidder. The French ambassador assured his own king that in diplomatic business 'it will be necessary to employ her, though I will not trust her further than is absolutely necessary'.[52]

Meanwhile, Sophia Charlotte, the king's half-sister, had died in 1725. Although she was perhaps the most intellectually curious and cultured member of George I's inner circle, she was underestimated to the last by the xenophobic British. Until her death, she'd held a weekly supper for her half-brother the king to which writers and wits were invited, occasions that have been overlooked when people describe George I as incurious and unintelligent.[53]

When he visited his family, the king had both ostentatious and discreet ways of getting around the palace. On the grand, public staircases, he always appeared with attendants: a Vice-Chamberlain holding up a candle to light the way, equerries like Peter Wentworth following on behind.

On other occasions he would cut conveniently through the behind-the-scenes areas and labyrinthine passages that were used by the palace's scurrying servants. The narrow 'back-stairs' to his private apartments were useful for making a discreet exit. The royal chamber pot descended down this secret staircase, and the king's most intimate visitors were brought up it when they came to visit him. Using the back-stairs circumvented the pomp, publicity and many watchful eyes ever present on the King's Grand Staircase. The enduring phrase 'back-stairs gossip', signifying insider information, was born in this part of the palace.

As time went by, more and more of the courtiers considered themselves to be entitled to the privilege of using the back-stairs. The result was that the little staircase became positively crowded, with constant 'contriving, undermining and caballing at the back-stairs, the great ones hurrying back and forward, and the little ones cringing after'.[54] One experienced diplomat thought that multitudes using the British back-stairs showed a shoddy lack of management: 'I have lived in four courts, and this is the first where I have ever seen anybody to go up the back stairs unless such as the Prince would have come to him unobserved.'[55]

Anyone trying to get up to the king's private chambers via the back-stairs would find one of the pages keeping guard. These gatekeepers to the king wielded enormous power, all the more so since Charles II had in the previous century delegated much control to one particular page. William Chiffinch, this favoured servant, became 'a man of so absolute authority' that even government ministers obeyed his commands.[56] Some people, knowing that his duties included bringing in women for the king, called him the 'Pimpmaster General'.[57]

Eventually, Chiffinch's unofficial power was acknowledged with an official title: the first among the pages became known as the 'Keeper of the King's Closet'. Exactly the same title was given to his successor, Mohammed, George I's chosen gatekeeper. That's why such a lubricious mythology grew up around the Turk. It was claimed that he too smuggled people in to fulfil the king's bizarre and excessive sexual desires, or even that he fulfilled them himself. But no evidence exists for this beyond salacious rumour.

The complex palace geography that Peter Wentworth and his colleagues found so familiar was difficult to learn, and journeys were inevitably hindered by the servants leaving upon the back-stairs 'a pail of dirty water with the mop in it, a coal-box, a bottle, a broom, a chamber-pot, and such other unsightly things'.[58]

One night, Wentworth witnessed an unusual bet between Princess Caroline and her courtier Lord Grantham about whether it was possible to reach a particular room without using the back-stairs. 'She bade him go and see,' Wentworth wrote. When he came back unconvinced, the princess took charge:

> 'Well', says she, 'will you go along with me if I show you the way?' 'Yes, madam,' says he. Up she starts, and trots away with one candle, and came back triumphant over my Lord Grantham.[59]

Many of the courtiers thought that Lord Grantham was a nin-compoop, possessing the 'animal gift of reasoning in so small a proportion that his existence was barely distinguished from a veg-etable'.[60]

To be fair to him, though, the back-stairs and passages were infernally complicated.

The characters inhabiting the warren-like world 'below stairs' had more influence than their position might suggest. As Lord Chesterfield recognised, a slighted servant could 'do you more hurt at court, than ten men of merit can do you good'.[61] 'No man', as the adage has it, 'is a hero to his valet,' and John Hervey begged an indiscreet correspondent not to leave his letters in a coat pocket, where they would inevitably be read by the nosy manservant giving the coat a brush.[62]

Peter Wentworth had to accompany the king on horseback if he left the palace, so he often had business in the stable yard. Peter the Wild Boy, too, took 'vast pleasure in conversation with horses', and had two 'intimate acquaintances in the king's stable'.[63] Making their daily way to the stables, Wentworth and the Wild Boy could take the temperature of the nether regions of the palace. The voices heard below stairs were doubtless different from those of the drawing room: perhaps rougher, perhaps warmer; maybe less articulate, maybe more direct. Lord Chesterfield considered that 'common people, footmen and maidservants, all speak ill. They make use of low and vulgar expressions, which people of rank never use.'[64]

In appearance, though, the superior servants were sometimes indistinguishable from their betters. Swept up in the eighteenth-century craze for fashion, an aristocrat might well have met 'a puppy at an assembly, perhaps who gets £50 or £60 a year, dress'd in his bag [i.e. his wig] and sword and the next morning you'll see him sweeping his master's doorway'.[65] He would also ape his master's arrogance: 'the servants of a great man are all great men. Wou'd you get within their doors, you must bow to the porter.'[66]

In the palace the only really clear visual distinction was between those who wore the lower household's livery and those who didn't. 'If she is Mrs with a surname, she is above the livery and belongs to the upper servants,' explained a correspondent of Henrietta Howard's, 'but if she be Mrs only with her Christian name, as Mrs Betty, Mrs May, Mrs Dolly,' then she will 'look as low' as anybody.[67]

One of the most important female servants at Kensington Palace was Mrs Jane Keen. In 1723, she purchased the reversion of the post of housekeeper against the time when the present incumbent, Henry Lowman, might die, and over the years she would become the motor that kept the palace running.[68] Princess Amelia poked fun at the Earl of Hardwicke for bowing just as low to Mrs Keen as he did to the king.[69]

The world below stairs could be rowdy, full of running feet and fists ready to throw a punch, while unsavoury characters lurked in its corners. Wentworth records the scuffle to get ready when the king 'took us at a surprise' by calling for his carriage with only an inadequate forty-five minutes' notice.[70] Then there were complaints that 'idle persons', 'vagrants & beggars' were 'commonly seen within the King's palace'.[71] A royal wedding was marred by 'bad company' and 'scrub people', and no wonder, for footmen were seen in the coffee houses beforehand, selling the tickets intended for peers 'to any who would purchase them for three shillings'.[72]

On one occasion Wentworth won 'immortal fame among the liverymen' for speaking up for a palace groom who'd beaten up a carter ('a very saucy fellow') obstructing the way of the royal coach.[73] More seriously, Princess Caroline had to sack one of her sedan chairmen because he was 'strongly suspected of having too good an understanding with some highwaymen'.[74] The bodies of condemned highwaymen and other felons were displayed at Tyburn Gallows, only a mile or so from Kensington Palace.

A kind of committee called 'the Board of the Green Cloth' was the mechanism for regulating these menial and sometimes troublesome reaches of the royal household. Its officers took their name from an actual table or 'board', covered with a green cloth, around which their predecessors had met since the reign of King Edward IV. Piles of tokens pushed across the table stood for provisions in and out.

The provisioning, cleaning and security of the palace was the responsibility of the Lord Steward, one of the great officers of the realm. He, along with the Treasurer, the Comptroller, the Master and the Cofferer of the household, plus clerks, made up the Board of the Green Cloth. Together they ran the entire below-stairs department, making contracts with suppliers and paying the bills.

And, importantly, the Board maintained discipline. It had

judicial responsibility for all offences committed in or near the court. Before the Board appeared disobedient servants, pick-pockets, prostitutes and the unruly scrum of chairmen touting for business and overcrowding the palace courtyards.[75]

Although he had a jester's traditional freedom of speech, the court comedian Ulrich Jorry's wayward attitude managed to land him in serious trouble from time to time. On one notorious occasion he complained to the Board of the Green Cloth that he'd been abused and attacked by two footmen 'belonging to the Countess of Portland' (governess to the little princesses).[76]

Court gossip, however, revealed that Ulrich had deserved his beating. He'd tried to kiss a certain 'damsel' or maid who worked for Lady Portland. The damsel's lover, a Welsh footman, had given Ulrich a punch in punishment. When the affair reached the king's ear, though, 'some of the biggest people at court' supported Ulrich's cause. This resulted in the footman being made prisoner in the palace guard room 'by His Majesty's particular direction'.[77]

Although Ulrich Jorry's attacker had been locked up, Ulrich appeared again before the Board of the Green Cloth the following day to make further accusations. Now he was pushing his luck, 'arraigning the justice of their proceedings' and 'behaving himself very insolent'.[78]

So Ulrich was threatened with imprisonment himself, for con-tempt of the Board, and he was taken off to the 'Porters Lodge'. But it looked like he would be able to use his charm to escape punishment, by 'begging pardon and acknowledging his fault'.[79]

Once again, however, the king came to hear of the matter, and this time he was disinclined to be lenient. George I ordered that Ulrich must be 'taken into custody by the guards' and put 'into the hole at Kensington' for a fortnight on a diet of bread and water.[80] In the event, this imprisonment only lasted twenty-four hours before there was a relaxation and Ulrich was released. Presumably he emerged having learnt that even favourites are not always above the palace rules.

There was a continual tension between the Lord Steward's

department (supervised by the Board of the Green Cloth) and the servants employed in the 'above-stairs' part of the palace, which was controlled by the Lord Chamberlain. The Lord Chamberlain's servants griped about the poor food provided by the Lord Steward's department: so little meat that they 'had much ado to make a dinner'. They also complained that the Lord Steward's men were so mean with candles that the courtiers ran 'their noses against the hangings' in the dark. 'Do not suffer us to be governed by the Board of Greencloth!' was a frequent cry to be heard among the Lord Chamberlain's servants.[81]

But this slapstick, knockabout type of conflict could become more serious, especially for the female employees. Punishments could be exceptionally harsh for servants caught stealing from the royal palaces. In 1731, servant Sarah Matts was put in prison for 'feloniously stealing a quilt' out of a palace guard room.[82] While incarcerated, she brought an accusation of rape against a guard. With heart-rending circumstantial detail, she reported how he 'thump'd me' and 'then he flung me a-cross the bed, so as my head hung down, and he tore my legs asunder . . . I scream'd, and cry'd out, Murder; but he would lie with me.'

A character witness who appeared in support of Sarah's assailant said that she was a prostitute, just 'a common vile woman' who deserved no better. He announced that she'd previously been seen 'in bed with a man, in the guard-room, at St. James's', and that 'the greatest black-guard may lie with her' for sixpence.[83]

It comes as no surprise, given the blackening of her character, that her attacker was found innocent and poor Sarah was subjected to a whipping.

Matters took an even worse turn for one Catherine Pollard, employed for thirty years in the silver scullery at Kensington Palace. She was accused of stealing four silver plates and selling them to a dealer who performed the treasonable action of filing off the royal arms. He, however, escaped punishment by giving evidence against Catherine herself, while she was tried for a capital felony at the Old Bailey.

The plea she made in her own defence was pitifully inadequate: 'I believe there was a spell set upon me, or else I was bewitch'd.'[84] She was condemned to death.

The court was constantly changing. In October of 1726, George I's trusty aide Mohammed fell ill. He had suffered from dropsy in the summer and sought to cure it with the waters of Bath. In the autumn it returned, and between 'thirteen and fourteen quarts' of fluid were drawn from his swollen body.[85] Two days later, on 1 November, he gave up the unequal fight.[86] He died, as he'd lived, at Kensington Palace.

Mohammed was widely mourned as a good man. His reputation for kindness and generosity was enhanced by his will, which included the instruction to spend money from his estate upon releasing three hundred debtors from prison. 'Forty years attendance upon COURTS,' it was said, 'those nurseries of flattery and deceit, made not the least impression upon him.' He also decreed that his children should inherit his property in Hanover, including 'tapestries, beds, chairs, tables, looking-glasses, pictures'.[87] His widow became very interested in the fate of a wallet containing 1,500 ducats, which she thought her husband had mislaid in the king's closet, but her quest for its restitution ended fruitlessly.[88]

Mohammed's duties – paying for the king's hats, suits and wigs, meeting the bills for theatre subscriptions, looking after the king's precious objects – were taken over by Mustapha, but there were only months to go before the death of the master they had both served for forty years.[89]

George I had felt a premonition of death in the same month that Mohammed passed away. His long-estranged wife, still confined in her faraway prison-castle at Ahlden, finally died after thirty-three years incarcerated. George I's reaction was to place the briefest of notices in the *London Gazette*, countermand the mourning dress that the court in Hanover had adopted, and to go to the theatre.[90] Nor would he allow his son Prince George

Augustus to wear mourning dress for the woman who was, after all, his mother.[91]

There was much whispered hearsay in London about a 'French prophetess' who'd predicted that George I himself would not long outlive his wife.[92]

On 20 December 1726, George I departed from Kensington Palace after what would prove to be his last extended residence there. Early in 1727, he returned to the palace for a brief tour with the housekeeper Henry Lowman. Ironically, it was during this final visit to the palace that George I looked forward to the completion of the project. William Kent's finished Grand Staircase 'pleased him much', and the king was happy to hear that the scaffolding would be taken down the following Monday.[93]

On the king's sixty-seventh birthday in May, John Hervey complained that 'the occurrences of all the Birthdays are alike'. There was 'a great crowd, bad music, trite compliments upon new garments . . . a ball with execrable dancers'.[94] The king's reign seemed somehow to be winding down. A few days later, on 3 June, he made his departure from England, intending to spend the summer in Hanover.[95]

George I travelled as usual by boat across the Channel and embarked upon the wearisome three-day coach ride towards Hanover. On the evening of 9 June 1727, he had a large and varied range of dishes for supper in the town of Delden, which is situated in the modern Netherlands. One theory had it that the melons he'd eaten at Delden caused the 'indigestion' that would play havoc with his body the following day, while an 'excess of strawberries and oranges' was proposed as an alternative hazard to an elderly digestive system.[96]

Mustapha would have known exactly what George I had eaten, for he was present as usual to look after the king. He was later able to inform the doctors that during the night the king had in fact visited the toilet several times and had not required any of his usual laxatives.[97]

The next morning, George I drank a cup of hot chocolate

before continuing his journey. Despite evident discomfort, he was determined to make progress towards Hanover. Mustapha was once again at hand when, later that day, the king collapsed completely. Everyone thought that he'd experienced a 'violent cholick of which he suffer'd very much'.[98] Rather than a digestive disorder, though, this event in the coach was probably a second and even greater stroke, for 'his hand fell down as if lifeless, and his tongue hung out of his mouth'.[99]

Instead of stopping, though, the king shouted at the coachmen to drive on in the direction of Hanover, the place that he had never really wanted to leave.

When he reached the town of Osnabrück later that day, George I finally admitted that he was unable to continue travelling towards home. He died there at about one in the morning of 11 June 1727. His last words were reported to be '*C'est fait de moi* [I'm done].' This final thought was as bald, factual, drab – and yet as honest and unpretentious – as the king himself had been.[100]

Melusine was summoned to the deathbed as soon as possible, but arrived too late to see her long-time lover alive. She was distraught and inconsolable, laid low by 'the signs of extreme grief'.[101] The king's cadaver was ceremoniously carried from Osnabrück along the rough road to Hanover. His funeral procession entered the town late at night, with servants on horseback carrying lighted flambeaux. Even Hanover's traditionally unemotional and phlegmatic townsfolk were moved to great grief at the sight. Despite the late hour, 'there was a great concourse of people from all parts to see, with tears in their eyes, this last honour paid to their late sovereign, once the joy and delight of his subjects'.[102] The natives of Hanover mourned their born ruler much more than did his adopted British subjects.

George I's corpse was eventually taken on to Herrenhausen, and lies today in the Hanoverian royal mausoleum, cloaked by oaks and situated on a rise looking out over his beloved gardens.

Back in London, the wigs and silver and crockery for the king's daily use were divided up among the former servants of his bed-chamber.[103] Now Prince George Augustus would become King George II, and Caroline his queen. The palaces of Kensington and St James's were theirs at last, and the battle between father and son was finally won. Yet there must have been a bleak streak in Prince George Augustus's victory: any lingering hope of a tender reconciliation between himself and his father was now extin-guished.

With the king's death, Peter Wentworth found himself once again changing employer. He remained at Kensington Palace as an equerry in Queen Caroline's household. This was his fourth royal job, as he'd served a prince, another queen and a king already.

Luckily, Wentworth had admired his new mistress ever since their very first encounter. It had taken place in the drawing room soon after Princess Caroline's arrival in England. Thanks to a kindly act of the Lord Chamberlain, Wentworth was beckoned through the crowd 'to kiss her Highness's hand; she repeated my name aloud and smilingly gave me her hand'.[104] Perhaps, like another lowly courtier introduced to Caroline, Wentworth found her compliments so 'very gracious that they confounded' him, and 'blunder'd out a great deal of nonsense' in reply.[105]

And now Peter Wentworth, like Peter the Wild Boy, found himself entering the special cadre of those whom Caroline cher-ished. She worked a kind of magic upon her favourite servants, drawing them into the circle of her charm, allowing them to see both her abundant affection for them and her private pain.

While many people lined up to puff and praise the new queen, Caroline was not universally liked outside her household. She pre-sented such a graceful, gracious front to the world that some peo-ple distrusted it. Unlike her husband, who could not hide his feelings and would 'kick whilst he obliged', Caroline 'would stroke while she hated'.[106] But her bright and easy social manner dis-guised a certain vulnerability. She was constantly begged for one favour or another, and had to defend herself against the draining strain of making constant refusals. Viscountess Falmouth, for example, was thrown into a frenzy by the news that Caroline might 'add some new ladies' to her household, and begged for a personal appointment to put her case for a position. 'I own to you', she wrote in desperate hope, 'I have been in such anxiety of mind, that I have not slept one wink all night.'[107]

Caroline may have been devious, guilty of empty smiles and empty words, but she needed to protect her vitality from these exhausting applications for help. When one lady arrived to beg for a rebel's life, Caroline 'could not bear to see her, but hastened out of ye drawing room into her own rooms and cried'.[108] It was this, her softer side, which really made people fall in love with the queen. 'I am so charmed with her good nature and good qualities', wrote one devoted lady-in-waiting, 'that I shall never think I can do enough to please her.'[109]

And now, as Peter Wentworth's and Caroline's paths converged, new hope was in sight for the unfortunate equerry. Ever since Caroline had 'smilingly' given him her hand, he had liked the princess, and in her service he would become her slave. He aspired to be one of the chosen few with whom Caroline would relax and become intimate. And, as a result, he resolved 'never to be concern'd in liquor again'.[110]

Queen Caroline offered Wentworth no promotion and no extra money. But she gave him something much more valuable: sympathy and attention. She told Wentworth that she didn't believe the occasional and perilous 'idle stories' of his being drunk on duty, because, as he said, 'she sees me every day sober'.

Her kind words soothed his spirit: 'Her Majesty has told me she knows none of my misfortunes has been my fault . . . She has said she pities me from her soul, & that I deserve a better fortune.'[111]

The neglected equerry had entered a warm new world.

SIX

The Woman of the Bedchamber

'In courts . . . the affections of the heart are as
much conceal'd as its substance.'[I]
(Lord Berkeley of Stratton)

In 1734, an uneasy love triangle existed at Kensington Palace. George II, the former Prince George Augustus, was by now well established as Britain's king, and Caroline as his queen. For nearly twenty years now Henrietta Howard had soldiered on in the unglamorous, unenviable and unpaid job of George II's acknowledged lover. She felt she'd seen quite enough of court life and yearned to escape.

The king, tired of his mistress, would have let her go. But Henrietta was a valuable servant to Caroline, and the queen wanted her to stay. This placed all three in an extraordinary dilemma.

The situation was most pressing, and most distressing, to Henrietta. She lived right at the very heart of the Georgian court. 'There is no politician who more carefully watches the motions and dispositions of things and persons,' people said, and she was legendary for her 'imperceptible dexterity' in negotiating court life.[2] Yet Henrietta's way of life was gradually taking its toll upon both her health and her happiness. Like all the courtiers, her daily struggle for survival at court meant that she was becoming a slave to deception.

Jonathan Swift, the outsider, was perceptive enough to notice the danger. He warned that Henrietta might 'come in time to believe herself' as she dealt out the courtier's habitual half-truths and flattery. If this happened, it could have 'terrible consequences' for her.

In a particularly striking simile, Swift feared that Henrietta's talents as a courtier would 'spread, enlarge, and multiply to such a

degree, that her private virtues for want of room and time to oper-
ate, must be folded and laid up clean like clothes in a chest'. All
that was best about Henrietta's character would remain hidden
away until 'some reverse of fortune' should 'dispose her to retirement'.[3]

Henrietta hoped to escape from court while her integrity still
remained intact and to put back on the 'clothes' of sincerity, wisdom and love that were so alien to a courtier's role.

But the story of her difficult life so far suggested that this might
be impossible.

Henrietta was born into the Hobart family of Norfolk. She'd been
baptised in London on 11 May 1689, but her family's main home
was Blickling Hall near Norwich.[4] Despite the grandeur of their
country mansion, the Hobarts' finances were precarious, and
became even more so after Henrietta's father was killed in a duel
in 1698. Left orphaned by the death of her mother shortly afterwards, Henrietta at the age of sixteen assumed that marriage to
the thirty-year-old Charles Howard would provide her with some
measure of security.

She made the terrible mistake of marrying him in 1706. In time
Henrietta would deeply regret placing her confidence in this
'wrong-headed, ill-tempered, obstinate, drunken, extravagant,
brutal' reprobate.[5] As one of her friends put it, 'thus they loved,
thus they married, and thus they hated each other for the rest of
their lives'.[6]

The couple were genteel paupers, their shortage of money made
all the more excruciating by the need they felt to hide it. Charles
spent his early married life in London in gaming houses and
brothels, while their lack of cash meant that Henrietta often felt
the 'smart of hunger'. 'Despised and abused' by her husband, she
would later recall that during her young adulthood she 'suffer'd all
that poverty and ye whole train of miseries that attend it can suggest to any one's imagination'.[7]

Her plan to travel to Hanover to look for work and escape a

wretched life was spurred on by the birth of her son, Henry, in 1707. She and her husband could hardly afford the journey. Their expenses were met by Henrietta selling even their 'beds & bedding', and she was offered eighteen guineas by a periwig-maker for her lovely long light brown hair. Her disagreeable husband's only reaction was to say he thought it worth not nearly so much.[8]

Once in Hanover, Henrietta did indeed find gainful employment: as a Bedchamber Woman to Princess Caroline and, soon after that, as a mistress to Prince George Augustus. The arrangement seemed acceptable, almost respectable, to everybody.

It would indeed have been more scandalous for the prince to have remained faithful to his wife. Lord Chesterfield recommended that every gentleman should take a mistress as an important part of his education. In preference to learning 'all Plato and Aristotle by heart', he advised a youth to fall 'passionately in love with some determined coquette' who would 'lead you a dance, fashion, supple, and polish you'.[9] For Henrietta's part, 'the sacrifice she made of her virtue' was for reasons more pragmatic than romantic: 'she had felt poverty, and was far from disliking power'.[10]

Princess Caroline, the wronged wife, was not too put out either. Writing to Caroline from Paris, the Duchess of Orléans was warm in her recommendation of separate sleeping arrangements for a royal husband and wife. 'It is nothing new for a husband to have a mistress,' she claimed, and 'you won't find one in ten thousand who loves no one but his wife. They deserve praise if they simply live on good terms with their wives and treat them kindly.'[11]

Double standards, though, were firmly in place where women's sexual activities were concerned.[12] Legal opinion had it that a man's wife was his possession just like his money, and for another man to sleep with her was 'the highest invasion of property'.[13] Men, then, would not put up with the infidelities that their wives had to tolerate: 'forgiveness on the part of a wife' was 'meritorious; while a similar forgiveness on the part of the husband would be degrading and dishonourable'.[14]

After the death of Queen Anne in 1714, Henrietta Howard –

both servant and mistress – accompanied the new royal family on its journey to England. She was retained as part of Princess Caroline's British household, earning £300 a year as one of the six Bedchamber Women, and her husband was made a Groom of the Bedchamber to George I. The couple initially shared an apartment at St James's Palace, but their attachment to different households would prove problematic when war broke out between the rival courts.[15] During these years, Henrietta found herself becoming friends with the sprightly literary spirits of the age: John Gay, Alexander Pope, Dr Arbuthnot and Jonathan Swift.

By then, Henrietta's husband had become a terrible burden to her. He took her money, and she was often in physical danger from his alcohol-fuelled violence. After she'd left him, Henrietta addressed to Charles Howard a list of the abuses she'd endured at his hands: 'you have call'd me names and have threatened to kick me and to break my neck. I have often laid abed with you when I have been under apprehensions of your doing me a mischief and sometimes I have got out of bed for fear you shou'd.'[16]

While everybody else seemed to tolerate her role as the Prince of Wales's mistress, her husband sought to benefit from it, pretending to be jealous and demanding to be compensated financially for his supposed shame.

Henrietta's plight was pitiable. While her husband lorded it over her 'with tyranny; with cruelty, [her] life in danger', she had no remedy in the eyes of the law. Society treated women abominably, Henrietta thought privately. 'If they have superior sense, superior fortitude and reason, then why a slave to what's inferior to them?' she asked. Her own husband was indeed 'inferior to all mankind', and Henrietta reasoned with herself that his neglect, alternating with brutality, negated their marriage contract: 'I must believe I am free.'[17]

Yet she recognised that the world would not agree. Only the exceptional voices of her time, like Lady Mary Wortley Montagu's, publicly exposed the unfairness of an unfaithful wife being universally condemned while a husband's adultery was overlooked:

For wives ill us'd no remedy remains,
To daily racks condemn'd, and to eternal chains.[18]

Henrietta's only comfort lay in her female friends and, when they were absent, their letters. Lady Lansdowne was typical in writing: 'Dear Mrs Howard, you & I shall live to see better days, & love & honour to flourish once more.'[19]

Despite the difficulties she had with her husband, Henrietta was remarkably well-suited to the job of royal mistress. She was never arrogant or indiscreet. Polite to everybody, she became known as 'The Swiss' because of her neutrality in court storms. If Henrietta were a book, wrote her friend Molly Hervey, she would be 'a complete treatise on subjects moral, instructive, and entertaining, perfectly well digested & connected, the style is admirable, the reasoning clear & strong'.[20]

There were a few people at court who disliked Henrietta, but they condemned her in the mildest of terms. 'The real truth is, that Mrs Howard was more remarkable for beauty than for understanding,' concluded an early biographer of Sir Robert Walpole, and he said that her becoming royal mistress was just a matter of convenience.

Henrietta was not even the first choice, he claimed, as Prince George Augustus had previously been 'enamoured' of the spirited Mary Bellenden. She'd boldly turned him down and allowed her friend Henrietta to pick him up instead.[21]

And Henrietta did not find the mistress's role at all delightful, even in the tender years of her relationship with Prince George Augustus before he became king. 'I was told', wrote Mary Bellenden to Henrietta as early as April 1722, 'that somebody that shall be nameless, was grown sour & cross & not so good to you as usual.'[22] There was certainly a greater frankness and affection between Henrietta and Mary than between either of them and their so-called lover.

The goings-on at George II's court are often described in almost cosy terms, as if the king could legitimately sleep with any number of jolly playfellows, and certainly there were plenty of women willing to taste 'the charms/ of love and life in a young monarch's arms'.[23] This was tolerated partly because George II made sure that his mistresses were perceived to be powerless – a sharp contrast to the despicable potent German wiles wielded by Melusine in the previous generation. 'He had seen, and lamented, that his father had been governed by his mistresses,' people said, and was therefore 'extremely cautious to avoid a similar error'.[24]

Caroline likewise treated 'those little episodes' of her husband's with indifference for the most part, and with some contempt. She knew that in reality George II 'reserved his heart, and his friendship' for her alone.[25] Sir Robert Walpole also claimed to perceive the real situation behind the royal marriage. In an arresting image, he said that those who cultivated Henrietta at the expense of the queen had the 'wrong sow by the ear'.[26]

Through the pens of her friends, Henrietta is shown to be a thoughtful, witty, warm and reasonable woman, far too intelligent to be satisfied as a member of the royal circus, where handing glasses at table and doing up dresses formed her chief duties. Mary Bellenden, who had resigned as a Maid of Honour upon a marriage made for love, wrote to her friend that 'it wou'd make one half mad' to think of the time they had both misspent in servitude.

'I am happy', she continued, '& I wou'd to God you were so. I wish . . . that you might leave that life of hurry, & be able to enjoy those that love you, & be a little at rest.'[27]

By 1734, after nearly two decades as the king's mistress, Henrietta herself was almost desperate to retire. George II and Caroline had been king and queen for nearly seven years, and this had been the busiest, most exciting and most successful period of their lives so far.

In the immediate aftermath of his father's death, there was a rumour that George II was planning to rescue his much-maligned mother's reputation, bringing her portrait out of storage and hanging it on the wall.[28] But another undercurrent of gossip rivalled it: that now, as king, with full access to the archives at Hanover, he'd discovered some of the letters written by his mother to her lover. These had shocked him, convinced him of her guilt and killed the affection in his memory of her.[29] The new king remained touchy on the subject and sought to destroy his mother's papers. In 1732, he used the diplomatic service to suppress an anonymous and scurrilous work about her called the *Histoire secrète de la duchesse d'Hanover.*[30]

The king discussed almost – but not quite – everything with John Hervey, now Vice-Chamberlain of the court. While he would freely dissect his difficult relationship with his father, he never mentioned his mother at all.[31] Only one thing is sure: the death of the disgraced mother he had not seen for so long, followed so soon by the demise of his hated father, must have caused a strange mixture of reactions. 'I am at a loss', he admitted, 'how to express myself upon this great and melancholy occasion.'[32]

George II was at first almost overwhelmed by his new responsibilities as king. A popular anecdote has it that the announcement of his father's death literally caught him napping and only half-dressed, 'with his breeches in his hand' and reluctant to give a hearing to the messenger who brought the news.[33] His first Parliament was similarly farcical, as one person present noted: 'I saw him make [his opening speech] today, I can't say heard, for his majesty was in so much confusion he could not put out his voice to be heard.' Likewise, with 'his crown he seemed a little awkward being ye first time of wearing it'.[34]

But George II's reign got off to a much more secure start than his father's. Even the Jacobites admitted that the new king, although 'passionate, proud and peevish', made a reasonably good first impression. His declared intention of 'turning off the Germans', for example, went down very well.[35] At his coronation, Handel's superlative musical setting for the ancient coronation text *Zadok the Priest* surged through Westminster Abbey for the first time; in following centuries it would become inextricably associated with the ceremony of crowning. 'I shall never forget the joy that swell'd my heart,' wrote one witness present.[36]

Another of the memorable sights seen by the coronation's hordes of spectators was the Countess of Orkney, the retired mistress of William III, exposing 'behind a mixture of fat and wrinkles, and before a considerable pair of boobies a good deal withered', along with 'a great belly'.[37]

Henrietta was there too, in Queen Caroline's train, making one of the 'finest figures of all the procession' in her scarlet and silver gown.[38]

The coronation feast took place in Westminster Hall, where William Kent had designed a festive triumphal arch. It was topped by statues of the new king and queen looking down upon the immense banquet spread below.

Kent would enjoy magnificent patronage from Britain's new rulers. Over time he became almost constantly 'called on for draughts' or designs, both at court and 'amongst people of quality'. In 1728, George II made Kent his official history painter and 'keeper or preserver of the paintings of the royal palaces for life'.[39]

George II and Caroline enjoyed joining Kent 'upon the scaffold' to see him at work in this new capacity. Once they even climbed up to the ceiling of the Banqueting House in Whitehall to inspect his ongoing restoration of its paintings by Peter Paul Rubens. Kent's own record of the occasion shows the contrasting gruffness of the king and the queen's elegant eloquence: 'his Majesty was pleas'd to tell me I had done them exceeding well', while 'the Queen told me I not only deserv'd thanks from the King', but from 'all lovers of painting'.[40]

Kent's success continued to infuriate Sir James Thornhill. The older artist had long ago paid for his presumption in setting himself up as an architect and for his insolence towards the Board of the Office of the King's Works. In the matter of the decoration of Kensington Palace he had managed to blend all parties 'against him in all his affairs'. As a consequence he had fallen so far from

fashion, and so suddenly, that he had 'long been unemployed' by
1734.[41] It would be the year in which he died.

With his customary versatility, Kent also designed much-
praised costumes for court masquerades: Tudor huntsmen in green,
for example, with bows and arrows and 'caps and feathers upon
their heads'.[42] In 1733, working as an architect, he'd completed a
splendid new 'Royal Mews' for the king's horses at Charing Cross.
But the most important of his works were by now taking shape out
in the garden, a new field of endeavour for him and one in which
he would become the country's undisputed master.

His most striking works so far had been a clutch of crazy and
inventive grottoes, summerhouses and other structures for
Caroline, to ornament the grounds of her summer residence at
Richmond. Kent's love was for 'natural' landscapes, a far cry from
the rigid alleys and clipped hedges of the previous generation's
baroque gardens. His friends cast scorn upon those old 'damned
dull walks', those 'cold and insipid straight walks which would
make the Signior sick'.[43] In the same spirit, Caroline had the great
formal baroque garden planted by Queen Anne at Kensington
Palace uprooted and replaced with a rolling lawn.

'The Signior' much preferred planning gardens to palace politics. A spoof letter from one of his clients describes the simple
pleasure to be found in masterminding the woodlands of a
Norfolk estate, contrasting his and Kent's joint enjoyment with
the machinations of the court:

> Here Kent and I are planting clumps
> Not minding whom our monarch rumps
> Or what Sir Robert's doing.[44]

Sir Robert Walpole was by now well ensconced in power, and cordially hated by those who resented his iron grip over people and
events. Now enormously fat, he was unkindly but memorably
described as 'the potent knight whose belly goes/ At least a yard
before his nose'.[45]

He was the leader of the Whig party, but this was still far from being a disciplined organisation with a defined membership. It was a relaxed coalition of politicians, generally opposed by the Tories with their more rural and conservative interests. Yet the Whigs clearly remained in the ascendant. The control they had over the disposal of offices allowed them to shower their loyal supporters with rich rewards. In the sometimes rather grubby elections of the early Georgian period, they had little difficulty in keeping the Tories out.

Disaffected Whigs harried and spat at their colleagues, though, while renegade Tories occasionally accepted Walpole's blandished offices, and parliamentary politics were lively and passionate. Peter Wentworth was left stunned by Walpole's eloquence in the House of Commons: 'shou'd I attempt to repeat after him I shou'd spoil the jokes ... I am angry at my unhappy memory that cannot retain them.'[46]

Sometimes those jealous of Henrietta's position as official mistress attempted to wound her by accusing her of consorting with Tory politicians. Yet she cleverly parried these attacks, carefully cultivating an image of herself as delightful but dim, and entirely without influence. Like Lady Mary Wortley Montagu, Henrietta accepted that a woman should 'conceal whatever learning she attains, with as much solicitude as she would hide crookedness or lameness'.[47]

Many of Henrietta's colleagues were openly confused by her mixture of sociability and apparent insignificance. 'She possessed every accomplishment and good quality which were ever the lot of a woman,' ponders one perplexed eighteenth-century historian, while at the same time recounting anecdotes that show Henrietta demonstrating her helplessness.[48] She sometimes ostentatiously asked people 'to procure a trifling' favour for her at court, asking them to keep her name out of the matter and saying, 'if it is known that I have applied, I have no chance of succeeding'.[49]

In fact, this pretence of powerlessness was a crafty strategy to maintain a low profile and stay safe.

Immediately after the coronation in 1727, it was found to be impossible that 'the Palace of St James's should be ready soon enough' for occupation.[50] So king, queen and all their households went off to Kensington Palace instead. Henrietta arrived at what would now become her regular summer home.

George II and Caroline wasted no time in altering the arrangements for the education of their daughters at Kensington: their cruel governess Lady Portland was sacked, and was reported to be sadly 'fallen away since her dismissal from Court'. Lady Deloraine, the former Maid of Honour Mary Howard, came back into the royal household as her replacement.[51]

Although George II and Caroline were now reunited with their elder daughters, family harmony was still strangely absent. It seems that the king thought the regained children had been somehow tainted by their time with his father; certainly he and they were no longer close.

For the next decade of George II's reign – the 1730s – we have the flamboyant, gripping and voluminous account of his and Caroline's lives as king and queen captured in the memoirs of John Hervey.

The most malicious, amusing and memorable spokesperson for the Georgian court, Hervey had a voice that was – and remains – simply unmistakable. He also looked increasingly odd. His golden, girlish good looks that had initially attracted Molly Lepell had decayed, and he was now a foppish, ill-ish man with bad teeth and sometimes a little too much make-up. 'This world consists of men, women and Herveys,' Lady Mary Wortley Montagu famously said.[52]

Hervey's pen portrait of Caroline, his royal mistress and much-loved friend, has given her stellar status among the British queens. As a result of Hervey's readability and wit, her reputation remains sky-high: a clever, loquacious woman, trapped by a trying husband and a frustrating job.

But John Hervey, her strongest advocate, can also be a treacherous guide to the court. His partiality for Caroline led him to caricature George II as an ignorant and insensitive boor in a crude,

John Hervey joked about his own cold and feline personality. He said his coat of arms should really be 'a *cat* scratchant, with this motto: "For my friends where they itch; for my enemies where they are sore"'

one-sided portrait which has dominated popular history.

To be fair, Hervey's stated aim in writing his memoirs of the court was much more modest than that of being its official historian. It was merely to capture a scene, to titillate a little and to amuse. 'I am determined to report everything just as it is, or at least just as it appears to me,' he wrote, 'and those who have a curiosity to see courts and courtiers dissected must bear with the dirt they find.'[53]

Although John Hervey is a brilliant sketch-writer, a cold and razor-sharp wit and an exaggerator of the ridiculous, the theatrical and the gothic aspects of the court, that doesn't mean that we can't believe him at all. At the heart of each of his brilliant word-pictures, with all their superfluous frills of absurdity, there probably lies a germ of truth. The events he describes really happened; the words were really spoken – though perhaps not in such a high-camp manner as he suggests.[54]

And Hervey was doubtless very close to the king and queen, and privy to their secrets. The summer of 1734 saw him:

in greater favour with the Queen, and consequently with the King, than ever; they told him everything, and talked of everything before him. The Queen sent for him every morning as soon as the King went from her, and kept him, while she breakfasted . . . generally an hour and a half at least.

Caroline called Hervey her 'child, her pupil, and her charge'. She also used to tell him that she permitted 'his being so impertinent and daring to contradict her so continually' only because 'she could not live without him'. 'It is well I am so old,' she often said, 'or I should be talked about for this creature.'

Was this flighty butterfly of the court emotionally engaged by Caroline in return, or was he simply unable to resist fluttering near to the flame of power?

However unlikely it seemed in the wicked world of the court, the truth lay in the former. Hervey 'really loved and admired' the queen. He gave up all of his 'time to her disposal', at the cost of neglecting his beautiful wife.[55]

We left Molly pursuing intrigues of her own, but she had dutifully produced a whole string of Hervey heirs. Named for the king, her own George was born in 1721, followed by Augustus. Molly also had two daughters, Lepell and Mary. Frederick, her third son, born in 1730, was a puny infant, and his grandfather thought his weak physique had been caused by the pregnant Molly's irresponsible fondness for 'dancing, morning suppers, sharp wines, china oranges, &c'.[56] Three more children would follow, making a total of eight. Yet Molly was distinctly unmaternal: 'I mortally hate children and am uneasy when they are in the room.'[57]

John Hervey was likewise uninterested in his children, and his passion for politics also separated him from Molly. Sir Robert Walpole, Hervey's great friend and ally, 'had formerly made love to her, but unsuccessfully . . . Sir Robert Walpole, therefore, detested Lady Hervey, and Lady Hervey him.'[58] In writing about this incident, John Hervey, a man of his time, seems to have valued the political bond that he shared with Walpole more highly than the relationship he'd once had with his wife.

As Caroline's strongest supporter, Hervey always made a point of running down Henrietta. Although Caroline 'affected to approve' of her husband's 'amours', she was in fact rather jealous of whatever vestige of influence Henrietta may have had.

So she made quite sure that the door to Henrietta's apartment 'should not lead to power and favour', and that the hopeful sycophants who traipsed through it should leave disappointed.[59] John Gay, for one, found that his friendship with Henrietta was worthless, and 'the queen's jealousy' prevented his ever being offered an important job at court.[60] Lord Chesterfield, too, fell from favour for the same reason: he was detected paying a night-time visit to Henrietta, ostensibly to deposit with her for safe-keeping a large sum of money won by gambling. Caroline discovered his perfidy, and Chesterfield paid the price of her displeasure.[61]

While Henrietta shrank away from political intrigue, Caroline clearly relished it. She and Sir Robert Walpole had a system of secret code words to use when the king was present, so that they could together change tack in conversation in a manner 'imperceptible by the bystanders'.[62] George II was blithely unsuspicious of the fact that he was being manipulated, and would sometimes 'cry out, with colour flushing into his cheeks' that Sir Robert was 'a brave fellow' who had 'more spirit than any man [he] ever knew'.[63]

As the satirists had it, Caroline was all-powerful:

> You may strut, dapper George, but 'twill all be in vain;
> We know 'tis Queen Caroline, not you, that reign . . .
> Then if you would have us fall down and adore you,
> Lock up your fat spouse, as your dad did before you.[64]

Yet the cunning Walpole boasted that he, not she, ultimately pulled the strings of this puppet king:

> Should I tell either the King or the Queen what I propose to bring them to six months hence, I could never succeed. Step by step I can carry them . . . but if I ever show them at a distance to what end that road leads, they stop short, and all my designs are always defeated.[65]

*

A satirical print called *The Festival of the Golden Rump*. Queen Caroline injects
magic medicine up a raving, satyr-like George II's backside in order to bring him
back under her control. Sir Robert Walpole looks on approvingly; the courtiers are
shown as bizarre savages taking part in an exotic ritual

When George II and Caroline first became king and queen,
Henrietta had lived for several weeks in real fear of being kidnapped by her violent husband. Charles Howard had hoped for
some time to win financial advantage for himself by threatening to
demand the return of his wife. He had even obtained a warrant
from the Lord Chief Justice giving him the authority to seize her
by force. But Henrietta 'feared nothing so much as falling again
into his hands', and consequently 'did not dare to stir' outside St
James's Palace.

The stout Caroline proved herself on this occasion to be a
doughty protector to Henrietta. When Charles Howard actually
attempted to storm the queen's apartment, in search of his wife,
Caroline boldly stood her ground. Afterwards she admitted that
she'd been 'horribly afraid', knowing him to be 'brutal as well as a
little mad, and seldom quite sober'. She thought him quite capable
of throwing her out of the window.[66]

Once Howard had been ejected from the palace, the whole matter was hushed up. He was given money to leave the king's mistress alone, 'and so this affair ended', the king reluctantly paying £1,200 in order to retain the lover he no longer desired, and Howard receiving the bribe 'for relinquishing what he would have been sorry to keep'.[67]

'Marriage is traffick throughout', claims a character in one of Henry Fielding's contemporary dramas, expressing views shared by Charles Howard. 'As most of us bargain to be husbands, so some of us bargain to be cuckolds.'[68]

Molly Hervey understood perfectly how Henrietta's fear of her husband compelled her to remain in her degrading relationship with the king, and commiserated with her about the long-drawn-out fading of George II's favour: 'the sun has not darted one beam on you a great while. You may freeze in the dog-days, for all the warmth you will find from our *Sol*.'[69]

Indeed, Henrietta became increasingly anxious to retire from the court, despite the protection that it offered against her husband. 'How soon it will be agreeable to you that I leave your family?' she asked George II in one undated letter, making an attempt to retreat from royal service. 'From your Majesty's behaviour to me, it is impossible not to think my removal from your presence must be most agreeable to your inclinations.'[70] But this storm, like many others, blew over, and Henrietta was obliged to stay.

In 1728, she finally succeeded in persuading her husband to sign a formal deed of separation, an extreme and very rare proceeding for her age and social class.[71] It was wonderful to be able to cut loose from him at last, but freedom came at a high price.

She had no chance of winning custody of her only child, and it seemed unlikely that she would ever see her beloved son again.

Kensington Palace was the backdrop to the world in which Henrietta had to live but longed to leave. Her apartment there was 'very damp and unwholesome', situated in a semi-basement

The south view of Kensington Palace, with courtiers gliding about the lawns

three feet underground. Insanitary and unhealthy, its floor produced 'a constant crop of mushrooms'.[72]

Surprisingly, the Georgian kings verged upon the miserly in the facilities they provided for their households. George II prided himself upon at least attempting to live within his means and shunned superfluous expenditure on palaces and parties. This was partly because the nature of monarchy itself was changing. People were beginning to query the need for the extravagant baroque architecture now to be seen across Europe, and to question the authority of the absolutist kings who commissioned it. According to William Hooper, writing in 1770, 'the glory of a British monarch consists, not in a handful of tinsel courtiers', but in the 'freedom, the dignity and happiness of his people'.[73] Henrietta and her colleagues paid for this attitude with slightly substandard accommodation.

Yet the palace in the park provided a snug refuge from life in London, where Henrietta would have found it hard to live in the civilised style to which she had grown accustomed. The previous year, a visitor to grimy London found it deeply disappointing, 'many of its streets being dirty and ill-paved, its houses of brick, not very high . . . blacken'd with the unmerciful smoke of coal-fires'.[74] Henrietta's court salary, £300 a year, would have been just enough to afford 'a pint of port at night, two servants, and an old maid, a little garden . . . provided you live in the country'.[75] Her pension, were she to leave court, would not support a London life of any pretension whatsoever.

Visitors to Kensington Palace drove from town across Hyde Park. At intervals along the way, posts were enchantingly topped with lighted lanterns 'every evening when the Court is at Kensington'. The enduring name of this road through the park, 'Rotten Row', is probably a corruption of the *'Rue du Roi'*, or 'King's Road', originally built for William III but improved for the Georgian monarchs.

The gardens surrounding Kensington Palace were now beginning to take on their final form, which remains recognisable today. A visitor in 1726 had found no fewer than fifty labourers hard at work making improvements to the palace's immediate surroundings.[76] The royal gardener, Charles Bridgeman, had been busy 'planting espaliers and sowing wood' all around the building, and the vast Round Pond was dug to provide a pleasing prospect from the drawing room's windows.[77]

The glades and avenues of the 'delightful' and 'glorious' Kensington Gardens were opened to the public on Saturdays, 'when the company appeared in full dress'.[78] Here Caroline indulged her almost superhuman love of walking. She often exhausted her ladies-in-waiting (one of them 'was ready to drop down she was so weary' after a royal ramble), but the devoted Peter Wentworth loved a 'good long limping walk' with his queen.[79] Sometimes he and she walked together 'till candle-light, being entertain'd with very fine french horns'.[80] It's understandable that Caroline loved gardens, where a little more freedom of movement and conversation might be possible than indoors. As John Hervey asked, 'is the air sweeter for a court; or the walks pleasanter for being bounded with sentinels?'[81]

This was truly the heyday of the palace proper at Kensington, with its water system, transport, cleaning and cooking arrangements by now well established and finely tuned. During the reign of George I, Kensington's state apartments had been used 'only on publick days' and otherwise left locked.[82] In the summer of 1734, though, the whole palace was buzzing with life and activity. 'My time at Kensington', wrote Peter Wentworth to his brother about his new life in Caroline's service, 'was very precious.'[83]

Wentworth also described the daily court routine: 'up every morning by six a clock and ride out by 8 or 9 till 11; then new dress for the *levées*, and morning drawing room'. Then, he said, 'we go to dinner at three and start from table a little after 5 in order to walk with the Queen'. At six, everyone returned and sat down to cards in the drawing room. Wentworth had recently been appointed to the paid position of managing the public lottery, and had begun to dare to hope again that his sober and assiduous attendance at court would result in a further promotion of some kind: 'if I don't make something of it at last I shall have hard fate'.[84]

In 1734, Mrs Jane Keen, now well settled into the job of palace housekeeper, made a survey of all the chimneys that needed sweeping, and her list gives a good idea of how the accommodation was laid out. All in all there were 246 chimneys in the palace, requiring a sweep 'every 14 or 21 days' when the court was in residence and the fireplaces 'in constant use'.[85] Mrs Keen began her tour of the palace at the 'porter's lodge' (one chimney), then moved on to the 'Stone Gallery' range, which was packed with courtiers' lodgings, including those of John Hervey (one chimney). There too was the apartment reserved for the 'Lord of the Bedchamber' in waiting at any particular moment (three chimneys).

Then Mrs Keen moved on through the state and private apartments of the king and queen. Henrietta's large, if damp, apartment (five chimneys) was in Clock Court, and it was separated from the King's Privy Lodgings (twenty chimneys) only by the wardrobe, a storage room for unused furniture.

George II's private apartments lay on the first floor, with a lovely outlook east over the gardens. Caroline, on the other hand,

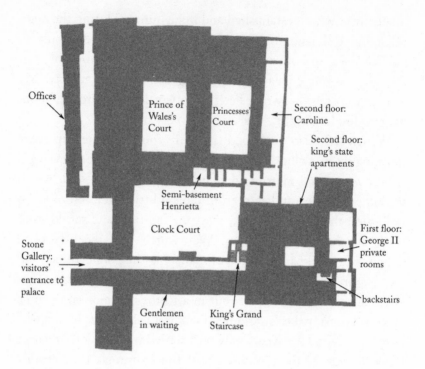

Offices

Prince of
Wales's
Court

Princesses'
Court

Second floor:
Caroline

Second floor:
king's state
apartments

Semi-basement
Henrietta

Clock Court

Stone
Gallery:
visitors'
entrance to
palace

First floor:
George II
private
rooms

backstairs

Gentlemen
in waiting

King's Grand
Staircase

The scene of the action: the king's, the queen's and the mistress's
apartments at Kensington Palace

was lodged in a rather poky suite with no views. The ladies in
'close waiting' at any given time spent their night right outside
Caroline's bedchamber, upon a bedstead with a feather mattress
and 'five fine blankets'.[86] When the king wanted to sleep with his
wife, he always came to her rooms rather than vice versa.

When the family was in residence and all 246 fireplaces were lit,
the building was toasty warm: 'in all ye rooms great coal fires
instead of wood'.[87] Fortunately the palace was by now well protected from fire, a constant concern both at Kensington and elsewhere in the wooden world of eighteenth-century London. The
palace had been terribly damaged in 1692, when a blaze caused by
'the carelessness of a candle' destroyed part of the south-west
range. On that occasion the fire engines were so slow to arrive from
Whitehall that the flames were eventually extinguished by soldiers

bringing up and breaking open bottles of beer from the cellars.[88] By 1734, Kensington Palace had its own fire engines.[89] These devices were tanks of water on wheels, and their crews pumped huge levers to create a flame-quenching jet. John Rowley, formerly master of mechanics to George I, had designed the fire engines at Kensington, Hampton Court and the House of Commons. His masterpiece was the 'great water engine' at Windsor Castle, which remained in working order for forty years.[90]

The accounts for the month of August 1734 show the prodigious quantity and variety of food that Henrietta and her fellow courtiers consumed. It was prepared in specialised departments round the Kitchen Court ranging from the 'Jelly Office' to the 'Herb Office', while outside on the green were the 'Feeding Houses for Fowls'.[91] Many of the employees of these various 'offices' lived in garrets immediately above their place of work.

The chosen suppliers of goods to the kitchens would provide produce on credit at agreed rates, and everything was carefully recorded by the clerks. Volume after volume of their work remains in the National Archives today: the 'credit accounts' listing all the food entering the Georgian kitchens, and the 'diet books' registering every single dish cooked and served to the royal family. The more exotic provisions to appear include olives, gherkins and

A cook, sketched by William Kent

mangoes; Bologna sausages and giblet pies; and udders, trotters and pig's heads.[92]

The courtiers were entitled to various allowances of food depending upon their rank. The more senior, like Molly Hervey, had 'three pats of Richmond butter and a quarter-pint of cream' every day by right.[93] Even the lowly sempstress, Mrs Purcell, enjoyed a daily bottle of claret.[94]

Despite the emphasis placed upon meat as food fit for kings, there was no shortage of vegetables available too. In two years, for example, the royal gardens provided

> 1684 salads. Above 6000 cabbage lettuces. 3541 cucumbers. 1088 arti-
> chokes. 4668 celery and endive. 1351 bundles of asparagus with
> radishes, peas, beans, French beans, carrots, savoys, cauliflowers,
> onions, sweet herbs, borecole [broccoli?] and great parcels of flowers.

This was as well as '4368 baskets of fruit of all sorts'.[95] Caroline was fond of fruit with sour cream in the mornings, and enjoyed 'a fine breakfast with the addition of cherries & strawberry'.[96]

Drinking was another important part of life at Henrietta's court. Hot chocolate was taken each morning. Later in the day tea soothed many a courtier's cares: a lover lost, a gambling debt gained. It was promoted by matrons as a cure for a broken heart: 'now leave complaining, and begin your *Tea*'.[97] But John Hervey's father thought it was 'detestable, fatal liquor', which had brought many people 'near to death's door'.[98]

Although tea was considered rather decadent, meals were always accompanied by something even stronger. Each day after dinner, we hear, the 'men remain at the table; upon which, the cloth being taken off, the footmen place a bottle of wine'. The servants present the drinkers 'with glasses well rinsed' and they 'always drink too much, because they sit too long at it'.[99] Lord Lifford on one occasion drank so much that he fell off his chair, and the next morning Caroline 'railed at him before all the Court upon getting drunk in her company'.[100]

Peter Wentworth found that this post-prandial ritual between three and five every day placed a sore strain upon his resolution to avoid taking even a single 'drop of wine too much'. His seventeen-year-old daughter Catherina's sudden and tragic death from consumption, the 'folly & extravagance' of his son George and anger at a villainous son-in-law who'd contracted syphilis still gave him the odd 'occasion to drown and stupifie [his] thoughts'.[101]

The year 1734 was one of panic about a new drinking craze among London's poor. Caroline, among others, was stridently in favour of Parliament's legislating against 'Mother Gin', or 'Madam Geneva' as it was also known. This strong and novel spirit was drunk by the pint, like beer, with devastating consequences, and was causing chaos in London. The streets were lined with the insensible bodies of the inebriated, while those still conscious showed the 'utmost rage of resentment, violence of rudeness, and scurrility of tongue'.[102] The lists of fatalities recorded in the newspapers began to include 'excessive drinking of Geneva' alongside the more familiar 'drowned accidentally in the river of Thames'.[103] Just two years later the draconian Gin Act was introduced, which sought – with limited success – to have gin sold only through recognised and licensed outlets.

While the rich condemned the poor for the miserable manner of their escape from the urban grind, Lord Chesterfield nevertheless considered drinking deeply to be 'a necessary qualification for a fine gentleman'.[104] The Maids of Honour likewise refused to stint themselves. They could order as many bottles of wine as they liked to drink with their dinner (although the under-butlers always inflated the total in the official record and drank the difference themselves).[105]

But Lord Chesterfield also warned his son to avoid becoming 'flustered and heated with wine: it might engage you in scrapes and frolics, which the King (who is a very sober man himself) detests'.[106]

Princesses like Caroline, sent to spend their married lives in foreign countries, inevitably missed their native food. The German-born Duchess of Orléans longed for German sausages in Paris.

She proudly claimed to have made smoked ham fashionable in France, along with 'sweet-and-sour cabbage, salad with *Speck*, red cabbage and venison'.[107]

George II likewise loved his German dishes. One Mr Weston, he announced, must have the job of 'first cook, for he makes most excellent Rhenish soup'.[108] But their Germanic fondness for Rhineland soup and sausages caused the Hanoverians much trouble and unpleasantness. Propaganda released by the Pretender, the so-called James III, claimed that he ate only English dishes such as roast beef and Devonshire pie, and drank only English beer.[109]

Unlike the king, some other foreigners were surprisingly enthusiastic about English cooking. Baron Pöllnitz, a Pole visiting London, wrote that 'there is excellent beef here; and I am in love with their puddings'.[110] 'Ah, what an excellent thing is an *English pudding!*' sighed a French visitor. '*To come in pudding-time*' means 'to come in the most lucky moment in the world'.[111]

The royal family's food reached their mouths via a lengthy chain of servants in which Henrietta was intimately involved. Unlike his reclusive father, George II was regularly willing to dine before spectators. This curious spectacle was almost like feeding time at a royal zoo, and left the watching crowds 'mightily pleas'd' with the show.[112]

Public dining for George II, Caroline and their children took place every Sunday, when their table was 'plac'd in the midst of a hall, surrounded with benches to the very ceiling, which are fill'd with an infinite number' of viewers.[113] Usually 'the room was so throng'd with spectators there was no stirring'.[114] The audience were mere members of the public who'd queued for admission. At one dinner attended by Sir John Evelyn, he found them rather coarse: 'very dirty and noisy'.[115]

George II and Caroline's personal servants found the pressure of the performance and of keeping the food flowing in a suitably respectful manner to be quite considerable. It was 'a very terrible fatigue' to the Lady of the Bedchamber whose duties included taking the covers off the dishes, carving the meat, kneeling down to taste the food for poison and, besides all that, 'giving the Queen drink'.[116]

Such a summer dinner served to Caroline in June 1735 consisted of a lengthy procession of beef, chicken and mushrooms, mutton hashed in a loaf, veal and sweetbreads fried, pullets and cream, a haunch of venison, cold chicken and pickles, peas and cucumber, a lobster, gooseberry and apricot tart, smoked salmon and prawns.[117] Henrietta's role, as Bedchamber Woman, was to form a link in the human chain that kept the Lady of the Bedchamber supplied with utensils. When Caroline wanted a drink, a page handed a glass to Henrietta, who gave it to the Lady, who finally presented it to the queen.[118]

All this etiquette meant that any grand dinner was fraught with potential insult. It was the host who determined whether his guests would be served on bended knee or not, and guests felt slighted if ceremonies were omitted. Caroline's daughters the three elder princesses once refused to stir from the antechamber before a dinner until 'the stools were taken away' and proper chairs carried in, and after the meal they 'were forced to go without their coffee' for fear that 'they might have met with some disgrace . . . in the manner of giving it'.

John Hervey, seeing through the charade as usual, thought this all quite ridiculous: 'squabbling and contesting with one another for trifles'.[119] But while correct he was also foolishly naive, for by what else could the princesses judge their status and success? Marriages, babies, chairs not stools: these were the stuff of their circumscribed world. When the Irish peers were excluded from a court procession, Lord Egmont thought the consequences potentially cataclysmic for his spouse. 'If this matter be decided against us,' he protested, 'I know not who will give our wives place or what they ought to insist on, in coming or going out of doors, at card tables, &c.'[120]

Despite all this attention to detail, the proceedings sometimes broke down into farce, and court dinners could be roisterous and rowdy. Once, so many people came 'to see their majesties dine, that the rail surrounding the table broke'. The people who'd been leaning upon it all fell over and 'made a diverting scramble for hats and wigs, at which their Majesties laugh'd heartily'.[121]

There was even more of a scrum at coronation feasts. After George I's, the newspapers carried pleas for the return of the silver 'dishes, trencher-plates, knives, forks, spoons, and salts' pinched by those present.[122] At the end of George II's own coronation banquet:

> the big doors were thrown open and the crowd allowed to enter and take possession of the remains of the feast, of the table linen, of the plates and dishes, and of everything that was on the table. The pillage was most diverting; people threw themselves with extraordinary avidity on everything that hall contained; blows were given and returned, and I cannot give you any idea of the noise and confusion that reigned. In less than half an hour everything had disappeared, even the boards of which the table and seats had been made.[123]

The historian Jeremy Black evokes this riotous image to illustrate how, despite the supposed gentility and elegance of the Georgian age, it was really characterised by 'unruliness just kept at bay'.[124]

Kensington Palace in 1734 was perhaps the liveliest it had ever been, with endless parties and pranks among Henrietta's companions. At all courts, the amusements veered towards the improper: 'blind man's buff, till past three this morning; we have musick in the wood, parties out of town; besides the constant amusements of quadrille and scandal which flourish and abound'.[125] The absent Molly Hervey wistfully recollected the japes of the Maids of Honour and their *beaux*: 'I really believe a <u>frizelation</u> [court jargon for flirtation] wou'd be a surer means of restoring my spirits than the exercise and hartshorn I now make use of'.[126]

Henrietta's Kensington Palace must have felt like the very centre of the world, because everybody who was anybody came to visit. Would-be guests had to send in their names to the Lord Chamberlain, then the Duke of Grafton.[127] Familiarly known as

'Booby Grafton', the smooth-talking Charles Fitzroy, second duke, was an illegitimate grandson of Charles II. His colleagues thought him an excellent courtier, 'beloved by all parties', and 'every court storm to which the climate is so subject broke at his feet'.[128] He had long been in love with Princess Amelia, despite being old enough to be her father. As no handsome prince had stepped forward to claim Amelia (or her younger sisters), a flirtation with the safe and familiar Booby Grafton seemed the most attractive relationship open to her.

The right of entry through the hallowed door into the drawing room was codified by unwritten rules. The kernel of those granted entry included the more important members of the royal household, the courtiers proper. Many of them were peers of the realm holding specific posts, usually attending in rotation for part of the year only. Then there were the two hundred-odd families of the peerage in general, most of whom attended on occasion, if not regularly.

Ambassadors and members of foreign peerages would also find access easy. But there were no hard and fast rules, and the next rank down – lawyers, rich merchants, country gentlemen – might well be allowed in. Even a penniless law student, relying on the impression created by his 'best clothes and lace ruffles', once managed to slip through the door in the wake of a grander personage walking just ahead.[129]

According to custom, the drawing room was still opened to visitors several times a week 'at ten o'clock at night'.[130] Then the king and queen would make a dazzling appearance: sometimes Caroline's 'stomacher was prodigiously adorn'd with diamonds . . . as broad as a shilling', while George II's 'coat was of blue velvet with diamond buttons'.[131]

Some of the guests came from elsewhere in Europe or from even further afield. The year 1729, for example, saw Handel and his cast of Italian opera stars perform at Kensington Palace before the king and queen.[132]

Sir Robert Walpole had kept Britain out of the costly European

War of the Polish Succession of 1733–4, hoping (in vain, as it happened) to become the arbiter of events once the European powers had exhausted themselves in combat. Nor did Walpole take much interest in Britain's empire. Across the Atlantic, the colony of Georgia, named for the king, had just been founded. (This had annoyed the Spanish in nearby Florida, and would lead to future trouble.) One visitor to Kensington from North America was a novel and curious creature. The governor of New England sent Caroline 'a young beaver alive', the representative of a species that had been hunted to extinction in Britain a hundred years before. The beaver joined the other animals in the palace menagerie, but Caroline was warned to keep it 'within stone walls, or iron bars, or to be chained, because it will eat through anything of wood'.[133]

The 3rd of August 1734 saw another remarkable sight at Kensington Palace: a party of chiefs from the Cherokee nation come to pay their respects to George II. Tomochichi, their king, led in 'his two War-Captains' and 'three others, called Chiefs'. Their faces were 'most hideously painted' in 'black and red, so thick that at a little distance they looked like masks'.[134]

Now William Kent's Presence Chamber at the top of the King's Grand Staircase came into use. Here George II sat upon his throne, which was actually an armchair covered with crimson velvet.[135] The Cherokee chiefs 'made their obeisances', delivered an incomprehensible speech and presented the king with animal skins and 'sticks with feathers on them, which are emblems of peace'.

After this forging of an alliance between the two nations, the Cherokees went through to the Gallery for an audience with Queen Caroline and all the ladies of the court. One of the chiefs 'was asked which he thought the finest woman there'. He made a very diplomatic answer, 'owning that all white people were so much alike to him, that he could not easily distinguish one from another'.[136]

So the kings of the New World came to pay homage to the king of the Old.

Every month or so, the evening drawing-room gathering was eclipsed by a splendid ball to celebrate one of the birthdays of the numerous royal children. Once again security was not particularly tight, and the resourceful law student also succeeded in infiltrating a court ball. He waited 'among a vast crowd of nobility and gentry' for the all-important 'opening of the door' to the dancing room. Then 'we all rushed in as fast as we could go and got in among the rest and got into a pretty good place'.[137]

One Georgian letter-writer gives us a gorgeous glimpse of the corpulent Caroline being swept up and carried away by an eager crowd of dancing courtiers. Wanting to introduce her to a visitor named Sir Paul Methuen, the dancers burst 'into the room, where the Queen was at play and danced round the table; upon which the Queen rose up, took Sir Paul by the hand, danced through all the rooms and so to the coach'.[138]

Peter Wentworth's young and aristocratic nephew once enjoyed a high-spirited children's birthday ball held for Caroline's youngest son, William Augustus. Little Lord Wentworth was taken along to court by his mother, and Caroline welcomed him with her usual warmth: 'the Queen cried out: "Oh! Lord Wentworth! How do you do? You have mightily grown! My lady, he is prodigiously well dressed. I hope you will let him come to our ball to night."'[139]

So the young lord was dressed in his best, and Mr Morin the hairdresser sent for to do up his hair.[140] The evening's events, much anticipated, were slightly marred by an accident befalling the new governess, Mary Deloraine. The very same day she 'fell in labour, and was just brought to bed of a dead son; so they could not have the room they used to dance in (it being next to hers)'. The young people enjoyed themselves nevertheless. Peter Wentworth's nephew was asked to dance by the forthright Princess Amelia, and was enjoined to eat a supper of cold chicken, tongue, jelly and sweetmeats. But on this occasion, as his mother reported, 'as well as my love loves eating, he says he ate but a leg of chicken, for he says he did not [think] it looked well to be pulling greasy bones about in a room full of princesses'.[141]

[165]

The year's most important ball, for the king's birthday at the end of October, was usually held back at St James's Palace. It signalled everyone's return to town after the summer. In 1734, an exceptionally magnificent entertainment marked the marriage of Caroline's eldest daughter, Anne, the Princess Royal, to the hunchback Prince William of Orange. Now twenty-four, she'd become so desperate to marry and escape the monotony of palace life that she claimed she'd have accepted a proposal even from a baboon.

William Kent was given the job of decorating the chapel for the ceremony, and pulled strings to have Sir James Thornhill's son-in-law, William Hogarth, banned from making potentially lucrative drawings of the wedding setting. Now that he was so snugly settled in the queen's favour, Kent found himself easily able to swat aside annoyances such as the infringement of an old enemy upon court ground.

To sniggering bystanders it appeared that Hogarth now regretted those discourteous 'caricatures' with which he had previously poked fun at Kent and 'which now he is like to pay for, when he least thought on it'.[142]

In the battle of the painters, Kent had finally had the last laugh.

What changes had kingship wrought upon the character of Henrietta's 'passionate, proud and peevish' lover, George II? By 1734, his earlier willingness to please was wearing off. Disaffected courtier Lady Mary Wortley Montagu summed him up as ardent but overindulged. She thought that he viewed 'all the men and women he saw as creatures he might kick or kiss for his diversion'.[143]

With the passage of time, George II had reverted to his German roots. 'Whilst the late King lived everybody imagined this Prince loved England and hated Germany,' it was said, but now his birthplace exerted more of a pull upon his affections. He could be heard complaining that no English cook 'could dress a dinner; no English confectioner set out a dessert; no English player could act; no English coachman could drive'. In Hanover, of course, 'all these things were in the utmost perfection'.

Henrietta's supposed lover frequently abandoned her to flee back to Hanover, and every three years or so he paid an extended visit of several months. Indeed, one of these absences was so prolonged that a mysterious paper was pasted up at the Royal Exchange, spoofing a court announcement: 'it is reported that his Hanoverian Majesty designs to visit his British dominions for three months in the spring'.[144]

As he entered his fifties, George II had become a stickler for minor matters of protocol. 'The least negligence, or the slightest inattention, reported to him, may do you infinite prejudice,' one would-be courtier was warned. The king was 'rigidly attached to etiquette', and seemed 'to think his having done a thing today, an answerable reason for his doing it to-morrow'.[145]

This turgid devotion to the same daily programme gradually ground his courtiers down into miserable, mind-numbing boredom. 'I will not trouble you with any account of our occupations,' John Hervey wrote in 1733, 'no mill-horse ever went in a more constant track, or a more unchanging circle.'[146] 'We go on as regular as ye clock,' confirmed Lady Burlington, 'we are now going on our evening's walk; from hence to lottery & so on.'[147]

His ponderous dedication to routine meant that George II would not pay his daily visit to his mistress one minute before the accustomed time. He was used to arriving in Henrietta's apartment at 7 o'clock exactly, and if he was early he would 'walk up and down the gallery, looking at his watch, for a quarter of an hour'.[148] Then he'd usually spend a couple of hours with Henrietta, but he did so more out of duty than desire. By now the courtiers were firmly convinced that the king had a mistress 'rather as a necessary appurtenance to his grandeur as a prince than an addition to his pleasures as a man'. He was overheard speaking to her in an 'angry and impatient tone', and replying to a mild question with 'that is none of your business, madam; you have nothing to do with that!'[149]

To Henrietta the situation was unbearable. As she put it, 'I have been a slave twenty years without ever receiving a reason for any one thing I ever was oblig'd to do.'[150]

On the increasingly rare occasions when he was at home with them rather than closeted with Henrietta or away in Hanover, his family had to endure George II's brusque and egocentric manner and his deadly dull lectures upon the esoteric German connections of their family. On one grotesque occasion at Kensington Palace he burst in and

> stayed about five minutes in the gallery; snubbed the Queen, who was drinking chocolate, for being always stuffing, the Princess Emily [Amelia] for not hearing him, the Princess Caroline for being grown fat, the Duke for standing awkwardly, Lord Hervey for not knowing what relation the Prince of Sultzbach was to the Elector Palatine, and then carried the Queen to walk, and be resnubbed, in the garden.[151]

Sir Robert Walpole's brother likewise found himself in perpetual disgrace for 'disputing a point of German genealogy' with the king.[152] George II could never laugh at himself. When he learnt about the Rumpsteak Club, whose members consisted of everybody he'd 'rumped' or snubbed in the drawing room, he simply exploded with wrath. '*Quoy!*' he bellowed with futile pride. '*Est qui se moque de moi?* [What! Are they laughing at me?]'[153]

According to John Hervey, who always took Caroline's side, the king's hideously bad temper was unjustified and unfathomable. He was 'abominably and perpetually so harsh and rough' that she 'could never speak one word uncontradicted, nor do any one act unreproved'.[154] But with true royal pride Caroline suffered silently and did her best to hide her hurt: 'she seldom forgot that she was a queen, and always kept up a due state both in public and private'.[155]

At least Caroline had other interests and hobbies to provide distraction and comfort, and at Kensington Palace these included her wonderful cabinet of curiosities. This was a room that in Germany might have been called a *Wunderkammer*, like the one assembled by George II's grandmother at the Hanoverian palace of Herrenhausen. An inventory of the contents of Caroline's curiosity museum at Kensington shows that it contained bizarre treasures such as a crystal cup containing a humming bird, 'two small unicorns' horns' and drawers full of vintage medals 'apt to jump out of their places' when opened.[156]

She constructed an even more grandiose exhibition of marvels and relics from the past in the gardens at Richmond, her country home. Here William Kent built her a curious chamber known as 'Merlin's Cave', and she filled it with waxworks of characters from ancient times. Caroline charmed the courtiers with her fondness for British antiquity, joking that 'she was always v. angry with the English when she was reading their history to see how violent and raging they were against one another'.[157] Her husband, of course, had no time for this whimsical activity and told her that she 'deserved to be abused for such childish silly stuff'.[158] Nevertheless, it was here, in her wonderland at Richmond, that Caroline enjoyed the historical and intellectual pursuits that were balm for her soul.[159]

She even went so far as to procure a real live hermit, Stephen Duck, the so-called Thresher Poet, to live at Richmond. Once his literary gift was discovered, he was plucked from an obscure life as a rural labourer, forced to leave behind his family and brought to settle in the gardens as a royal pet. Unfortunately the forced transplantation was not a success, and he later committed suicide.[160] And another human oddity likewise spent part of his time down at Richmond. The accounts of the money expended at Caroline's residence there include payments 'for the maintenance of Peter the Wild Boy'.[161]

Some of the most intense scenes in the breakdown of the eccentric but enduring love triangle between George II, Caroline and Henrietta were played out between the two women in the bedchamber, during the queen's toilette.

George II and Caroline submitted with good grace to the

dressing ceremonies expected of monarchs, and their bedcham-
bers were opened daily to the court. George II allowed the senior
members of his household to dress him of a morning, and then in
surged the 'gaping crowd' for the meeting, greeting and business
talk that comprised the official levee.[162] From 1714, Henrietta had
served Caroline as a Bedchamber Woman, an honour paid for
with difficult and sometimes demeaning duties.

When the Ladies of the Bedchamber had renounced their obli-
gation to do real work, they'd nevertheless tried to maintain their
right of access to Caroline's bedroom. Some of them were quite
astoundingly persistent. Caroline's recovery from the birth of a
stillborn son in November 1716 was made no easier by one such
quarrel about access. Despite the fact that the princess was desperately ill, the Countess of Manchester was adamant that her position still entitled her to enter. Her insistence on such a thing at
such a time incensed even the etiquette-obsessed court: 'everybody knew she was a fool'.[163] But on normal occasions the
courtiers were absolutely convinced that such trivia were indeed
matters of life and death.

The position of Bedchamber Woman was not physically
demanding, but the long hours of waiting, the boredom and the
necessity for total self-possession took their toll. Molly Lepell
once said that 'the life of a Maid of Honour was of all things the
most miserable' and she 'wished that every woman who envied it
had a specimen of it'.[164] Both jobs could often be quite mind-
bendingly tedious.

In fact, these posts in the royal household, once the pinnacle of
aspiration, were slowly declining in terms of prestige. With the
passing of greater power to Parliament the court was gradually
becoming a backwater, and the ambitious no longer vied for the
great court offices such as Groom of the Stool. By the early years
of the nineteenth century, the offices would become something of
a joke.[165] Reformer John Wade in 1831 had quite a rant upon the
subject: 'to what public purport . . . are the offices of groom of the
stole, master of the hawks, master of the buck-hounds, master of

the horse, or grooms and lords of the bedchamber?' He thought them merely 'menial offices, and unbecoming to the dignity of a nobleman'.[166] Indeed, in 1837, a quiescent House of Commons heard that no Groom of the Stool was to be appointed to the new household of Queen Victoria. The only recorded comment heard in the House was 'a laugh' at the very idea.[167]

Henrietta, though, belonged to a generation that still broadly considered personal service to the monarch to be honourable and valuable.

But her duties were made more than usually onerous by the psychological background to her employment. If anyone mentioned her role as royal mistress in Caroline's presence, the queen sharply rebuked the speaker and reminded him or her that he or she 'was speaking of the King's servant, and to the King's wife'.[168]

So Henrietta went every morning to Caroline's bedchamber to help the queen prepare for the day. Her duties did not include the bringing of water and the emptying of the chamber pot, jobs which were done by the 'necessary women'. (They were reimbursed for their mops, brooms and brushes in addition to their wages.[169]) The use of chamber pots at court was not necessarily restricted to private moments: the French ambassador's wife, for example, was notorious for the 'frequency and quantity of her pissing which she does not fail to do at least ten times a day amongst a cloud of witnesses'.[170]

Henrietta did have to hold the basin of water while Caroline washed, beginning with her teeth. The current method was to use 'a soft spunge and warm water, for four or five minutes; and then wash your mouth five or six times'.[171] Rather repulsively for Henrietta, 'The basin takes whatever comes/ The scrapings of her teeth and gums.'[172] Of course, tooth decay could not be avoided completely. Poor Princess Anne's new husband, William of Orange, possessed breath 'more offensive than it is possible for those who have not been offended by it to imagine'.[173]

Sometimes, but not always, the washing of other body parts

followed. In 1750, John Wilkes observed that 'the nobler parts are never in this island washed by women', and John Hervey described a typical drawing-room gathering as 'sweating and stinking in abundance as usual'.[174] Caroline, however, bathed rather more frequently than her contemporaries. Her necessary woman, Susanna Ireland, would lug up ewers of hot water to fill her bath. The queen would remain dressed throughout in a yellow canvas shift.[175]

Lord Chesterfield gave his son a piece of advice that reveals the general state of eighteenth-century fingernails: 'you must keep the ends of them smooth and clean, not tipped with black, as the ordinary people's always are'.[176] Caroline likewise liked her servants to be well-manicured, and Peter Wentworth grumbled that once 'when I did not think she saw me, I was biting my nails. She called to me and said: "Oh fie! Mr Wentworth, you bite your nails very prettily."' He begged her pardon, and explained that he was trying to save the money the doctor demanded for cutting them.[177]

Caroline maintained a show of polite friendliness while Henrietta stood by with the basin and towels, and made a point of calling her servant her 'good Howard'.[178] But the fact that Caroline's hostility was concealed behind a veneer of charm made Henrietta's life even more desolate. Caroline also used to call Henrietta 'by way of banter, her sister Howard'. It might have sounded kind, but in reality it was 'the strongest mark of aversion and contempt'.[179]

The false friendship of the queen and the increasing coldness of the king must have made Henrietta's burden far heavier than the actual basin she was supposed to hold. As John Hervey put it, her task was utterly thankless: 'she was forced to live in the constant subjection of a wife with all the reproach of a mistress'.[180] But she did so with wonderful grace. Alexander Pope wrote that Henrietta had 'as much good nature' as if she'd been 'bred among lambs and turtle-doves, instead of princes and court-ladies'.[181]

And Caroline had no qualms about letting her real feelings

flash through at any sign of insubordination. On one occasion (in Caroline's words) Henrietta attempted to pick

> a quarrel with me about holding a basin of ceremony at my dressing, and to tell me, with her fierce little eyes and cheeks as red as your coat, that positively she would not do it; to which I made her no answer in anger, but calmly, as I would to a naughty child: 'Yes, my dear Howard, I am sure you will; indeed you will.'[182]

Exasperated by these 'demeaning' duties, the 'most servile offices' that Caroline could dream up, Henrietta took the trouble to consult precedent about the responsibilities of the Bedchamber Woman.[183] She asked her friend Dr Arbuthnot to extract the exact job description from a retired predecessor who had served under Queen Anne. She hoped to find evidence that she need not hold the basin and thereby could avoid her daily ordeal.

After Caroline had washed, Henrietta handed over the queen's garments, one by one, to the more important Lady of the Bedchamber, who then gave them to the queen. Mary Cowper explained how the dance of dressing commenced: 'the Duchess of St Albans put on the Princess's shift, according to court rules'.[184] Another ex-member of the bedchamber staff likewise recalled that 'the Bedchamber Woman gave the fan to the Lady', who then handed it to the queen.[185] These nuances of role between the 'Lady' and the 'Woman' were considered to be of cut-throat importance.

The shift that Caroline wore next to her skin was made of very fine Holland linen.[186] Over it went a quilted white dimity petticoat, then a set of soft stays with silver hooks, and then a set of crimson whalebone hoops to support the skirt of her patterned silk dress. Caroline liked to wear the mantua, a coat-like dress worn over wide hoops, and bought no fewer than fourteen different models between 1730 and 1734.[187] The queen's clothes-shopping was prodigious: twenty fans a quarter; four silver girdles in a single month. Finally, the finishing touches were required: the Bedchamber Woman 'pulled on the Queen's gloves' and 'the page of the backstairs was called in to put on the Queen's shoes'.[188] She favoured slip-on mules rather than shoes, and her 'walking slippers' had red heels.[189]

Next Caroline's hairdresser, Mrs Purcell, would spread a short muslin cape over the queen's shoulders to protect her dress while her hair was arranged into a high bun. Once a conical 'powder mask' had been placed over Caroline's face, her tight curls were 'clotted all over' with white particles.[190] Hairdressing was not terribly hygienic, and a Georgian lady could find her head being patted with 'a paste of composition rare/ sweat, dandruff, powder, lead, and hair'.[191] Next one of Caroline's 'heads' or 'hoods' of gauze or lace from France or Brussels would be settled over her hair; these were among the most expensive items in her wardrobe.[192] During these closing stages of the toilette, George II would sometimes come in and criticise Henrietta's work, snatching off the handkerchief from round Caroline's shoulders and crying, 'because you have an ugly neck yourself, you love to hide the Queen's!'[193]

Finally, painting the face was a necessity for most courtiers, men as well as women. Rouged cheeks were daringly fashionable: as Lady Mary Wortley Montagu put it, 'falsehood, like red on the face, should be used very seldom and very sparingly'.[194] A cut and wet red ribbon sometimes did the trick. Caroline wore few cosmetics, although she did favour 'patches' (she purchased six 'papers' of patches in 1733, for example) to cover her smallpox scars.[195]

Unfortunately for Henrietta, Dr Arbuthnot's researches confirmed that the Bedchamber Woman certainly was required to hold the basin, and that it was indeed her duty to pour 'the water out of the ewer upon the Queen's hands'.[196]

Once precedent had spoken in this dispute over etiquette, Caroline had no hesitation in reminding Henrietta that she was powerless. She first showed the velvet glove: 'I told her I knew we should be good friends again.' But then she gave a glimpse of the iron fist beneath, reminding Henrietta 'that it was in my power, if

I had pleased, any hour of the day, to let her drop through my fingers – thus –'[197]

The querulous queen, now nearly fifty, was not easy to dress elegantly, for her figure was decidedly overripe. Some people even called her the king's 'great fat-arsed wife'.[198] Henrietta, at forty-five, had retained her charms rather more effectively. She dyed her hair blonde, and could still make Lord Peterborough, for one, tremble with lust: 'When she comes in my way – the motion, the pain/ The leapings, the achings, return all again.'[199]

Despite her formidable powers of attraction, Henrietta was suffering from various health problems, including dreadful headaches and a hearing impairment. She had 'a most intolerable pain in one side of her head', while an operation upon her jaw caused 'many weeks misery'.[200]

In 1731, though, had come a great stroke of luck which enabled her to begin to consider a plan for escape. Even after separating from her husband, she'd remained close to his much more respectable brother, the Earl of Suffolk. The earl died on 22 June of that year. Having had no intention of letting his wastrel younger brother Charles inherit and squander his money, he left a considerable sum to his sister-in-law Henrietta instead.

His death also meant that she became the Countess of Suffolk. At first Henrietta was rather embarrassed by all the bowing and scraping that she now received, and commanded her friend John Gay to stop calling her 'Your Ladyship' under threat of being sent supperless to bed.[201] However, it was impossible that a peeress should remain in the menial position of Bedchamber Woman, and promotion for Henrietta was inevitable.

It was also inevitable that Henrietta's husband Charles would challenge his brother's will. Disgusted by Charles's nastiness, though, the old Earl of Suffolk had sewn up his estate so cleverly that Henrietta received her money intact. Indeed, Charles himself had only a couple of years more to live.

Henrietta, now Lady Suffolk, bargained carefully for her new job in the royal household. People reported that she 'was offered to be Lady of the Bedchamber, which she declined'.[202] She held out for a more important post, Mistress of the Robes, and on 29 June 1731 she told John Gay that she had finally 'kiss'd hands' for her new place.[203] Now her duties would be far lighter: in fact, her only task was 'to give the Queen her jewels'. Her salary remained the same, because previously she'd received an extra hundred pounds a year on top of a Bedchamber Woman's salary 'for buying the Queen's clothes'.[204]

The lifting of the burden of constant service elated Henrietta. As she enthused to John Gay, her new situation promised 'more happiness for the latter part of [her] life than [she'd] yet had a prospect of'. 'My time is become very much my own,' she wrote. And the money she had inherited would enable Henrietta to enjoy herself.

She had 'at this time a great deal of business' upon her hands, not from her court job, but from a much more pleasurable project. She was supervising the building of a little house for herself by the Thames west of London, at Marble Hill.[205] She'd purchased the site in 1724, and three years later she'd obtained and been greatly influenced by William Kent's architectural book, *The Designs of Inigo Jones*. Nothing made her happier than inspecting the workmen's progress upon her proposed Palladian villa. Peter Wentworth thought Henrietta's good fortune had even ameliorated her deafness: 'she's so well pleased that she hears better already'.[206]

So Henrietta now blossomed. The summer of 1734 saw her taking advantage of something that she'd never previously experienced: a holiday. She favoured the resort of Bath with her presence for six weeks. Because no one could remember Henrietta ever leaving the court before, it caused a sensation, and 'occasion'd as much speculation in the family at Kensington as the removal of two or three minor Ministers would have done'.[207]

But when she returned in October from her jaunt in the pump rooms and ballrooms of Bath, Henrietta found George II even less eager than before to share her company. Suspecting her of having consorted in Bath with his political enemies, he cut her dead in the drawing room. And that 'the King went no more in an evening to Lady Suffolk was whispered about the court by all that belonged to it'.[208]

To enter the royal household was difficult, but to leave it contrary to royal will was even harder. Henrietta had first sought to quit the court nearly ten years previously, but she'd been forbidden from doing so.

Now, armed with what she thought was clear and incontrovertible evidence of the king's disapproval, she sought a resignation interview with Caroline. She found herself in possession of 'above an hour and a half alone' with the queen in the bedchamber where so many of their previous showdowns had taken place.[209]

The conversation was so painful and so important to Henrietta that after it was over she wrote it down. At first Caroline claimed that she hadn't noticed Henrietta's cold reception since her return from Bath: 'You surprise me. What do you mean? I don't believe ye King is angry . . . Child, you dream.'

And she refused to listen to Henrietta's complaints of court intrigue and the king's coldness: 'Come, my dear Lady Suffolk, you are very warm, but believe me I am your friend, your best friend. You don't know a court. It's not proper of me to say this, but indeed you don't know a court.' She told Henrietta not to mind court gossip, and reminded her how cold the world would seem outside the court bubble.

But now Henrietta showed that she still had her integrity hidden away beneath her courtier's shell, and she insisted that she wanted to leave. 'Some people may shew me it was ye courtier and not me that was liked,' she replied. 'I can't say that to keep such an acquaintance will be any argument for me to stay at court.'

When the queen perceived that her scoffing was having no effect, she was forced to try a different tack to persuade Henrietta to stay: 'For God's sake consider your character! You leave me because the King will not be more particular to you than the others?'[210]

Defeated at last, though, by Henrietta's solid opposition in this game of verbal chess, Caroline could only play for time.

'Oh fie, Lady Suffolk, upon my word,' she expostulated. The idea of resignation was only 'a very fine notion' out of a novel. 'Pray consider, be calm,' the queen implored. 'Stay a week longer, won't you stay this week at my request?'[211]

Having won this week's grace, Caroline tried to have her husband the king prevent her meekest, mildest and most useful servant from leaving court. By now, though, he was as anxious to let Henrietta go as she was herself to depart. 'What the devil did you mean by trying to make an old, dull, deaf, peevish beast stay and plague me when I had so good an opportunity for getting rid of her?' was one account of what he shouted at his wife.[212]

Another account – less dramatic but no less nasty – reported that his words were: 'I don't know why you will not let me part with an old deaf woman, of whom I am weary.'[213]

Henrietta ended their long relationship with a grace that was in a different realm altogether, conceding in a letter to him that 'the years to come must be employ'd in the painful task to forget you as my friend; but no years can ever make me forget you as my King'.[214] The truth of her statement would indeed be tested, decades later.

Having served her week's notice, Henrietta 'had another audience, complained again of her unkind treatment from the King, was very civil to the Queen, and went that night to her brother's house in St James's Square'.[215]

So it turned out that when the king, queen and all their servants had vacated Kensington Palace at the end of the summer, Henrietta had been leaving it for the last time ever. On 22 November, amid wonder, disbelief and shock, she departed from St James's en route for her newly built villa by the river Thames at Marble Hill and for a private life.

*

Henrietta's departure also signalled the breaking up of the cheerful, prank-prone band of the Maids of Honour, although many of them had by now married. ('We wild girls always make your prudent wives and mothers,' laughed Lady Mary Wortley Montagu.[216])

Some Maids of Honour, though, were less lucky or wise. Miss Anne Vane was described as 'a maid of honour who was willing to cease to be so upon the first opportunity', while aspirant Maid of Honour Peggy Bradshaw boasted in correspondence to Henrietta that the king 'I daresay will like me for my boobies are mightily grown'.[217] Peggy also had in hand a gentleman worth £300 per year who fancied her 'extremely', but unfortunately he was engaged to someone else. 'I live in hope', she concludes, 'that a loose man may come.'[218]

Illegitimate children were far from unknown at St James's Palace, and the Maids of Honour often seemed to have insider knowledge about their origins. For example, the chapel archives record the evening baptism of 'a female child about four weeks old' that was mysteriously 'dropped in the court'. Two of the Maids of Honour, Miss Tyron and Miss Meadows, were roped in 'to stand as godmothers'.

Margaret Cuyler, who grew up to be a courtesan and actress, claimed in later life to be the daughter of an unnamed Maid of Honour and to have played with the royal children. Her assertion rings true because she always seems to have been welcome at court despite her dubious reputation and promiscuous life.[219] Even the wise Molly Hervey, on one occasion before her marriage, was 'drawn into a fine scrape' and had to seek Dr Arbuthnot's help: 'what I am to do in the matter God knows, not I. [I] beg your advice in it.'[220] What this 'scrape' was and what medical advice was offered remain mysterious but guessable.

But not everyone got away with 'dropping' a child. While Henrietta negotiated a smooth exit from the court, others were brutally expelled: Maid of Honour Sophy Howe, for example, was crushed like a butterfly after her seduction and abandonment by Lord Lonsdale's brother 'Nunty'.

Sophy's high spirits had always brought her into conflict with the restrictions round court life, and her crush on Nunty Lowther encouraged her to kick over the traces altogether. She ran away from the palace 'dressed in men's shoes and breeches' and made her way to Lowther's house in town. Here her so-called lover – 'who she is in love with, and by the way, the town says she is with child by' – escaped through the back door, while his conniving porter detained Sophy on the front step. The authorities 'were forced to send to her mother and friends, and they have confined her'.[221]

This was the end of Sophy's career: 'her pining cheek betray'd her inward smart/ her breaking looks foretold her breaking heart'.[222] Yet Sophy was quickly old news at court, and the courtiers complained that 'poor Howe's misfortune, is all our theme, and that is almost worn out, so you must send us something new'.[223] It showed the truth of John Hervey's opinion that it was rare for a personal disgrace at court to be 'anything more than the novel of a fortnight, which everybody would recount and everybody forget'.[224]

The Maids of Honour had also lost their old crony, poet John Gay, who'd eventually given up the search for court office in disgust. Driven at last by financial need to real effort, he wrote the spectacular theatrical success *The Beggar's Opera*, with its wicked digs at Sir Robert Walpole.

Dr Arbuthnot could not deny that Gay's masterpiece contained 'a great deal of true low humour', but the outrage and trouble it generated made it much harder and riskier for writers and theatres to stage political plays.[225] When Gay himself tried to bring out a sequel, *Polly*, Walpole promptly had the work banned. John Gay did not long outlive his disappointment, for in 1732 Dr Arbuthnot attended his old friend's deathbed. He reported that Gay 'dy'd of an inflammation, and I believe at last a mortification of the bowels; it was the most precipitate case I ever knew, having cut him off in three days'.[226]

At the time that Henrietta left court, John Gay's old flirting partner Molly Hervey was spending a much-needed three-month break in France. This left the coast clear for her husband John to deepen his acquaintance with Anne Vane. Mistress Vane was the poor deluded Maid of Honour who had been taken up and cast aside by a number of courtiers, including some of the very highest rank. She and John Hervey went swiftly from 'ogling' each other to sending 'messages, from messages to letters, from letters to appointments, and from appointments to all the familiarities'. Anne Vane would wrap herself in a cloak and slip on foot into the Hervey household, where 'they often passed the whole night together'.[227]

Molly now expected nothing from this unreliable husband of hers, and they were described as living 'as if not married at all' in a loose, uninterested union.[228] 'Marriage is like drinking,' John Hervey said, 'it begins with being our cordial & ends with being our poison.'[229] Sadly the glow of the court's former *Schatz* (or 'treasure') was now extinguished by domestic duties: she was 'a fatigued nurse, a grieved sister, and a melancholy wife', marooned when in England with her children on the Hervey family estate, Ickworth in Suffolk.[230]

'I know laudanum can at any time lend me a stock [of good spirits] for present use,' Molly admitted, but she understood its risks: that repeated indulgence would run her 'greatly in arrears, and considerably lessen [her] principal, which is already too much impaired to bear a further diminution'.[231] She was right to be careful: laudanum is a powerful and addictive mixture of alcohol and opium.

She was much better off with her old pastime of illicit reading, being on occasion happily and 'mightily taken up with a book' of Elizabethan letters.[232]

'The number of stories & contradictory reasons given for Lady Suffolk's removing from court wou'd fill more than an ordinary length of one of my letters,' wrote one courtier soon after the great event.[233] Queen Caroline condemned Henrietta's departure as 'the

silliest thing she could do', while the newspapers thought it repre-
hensible, desirable and incomprehensible in equal measure.[234]

But the real explanation was that the death of Henrietta's husband had removed the 'danger of falling into his hands', and that
Henrietta herself was 'desirous to have liberty & a little more time
at her own command'.[235] Her true friends thought that 'not only
her master & mistress but her very enemies will have reason to
repent the part they have acted by her'.[236]

After her resignation had created the sensation of a fortnight,
though, the waters began to close over Henrietta's memory.
Returning to London in January 1735, John Hervey 'expected when
[he] came to town to hear a great deal about Lady Suffolk; but they
talk of her no more than if she did not exist, or than if she never
had existed, one might as well ask questions about Henry II and
Fair Rosamund; it would hardly seem a story more out of date'.[237]

Despite her loss of position, fame and untold opportunities for
'frizelation', it seemed that Henrietta had made a lucky escape.
Some of her old colleagues commiserated with her loss of station:
'all ye *beau-monde* that us'd to crowd about your *toilettes* will avoid
you, as if you had got ye plague'.[238] Yet it seems very doubtful that
Henrietta much missed the beau monde's shallow company.

As Jonathan Swift said of his friend, she'd had little need of her
numerous virtues at court.[239] The loss of the king's favour had at
first seemed like a setback, but with it the stage was set for her
redemption. Henrietta could at last unpack from her chest of
virtues her talent for writing and wit and friendship. She would
also now have the good fortune to discover which of her acquaintances were really loyal and true to her, something she 'cou'd never
have found out without this change'.[240]

And there was also another, hidden, reason driving Henrietta
forward on her path of propulsion from the court. While the king
had been falling out of love with her, Henrietta was herself falling
in love with somebody else.

The next scandal at court was to be the news of her unexpected
and very hasty marriage.

*

The court was once again electrified by the news of Henrietta's swift wedding to Member of Parliament George Berkeley. It took place on 26 June 1735, consummating a relationship that had begun in secret well before her delicate negotiation of her exit from the palace. As the wedding was so unexpected, there was a torrent of gossip: 'the town's surpris'd, & the town talks, as the town loves to do on these ordinary extraordinary occasions'.[241]

In John Hervey's opinion, 'Mr Berkeley was neither young, handsome, healthy, nor rich', and he heard people wondering what had induced Henrietta 'to deviate into this unaccountable piece of folly'.[242] Others joked cruelly about 'her deaf-ear, & his lame-leg' and thought it repulsive that such old people should retire together to the 'bed on purpose bought, for ye unexpected nuptials'.[243] But George Berkeley was nevertheless only forty-two to Henrietta's forty-six, and her escape from court life had left her looking 'better than [she] did seventeen years ago'.[244] One of Berkeley's relations congratulated him upon his wise choice of wife, in which 'the most agreeable beauties of the mind are joined to those of the body'.[245]

Some imagined that the marriage 'was to pique the King', but if indeed it had been, Henrietta's aim was confounded. He wrote to Caroline that '*ma vieille maîtresse*' had married '*ce vieux goutteux George Berkeley*', and that '*je m'en rejouis fort!*' [My old mistress has married gouty old George Berkeley, and I'm really happy about it!].[246]

In fact, Berkeley was kind, loving and honest, and his correspondence with his wife shows they shared a deep bond that was admired by all their friends. And, far from being cut by the fashionable world, the couple hosted that summer 'a greater court now at Marble Hill than at Kensington'.[247]

Safe, happy, in love at last, Henrietta had nothing to regret about leaving the court. She had also picked the perfect moment to leave, barely escaping the explosion of the most violent royal quarrel yet.

SEVEN

The Favourite and His Foe

'You and I know enough of courts not to be
amaz'd at any turns they may take."
(Lady Mary Wortley Montagu)

Back at the palace, a huge new row was brewing within the royal family. George II had spent years wrangling with his father, and now it seemed that history was repeating itself: 'it ran a little in the blood of the family to hate the eldest son'.[2]

The family's frightful feuding spelt danger for the whole British nation. In the words of Sir Robert Walpole, 'divisions in the palace' would lead inevitably to 'divisions in the kingdom', a situation 'much more terrible to think of than difficult to foresee'.[3]

On the night of 31 July 1737, events in the king's embattled relationship with his own heir, Prince Frederick, came to a head. A 'very extraordinary quarrel at Court' saw a heavily pregnant princess being rushed dangerously through the night by coach.[4]

It was the culmination of yet another battle royal, and at its centre was yet another royal baby.

As the story unfolded over the summer of 1737, John Hervey was once again present to record its every twist and turn. By chance he'd also witnessed the very inception of the quarrel, which lay more than twenty years in the past.

Long ago, Henrietta Howard had gone to Hanover to seek her fortune, and the youthful John Hervey had made a similar journey to Germany. Exactly like her, he'd hoped to make important connections to help along his future court career.

In 1716, aged nineteen, John set out upon a young aristocrat's conventional grand tour of the sights of Europe. His first stop was Paris, and Hanover was to be his second.

Business in the principality had proceeded as usual after George I had decamped to Britain in 1714. The small, dull, provincial state continued to support the two royal palaces, one in the city on the River Leine, the other in the country at Herren - hausen, and there was a rural hunting lodge at Göhrde. The state's silver mines kept its Elector personally wealthy, while his subjects were stubborn and hard workers in the fields.

Because of its ruling family's connection with Britain, Hanover after 1714 had become accustomed to being overrun with English tourists. The sightseers squabbled over the limited lodgings available in the town, while their coaches whipped up the dust that coated the leaves of the long lime avenue leading out to Herren-hausen.

John Hervey hurried on his way to Hanover in 1716 so that his visit would coincide with one of George I's extended holidays at his former home. Soon he had an appointment to wait upon the king (and, with youthful thoughtlessness, neglected to take his tutor with him).[5] He also got himself an introduction to the king's grandson, the then nine-year-old Frederick, Prince of Wales (1707–51). Prince Frederick headed Hanover's permanent court and generally welcomed royal or other important visitors to the town when his grandfather and parents were away in Britain.

This meeting with Prince Frederick in 1716, made out of a careful calculation of future gain, would prove an important turning point in John Hervey's emotional life as well as his career.

He and the prince immediately took to each other. Hervey's father advised that he should get to know the boy and leave Hanover only when his 'foundation in Prince Frederick's favour' was laid 'indelibly'; this proved easy to achieve.[6]

Just like his marriage to Molly, though, Hervey's initially adoring relationship with Prince Frederick would eventually become mired in misunderstanding. Unlike his marriage, this would become one of the most significant relationships of his life.

In this chapter, for the first time in our story so far, we will see John Hervey in pain.

Both John Hervey and the boy prince were slight and feminine in

Frederick, Prince of Wales: his 'face fair but not
handsome; his eyes grey like a cat'

appearance. Prince Frederick – also known as 'Fretz' by his family
– had hair 'with a yellowish cast' and a 'face fair but not handsome;
his eyes grey like a cat and very dull'.[7] His legs were spindly
because he'd suffered from rickets.

Unable to find much to praise in his appearance, courtiers
describing Prince Frederick tended to fall back upon his charm.
One observed that he had that certain 'something so very engag-
ing and easy in his behaviour', as well as 'the fine fair hair' of his
mother Caroline.[8] Another found him not the least bit handsome
but still 'the most agreeable young man it is possible to imagine . . .
his person little but very well made and genteel', an indescribable
liveliness in his eyes.[9] The prince certainly had a captivating and
amusing manner: 'the Lord knows what a mimic!'

But Prince Frederick was a little short-sighted, in two senses.
His slightly protuberant eyes were myopic, and he was also a little
lazy in his outlook upon life. He lacked integrity and tended to
take the easy way out of problems. 'His best quality was generosity,'
it was said, and 'his worst, insincerity, and indifference to truth'.[10]

The sharp and cynical John Hervey, witness of Prince Frederick's formative years, was certainly not the best person to provide firm moral guidance. With kind guardianship and good advice, this boy could have been a fine king. Yet Frederick's childhood was even more damaging than that of an orphan: he was a child deserted and positively disliked by his parents.

His birth had taken place in Hanover's Leine Palace in 1707, and he was dogged by rumour about its exact circumstances. Because of the coolness between Queen Anne and the Electoral family of Hanover, there had been no official British witness present during Caroline's labour. The English envoy to Hanover found this 'unaccountable' and 'very extraordinary'.[11]

It would indeed have been a wise precaution to have had one present, given all the trouble that rumours about an impostor baby had caused when the unpopular James II's son was born. When his Catholic wife, Mary of Modena, had fortuitously produced a healthy boy, English Protestants claimed that a lapse in palace surveillance had allowed a live infant to be slipped in to replace a dead, miscarried child. The king's enemies spread it about that a surrogate baby boy had been smuggled into the queen's bed in a warming pan. Many people believed the scandal, and the incident became an important step along the road to James II's eventual overthrow.

Still, such rumours usually originated from political enemies. It reveals the depth of George II's bad feeling towards Prince Frederick that he referred to his own son as a '*Wechselbalg*', or changeling, or as 'the *Griff*'. The latter may have simply meant that Frederick looked like a griffin, but the word can also mean a person of mixed race (a suggestion which cast grave aspersions upon Caroline's character and conduct).[12]

In 1714, when the Hanoverians came over to London en masse, George I insisted that Frederick's parents should leave their seven-year-old son behind. There were actually very good political reasons for this. A significant figure from the family was needed as its representative in Hanover, and Caroline was expected to have British-born heirs to follow. Yet to the little boy it must have felt like his parents were abandoning him.

Prince Frederick was placed in the care of his uncle, George I's younger brother. Hanover remained his main concern, although he was also taught English and sent packets of parliamentary papers and models of British warships in preparation for his future role as king of Britain.[13] Tittle-tattle claimed that Frederick's sexual education was provided by one Madame d'Elitz from the Schulenburg family, completing a hat-trick that she'd begun by seducing Frederick's grandfather, George I, and then George II.[14] ('There's nothing new under the sun, or the grandson either,' people said.)

During the long summer holidays, when George I returned to lime-lapped Herrenhausen, grandfather and grandson grew close. Prince Frederick called his grandfather his 'best friend', demonstrating that they had an intimate relationship which his absent father inevitably resented.[15]

When George I died, Frederick was left to languish in Hanover until his father's bewilderingly sudden command to uproot himself and come to England for the first time at the end of 1728, when he was twenty-one.

There was some compensation for Prince Frederick in the thought that in London he might have more chance of meeting his dashing, grown-up friend John Hervey once again.

And now, with Prince Frederick in England, the trouble really began. Just as George II in his own day as Prince of Wales had formed the focus for the Opposition in Parliament, all the politicians opposed to Sir Robert Walpole's long regime began to gather round the prince.

The sound political reasons for having left Prince Frederick behind in Hanover for so long were lost in a fog of resentment on Frederick's side, and impatience on his father's. By 1734, it was thought that the 'misunderstanding between the father and son had increased to a very alarming degree' and that Prince Frederick had been 'encouraged by the opposition' to create an 'open rupture'.[16]

To outsiders it was obvious that the politicians hoped to divide, and therefore to rule, the royal family.[17] But Prince Frederick's rather passive stupidity meant that he was putty in the hands of his advisors. As Molly Hervey observed, his very servants sought 'to aggravate everything'. 'Poor man!' she exclaimed. 'He does not see that every stroke that is aimed at his father recoils upon him.'[18]

Opinion was sharply divided on Prince Frederick, and even in the present day there is no clear consensus. His doctor enjoyed his 'pleasant facetious humour, which is easy and natural to him'.[19] The novelist Tobias Smollett found him 'a tender and obliging husband, a fond parent, kind master, liberal, generous, candid and humane'.[20] All this was to the prince's credit, and perhaps in any other family he could have flourished.

At the same time, diametrically opposed views of Prince Frederick also existed. A potential bride of the prince's was warned that he had a 'very narrow mind' and no self-discipline. 'Provided you can have the complaisance to put up with his debauches,' she was told, 'you may then govern him entirely' and 'be more king than he'.[21] His old tutor thought the prince possessed 'the most vicious nature and the most false heart that ever man had, nor are his vices the vices of a gentleman, but the mean base tricks of a knavish footman'.[22] His parents – and eventually even his friend John Hervey – came to share this view.

It was becoming horribly clear that conflict between a king and his son would form the permanent backdrop to eighteenth-century court and political life. In private the courtiers tried to please the king by describing his son as 'so awkward a fellow and so mean a looking scoundrel'.[23] In public, though, Prince Frederick was 'no more talked of now than if he had never been born'.[24] Whenever he appeared in the same room as his father, he went unacknowledged: 'it put one in mind of stories one has heard of ghosts that appear to part of the company and are invisible to the rest'.[25]

In the Hanover that Prince Frederick had now also left behind, business continued to tick over smoothly. Money sent from

Britain kept its army strong, its residents were far better-educated than their British equivalents, and Hanover's well-organised burghers planned European firsts such as systematic street signs and gas street lighting. At the royal palace the table was laid each day as if the family were still in residence, and, although absent, George II maintained 'the same number of gentlemen, pages, domestics, and guards; and the same number of horses, grooms, &c. in his stables'.[26] Like George I, he returned to this haven of prosperous and peaceful deference as often as possible for holidays.

Relations between Britain and Hanover certainly lay at the forefront of his mind when his father died in 1727, and this was evidenced by the strange affair of George I's will.

The document was produced by the Archbishop of Canterbury at a council meeting early on in the new king's reign, but George II grabbed it and made sure that it was never seen again. He also searched out and destroyed copies lodged on the continent. A pension paid to the Dowager Duchess of Brunswick was assumed to have been a payment for conveniently 'losing' the copy deposited with her husband.[27]

The historian Horace Walpole (son of Sir Robert) would later call this suppressing of the will 'an indelible blot' upon George II's memory.[28] He assumed that the king had wanted avariciously to avoid handing over the various legacies his father had dictated.

However, one of these legacies was indeed paid, at least in some small part. The Duchess of Kendal, George I's former mistress Melusine von der Schulenberg, received a bequest from the king, and used it to buy a villa in Isleworth, Middlesex.

One of her and George I's daughters made a respectable marriage to Lord Chesterfield. But Melusine's new son-in-law considered that she and her daughter had been cheated of a much larger intended legacy through the mysterious business of the missing will. After he had fallen from favour at court, Chesterfield had nothing to lose by challenging the generosity and legality of the payments made to his mother-in-law, and eventually he accepted £20,000 to settle the matter out of court.[29]

However, the real reason why George II concealed the contents of his father's will was that it contained the radical proposal to separate the countries of Britain and Hanover. The will decreed that after Prince Frederick's death the territories should be divided, Britain going to Frederick's (as then unborn) elder son and Hanover to a younger son. Whether the Act of Settlement actually allowed George I to make these decisions is questionable.[30]

Modern historians think that George II suppressed this will because he had a quite different plan in mind: for Prince Frederick to take over Hanover, while Frederick's younger and more favoured British-born brother, William Augustus, would rule Britain.[31] It would indeed have been sensible to separate Britain and Hanover, given their very different needs, but it also looks like George II was motivated by spite to do Prince Frederick down and to give his second and preferred son the bigger, better job. He didn't trust his eldest son to become a successful king of Great Britain.

In the event, interest in the issue of separating the two countries melted away. Prince Frederick's son and grandsons, George III, George IV and William IV, would go on ruling both of them. Britain and Hanover had a single ruler until 1837, when Queen Victoria lost the German state only because of her gender. Salic law, current in Germany, decreed that women could not inherit. Hanover eventually went its own separate way under one of Queen Victoria's numerous uncles.

The relationship between Prince Frederick and his mother Caroline was even more complicated. When she had first been forced to abandon him in 1714, Caroline felt acute pain at being parted from her first-born child. She would closely question returning travellers who had seen him – 'the Princess sent for me in private, and ask'd me a thousand questions of her little Frederick' – and begged all her European contacts for frequent updates.[32] The Duchess of Orléans, for example, fished for news that Prince Frederick was well, so that she could at least 'give his poor mother that much comfort'.[33]

Little by little, though, Caroline came to love her newer, British-born children. And, over time, Prince Frederick became associated in her mind with her hated father-in-law, George I, because of the summer holidays the two of them spent alone together in Hanover.

Frederick's arrival in London at the end of 1728, and his reunion with his parents, was very low key. He came 'privately in a hackney coach' to St James's Palace and almost sneaked inside through the back door.[34] Despite being fully grown, Frederick was not given a home of his own but lived with his younger brother and sisters in the various royal establishments.

After six years of this subordinate life, he arranged an audience with his father to ask for various improvements to his situation. But Prince Frederick's request to fight the French was turned down, his demand for a greater income of his own was met with silence and his desire to get married was parried with the suggestion of the mad (and to Frederick unacceptable) Princess Charlotte of Denmark.

Prince Frederick had nevertheless set his heart upon marriage, which would bring with it an indisputable need for him to have a separate establishment and larger income. He was rather reckless with money and had left many debts in Hanover. So, after the Danish fiasco and further harassment, George II came up with a second and sounder suggestion for a bride.

During the king's trip to Hanover in 1735, Princess Augusta of the tiny state of Saxe-Gotha had come to his attention as a potential daughter-in-law. Within a year, the flaxen-haired but otherwise unprepossessing Princess Augusta – 'pretty much markt with the small pox' – was brought from Saxe-Gotha into this most dysfunctional of royal families.[35]

One courtier described Augusta's figure as 'a good deal awry, her arms long, and her motions awkward'. In spite of all her fine jewels and brocade, the princess had a touchingly 'ordinary air, which no trappings could cover or exalt'. Augusta made up for her lack of grandeur with an amiable personality: she had 'a very modest and good-natured look'.[36] Another observer also confirmed that 'the Princess is neither handsome nor ugly, tall nor short, but has a pretty lively countenance enough'.[37] In addition to these qualifications, she looked likely to 'deliver robust children' and had started menstruating at the early age of eleven.[38]

The April wedding of Prince Frederick and Princess Augusta was the great event of 1736, and consisted of the usual parade of fabulous fashions and immensely long parties. Even a family celebration, though, created tension between father and son, for George II fell into a rage at the drawing room's 'thin appearance on his birthday'. People were not more richly dressed, he was tactlessly told, because they were saving their fine clothes for his son's wedding. This was certain to trigger jealous ructions, as 'His Majesty's temper', whenever sharpened, 'was seldom put in a sheath'.[39]

Poor, pleasant Princess Augusta was married to her not-particularly-handsome prince, a man she'd barely met, a mere forty-eight hours after landing in England. The ceremony took place in the chapel at St James's Palace. Augusta's trembling neck could barely support her weighty new crown, 'set all over with diamonds'. Her heavy robe was 'crimson velvet, turn'd back with several rows of ermine', and her train carried by four silver-clad ladies.[40]

It was clear she didn't understand what was going on. In the backwater of Saxe-Gotha, Princess Augusta's mother had neglected to include English lessons in her daughter's educational programme, wrongly assuming that the Hanoverians would have had everyone in England speaking German after so many years in charge. In consequence Princess Augusta had 'not one word of English, and few of French'.[41] Queen Caroline had to translate the wedding service into her ear, and prompt her responses.

Caroline also gave the bride a piece of pragmatic but depressing advice. 'Avoid jealousy,' she told Princess Augusta, and 'be easy in regard to amours'.[42] Caroline explained that her own happy marriage was entirely due to this. Her daughter-in-law must have felt that her new life as Princess of Wales was going to be far from a fairy tale.

At the wedding feast Prince Frederick ate an extraordinary amount of jelly because it was thought to have aphrodisiac qualities, and afterwards the wedding guests had the dubious pleasure of trooping into the newly married couple's bedchamber 'to see them abed'.[43] Caroline's daughters the princesses had undressed Augusta, and all the 'quality were admitted to see the bride and bridegroom sitting up in bed surrounded by all the Royal Family'.[44] Prince Frederick's nightcap, according to his disparaging mother, was ridiculously tall.

Caroline also thought that Princess Augusta looked surprisingly well rested the next morning, as if her son had failed to do his marital duty.[45]

Despite this inauspicious beginning, the ingénue Augusta was rather a success as Princess of Wales. Prince Frederick grew very fond of her, and Caroline, feeling sorry for her, gave her generous presents, such as 'a most beautiful hat, curiously made of feathers in imitation of a fine Brussels lace'.[46] Princess Augusta set to work upon her language skills and was soon able to 'talk freely to the ladies in good English, which entirely won their hearts'.[47] In fact, her English was quickly superior to the rest of the royal family's, despite their long residence in Britain.[48]

She even managed to stay on reasonable terms with her parents-in-law by acting as Prince Frederick's submissive and innocent little wife. Augusta was careful to be always 'very modest and very respectful', and, in Caroline's opinion, 'there was no sort of harm in her'.[49]

People jokingly began to call her 'Princess Prudence'.

Caroline and her son, though, remained constantly at odds. This was partly because they still lived almost on top of each other.

Prince Frederick and Princess Augusta were often (if not contin-
uously) in residence at Kensington Palace. They moved there in
May 1736 to begin their married life alongside Caroline and the
other royal children, and Princess Augusta 'kept her drawing-
room and he his *levée* there constantly every Monday morning'.[50]

No wonder hatreds ran high in such a closed little world. As
John Hervey wrote from Kensington, 'I hardly ever go out of these
walls, which, by the identity of faces they enclose, one should
imagine belonged rather to a Turkish Seraglio than an English
Palace.'[51]

Nevertheless, Prince Frederick and Princess Augusta occupied a
very commodious apartment, a large, almost self-contained house
built in the 1720s to the north-west of the main palace complex (it
would later become the conjugal home of the present-day Prince of
Wales and his first wife Diana). This house of Prince Frederick's,
with its own 'Great Stair', its 'Presence Chamber' and its 'Coffee
Room', gave its name to 'Prince of Wales's Court' in the palace.[52]

Prince Frederick was a talented performer upon the violoncello,
although he had to squint hard to read the music with his feeble
eyes. He occasionally gave informal evening concerts at Kensington Palace. In John Hervey's opinion this was a lowbrow, inelegant
and unseemly hobby for a prince, but there is much to savour in
his snapshot of Frederick at Kensington, 'seated close to an open
window of his apartment, with his violoncello between his legs,
singing French and Italian songs to his own playing for an hour or
two together, whilst his audience was composed of all the under-
ling servants'.

As darkness fell, the lights of the apartment illuminated Prince
Frederick beautifully, and the court below gradually filled up with
all the servants, grateful for the music:

> the colonnade below being filled with all the footmen, scullions, pos-
> tillions, apple-women, shoe-boys and lower order of domestics, whilst
> the first floor windows were thronged with chambermaids and *valets
> de chambre*, and the garret, like the upper gallery, stuffed with laundry
> maids and their gallants.[53]

Music alone could unite the different ranks of court society in attentive quiet.

Kensington Palace was not Prince Frederick's only home. In 1730, he had acquired an old country house at Kew, and had chosen none other than William Kent to remodel it. The property was extremely dilapidated (the prince's 'Rat Physician' captured more than five hundred rodents in the house before work began) and became a major project for Kent.[54]

Escaping from the royal palaces and building this practically new house made Prince Frederick feel more independent from his parents, and for Kent this was really his first venture into designing a whole edifice, as opposed to the purely decorative work he had done at Kensington. Frederick was evidently delighted with Kent's ideas: a green and gilded study lined with 'panels of Japan', a gallery decorated with grotesque work, and a red damask bed in a scarlet bedroom.[55]

In 1735, William Kent received yet another promotion, becoming Master Mason and Deputy Surveyor of the Office of the King's Works, as well as architect to the heir to the throne.[56]

This foolish, malleable, musical prince, now happily married, nevertheless remained set upon a collision course with his parents over the issue of money. Prince Frederick thought that his income should be doubled to support his new married state, and was quick to emphasise that his father in his own day as Prince of Wales had enjoyed £100,000 a year. Somewhat understandably, Frederick wanted the same amount.

Augusta's refuge from the in-laws: the house that William Kent created for the Prince and Princess of Wales at Kew

Meanwhile, he stirred up more ill will by failing to appear in the queen's drawing room, by consorting with the king's political enemies and by drinking crowd-pleasing toasts to 'Liberty' in Pall Mall. 'My God,' said Caroline, conveniently forgetting how dexterous she was at tweaking her own public image, 'popularity always makes me sick; but Fretz's popularity makes me vomit.'[57]

Prince Frederick also exploited the enormous opposition to the government's new Act intended to control the havoc created by the abuse of gin. He signalled that he too thought the legislators meddlesome spoilsports by ostentatiously raising a glass in the taverns while shouts of 'No Gin! No King!' echoed round London. By contrast, his mother Caroline was a strong supporter of the (ultimately futile) Gin Act that was supposed to regulate spirit sales. The Act's becoming law in 1736 was celebrated with many mock funerals: 'last Wednesday . . . several people made themselves very merry with the death of "Madam Gin", and some of both sexes got soundly drunk at her funeral, of which the mob made a formal procession with torches'.[58]

The prince's advisors also urged him to take offence at all sorts of imagined slights from his parents. They were furious in May 1736, for example, when George II went off to Hanover but appointed his wife, not his son, as his British regent. And when the king dallied overlong overseas, to the disappointment of his British subjects, Prince Frederick was visited by 'the chiefs of the discontented party', who discreetly encouraged him to attempt a coup.[59] But in this case he had the wisdom to refrain.

Caroline, however, had no such expectation of her son. 'I hear that yesterday, on his side of the house,' she spluttered, 'my good son strutted about as if he had been already King.'[60] By January of the year 1737, when George II cancelled the court ball that Prince Frederick expected for his birthday, people refused to accept the official excuse – Caroline's gout – but chose instead to believe that the king did not want people to show their respect to Frederick 'at this time of misunderstanding between him and his father'.[61]

The animosity over Prince Frederick's allowance grew more

and more intense, and the royal family were once again becoming dangerously oblivious to everything but their own disputes. Fed up with his father's intransigence, Frederick eventually decided to go behind the royal back. He tried to get his money directly from Parliament, and in February 1737 the Opposition lost the measure to increase Frederick's income by a mere thirty votes. Given that there were only 438 members, this was terrifyingly tight for the king's supporters, and it demonstrated the political price to be paid when a prince had what was a kind of parliamentary party of his own.

George II, meanwhile, was laid low with haemorrhoids, the embarrassing illness to which his father had also been a martyr. When the news of Frederick's temerity and the closeness of the vote arrived at the royal apartments, John Hervey begged Caroline to keep it from the king. He was still very weak, and it might have 'put him in such a passion' as would go a 'good way towards killing him'.

In the event, the king's rage seemed to act as a tonic and he began to recover, 'though he looked pale and was much fallen away'.

Caroline and John Hervey were still in the habit of chatting and idling the morning away together in her apartments. One day, they happened to be looking out of Caroline's dressing-room window when Prince Frederick passed by below. The sight prompted Caroline to snarl: 'Look, there he goes – that wretch! – that villain! – I wish the ground would open this moment and sink the monster to the lowest hole in hell.'[62]

These were horrendous things for a mother to say about her son, but Caroline admitted John Hervey to nearly all of her most intimate and secret thoughts. She found him clever, amusing, adoring and familiar: everything that Prince Frederick was not. Hervey had by now almost taken the place of the queen's eldest child, while her real son was loathed rather than loved.

Caroline, whose maternal instincts had been so strangely

subverted, was also possessed by a prurient curiosity about her son's sexual activities. She could not decide whether to believe that Prince Frederick was impotent or to give credence to the rumours that he was promiscuous and 'often got nasty distempers from women'.[63] His marriage to Princess Augusta brought the issue higher up the list of Caroline's concerns as she was worried about the fate of her potential grandchildren.

The usual royal paranoia about the provision of a true heir had Caroline firmly within its grip. She asked John Hervey to investigate the matter for her by seeking information from the licentious Lady Dudley. She had 'lain with half the town as well as Fretz, and consequently must know whether he is like other men or not'.

Paranoia also led Caroline and Hervey to indulge in one particularly morbid and gothic flight of fantasy. They tried to imagine whether it might be possible for Prince Frederick to insinuate a man more virile than himself into Princess Augusta's bed, without Augusta noticing the difference, in order to father a child. Hervey thought it might just be possible, if Frederick prepared well: falling into a habit of going 'to bed several hours after his wife', getting up 'for a flux several times in the night' and perfuming 'himself always with some predominant smell'. He reckoned that these tricks could help the prince to put 'any man near his own size upon her that he pleased'. Hervey thought that he could probably even impregnate Augusta himself.

'I know not what to think,' concluded Caroline, 'but altogether I know it makes me very uneasy.'[64]

Deviant, topsy-turvy, almost unbelievable: these strange speculations were really caused by the reversionary problem, which set generations of the royal family against each other at the very deepest level.

But there was also another angle to the mystery underlying this seemingly shocking perversion of normal family relationships. It's all tied up with the explanation of why John Hervey hated Prince Frederick so passionately, when they had once been the closest of friends.

*

Although John Hervey had been away on a continental tour when Prince Frederick arrived in Britain in 1728, his earlier spadework in Hanover meant that he quickly became part of Frederick's inner circle when he returned to London. Intriguingly, the relevant part of Hervey's memoirs, which might explain why this close friendship turned into equally passionate hatred, is missing.

Perhaps, like so much palace scandal, the quarrel between Prince Frederick and his former favourite had its roots in the apartment of the Maids of Honour. John Hervey was not the only person to enjoy the favours of Anne Vane, Maid of Honour, and his rivals included the prince himself. This certainly caused a falling-out between the friends.

Anne Vane had long since lost her despised virginity, and counted Prince Frederick among her numerous lovers. She gave birth to a baby that was probably his son, a fact that she stressed by giving her child the name Cornwall FitzFrederick. The beau monde was secretly delighted, and scurrilous ballads circulated:

> Of a hundred amours, she (at least) was accused.
> A hundred! (she cries) Heavens how I'm abused,
> For I'll swear the dear Babe (or else I may starve) is
> The Prince's, or Stanhope's, my footman's or Hervey's.[65]

(This poem draws attention to the fact that 'Hervey' was pronounced 'Harvey'.) Although Prince Frederick was growing tired of Anne, he was nevertheless rather put out when John Hervey took her off his hands. One of Hervey's friends sympathetically depicted the Vane incident with an animal metaphor: Prince Frederick was a poor puppy, with a bottle (Anne Vane) cruelly tied to his tail; Hervey made a kind effort to free the puppy by removing the bottle but was repaid only with a vicious bite.[66]

Anne Vane herself, defenceless, exploited, more sinned against than sinning, came to a bad end and died young.

The more perceptive courtiers, though, noticed that on the subject of sex Prince Frederick 'talked more of feats this way than he acts'.[67] And there is another, rival explanation for the quarrel between Prince Frederick and John Hervey: a homosexual relationship gone wrong.

People in the eighteenth century had no notion of a person's being 'homosexual' as we would understand it today. But sexual relationships between people of the same gender nevertheless took place, and there's no question that John Hervey was sexually attracted to both women and men.[68]

He was absent from England at the actual moment of Prince Frederick's arrival because he'd abandoned his promising political career in order to make a tour of Italy. This was partly for his health and partly to pursue his passion for his fellow traveller Stephen (or Ste) Fox, the young man who had superseded Molly in his affections.

The British courtiers thought that Italy was the home to unnatural vice. 'Both the word and the thing came to them from Italy, and are strangers to England,' it was said, while the English themselves 'love the fair sex too well to fall into such an abomination'.[69] The author of *Plain Reasons for the Growth of Sodomy in England*, published in 1728, thought homosexual proclivities must be caused by deficiencies in the education of boys, the growing effeminacy of men's dress, the 'barbarity' of women and the increasing popularity of the Italian opera.[70] Italy was a congenial place for the young aristocrats, both for its culture and its moral laxity.

And now we begin see the vulnerability beneath John Hervey's sarcastic, witty, courtly facade. Hervey the courtier did his best to disguise Hervey the lover. Yet just sometimes, as his shotgun marriage to Molly had shown, the lover threw off the courtier's mask. Hervey, who so often seems to have been born with a splinter of ice in his heart, was totally floored by his relationship with Ste Fox: 'I love you & love you more than I thought I could love anything.'[71]

Georgian aristocratic men often prized their male friendships above their relationships with their wives, and clearly had little in common with the established subculture of homosexuality that

George I, George II and their courtiers favoured Kensington Palace, surrounded by its famous gardens, as a healthy summer holiday home.

Courtiers having tea at Lord Harrington's house. Henrietta Howard (wearing a gold-coloured dress), the king's mistress, is sitting at the card table in the centre. Her head is inclined towards the man near the fireplace: George Berkeley, the true love of her life. He was first her secret lover and then her second husband.

The King's Grand Staircase, leading up to the state apartments at Kensington Palace. Everyone of influence in Georgian England came up these stairs, hoping to speak to the king. Forty-five members of the royal household observe the king's visitors from the painted walls.

Peter the Wild Boy has curly hair and holds up a sprig of oak: a reminder of his feral life in the forest before he was found and brought to court as a pet. To the left, Dr Arbuthnot, satirist, medical doctor, and Peter's tutor and friend, leans on the stout stick he always carried because of his limp.

Mohammed (left) has a blue cloak. His colleague is Mustapha (right), with white turban and beard. These two were among George I's most trusted servants, and their intimacy with the king aroused much envy. Gossipy Londoners reported that the king 'keeps two Turks for abominable uses'.

Is this Mrs Tempest? We know that Queen Caroline's pretty milliner is shown somewhere on the staircase, and this lady has a hyper-fashionable black hood as a milliner might. There's a rumour that the page boy in blue worked for Henrietta Howard.

Robert and Franciscus: the assistants who helped the pushy painter William Kent to complete the staircase with its portraits of the servants at court.

The staircase still holds many secrets, such as the identities of these ladies. According to the secret language of the fan, William Kent jokingly depicted several of the women servants signalling a series of similar messages: 'I am married', 'leave me alone' and just plain 'no'.

A shy and apparently grumpy man, King George I was widely misunderstood by the English courtiers. Only his servants and mistress saw him off duty, when he was relaxed and good company. But it is true that he could be exceedingly cruel: he imprisoned his wife for adultery, hated his son and kidnapped his grandchildren.

Sir James Thornhill: the older, well-established painter who had fully expected to decorate Kensington Palace. His nemesis William Kent ousted him from the commission in the cut-throat battle of the painters which unfolds in Chapter Three.

The Cupola Room at Kensington Palace: commissioned by George I in the hope of hosting parties even more lively and popular than his son's. The job of painting the room was won by the cheeky upstart William Kent. This was an early project for the artist who went on to create the definitive look of the Georgian age.

The coming man: the talented and bumptious William Kent, with his actress-mistress, Elizabeth Butler. William Kent, 'very hot and very fat', eventually died of 'a life of high feeding and much inaction'.

Herrenhausen: the beautiful garden palace outside Hanover where George I invested much money and effort. He missed this place dreadfully when he inherited the crown of Great Britain, and was travelling back to it at the very moment of his death. Below is his mausoleum, overlooking his beloved gardens.

George I's wife had a prolonged and flagrant extra-marital affair with a Swedish count. Legend tells that George I had his wife's lover murdered, and the body thrown into the River Leine at this very spot. George I's son, George II, never saw his mother again after she was imprisoned for adultery.

Mustapha and Mohammed in the garden of a German hunting lodge. Born in the Ottoman Empire, the king's two Turks were captured in war and taken to Hanover, where they converted to Christianity and entered royal service. In the final stage of an amazing journey, they came with George I to Kensington Palace in 1714. One of Mohammed's tasks was to treat the king's haemorrhoids, and Mustapha administered his laxatives.

Flawed but fascinating, George II and Queen Caroline were real human beings trapped in their royal roles. George II could fly off the handle but could write a good love letter, while Caroline, fat and funny, was the cleverest queen consort ever to sit on the throne.

Frederick, Prince of Wales and his sisters. These are the three 'little princesses', Anne, Amelia and Caroline, whom George I snatched from their parents during the terrific quarrel of 1717. Goggle-eyed and musical Fred, so passionately hated by his parents, performs with his sisters in the garden of Kew Palace.

William Hogarth's painting of a theatrical performance, with Queen Caroline's younger daughters in the audience. The lady reaching down to the floor is Mary Deloraine. She was a later mistress of George II's: sad, selfish and a hopeless alcoholic.

John Hervey, holding his ceremonial purse of office as Lord Privy Seal. He was the vice-chamberlain of the court and had many vices, including chronic indiscretion. He abandoned his beautiful wife Molly in favour of an unhappy series of male lovers.

John Hervey's letter book has had thirteen pages mysteriously cut out. A prudish Victorian descendant probably wished to destroy the evidence of his affairs with men.

Peter the Wild Boy's collar shows his name and address so that strangers could bring him home.

The strangest royal love triangle in history. In one corner, Queen Caroline. In later life the immensity of her bosom was legendary. When she sat for this portrait in 1735, aged 52, she was already suffering in secret from the umbilical hernia of which she would die two years later.

Henrietta Howard at the age of 35. Beautiful, melancholy and hard-of-hearing, she was both Queen Caroline's servant and King George II's mistress. She maintained this delicate balancing act for many years, but at high cost to her sense of self-worth and integrity.

George II in old age, standing at the top of the King's Grand Staircase at Kensington. In this portrait he looks kindly and relaxed, quite unlike his younger tempestuous self. He became rather sentimental in his old age, once he'd lost everyone he'd ever loved.

would form in centuries to follow. They believed that their sexuality formed no part of their public personas. Yet John Hervey and Ste Fox nevertheless shared a physical relationship that would in modern terms be considered homosexual, for at least some of the many years of their friendship. Hervey wrote of 'favours' or bruises received from Ste, 'written in such lasting character upon every limb, that 'tis impossible for me to look on a leg or an arm, without having my memory refreshed'.[72]

They had to be careful to keep their relationship secret. In the eyes of a contemporary pamphlet-writer, men kissing men, even in polite greeting, was a 'detestable' practice.[73] In the eyes of the law, sodomy was still punishable by death. The over-articulate John Hervey often expressed his love in letters and lived in constant fear of being discovered through a written indiscretion. He warned Ste Fox that a recent letter 'had been opened, as every one I have written or received since I came to England has been; so take care what you say'.[74]

While copies of many of the letters sent by Hervey to his Ste survive, some of their number have been mysteriously removed from Hervey's letter book.[75] This was probably because of their sexually explicit content, and likewise there is a curious gap in John Hervey's memoirs.

Hervey himself never published this work. Usually known as *Some Materials Towards Memoirs of the Reign of King George II*, it remained in manuscript form for a century after his death. He started to write in 1733, first going back in time to cover events since 1727. The text covering the period from May 1730 to the late summer of 1732, during which his relationship with Prince Frederick was at its closest, is the very part that's mysteriously missing.

The excision and destruction of these pages of the original manuscript is usually blamed on a prudish nineteenth-century descendant of John Hervey's, the first Marquess of Bristol. He's thought to have removed all references to a homosexual relationship in order to protect the family reputation. It was he who authorised the publication of a sanitised version of the memoirs in 1848.

If this is true, who was the other man in the relationship that John Hervey described? There's a very strong case that it was none other than Prince Frederick himself.

In 1780, Horace Walpole reported gossip that Hervey's son had banned the publication of his father's papers in order 'to prevent disagreeable truths appearing' with regard to Frederick, Prince of Wales.[76]

And some historians argue that the few letters between Hervey and Prince Frederick which do survive from the period of the 'missing' memoirs are highly suggestive. In them Frederick refers to himself and Hervey as 'Orestes' and 'Philades', inseparable friends, and Hervey casts himself as 'Hephaistion' to Frederick's 'Alexander' (a well-known same-sex couple), choices that tell their own tale of love and lovers.[77]

Among John Hervey's circle of witty, often married male friends there was nothing particularly unusual about having a short but intense physical relationship. A discreet, close male friendship would not automatically become subject to suspicion until the nineteenth century. What was less acceptable, and what would have invited condemnation if more widely known, was the possibility that Prince Frederick had an exclusive male favourite. The phenomenon of the favourite had been feared and despised throughout history, so the real reason for secrecy was this, plus the fear of public prosecution. The aristocracy's private moral code would have found nothing wrong.

Caroline later scolded her favourite for having hoped to draw lasting nourishment from his relationship with her unreliable son. She thought John Hervey ridiculously foolish 'for having ever loved him' and for thinking 'that he had been ever beloved'.[78]

By December 1731, whatever affection there may have been between 'Alexander' and 'Hephaistion' had clearly soured. 'That fool 7 [Frederick, according to their agreed cipher] plagues my heart out,' John Hervey complained to Ste Fox. 'He is false, too, as he is silly.'[79] Maybe he was bored with the puppyish prince, or maybe this was hurt pride speaking if Prince Frederick had been the one to break off the relationship.

And Frederick clearly came nowhere near to Ste's privileged position in John Hervey's heart. Even in the affectionate phase of his relationship with the prince, Hervey wrote to Stephen that

> when I said I wish'd I loved 7 as well as I do you, I lied egregiously; I am as incapable of wishing to love anybody else so well . . . God forbid any mortal should ever have the power over me you have . . . since I first knew you I have been without repenting and still am and ever shall be undividedly and indissolubly yours.[80]

Molly Hervey, meanwhile, had to accept that she would never again be 'undividedly and indissolubly' her husband's. While Ste and her spouse were jaunting round Italy together in 1728 in search of a cure for John Hervey's gall-bladder complaint, Molly wrote a pitiful letter to Ste, timidly asking for an honest account of the invalid. It is painful to see the poised and polished Molly reduced to asking her husband's lover for news, afraid that Ste will think her very troublesome, begging for information about John's health and requesting that he 'mayn't know' about her letter for fear of her being a bother.[81]

Molly was last heard of by us taking a tour of France while John Hervey was taken up with Anne Vane, and in fact in France she would find something like salvation.

She began to spend increasing amounts of time there, an eccentricity which embarrassed her children. She started to pick up lofty French mannerisms and to behave with 'a foreign tinge, which some call affected'.[82] She sometimes came back to court during her periodic returns from the continent. Regulars at the palace drawing room were once actually disappointed that she appeared there 'drest quite English' and had 'not much more paint on, than usual'.[83]

Molly's drawing-room manner, always so problematic, continued to disguise her uncertainty and shyness: 'I affect an air of grandeur which does not suit my stature, and makes me appear haughty and disdainful.'[84] At least her proud habit of reserve prevented her from gaining a reputation as a loose woman as well as an abandoned wife: 'her total, real indifference to mankind has prevented her ever having a lover. For I am sure it was not love to her lord that prevented her.'[85]

Abroad, alone and now estranged from her old employers in the Hanoverian court, Molly felt freer to expose the Stuart-supporting sympathies which came naturally to her. She'd had to keep these deeply buried while in Caroline's employment, but now it began to be said that 'notwithstanding her constant close connexion with the old court, she was, at heart and in opinion, a zealous Jacobite'.[86]

Like the other great English eccentric, Lady Mary Wortley Montagu, who found peace at last in an Italian garden, Molly Hervey was simply too extraordinary for a limited life in London.

Her extraordinary husband, meanwhile, continued as Vice-Chamberlain at court, where his sexual preferences were tacitly tolerated. Sir Andrew Fontaine, one of Caroline's Vice-Chamberlains, was equally welcome at court despite having been accused of effeminate vices by both Tobias Smollett and Alexander Pope.[87]

But John Hervey's frail and increasingly effete appearance meant that he was vulnerable to damaging speculation about his sexuality. His girlish face was painted to cover up the scar left by an operation to remove a tumour, he was infamous for his light verse and he constantly chatted with the court ladies almost as one of their own number. His enemies began to call him 'Lord Fanny'.

What would have made London life impossible for Hervey were public accusations of homosexual acts. Indeed, back in 1731, again during the time of the missing memoirs, such accusations had led to another close comrade nearly killing him in a duel.

John Hervey's relationship with the rival politician William Pulteney, formerly a great friend, turned nasty when their previously political disputes became personal. They had been fighting a lively and enjoyable duel of words through a series of anonymous pamphlets. But Pulteney went too far. He referred to Hervey in print as 'Mr *Fainlove*', 'a *delicate Hermaphrodite*' and a 'pretty, little, *Master-Miss*'.[88] Hervey was forced to insist that the debate be continued with drawn swords in Green Park. They met there early in the misty morning of 25 January 1731. At first they seemed evenly matched and each of them managed to wound the other. But Pulteney gained the advantage, and their seconds intervened just before he gave Hervey a fatal blow.

So John Hervey's honour was sadly dented. Much to the detriment of his lasting reputation, Pulteney's insinuations were also repeated and exaggerated by Alexander Pope. The poet created the renowned and enduring picture of John Hervey as a noxious queen:

> His wit all see-saw between *that* and *this*,
> Now high, now low, now Master up, now Miss,
> And he himself one vile antithesis:
> Amphibious thing! that acting either part,
> The trifling head, or the corrupted heart,
> Fop at the toilet, flatt'rer at the board,
> Now trips a Lady, and now struts a Lord.[89]

The savagery of this caricature is breathtaking and – fair or not – it set the tone of how Hervey would be remembered in future centuries.

This spat with Alexander Pope also had its origin in sexual matters, for long ago Pope himself had been among John Hervey's rivals for Molly's heart. He thought that Hervey, having been fortunate enough to win the hand of the court's beloved *Schatz*, had behaved criminally in tossing aside such a wondrous treasure.

Prince Frederick, homosexual or not, managed to get his wife Augusta pregnant, and the tangled ties between him, his family and John Hervey tightened towards their crisis in 1737.

As she began to pick up English, Princess Augusta became one of the more popular members of a tarnished royal family, but often found herself in the role of pawn rather than princess. She was drawn into disputes about palace access and etiquette. Caroline, for example, sent orders that Augusta must use a secondary entrance to the chapel, because the princess had caused great inconvenience in 'crowding by the Queen'. Prince Frederick therefore commanded his wife to stay away from the chapel altogether. On this occasion he disdained to argue because he was saving his energy to dispute his allowance instead.[90]

But never was Princess Augusta more at the mercy of her quarrelsome new family's rivalries than upon the night her labour pains began. Queen Caroline and Prince Frederick had very different ideas about the location and circumstances in which her baby would be born.

On the evening of Sunday, 31 July 1737, Princess Augusta, her husband and her parents-in-law were at Hampton Court Palace, where they had all spent the summer. Caroline was determined to be present when Augusta gave birth to her grandchild, although she suspected that her son might well attempt to prevent it. 'At her labour I positively will be,' Caroline was heard to say, 'let her lie-in where she will; for she cannot be brought to bed as quick as one can blow one's nose and I will be sure it is her child.'[91]

The evening began like any other, hot and humid, as it was the 'warmest season that anybody now alive remembers to have felt'.[92] Evenings with George II were a particularly trying time of day. On this particular Sunday, the royal family had spent the morning at chapel, had 'dined afterwards in publick, as usual, before a great number of spectators', and had then retired to their private apartments for their usual hours of twilight entertainment, if 'entertainment' is the right word for something so humdrum and predictable.[93]

George II, Caroline and their close circle were by now accustomed to tamer pleasures than the wild parties they'd enjoyed in their younger years. 'At night the King plays at commerce and backgammon, and the Queen at quadrille,' writes John Hervey.

> The Duke of Grafton takes his nightly opiate of lottery, and sleeps as usual between the Princesses Amelia and Caroline; Lord Grantham strolls from one room to another (as Dryden says) *like some discontented ghost that oft appears and is forbid to speak* . . . At last the King comes up, the pool finishes, and everybody has their dismissal: their Majesties retire.[94]

But John Hervey, the favourite, was not allowed to escape even then, when the formal part of the evening was over. He would spend the hours between nine and eleven in the queen's dressing room. Here Caroline would sit 'yawning' over her needlework, while George II would take a candle and recite to Hervey the subjects of all the pictures on the walls in their fine gilt frames. Hervey, while 'peeping over His Majesty's shoulder' at the paintings, would also be 'shrugging up his own, and now and then stealing a look to make faces at the Queen', who was 'a little angry, and little peevish, and a little tired' with her husband's endless soliloquies.[95]

On this particular evening, with a day of exhausting public appearances in the chapel and dining room over at last, everyone eventually began to prepare for bed, candles were snuffed and silence fell.

Then – at 7 o'clock according to some accounts, at 11 o'clock according to others – things began to happen.

The trigger was Princess Augusta's waters breaking. She could have now expected midwives to be summoned, pans of water heated, clean linen put onto her bed and the necessary witnesses – the queen, members of the Privy Council – to be called.

But none of this took place. Prince Frederick, with a callous disregard for the health of his eighteen-year-old wife and unborn child, insisted instead on bundling Augusta through her bedchamber door and down the stairs. He wanted her out from under his parents' roof before the baby was born.

To get the wailing princess to descend to the waiting coach, Frederick pushed from behind, while his dancing master and one of his equerries pulled at each of her arms. Meanwhile, Lady Archibald Hamilton, one of Princess Augusta's ladies, begged 'for God's sake' that 'the Prince would let her stay in quiet where she was, for that her pains were so great she could not set one foot before the other, and was upon the rack when they moved her'.[96]

Considering the complicated nature of royal households, it comes as no surprise to learn that Lady Archibald Hamilton was another old flame of Prince Frederick's. But her pleas on Princess Augusta's behalf were in vain. The prince insisted that his wife be packed into the vehicle with Mrs Clavering and Mrs Paine, two of her dressers, while Vreid, his faithful valet and a trained surgeon, sat on the box. They now drove hazardously through the night to St James's Palace.

Prince Frederick would later put it about that it was at Princess Augusta's own 'earnest request' that they rushed away from Hampton Court. The journey was absolutely necessary, he claimed, because 'there was neither midwife, nor linen, nor nurse at Hampton Court', while all things were available in London.[97]

And it was certainly true that Frederick was an anxious and jumpy father-to-be: in the weeks before the birth, he had been 'twice or thrice in town to get advice of his physicians, and Mrs Cannon, the midwife'.[98] They'd assured him that the intermittent pains Princess Augusta was feeling were caused only by colic. He may have married her in order to increase his allowance, but the prince did have tender feelings towards his wife.

But nobody was fooled by this explanation that the journey resulted from the fears of a 'wise and tender' husband concerned for his wife's safety: it was 'far from truth'.[99] Indeed, nothing could have been less likely than Princess Augusta herself choosing to endure her first labour in a coach, and 'she cried and begged not to be carried away in her painful condition'.[100]

Her husband's tetchy reply was, 'Come, come, all will be soon over,' and 'Courage! Courage! Ah, quelle sottise! [Ah, what foolishness!]'[101] Prince Frederick was absolutely determined that he would deny his detested parents their privilege of witnessing the birth of an heir.

The smuggling of the pregnant princess out of the palace took place while Caroline and George II's evening was winding down, and the king and queen remained completely unaware of the commotion. As John Hervey described it, all was 'just as usual' until they separated 'at ten of the clock; and, what is incredible to relate, went to bed all at eleven, without hearing one single syllable of the Princess's being ill, or even of her not being in the house'.[102]

For once Prince Frederick had managed to seize the initiative in the battle with his parents. In his desperation to make an impression on his implacable father, he willingly risked two lives. 'Had he no way of affronting his parents but by venturing to kill his wife and the heir of the crown?' was one verdict on this adventure. 'A baby that wounds itself to vex its nurse is not more void of reflection.'[103]

The journey in the coach must have been frightful. They covered the fifteen bumpy miles in only an hour and a quarter,[104] and Prince Frederick and the three ladies had to hold down the screaming princess. (Frederick later complained that the force he'd been compelled to use had given him a terrible ache in his back.) They were 'oblig'd to stop several times whilst she took her pains', a treatment considered most 'cruel' by those who heard of it afterwards.[105] While they were on the road, Frederick dispatched messengers to Chiswick and Lambeth to fetch Lord Wilmington and the Archbishop of Canterbury, the most convenient members of the Privy Council. He needed witnesses to the birth.[106]

Although they thrust many handkerchiefs up Princess Augusta's petticoats, her skirts were slowly soaked with 'the filthy inundations which attend these circumstances'. When the coach eventually reached St James's Palace, Prince Frederick ordered all the lights to be put out so that the servants there could not see this gruesome evidence of 'his folly and her distress'.[107]

Of course, nothing at St James's was prepared, so they had to
send out to the neighbours for napkins, warming pans and other
'necessary implements' for the operation of birth.[108] One account
of the evening presents the ludicrous spectacle of Prince Frederick
and Lady Archibald Hamilton together airing the sheets for
Princess Augusta's bed, which turned out to be damp, forcing
them to use tablecloths instead.[109] Arriving all of a sudden, the little baby – 'about the bigness of a good large toothpick case' – had
to be wrapped in a napkin.[110]

In a final touch of farce, the official witnesses arrived too late,
the Archbishop fifteen minutes after the child was born.

The baby princess, to be named Augusta like her mother, was
born at about eleven or midnight (accounts vary), and a messenger bearing the news was immediately sent post-haste to
Hampton Court.

There must have been much anxious discussion among the
queen's servants before, at half past one in the morning, Caroline
was woken by her Bedchamber Woman Charlotte Amelia
Titchborne. Caroline's first thought was that the palace must be
on fire. But no, Mrs Titchborne explained, it was just that Princess
Augusta's labour had begun.

The queen called for her nightgown, expecting to go to her
daughter-in-law's apartment a few metres away. 'Your nightgown,
Madam,' replied Mrs Titchborne, 'and your coaches too; the
Princess is at St James's.' 'Are you mad?' Caroline interrupted, 'or
are you asleep, my good Titchborne?'

All was soon explained, and the eruption of George II's wrath
when he heard what had happened must have been one of the
most spectacular ever.

Baulked from being present at the actual birth, Caroline was
anxious to get there as soon as possible afterwards. Very grim and
sober, she called for her coach and for John Hervey, and together
they drove off to St James's in a kind of tragicomic chase. Of
course, no one at St James's Palace was expecting them, so when

they arrived Caroline had to sit waiting in the dark 'till a footman was found who had a candle and lighted her up to the Princess's apartment'.[III]

Upstairs in Princess Augusta's rooms Caroline found the baby girl wrapped in table linen. 'God bless you, poor little creature!' the old queen said to her granddaughter. 'You have come into a disagreeable world.'[II2] This was a rare and brief moment for grandmother and baby to bond, a tiny lull in the war between the generations.

After drinking hot chocolate with John Hervey, Caroline departed from St James's at about 4 o'clock in the morning. Back at Hampton Court she found her husband still 'in an infinite passion' at Prince Frederick's sneaking away with 'no notice to him or the Queen of his design'.[II3]

The king's terrible tantrum continued all the next day, and a courtier returning to the palace to begin a week on duty 'found all the folks here in a comical sort of way, with their being call'd up in the night'. Information about what had actually happened was hard to come by: 'everybody here being dealers in mysteries', while 'all the sycophants and agents of the Court spread millions of falsities'.[II4]

But everybody agreed that this was indisputably an act of war.

This action of Prince Frederick's was more than a foolish risk taken with his child's life; it was a deliberate piece of the most extreme provocation. Nothing could have been calculated to give more offence than tricking George II and Caroline into missing the birth of their grandchild by whisking their daughter-in-law away from the palace without a word. The king 'swells, struts and storms' with rage, wrote one courtier.[II5]

Over the next few weeks, Caroline steadfastly visited her granddaughter at St James's, but observers noticed that she never addressed her son, nor he her. When his mother was leaving the palace, though, Prince Frederick took advantage of the crowd of spectators in the courtyard to sink ostentatiously to his knees, 'down in the dirt', and to kiss her hand with a false but 'most respectful show of duty'.[116]

He was not the only one acting a part in order to win the war for public approval. Despite her gruelling night-time journey and repeated visits to her daughter-in-law, Caroline too admitted privately that 'one does not care a farthing for them, the giving oneself all this trouble is *une bonne grimace pour le publique* [putting on a good show for the public]'.

After several solicitous visits she could bear it no longer. George II was glad that she stopped going, telling her she was 'well enough served for thrusting her nose where it had been shit upon already'.[117]

Part of the reason for Caroline and George II's fury was their obsessive suspicion that they might have had a fraudulent heir thrust into their family, a fear that had been rife in royal circles since the birth of James II's son, the Old Pretender, in 1688. George II and Caroline were worried that Prince Frederick, by arranging for Princess Augusta to give birth in private, might have likewise introduced an impostor. 'A false child will be put upon you,' the king thundered at the queen.

Having seen Augusta's baby girl, though, Caroline did not suspect her son of having planted someone else's child upon her. 'I own to you, I had my doubts upon the road that there would be some juggle,' she said to John Hervey later, and 'if, instead of this poor, little ugly she-mouse, there had been a brave, large, fat, jolly boy, I should not have been cured of my suspicions'.[118]

Now it was openly acknowledged that 'the two Courts of the King and the Prince, over which a cloud has hung for some time', were 'at last quite separated by a storm that has broken out upon the lying-in of the Princess'.[119] A stand-off through the medium of letters commenced, just as it had in the 'christening quarrel' of 1717.

Prince Frederick fired off a volley of what he thought were submissive missives apologising for his behaviour, but it was inevitable that his parents failed to find them sufficiently remorseful.

On 5 August 1737, Hervey wearily reported to Ste Fox's brother Henry (also an old friend) that 'yesterday's letter' from Prince Frederick to George II 'was to desire earnestly to be re-admitted into the King's presence, protesting the uprightness of his intentions, and not owning himself in the wrong at any step'. It gave offence for including 'not a word *of* or *to* the Queen'. The king's answer was that 'as the purport of the letter was the same as that which Lord Jersey brought the night before, it required no other answer than what had been given to that'.

Poor John Hervey understandably complained that he was 'tired to death of hearing nothing but this sort of stuff over and over again; it *ennuies* me to a degree that is inconceivable'. 'I shall see you tomorrow,' he wrote to Henry Fox, 'and I suppose you, not being so tired of the subject as I am, will make me talk it all over again.'[120]

In the earlier 'christening quarrel' George II had been kicked out of the royal palaces, and now he found himself expelling his son in exactly the same manner. On 12 September, the order went out to 'all peers, peeresses, Privy Councillors and their ladies and persons in any station in the service of ye King and Queen that whoever goes to pay their court to their Royal Highnesses the prince or princess of Wales will not be admitted into their Majesty's presence'.[121]

Meanwhile, just as before, 'whoever was unwelcome at St James's, was sure of countenance at the Prince's apartments'.[122] Again the courtiers had to choose their allegiance, and one of them found this 'melancholy prospect' made him 'almost burst into tears'.[123] The doomsayers inevitably predicted the end for the House of Hanover: with all these silly quarrels, the crown would 'be lost long before this little Princess can possibly enjoy it'.[124]

So Prince Frederick, Princess Augusta and their servants prepared to leave St James's Palace for the last time, their clothes hurriedly tossed into wicker laundry baskets rather than being properly packed.[125] The soldier on gate duty was one among the many who found themselves torn in two at the sight. He'd been

ordered by his captain 'not to salute the Prince on his departure
(for the King had given that command)'. He would have saluted
anyway, had not the eagle eye of his captain been 'particularly on
him'. The salute was left unmade while 'the tears trickled' down
his cheeks.[126]

Now George II deployed exactly the same weapons against his
son as his own father had used in earlier years. Prince Frederick's
cohort of official guards was withdrawn, so that he and Princess
Augusta were forced to creep out of the house 'like private people',
with a mere footman to attend them.[127] During the preceding
quarrel, George II had retired from St James's to Leicester Fields.
Extraordinarily, his son would also eventually settle down in the
very same house, earning it the nickname of the 'pouting-place of
princes'.[128] Kew Gardens also became a more frequent rural residence for the prince.

But there was one big difference between the quarrels of 1717
and 1737. Despite his numerous supporters, Prince Frederick was
never remotely likely to win a popularity contest against his father.
George II and Caroline were considerably more beloved by their
subjects than George I had been.

Frederick may have had wit, charm, a healthy young family and
the prospect of great future power, yet he lost something
immensely valuable by his rash act: his reputation. His good qualities were now submerged beneath the deluge of condemnation
that was poured upon him for his selfish insubordination. As a
result of this, history would come to remember him as a failure,
hated by his parents, damned by the poisonous pen of John
Hervey.

Yet weak, foolish Frederick – appropriately nicknamed 'Poor
Fred' by historians – was really something of a victim. He felt
forced by his parents' revulsion into taking this desperate step, but
in doing so he only confirmed their low opinion of him.

As the weeks turned into months, though, Frederick began to
think regretfully about the wrong turns taken in his relationship
with his mother. Perhaps having a child of his own made him

begin to take a more tolerant view of his parents' behaviour. Slowly, secretly but surely, he started longing to see Caroline once again.

But the period of time left for any possible reconciliation to take place was shorter than anyone could have guessed.

EIGHT

The Queen's Secret

'May Caroline continue long
For ever fair and young! – in song.
. . . the royal carcass must,
Squeezed in a coffin, turn to dust."
(Jonathan Swift)

The appalling family wounds of summer 1737 remained unhealed that autumn, and Caroline was still eaten up with hatred for her son.

But the next conflict at court would be fought between mightier forces than the warring royals. A battle between eighteenth-century medicine and mortality was about to begin, and the scene of the struggle was to be the bed of the weakened queen.

Her fight for life would take place back at St James's Palace, which was still in the same unsatisfactory condition as it was when the Hanoverians first came to England. Foreigners considered that there were 'few Princes in Europe worse lodged than the

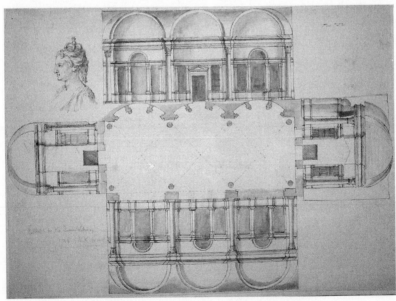

Caroline's 'room of her own': the library William
Kent designed for her at St James's Palace

King of England', and once the royal family was temporarily forced out of the palace by the 'stench of a necessary house' belonging to the tavern next door.[2]

After many trying years as queen, the balance of Caroline's life had shifted and was now weighted towards despair. By the later 1730s, she was feeling neglected by her husband as well as her son. As time went by, George II's summer holidays in Hanover grew longer and longer, so much so that his family and his adoptive British subjects felt that they hardly saw him at all. Caroline constantly dwelt upon her failures as a wife and a mother: 'her Majesty is exceeding uneasy and often weeps when alone'.[3]

Caroline decided to comfort herself during one of the king's unaccountable extended absences by beginning to build herself a new library at St James's Palace. This was to be a room of her own, a consolation; it was a private project that would be of no conceivable interest to her husband. And it was not surprising that she turned for soothing discussions about the necessary decoration to the jovial and familiar William Kent.

Together they agreed upon a rich cornice, twenty-one bookcases, busts of philosophers and green couches trimmed with silver lace.[4] In her library, this peaceful and private place, Caroline planned to cure her cares with literature. She was certainly fond of

William Kent doodled this lovely portrait of the mature Queen Caroline at the edge of his page. She stoically insisted that she minded her husband's infidelities 'no more than his going to the close stool'

her three thousand books: on various occasions we hear of her laughing at *Gulliver's Travels*; listening to literature read aloud during the tedious hours at her toilette; and sending out a Lady of the Bedchamber to get her 'all my Lord Bacon's works'.[5]

Caroline was impatient to put her temple of learning to use, and John Hervey was annoyed when the builders promised her unachievable progress. He wrote crossly to Henry Fox, who'd recently been put in charge of the unimproved and still inefficient Office of the King's Works: 'which of the devils in Hell prompted you to tell the Queen that everything in her Library was ready for the putting up of her books? – Thou abominable new broom, that so far from sweeping clean, has not removed one grain of dirt.'[6]

It was in her unfinished library, on 9 November 1737, during her fifty-fifth year, that Caroline collapsed to the floor with an unbearable pain in her stomach.

What are we to make of the many and varied dispatches from the front line of Caroline's battle with death, penned over the next few days as the whole nation waited with baited breath and snapped up every crumb of information available?

John Hervey's account of the following week of Caroline's life, covering the progress of her illness, is the great set piece of his memoirs, the most memorable, most melodramatic and blackest of all his sketches of court events.

Although it is Hervey's horrifically gory account that has become the best known, other contemporary descriptions of Caroline's illness were more reverent, noting that she bore pain 'like a heroine' and with 'a Christian firmness and resignation of mind'.[7] And indeed the minor but telling details of the next few days would make a great impression upon the nation: 'these little circumstances are too trivial in themselves to relate, but when they concern the last moments of Princes, are to be taken notice of'.[8]

All the accounts of Caroline's final few days, whether sensational or instructional, agreed that this uniquely testing time would reveal her 'greatness of soul'.[9] The queen would find her greatest strength in her weakest hour.

Despite the public's unquenchable thirst for information, royal health was surrounded by secrecy. George II took great pains to disguise any chink of weakness, and John Hervey noted

> a strange affectation of an incapacity of being sick that ran through the whole Royal Family . . . I have known the King get out of his bed, choking with a sore throat, and in a high fever, only to dress and have a *levée*, and in five minutes undress and return to his bed.[10]

There were actually very good reasons for the king to maintain even a 'ridiculous farce of health'. If the news of an illness leaked out, it would 'disquiet the minds of his subjects, hurt public credit, and diminish the regard and duty which they owe him'.[11]

Earlier in 1737, George II had suffered horribly from haemorrhoids, and he'd eventually undergone the painful operation to have them cut out. He had endured 'violent inflammation and swelling', and 'his surgeon was forced to attend him with alternate applications of lancets and fomentations'.[12] The king could not bear to speak of his humiliating illness. He dismissed his solicitous servants as 'troublesome, inquisitive puppies' who were 'always plaguing him with asking impertinent, silly questions about his health like so many old nurses'.[13]

Caroline also suffered from the necessity of having to be present and correct in the drawing room whatever the circumstances. In the past her health had often given cause for concern. At one court occasion, 'she found herself so near swooning' that she had to send a message 'to the King to beg he would retire, for she was unable to stand any longer'. That night he nevertheless made her go to a ball, and kept her there until eleven.[14]

Peter Wentworth, standing and watching from the sidelines as usual, frequently found his heart smarting with concern for Caroline's heroic fortitude. He described how he was 'often in great pain for my good Queen, but it is not the fashion to show any [weakness] at Court'. After another, earlier illness, he over-heard her telling another courtier 'that she had really been very bad and dangerously ill'. It was her own fault, Caroline said, for she'd kept her fever a secret and soldiered on with her social duties. 'She owned she did wrong,' Wentworth recalled, and she promised that 'she would do so no more, upon which I made her a bow, as much as to say, I hoped she would do as she then said. I believe she understood me for she smiled upon me.'[15]

The pain that Caroline felt in her new library, though, was too severe for her to deceive anyone: a vicious cramp in her stomach accompanied by 'violent vomiting'. Her doctors eventually resorted to Sir Walter Raleigh's Cordial. This powerful sedative made from alcohol and a compound of forty different roots and herbs 'gave her some ease, and was the only thing stayed with her . . . She continued all night so ill that the King, the Duke and Princesses sat up with her.'[16]

Like Peter Wentworth, Sir Robert Walpole hoped that Caroline's collapse would force her to begin to take better care of herself. The day after her attack in the library, he spent an anxious hour begging her to be careful, saying, 'Madam, your life is of such consequence to your husband, to your children, to this country, and indeed to many other countries, that any neglect of your health is really the greatest immorality you can be guilty of.'

Only she could control the king, Walpole said, she alone held the reins 'by which it is possible to restrain the natural violences of his temper'.

'Should any accident happen to Your Majesty,' Sir Robert con-cluded, 'who can tell what would become of him, of your children, and of us all?'[17]

As the queen's battle against this mysterious stomach ailment commenced, she had the comfort of knowing herself to be a brave, if bloodied, warrior in the field of medicine, and she had previ-ously won some fabulous victories against the ignorance and con-servatism of contemporary doctors. She is most renowned, medically speaking, as a strong supporter of the practice of inoculating children against smallpox.

The mild discomfort of a few days of artificially induced illness was well worth it to avoid the full-blown version of a disease which had such a high risk of death. Smallpox first appeared as a red rash, then liquid-filled pustules gradually covered the sufferer's entire body. The mouth, eyes and even the sexual organs became so swollen that the patient couldn't be recognised and fought for breath as his or her throat and nose narrowed. After a week or so, the liquid in the pustules turned to yellow pus, and feverish delirium set in.

When the pustules burst they filled a sickroom with 'a stink so intolerable, that a thousand old rotten ulcers, with their united stench of Midsummer, could not equal it'. One medic reported that he'd put a vinegar-soaked sponge in his mouth as protection against the putrid smell, but even that was inadequate: 'as if struck with a thunder-bolt, I was instantly seiz'd with a trembling over my whole body'.[18]

If the patient survived the bursting of the pustules, the prognosis was good, for then they formed incredibly itchy but harmless scabs. These slowly flaked away, leaving behind brown and finally white permanent pits in the skin. The scarred survivors known to Caroline included her own daughter Princess Anne and Lady Mary Wortley Montagu (who'd lost her eyelashes to the disease).[19] And Caroline herself had suffered in her youth. It was said that she 'was esteemed handsome before she had the small-pox, and became too corpulent'.[20]

Meanwhile, far away in Asia, the secret to surviving smallpox safely had been discovered. Lady Mary Wortley Montagu, a former drawing-room regular, had travelled to the East as the wife of Britain's ambassador to the Turks. In Constantinople she'd learnt how to introduce a tiny amount of smallpox pus into a child's body to bring on a mild form of the disease, with the intention of immunising the adult against more virulent strains. The method to be followed was to take a child of any age under ten years old, the younger the better . . . and find out a person that is sick of a favourable sort. When the pustules are ripe . . . lance some of them, and receive the matter into a nut-shell, and carry it to the place where the child is. Then with a needle, that hath been dipt into this pocky-poison . . . prick the fleshy part of each arm and each thigh, deep enough to fetch blood. In a little time each of these punctures begins to inflame, and rises up into a great boil, which ripens, breaks, and discharges abundance of matter. About the seventh day the symptoms of the small-pox begin to appear [but] neither the life nor the beauty of the patient is in any danger.[21]

This technique – so completely counterintuitive – would never have caught on in England without the support of George II and, especially, of Caroline. It was probably Sir Hans Sloane, the royal doctor, who drew their attention to this remarkable new way of saving lives. At Caroline's request, George II allowed Sloane to try out inoculation on a group of prisoners awaiting execution in Newgate Jail. They were promised freedom if they survived the experiment.

The positive results convinced Caroline that the treatment was good enough for her to give it the ultimate seal of approval: she had her own children – Princesses Amelia, Caroline, Mary and Louisa – inoculated.[22]

This news was widely publicised, and the same edition of the newspaper announcing Peter the Wild Boy's arrival at court in 1726 also informed its readers that 'last Saturday night the Princess Mary was inoculated for the small pox'.[23] Other court mothers including Mrs Titchborne followed Caroline's example and had their children treated too.[24] Sarah Osborn described her own son's intense misery during the experience: 'his swelling under his arm is still open'.[25]

Inoculation was, and remained, deeply controversial. In Paris, the Duchess of Orléans confessed that she was 'worried a great deal' by Caroline's proceedings. 'If my children were quite well I couldn't possibly steel myself to make them ill,' she admitted. 'My doctor doesn't think this remedy is safe, he says he doesn't understand it.'[26]

Nevertheless, it was soon reported at the British court that 'the three young Princesses' were seen dancing, 'which is a sign they got over their inoculating very well'.[27] A doctor was dispatched to Hanover, where the young Prince Frederick was still living, in order to inject the heir to the throne. He complained heartily about the 'soreness all over his skin' from the 500 pustules he developed. Yet he was still able to crack jokes and to eat baked rice pudding with a good appetite.[28]

These events, widely reported in the press, sent out a powerful message about the modern, enlightened nature of the Georgian monarchy. Opponents of inoculation often took the line that it was bound to fail, associated as it was with foreigners (the Turks) and females (Lady Mary Wortley Montagu). Indeed, one senior doctor thought it extraordinary that 'an experiment practiced only by a few *ignorant women*, amongst an illiterate and unthinking people' should suddenly be 'receiv'd into the *Royal Palace*'.[29] And its adoption or rejection by doctors tended to follow political lines: Dr Arbuthnot, Peter the Wild Boy's tutor, was the single exception to the rule that all Tory doctors were against inoculation.[30]

Their support of medical science differentiated George II and Caroline from the exiled Stuart claimants to the throne. The Stuarts, as mystical, divinely appointed monarchs, believed that the power to heal lay in the very touch of their hands. Sufferers of the illness called scrofula, a disorder of the glands, had queued for hours to be 'touched' by the seventeenth-century Stuart kings and queens in hope of relief.

While the Stuarts had claimed to cure through a kind of magic, the Georgian kings trusted science instead. Unlike the Pretender, George II would never be found 'touching' victims of scrofula. This was of incalculable significance. In the seventeenth century, people used simply to hope that divine providence would cure their ills; now they began to place themselves in the hands of doctors and scientists.[31]

Despite these steps forward, eighteenth-century doctors could still be violent and misguided, doing more harm than good. Many of them continued to think that sickness was the result of an imbalance in the body's four constituent 'humours' – black bile, choler, phlegm and blood – so purges of the digestive system, morphine-based drugs and bleeding to restore a supposedly lost equilibrium remained the commonest medical treatments.

In reality, bleeding sapped the body of strength and much-needed oxygen. Caroline herself was drained of no less than 'thirty ounces of blood' during the first twenty-four hours of her illness.[32] And the treatments she was given would continue to suggest that Georgian doctors could do more harm than good.

Caroline fell ill on Wednesday 9 November, but it wasn't until 4 o'clock in the morning of the following Saturday that her doctors finally worked out what was wrong with her. Until then they could come up with no better explanation of her illness than 'gout in the stomach'. Diagnosis was made all the more difficult because of their customary lack of permission to examine her body, and they were doubly confounded by a conspiracy of silence about a dread secret.

No one had seen Caroline naked for over ten years. Part of the reason for this was the eighteenth-century habit of wearing a shift practically all the time, even in the bath. Yet Caroline also had a grotesque problem with her stomach that she'd taken care to keep to herself and only a very few others.

It was her husband who finally gathered the strength to be honest with the royal doctors, breaking a promise he had made to his wife and overcoming his scruples about invading her privacy.

Now, because 'the King absolutely insisted upon it', she admitted that for many years she'd had 'a rupture under her navel'.[33]

This rupture, or hernia, was caused by Caroline's last pregnancy, and her whole medical history was full of the frightening incidents attendant upon the need to secure the future of the dynasty by providing heirs.

Her obstetric troubles had begun more than thirty years previously, soon after her marriage in 1705. Following the wedding, her husband had revealed a desire to go to war, but it was reported that the 'Court is against it, and will not give their consent to let him go into the field till he has children'.[34]

From the very beginning of her married life, Caroline's duty to provide a son had been made more than clear.

Yet, in the early years, she had difficulty in fulfilling it. In January 1707, some sixteen over-long months after her marriage, Caroline finally appeared to be pregnant. But the court of Hanover had 'for some time past almost despaired' of her ever 'being brought to bed'. They feared that the bulge in her stomach was 'an effect of a distemper' rather than an unborn child.

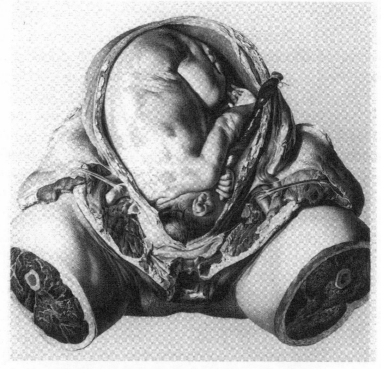

William Hunter's engraving of an unborn baby, 1752

However, Caroline was finally 'taken ill' one dinner time, and subsequently 'delivered of a son'.[35] This was Prince Frederick, who would cause so much trouble.

Working women found that breastfeeding their children for up to two years had a contraceptive effect that allowed them to space out their pregnancies. But no one had the slightest notion that Caroline should breastfeed her children. Aristocratic or royal women, constantly under pressure to produce heirs, used wet nurses instead. As a result, they could find themselves almost continually pregnant. John Hervey's mother, the Countess of Bristol, had seventeen children, of whom only eleven survived beyond babyhood.

Princess Anne followed Frederick two years later, and Caroline's husband was greatly relieved that she'd made a second safe passage through the dangers of childbirth. 'The peace of my life', he wrote to her, 'depends upon knowing you in good health, and upon the conviction of your continued love for me. I shall endeavour to attract it by all imaginable passion.'[36] Princesses Amelia and Caroline followed in due course in 1711 and 1713 respectively.

In 1716, after she'd come to live in London, Caroline found the last stages of a difficult pregnancy made worse by the customary disputes about personnel and presence at the birth. For nine months she had been 'mightily out of order', 'extremely weak and subject to continual faintings'.[37] Endless streams of worriers came to wish her well. The back-stairs to her room were 'always so crowded' that it was hard to get through, and her Ladies of the Bedchamber were worn out with answering questions.

But even Caroline's precarious state of health had no effect upon the bickering German and English factions among her courtiers.[38]

When labour seemed imminent, the English ladies took against Caroline's German midwife. They 'all pressed to have the Princess laid by Sir David Hamilton' instead, but Caroline 'would not hear of it'.[39] The German midwife herself persuaded Caroline to keep the doctor at a distance and, significantly, encouraged 'the aversion of the Princess to have any man about her'.[40] It would be many years until the male accoucheur with his iron tongs was a fixture at babies' births.

Eventually, though, the German midwife lost her nerve. Daunted by her responsibilities, she 'refused to touch the Princess unless she and the Prince would stand by her against the English'. She said they were 'high dames, and had threatened to hang her if the Princess miscarried'.

Prince George Augustus, naturally enough, fell into such a frenzy at all this silly squabbling that he threatened to throw them all out of the window. But it was only several days later, with Caroline clearly 'in ye utmost danger', that the courtiers became frightened enough to quell their quarrels. A new and sombre tone emerged, with nothing 'talked of but the Princess's good labour and safety'.[41] The Ladies of the Bedchamber transformed their attitude towards the German midwife, 'squeezed her by the hand, and made kind faces at her: for she understood no language but German'.

But it was too late, and the labour went badly wrong. 'The poor Princess continued in a languishing condition till Friday night, when she was delivered of a dead Prince.'[42] The Duchess of Orléans was vastly relieved that Caroline at least had survived: 'I was very shocked that our dear Princess of Wales had such an unhappy lying-in, and cried bitterly, but God be praised that she is still alive and out of danger.'[43]

Only a year after her miscarriage of 1716, Caroline was ready to give birth again. On 2 November 1717, 'a little before six a clock in the evening' was born the short-lived baby, George William, whose christening had caused the disastrous division between George I and his son. On this occasion there was a considerable crowd present in the room:

His Royal Highness the Prince of Wales
The Lord Archbishop of Canterbury

The Duchesses of St Albans, Mountague and Shrewsbury
The Countess of Dorset
The Lady Inchinbroke
The Lady Cowper, being the Ladies of Her Royal Highness's Bed-
    Chamber
The Duchess of Monmouth
The Countess of Grantham
The Countess of Picbourg
The Governess of their Highnesses the young Princesses
All the Women of her Royal Highness's Bed-Chamber
Sir David Hamilton
and Dr Steigerdahl, physician to His Majesty.

That evening 'a universal joy was seen' among 'all sorts of people throughout London and Westminster, of which the greatest demonstrations were shown by ringing of bells, illuminations and bonfires'.[44]

When William Augustus, Duke of Cumberland was born in 1721, Caroline took the trouble to consult the authorities about who really had the right of admittance to her bedchamber. She was delighted to discover – despite rumour to the contrary – that 'neither the law, nor any rule or custom' decreed anything definite upon the subject of witnesses. The Lord Chancellor told her that she was 'at her perfect liberty to choose who she pleases to have present'.[45]

Prince William Augustus was followed by Princess Mary, and the arrival of Caroline's last daughter, Princess Louisa, in 1724 was accompanied by relief all round: 'we think it such a blessing her being safe & well that we don't repine at our not having a Prince'.[46] Each pregnancy was a major threat to life, and indeed in 1736 Caroline's own eldest daughter, Princess Anne, was 'so ill in labour that the midwife was forced to squeeze the child extremely to deliver her, which kill'd it'.[47]

Following the birth of Louisa, her last child, Caroline had suffered an umbilical rupture, or hernia. There's a natural weakness around the belly button in anyone's 'rectus sheath', or stomach muscles. In Caroline's case, repeated pregnancies had placed great pressure upon her stomach. As she grew older, and fatter, the muscles got weaker and a painful hernia, or hole, appeared.

This explains why Caroline's clothes accounts, which Henrietta had kept so carefully between 1730 and 1734, include payments for numerous whalebone hoops but only one set of stays, the waist-stiffening corset that would have been agonising to wear in the queen's condition. Understandably, Caroline much preferred the soft stays usually confined to casual dress or to pregnancy.[48]

Her condition came to a crisis in 1737 because a loop of her bowel had squeezed its way out through the hernia and become trapped there.[49] This had caused a blockage in her digestive system. Caroline preferred silence to revealing such an immodest, embarrassing problem, and 'kept this so great a secret that neither her children nor any of her servants who dress and put on her shift ever knew it'.[50] During the ceremony of dressing, Caroline had long been careful to divert suspicion by standing for 'some minutes in her shift talking to her ladies'.

Once the secret was out, various of Caroline's acts and words came to be seen in a new light. Sir Robert Walpole, for one, had some earlier suspicions confirmed. When Walpole's wife had died, Caroline had questioned him closely about her declining health, and time and time again had 'reverted to a rupture'. Walpole had rightly guessed that only a fellow sufferer could have taken such an interest in other people's hernias.[51]

'You lying fool,' said Caroline to her husband when she discovered that he'd revealed her secret, but now she could not escape Dr Ranby's examination. He insisted that she 'put her hand where the pain was' and, 'following her with his hand, found it was a very large rupture'.[52]

'There is no more time to be lost,' he said. 'Your Majesty has concealed it too long already.'[53]

And indeed the risk to Caroline's life had become much greater because the hernia was by now infected. It was whispered around the court that Caroline's 'rupture of the bowels' might have 'been easily reduced, if she had not delayed the disclosure of it till a mortification took place'.[54]

'Will it ever be believed', asked an exasperated Sir Robert Walpole, 'that a life of this importance . . . should be lost, or run thus near, by concealing human infirmities?'[55]

Caroline was not in the right state of health or mind to battle boldly against her affliction. She was by now, in 1737, worn out by gout, the pressure of making constant public appearances as queen and nine pregnancies. People said that she had been 'one of the most beautiful princesses of Europe' but that she had now 'grown too stout'.[56]

She could no longer walk because of her gouty feet and was rolled regally 'in and out of the Drawing Room every day' in a decorative wheelchair. (It had been originally made for a masque at Kensington Palace, and Lady Deloraine had used it to appear in the character of a 'Sea-Goddess'.[57]) Because she could no longer take her customary long walks, Caroline had grown so obese that she was afraid to turn herself in bed and had to be rolled over by a servant.[58]

She'd given birth to seven surviving children, and no more were planned. Contraception by the use of an animal-gut prophylactic, tied on with a silk ribbon, was certainly possible by this period, and '*Cundums*' were being sold in St James's Park in 1708.[59] (James Boswell described his first encounter 'in armour', with a seventeen-year-old prostitute in St James's Park, as providing only a 'dull satisfaction'.[60]) Instead of using contraception, though, George II simply abandoned Caroline in favour of other women.

In John Hervey's opinion, Caroline's silence about her hernia was not just due to modesty. It was also a refusal to face the fact that her sexual powers were in decline. She was dismayed to find that she was losing her sexual sway over the king, because 'power over him was the principal object of her pursuit'.[61] In the past Caroline had tolerated Henrietta and his other mistresses – his 'little corporeal excursions' – because he had always eventually grown weary of them and had returned to his wife with relief.[62]

For her part, Caroline had never been able to keep her hands off her husband and had 'the most extravagant fondness for his person'. After Princess Louisa's birth, she was far from considering herself freed from a distasteful task by no longer having to sleep with him. On the contrary, she deeply regretted her loss of pleasure.

Hervey records Sir Robert Walpole's very intimate conversations with Caroline, during which they freely discussed her fears about her declining sexual magnetism. Walpole advised her that 'she must not expect after thirty years' acquaintance, to have the same influence that she had formerly; that three-and-fifty and three-and-twenty could not more resemble one another in their effects than in their looks'. In fact, in his view, 'she should no longer depend upon her person, but her head, for her influence'.[63]

It sounds remarkable that John Hervey and Robert Walpole should describe and discuss the queen as a sexually voracious woman, but this was just before the important shift in the mid-eighteenth century, when attitudes towards female sexuality were transformed. Until this point, feminine desire was perceived as limitless, all-consuming and, in fact, downright dangerous to men. 'Women are by far more lascivious and more amorous than men,' it was confidently said, and indeed this was most worrying: 'how can a man be fit to do his duty . . . after being exhausted in excess of conjugal embraces?'[64]

The successive editions of the medical manual called *The Ladies Physical Directory* begin to reveal a change of attitude. First published in 1716, the text of the 1742 edition was amended to include a new paragraph in which it was now claimed that women were clearly 'of a much colder temperature than men, and of course much less inclin'd to venery'. Nor were they 'able to bear coition (to full satisfaction) half so often as men'.[65] This is one example of a wider alteration in attitudes, described by the historian A. D. Hervey as 'the waning of female lust'.[66]

Caroline was a member of the last generation of women to live before a curtain was drawn down over the female libido. For the rest of the eighteenth and nineteenth centuries, females were considered incapable of wanting or enjoying sex. By 1850, a writer in the *Westminster Review* could claim that men's 'sexual desire is inherent and spontaneous', while in women it is 'dormant, if not non-existent, till excited'. He thought that women whose 'position and education' protected them from encountering any 'exciting causes' would therefore never become sexually aroused.

'Happy for them that it is so!' was his conclusion.[67] Caroline would have found this as bizarre as it seems to twenty-first-century eyes.

But this seemingly retrogressive step was actually the result of scientific progress. Pre-Enlightenment doctors thought that women were just weaker versions of men and that their sexual organs (inside their bodies) were simply another version of what men had on the outside. For conception to take place, then, the female orgasm was thought absolutely necessary, just as the male orgasm was (and is). Once people began to understand that the female orgasm was *not* essential for conception, female sexual satisfaction became much less of a priority. That's why Victorian doctors doubted that females even experienced orgasms, whereas their predecessors had thought them a critical part of human reproduction.[68]

The waning of her sexual potential made the 1730s seem like dangerous days of decline for Caroline.

Yet the more the king neglected her, and the worse he treated her, the more respect and pity she earned from the people in general. Her heroism in bearing children and her toleration of the king's latest new mistress – a Hanoverian named Amalie von Wallmoden – elevated her to an almost saintly position in the eyes of her subjects. George II's image began to suffer as the 'ordinary and the godly people took the turn of pitying the poor Queen, and railing at His Majesty for using so good a wife . . . so abominably ill'.[69]

The king was left in no doubt about his growing unpopularity.

One day, protesters climbed over the wall into Kensington Gardens to hand him a petition of complaint.[70] Then a Thames waterman travelling past Hampton Court by boat yelled curses at the king 'and all his Hanover dogs' as he walked in the palace's riverside garden. Meanwhile, Caroline bravely put it about that she cared nothing for her husband's infidelity: she was 'sorry for the scandal it gave others, but for herself *she minded it no more than his going to the close stool*'.[71]

Even when George II was at home alone with her, Caroline had much to endure. He wanted chat, entertainment and unrelenting attention from his wife, 'twenty hours in the twenty-four'. If Caroline failed to please in any way, his bad temper 'used always to discharge its hottest fire, on some pretence or other, upon her'.

John Hervey, always chivalrously attentive to Caroline's feelings, recorded the increasingly miserable evenings which he had to spend with queen and king. He was forced to endure lengthy royal rants while Caroline tried to occupy herself with needlework. One night in 1735, Hervey and Caroline had to listen to George II's ill-informed complaints upon a variety of barmy subjects: his objections to Bishop Hoadley, Caroline's stupidity in spending her time and money on Merlin's Cave at Richmond and her vacuity in visiting her friends, like 'an old girl that loves to go abroad, no matter where'. Hervey observed that Caroline 'coloured, and knotted a good deal faster during this speech than she did before, whilst the tears came into her eyes, but she said not one word', and he tried to deflect the king's attacks.

The next day, he tenderly acknowledged Caroline's proud refusal to admit to the absence of love and respect in her marriage. When she twitted him for pitying her, he pretended that he hadn't seen the tears in her eyes. He made believe that he'd looked away because, if their eyes had met, they would have disgraced themselves by laughing.[72]

So Caroline exchanged loving lies with John Hervey, the person in the world who at this point knew the most about her heart.

They kept up a pretence that she'd choked down a giggle, not a sob.

When Caroline's great and terrible suffering began, however, the crosspatch king began to reveal himself capable of quite unexpected depths of feeling.

Despite his brutish reputation, George II had always found it easier to get on with women than with men. His passionate but short-lived rages alternated with equally strong sensations of empathy and compassion. His heartfelt condolences upon the death of her son brought the Countess of Hertford to tears, as he showed so much distress on his face and in the sorrowful 'tone of his voice'.[73]

This 'high degree of sensibility', which the king usually tried to keep hidden from view, would have seemed simply 'incredible' to those who hadn't witnessed it themselves.[74] It was quite characteristic that the king punched one of the doctors who'd dared to suggest that Caroline's illness was terminal. But his courtiers found the king's anger completely understandable, and attributable to 'the violent concern he had for her, and his disorder for want of sleep . . . having sat up with her three nights running'.[75]

George II's initial wooing of Caroline had been shrouded in romance and mystery. He'd made a midnight journey in disguise to Celle in Germany in order to spy upon the beautiful blonde princess as she passed through the town on a journey of her own.[76] Having set eyes upon Caroline, he was overwhelmed with 'desire' and found himself 'most eager to marry her without delay'.[77] Caroline was 'surprised and agitated' when she received the envoy bearing his marriage offer on 22 June 1705.[78] But she soon composed herself to accept.

The whole affair – 'which hath hitherto been conceal'd with so much care' – was finally made public, and their betrothal was widely celebrated.[79] Caroline's lover wrote to her with passion: 'I desire nothing so much as to throw myself at my Princess's feet and promise her eternal devotion; you alone, Madam, can make me happy.'[80]

And in some sense this was still true, over thirty years later. For, despite his infidelities, his sulks and his casual cruelties, this king still loved his queen.

Indeed, when he suffered a near-drowning during a rough return from the continent in early 1737, George II's thoughts turned immediately to Caroline. He wrote a letter showering her with 'the warmest phrases that youthful poets could use in elegies to their mistresses'. Back on dry land after an unsettling few days, he felt never 'more desirous than at that moment of opening his heart to her, because it had never felt warmer towards her'.

Despite his many faults, George II could write a good love letter. In competition for a woman like Caroline, who could be won with words, a literary gentleman would rather have had 'any man in the world for a rival than the King . . . in the gift of writing love-letters [no] man ever surpassed him'.

Caroline was so proud of the letter written after the stormy voyage that she showed it to John Hervey and Sir Robert Walpole, with the warning: 'do not think because I show you this that I am an old fool and vain of my person and charms'. But Hervey was not deceived and saw that really she was delighted by her husband's continued 'passion and tenderness'.

Now it was the writer of love letters, 'the easiest, the most natural, the warmest' of men, who fell in love with his wife once again as she lay sick.[81] From the first moment of her illness, he devoted himself to Caroline's care with surprising constancy.

When Caroline's illness was at last successfully diagnosed in November 1737, her doctors made a terrible mistake.

A 'mortified', or decayed, part of her bowel was now poking out through the wall of her stomach. The Royal Society had recently approved the surgeon Mr Stuart's book entitled *New Discoveries and Improvements in the most considerable Branches of Anatomy and Surgery*, which included 'ruptures of all kinds cured without cutting'.[82] The doctors should really have pushed the bowel back inside and sewn up the hole.

Instead, they cut it off.

Her late father-in-law had been accustomed to call Caroline *cette diablesse la Princesse* [that devil-woman the Princess]', a description which hints at the steely soul hidden inside her plump exterior.[83] And Caroline's tenacity, resignation and resolution during the terrible days that followed were spectacular.

She now underwent almost daily surgery in her bedchamber, under the knife of Dr John Ranby and his assistant, without the benefit of opium. The energetic Dr Ranby sometimes had to change his cap and waistcoat halfway through an operation because he'd soaked them in sweat.[84] Peter Wentworth reported that Caroline bravely cracked jokes before he began work each day. 'Before you begin let me have a full view of your comical face,' she would say to Dr Ranby, and, while his blade went in, she'd ask: 'what wou'd you give now that you was cutting your wife'?[85]

Dr Ranby, the son of an inn-keeper, had been a member of the Royal Society since 1724. As a surgeon, he was lower in status than a general physician, but he had perhaps more practical skills. Surgeons trained on the job for seven years, rather than attending university and winning a degree as did the socially superior branch of the medical profession. They were supposed to restrict themselves to 'internal' medicine only, but had branched out into treating sexually transmitted diseases as well. Their activities were closely linked to those of the barber, and were regulated by the Company of Barber-Surgeons. Surgeons usually plied their trade in shops and backrooms, working as quickly as they could on patients lashed down and often anaesthetised only with alcohol.

Physicians, on the other hand, jealously guarded their right to make expensive house visits. Poorer people had to make do instead with the advice of the apothecary in his shop full of herbal cures and the traditional symbolic stuffed alligator.

Caroline teased Dr Ranby about his wife, 'cross old' Jane, because in November 1737 he was seeking from her not only 'a separation, but a divorce'.[86] Ranby's only son was illegitimate, but his irregular personal life had proved no obstacle to his becoming sergeant-surgeon to the royal family.

Despite an aggressive and abrasive manner, Dr Ranby enjoyed considerable professional status. He'd published accounts of the medical oddities he had seen during post-mortems, such as a bladder containing sixty stones, a boy with an outsize spleen weighing two pounds, and a man whose swollen testicle contained four ounces of water.[87] Tradition has it that Dr Ranby was the inspiration for the uppity surgeon in Henry Fielding's novel *Tom Jones*, a character who 'was a little of a coxcomb' but 'nevertheless very much of a surgeon'.[88]

For his operation upon Caroline, Ranby had requested the aid of a comrade. Wise old Dr Bussier, formerly George I's doctor and now 'near the age of ninety', stood near to Dr Ranby to direct him in 'how to proceed in cutting Her Majesty'. Unfortunately this Dr Bussier 'happened by the candle in his hand to set fire to his wig, at which the Queen bid Ranby stop awhile for he must let her laugh'. The three of them proceeded with the bleak, black humour of medical students.

The incision into the infected area of Caroline's stomach had dramatic results. Given an outlet at last, the wound 'cast forth so great a quantity of corruption' that it created a horrific stench throughout the room. The doctors still did not quite understand what was going on: they thought that Caroline's stomach contained an abscess that would grow unless removed.[89]

So they cut away at Caroline's bowel. If the intestine had been pushed back inside and the rupture sealed up, all may have been well. Cutting the bowel, though, destroyed Caroline's digestive system, and with it all hope of her recovery.

Even at the time her treatment was recognised to have been flawed. She'd been attended, people said, by 'a throng of the killing profession trying their utmost skill to prolong her life in adding more torment to it'.[90] She would not be the first, nor the last, person in eighteenth-century London to have 'died of the *doctor*'.[91]

The doctors had an arsenal of mass-produced medicines from

which to choose to ease Caroline's pain, including Dr Ward's Pills, Sir Walter Raleigh's Cordial and Daffy's Elixir and its many rivals ('Mrs Daffy is pleased to call my *Elixir* spurious, and insinuates as if it were hazardous to the lives of men'[92]). Caroline was also offered snakeroot and brandy, usquebaugh (Irish whiskey) and mint water. Of all these, mint water was the only sensible treatment for a digestive complaint, and it is still administered in cases of colic today.

But Caroline could not keep these palliatives down long enough for them to take effect, and suffered on stoically without them. In the middle of his undoubted concern for his wife, George II could still be brusque with her, asking why she bothered to eat the food that she vomited up again and irrelevantly demanding that 'his last new ruffles' be 'sewed upon the shirt he was to put on that day at his public dressing'.[93] Even in this great crisis, George II remained something of his pettifogging self.

During her illness, Caroline's world shrank. It now consisted of only her bedchamber overlooking the courtyard in St James's Palace and her sumptuous bed, with its fifty separate textile components, including no fewer than five mattresses.

This little world was nevertheless still accessible to a surprising number of people. For a start, her family rallied round:

> Princess Caroline went to bed at night in her own apartment; the Princess Emily sat up in the Queen's bedchamber; Lord Hervey lay on a couch in the next room, and the King had his own bedding brought and laid upon the floor in the little room behind the Queen's dressing room.[94]

John Hervey also records the many and various people present and the jobs performed in the queen's private apartment during normal times. John Teed, her chocolate-maker, milled the ingredients for her morning drink.[95] Mrs Purcell, her hairdresser and laundress ('a forward, pert, silly woman'), brought it to her. The French Lady Charlotte Roussie and the German Mrs Schütz,

Caroline's attendants, were accustomed 'like angry monkeys' to chatter, 'none guessing what's the language or the matter'. As she was dressed at noon each day by her Women of the Bedchamber, Caroline's chaplains prayed in the next room. At night, after she had finished playing cards, the page of the back-stairs named Shaw snuffed out the candles, and a servant called La Behn read aloud to the queen until she fell asleep.[96]

After Caroline fell ill, members of Prince Frederick's household repeatedly tried to inveigle their way into St James's. Some of them almost managed to breach her bedchamber itself, so eager were they to bring back accurate news to their master. As tension mounted, special orders were given to exclude as many people outside the immediate family as possible. Caroline constantly called her children in to give them last words of love and advice. To the Princess Louisa, for example, she said (with strange prescience): 'Louisa, remember I die by being giddy, and obstinate in having kept my disorder a secret!' Louisa would die of a rupture very similar to her mother's, similarly concealed.[97]

George II answered Prince Frederick's frequent messages of concern and requests to visit with more angry denials: 'No, no! He shall not come and act any of his silly plays here, false, lying, cowardly, nauseous puppy.' According to Frederick's arch-enemy, John Hervey, Caroline gladly faced death without forgiving her son. 'At least I shall have one comfort in having my eyes eternally closed,' he reported her to have said, 'I shall never see that monster again.'[98]

But hints given by other, less hostile, witnesses suggest that Caroline secretly longed to be reconciled with her son and that he was often on her mind. Lord Egmont heard tell that 'she forgave him everything he had done against her, but could not see him while he continued his favour to the King's enemies'. Egmont's diary for the period of Caroline's illness also contains a milder version of George II's response to Frederick's request to visit: 'The King said he took it kindly, and went to acquaint the Queen with it, leaving her to do in it as she pleased: but Her Majesty declined it, saying *I forgive him with all my heart the injuries he has done me*.'[99]

Egmont also reported that Caroline had made a poignant plea to her husband: 'though she did not see the Prince, we hear she desired His Majesty not to forget he was her son'.[100]

So the quarrel looked set to continue into the grave, with regret on both sides. Caroline ruefully warned her sixteen-year-old second son, William Augustus, to be 'always dutiful to his father, & never to listen to anyone, who might be wicked enough to insinuate to him, that they cou'd have separate interests'.

There was more satisfaction to be found in being a good son, Caroline said, 'than in the possession of all the empires of the world'.[101]

After the operation to remove the mortified part of the queen's intestine, the court's spirits lifted a little. Every hope was pinned to her successfully 'passing' something through her digestive system, as this would demonstrate that her bowels were still in working order. Enemas were used to help the process and, encouragingly, 'came away with some excrement'.[102]

'I am in great hopes,' wrote Peter Wentworth, 'for God be praised the Queen [is] in good spirits.'[103]

For days Caroline lingered on with her bowels half in and half out, until, on Thursday 17 November, the news turned decidedly bad. Now her stomach practically exploded: 'the Queen's vomitings returned with as much violence as ever, and in the afternoon one of the guts burst in such a manner that all her excrement came out of the wound in her belly'. The 'running at the wound was in such immense quantities that it went all through the quilts of the bed and flowed all over the floor'.[104] Despite the news blackout, Alexander Pope somehow found out about these latest events:

> Here lies wrapt up in forty thousand towels
> The only proof that Caroline had bowels.[105]

Two days later, on Saturday 19 November, the end seemed near when 'more than a chamber pot full of corruption came out of the wound', although Caroline also managed to sleep and to eat some chicken.[106]

At 10 o'clock that night things were looking decidedly bleak: John Hervey's mother Lady Bristol told her husband that 'the Queen's vomiting is returned, which has been ceased for three days . . . I am afraid to say what I think; I am going back to my post'.[107]

Throughout her ordeal, Caroline remained stronger than those around her. 'She had not the least fears of the pains she endured,' it was said, nor was she frightened 'of the last closing scene'. Her only concern was 'for the King's affliction', which was 'certainly as sincere and intense, as ever human nature sustain'd'.[108]

In one of Caroline's last lucid conversations with her husband, she returned to him a ring he had once given her, saying that she owed everything to him. She begged him to marry again after her death, but 'wiping his eyes, and sobbing between every word', he stammered out his response to her suggestion: '*Non – j'aurai – des – maîtresses* [No . . . I will have . . . mistresses]'.[109] He might take lovers, he said, but he would never take a second queen.

Then he kissed her face and her hands a hundred times.

The end came on Sunday 20 November at 11 o'clock, when Caroline asked for one of the Bedchamber Women to take away the candle that stood by her bed. Her husband asked her if the light was hurting her eyes. 'No Sir,' she said, 'I wou'd spare you the affliction of seeing me die.'[110] Caroline lay quietly in the dark for a quarter of an hour, before asking her daughter Amelia to kneel by her bed and read a prayer. Before Amelia had finished, Caroline whispered, 'I am going,' and covered her mouth with her hand.

It was her last gesture. As she died, 'the King's hand was in hers'.[111]

'Like an earthquake', Caroline's death was a 'shock to the nation'.[112] Her last moments were talked about, written about, debated and endlessly reinterpreted. It was said that she 'died very heroically', yet at the same time with 'all the resignation imaginable'.[113] Her chaplain, Dr Alured Clarke, founder of hospitals, sought and found evidence of her Christian belief when he wrote at length about the prayer she'd said 'of her own composing', which 'demonstrated the vigour of a great and good mind'.[114] On the other hand, the old Duchess of Marlborough, with her customary plain speaking, said that Dr Clarke had written a 'nauseous panegyric' aimed at earning its author 'the first bishoprick that falls'.[115]

Others preferred to believe that, like a true queen of the Enlightenment, Caroline had refused the sacrament on her deathbed and that the Archbishop of Canterbury had covered up for her, discreetly fudging the matter by telling those who asked that she 'was in a heavenly disposition' rather than directly answering the question of whether she had taken it or not.[116]

Some people thought, rather unsympathetically, that 'the Queen's death was wholly owing to her own fault', and John Ranby (with a justifiable concern for his reputation) was heard to declare that if he'd been told about the rupture 'two days sooner, she should have been walking about the next day'.[117] Still others found consolation for their own lowly status by reflecting on the fact that even the 'glaring mask of Royalty' hid only 'flesh, however dignified or distinguished'.[118]

But the last word may go to Dr Clarke, who here sums up the views of many:

> it was truly said of her, that the same softness of behaviour and command of herself, that appeared in the drawing room, went along with her into her private apartments, gladdened everybody that was about her person . . . did not fail her even in the hour of death itself.[119]

Orthodox believer or religious radical, everyone found something to emulate in this horrible but admirable death.

Now Caroline's corpse was treated with the greatest respect and embalmed 'in the manner of the Egyptians, at the expense of between 5 and £600'. 'Her whole family' of children and servants attended it, just 'as if she was alive'.[120]

The queen's Ladies of the Bedchamber, Lord Chamberlain and

The obese Queen Caroline, sketched on her deathbed by one of her ladies.
Alexander Pope wrote of this picture: 'ALAS! what room for Flattery, or for
Pride!/ She's dead! – but thus she looked the hour she dy'd'

Master of the Horse watched over her body by day, while two
Maids of Honour, two Bedchamber Women and an equerry kept
guard at night.[121] Peter Wentworth reported that the servants were
on vigil from noon till nine, with a break of three hours for dinner;
'this to be continued till she's bury'd'.[122]

At Caroline's funeral there were twelve Yeomen of the Guard to
carry her coffin to Westminster Abbey.[123] It was preceded by her
crown, carried by her chamberlain on a black velvet cushion, and
followed by a procession of her ladies in black crape.[124] Because
Prince Frederick was still in disgrace, Princess Amelia was chief
mourner, and it was 'never heard that children grieve[d] more for
a mother' than she and her sisters did.[125]

For many weeks, George II was unable to speak of his wife without weeping, and 'look'd as if he had lost his crown'.[126] Sir Robert Walpole found the king 'with a flood of tears gushing from his royal eyes'. With agonised sobs, he reminisced how his wife's sweetness had softened even 'his own harshness and resentment'.[127] His daughters ordered the queens to be taken out of the pack of cards for the king's evening game because the sight of them 'put him into so great a disorder'.[128] One sad day he borrowed a portrait of Caroline from a courtier in order to meditate with it for two hours in his bedchamber. At the end of this time, he had to some extent come to terms with his loss. 'Take this picture away,' he said. 'I never yet saw the woman worthy to buckle her shoe.'[129]

Given that his mistress Henrietta had, for so many years, been almost literally in the position of buckling Caroline's shoes, it is clear where the king's true passion lay.

And on into the new year of 1738, the bereaved king remained troubled by disturbing dreams. According to court gossip, he made a midnight journey to Westminster Abbey and visited Caroline's vault, ordering her coffin to be broken open so that he could see her embalmed body by candlelight. He needed to reassure himself that she really was dead after seeing a vision of her walking abroad once more.[130]

Others were equally hard hit. It was said that John Hervey was strangely tranquil, 'as calm as ever . . . but afflicted to the greatest degree'. He looked upon Caroline's death 'as the greatest misfortune that could befall him'. In fact, 'the loss of so much of the pleasure of his life' made 'the rest not worth thinking of'.[131]

When his icy calm broke down, it did so dramatically. At one court party Hervey found that even the queen's death could not curb the high spirits of the Maids of Honour. Totally unlike his usual urbane self, he simply swore at them in the foulest language.[132]

John Hervey had written, with all the sincerity of which he was capable, that Caroline was the only person who could control or steer him:

> My gracious Queen, who, angry, spares
> And, whilst she chides my faults, my folly bears
> Whose goodness ev'ry day and hour I prove
> And look upon, like heav'n with fear and love.[133]

He and she had been linked by a strange friendship that vaulted the chasms between them: a gap in age, between royalty and commoner, between German and English, between male and female. Never again would he hear his crony exclaiming her characteristic 'Oh, *dummer Teuffel*! [Oh, dull devil!]' about a tiresome courtier, hear her contagious laugh or see her dancing, dangerously, in her slip-on mules.[134]

John Hervey was one of the few people who understood just how much the constant compliments and complaints of court life bored and blunted Caroline. He railed against the stereotypical courtier or 'court-brute' who failed to understand that one 'should never lead a Queen but by the hand'.

Both of them were interminably tired by a life that underused their considerable minds, and Hervey thought that there was little more to keep him in the trivial, repetitive role of Vice-Chamberlain, 'fit for nothing but to carry candles and set chairs all my life'.[135] His relationship with Caroline was in many ways the most significant of all his days, because for once he'd had no hand in ending it.

Now he wrote, tenderly, of his lost friend: 'sure in sleep no dullness you need fear'.[136]

And while he had been devoting his time to keeping Caroline amused, John Hervey had let the other great love of his life slip away. On 15 March 1736, Stephen Fox had made a sudden and startling marriage, to the heiress Elizabeth Strangways Horner. 'The Town', it was reported at the time, 'is at present very much entertain'd with little Ste: Fox's wedding, who on Monday night last ran away with the great fortune Miss Horner, who is but just thirteen years old & very low and childish of her age.'[137] If John Hervey had been expecting his lover to make a marriage of convenience, for form and money's sake, he was disappointed, for Ste seemed distressingly affectionate towards his child bride.

Having lost his wife, his queen and the man he loved best, John Hervey was now left alone.

Peter Wentworth was similarly stricken by Caroline's death. 'I am obliged to tell you', he wrote to his brother, 'that the best of Queens died Sunday night between ten and 11.'[138]

Caroline had loved to embarrass the bemused and blushing Wentworth with her affection. Her characteristic tease had been to call him '*une tres bon enfant*' and to josh him with a mixture of mockery and kindness: 'we are speaking of you; you know I love you, and you shall know I love, I do really love you!' Wentworth was always left speechless by her adoration, being able only to make 'low bows', as he 'had not the impromptu wit nor assurance to make any other answer'.[139]

Wentworth's shell of shyness had been shattered by Caroline alone: 'I swear by all the Gods, if it had not been for the Queen's extreme goodness to me, my heart had been broak,' he had said.[140]

Unfortunately, the cure for a broken heart would now seem to Wentworth only to lie at the bottom of a 'bumper of Burgundy'.[141] He even attached little importance to his humorous, lively, merry letters. 'What I writ', he stated, 'goes for the writing of a drunk fellow, & as such ought not to be valued.'[142]

'A drunk fellow' who was 'not to be valued' was exactly how he saw himself.

George II had promised his wife that he would look after her servants, and he kept his word. Like the others, Peter Wentworth found that his place and salary were assured, for he was to be kept on 'to do duty about the Princesses'.[143] Lady Bristol described how the king broke the news about their futures to the servants: 'I think in all my life I never saw anything in a tragedy ever come up to it; his tears flowed so fast he could not utter a word, nor was there a dry eye in the room . . . my spirits have been more than ordinary sunk ever since.'[144] Mrs Purcell, the late queen's dresser, agreed that they had 'lost the best queen, friend & mistress, that ever servants had: yet still all my faculties seem benumb'd as if seized with a palsy . . . what one suffers with *La Coeur Serré* [a heavy heart]'.[145]

Caroline's loss was deeply felt outside the household, too, with naughty posters again appearing round town:

> Oh death, where is thy sting?
> To take the Queen, and leave the King?[146]

London became 'the most dismal of places', for all plays and operas were forbidden for three months after Caroline's death.[147] George II grimly pressed on with his job and managed to host a drawing-room party in January 1738. But he appeared in public for a mere two minutes, with 'grief still fixed on his face'.[148]

The Opposition claimed that the court's mourning was over the top and injurious to trade. Lady Mary Wortley Montagu ingeniously argued the other side of the case: as people were forbidden from wearing foreign silk for the duration, a great boost would be given 'to the woollen manufacture, the staple commodity of these kingdoms'.[149]

Caroline's death also meant that no one at court had any further use for Peter the Wild Boy, so he was honourably retired to the country farm in Hertfordshire where Bedchamber Woman Mrs Titchborne had been accustomed to spend her summer holidays.[150] The year 1735 had seen the death of his tutor, Dr Arbuthnot, who'd remained to the end 'unalterable, both in friendship and quadrille', and who was sincerely missed by his buddies for 'the excellence of his heart'.[151] But nobody at court much missed the 'merry Doctor with his Wild Pupil' in the face of their greater loss.[152]

Sir Robert Walpole was also left 'in the utmost distress' by

Caroline's death.[153] And he may have the final thought on its cataclysmic significance.

'Oh! my Lord,' he exclaimed,

> what a scene of confusion there will be! Who can tell into what hands
> the King will fall? Or who will have the management of him? I defy
> the ablest person in the kingdom to foresee what will be the conse-
> quence of this great event.[154]

NINE

The Rival Mistresses

'A man at his time of day to be playing these youthful pranks,
and fancying himself in love, was quite ridiculous.'[1]
(John Hervey)

It took five years for the answer to Sir Robert Walpole's riddle to emerge.

In 1742, the drawing room at Kensington Palace would witness the deadliest duel yet in a long-running battle to establish who would 'have the management' of the monarch. Two main contenders had emerged, and two rival mistresses were fighting for the prize of Caroline's vacant place in the king's heart.

At the time of her death, some people had thought that George II would certainly die of grief, but others envisaged some eventual form of recovery. 'Though he is certainly extremely dejected by the great loss,' observed the Duchess of Marlborough, 'a heart is a long time a-breaking; and I have known very few instances of dying from the passion of love.'[2]

Still others predicted that the king would mourn Caroline 'for a fortnight, forget her in a month' and then get hold of 'two or three women . . . to lie with now and then'.[3]

But all the candidates for the position of royal lover hoped to become the main mistress, or *mistress en titre* as she was known in the continental courts. In that competition there could be only one real winner.

Sir Robert Walpole was extremely worried about who might end up on top: she might be avaricious; she might be ambitious; she might get the king into all sorts of scrapes. The sight of the elderly king hunting for women was beginning to amuse and to horrify: observers thought he was simply getting too old for japes of this kind. He was now nearly sixty, a considerable age by the standards of his century. People began to say that for an old man 'to be playing these youthful pranks, and fancying himself in love, was quite ridiculous'.[4]

Ridiculous it may have been, but George II had warned his dying wife that he needed female company. And he didn't just want sexual services. Despite his very public tantrums, in private he required constant reassurance and soothing, just like a cross little boy. It would be a tall order for any one woman to provide it.

The battle lines were clearly drawn in the years following Caroline's death, and by 1742 just two strong contestants remained in the field. With John Hervey once again observing from the sidelines, the struggle was near its conclusion.

Which of the two rival mistresses, Hervey asked, could quench the king's 'amorous heat, so unexpectedly diffused through his veins at such years'?[5]

The battle of the mistresses came to its climax one drawing-room evening in October 1742. On one side was the plump and placid Amalie Sophie Marianne Wendt, who bore the married name of von Wallmoden. Dark-haired and twinkling-eyed, she had many aces in her hand.

Not least among them was the support of first minister Sir Robert Walpole. 'I am for Madame Walmoden,' he declared against all her rivals. 'I'll have nothing to do with your girls.'[6]

George II had met and fallen for the German Amalie well before Caroline's death, during his summer visit to Hanover in 1735. Back then she was thirty-one, the daughter of an army family. Considering the close-knit nature of the Hanover community, it is not entirely shocking to discover that her grandmother had been an early mistress of George I's.[7] Amalie was married to a magistrate named Adam Gottlieb von Wallmoden, and the couple had a son and daughter, Franz Ernst and Friderike. But happily, von Wallmoden proved a complaisant husband when his wife caught the king's eye.

George II dallied with Amalie in Hanover long enough to cause serious dissatisfaction back in Britain. 'The people belonging to the Court were uneasy at it, as it made the Court so much more unpopular,' and 'the tradesmen were all uneasy' too because it was bad for business.[8] Court events brought their best customers into town from their country estates, and they were not held when the king was away.

It seemed that this time George II might have been seriously wounded by Cupid's arrow.

As was his usual habit, he had kept his wife fully abreast of this latest affair. 'I know you will love the Wallmoden, *because she loves me*' was one tactless phrase from him to her which the courtiers treasured.[9]

Caroline had also been treated to a full description 'of Madame Wallmoden's looks, brains and character'. His new lover was nowhere near beautiful, the king admitted, and she lacked a dazzling wit. But she was charming and possessed 'a very agreeable countenance' indeed.[10]

Those who knew Amalie remarked upon her 'fine black eyes, & brown hair'.[11] Short and 'inclined to be corpulent', she had a round face, large eyes and elegant hands. While she was certainly not 'a perfect or a blooming beauty', John Hervey found her stylish and charming: 'a young married woman of the first fashion'.[12] In fact, her succulent curves, combined with her restful, turtle-dove character, made it 'impossible for any man of taste and sensibility to avoid being in love' with her.[13]

Despite the delight he found in Amalie von Wallmoden's company, guilt finally forced George II into coming home after his Hanover visit of 1735. He made his way back to London at top speed, once again to fall into the wide-open arms of his Caroline. She welcomed him warmly and without reproach, 'glueing her mouth to his hand'.[14] But thinking fondly of his beloved Hanover and his adored Amalie, George II was heard to grumble that the English were nothing but a race of 'King-killers and republicans', and that he had to pay them 'not to cut his throat'.[15]

On his return to St James's Palace, the king had Amalie's portrait hung up at the foot of his bed. The compliment demonstrated 'the violence of his love', people thought, but they also murmured that he really might have constrained himself out of consideration for his wife and daughters.[16]

His daily habits changed. Previously he'd spent each morning until eleven with Caroline. But now he abandoned his wife in order to write instead 'for two or three hours to Madame Wallmoden, who never failed sending and receiving a letter every post'. Understandably, this was the period during which Caroline began to fall prey to doubt and depression.

By May 1736, George II was determined to return to Hanover, in order to keep a promise he'd made to Amalie to be back for her birthday on the 29th of that month.[17] When he arrived, he was presented with a newborn baby: Johann Ludwig von Wallmoden. He would never openly acknowledge this child as his son, but he was widely assumed to be the father. Certainly Amalie told George II that this was the case, and his 'silly vanity' in his senile virility cemented her position even further.[18]

Once again the king dallied overlong in Hanover that summer, reliving the gratifications of having a young wife and family. Back in London yet another satirical poster mysteriously appeared on the gate of St James's Palace:

> Lost or strayed out of this house, a man who has left a wife and six children on the parish; whoever will give any tidings of him to the churchwardens of St James's Parish, so as he may be got again, shall receive four shillings and sixpence reward.

> N.B. This reward will not be increased, nobody judging him to deserve a Crown.[19]

When the king finally arrived back home early in 1737, it was actually to spend his last few months, and to become reconciled, with Caroline. Yet he planned to invite Amalie to come to Britain as well so that he need not be parted from either his wife or his mistress.

Perhaps surprisingly, Caroline had agreed to this proposal. Having

endured the *ménage à trois* with Henrietta for so many years, she'd
accepted Sir Robert Walpole's advice that she should once again
be tolerant. 'If you can but once get this favourite to St James's,' he
argued, 'she will in three months be everything Lady Suffolk was,
but deaf.' Walpole faced Caroline with an unenviable choice:
'whether you will fear her at a distance or despise her near'.[20]

So, when George II proved to be incapable of dragging himself
away from Hanover in time to return to London for his birthday
in 1736, Caroline had begged her husband to bring Amalie back
with him too.[21] She was stoutly welcoming in attitude, and promised to 'get Lady Suffolk's lodgings ready immediately'. She even
planned to put her own books into storage so that Amalie could
have more space.

In addition to the support of Sir Robert Walpole, then, Amalie
von Wallmoden also had the (reluctant) blessing of the queen.

But Caroline did not really want Amalie in the palace, and
everyone knew it. The Ladies of the Bedchamber were overheard
'saying they hoped never to see this saucy whore brought under
Her Majesty's nose', and in private Caroline 'dreaded' Amalie's
arrival. She now regretted having driven away Henrietta, who had
been 'powerless, and so little formidable'.[22]

Amalie, in fact, failed to appear in England during Caroline's
lifetime, rightly fearing that she would be far from universally
welcome. Wilder London gossip claimed that the king could not
afford the £50,000 she'd demanded as a fee for coming (as she was
German, everyone assumed that she must be greedy).[23] And then,
of course, Caroline had fallen ill, and her husband's love for her
had been reignited, burning stronger than ever. When he was left
bereft by Caroline's death, it was with some hope of cheering him
up that Sir Robert Walpole finally sent for the abandoned Amalie
the following year.

In June 1738, Amalie and a few attendants crossed the Channel
and arrived in London. She lived at first in 'a mighty mean dirty
lodging in St James's Street', but this was only while the official
mistress's lodgings were being prepared for her at St James's.[24]

George II with his late-life mistress, Amalie. Caroline's portrait looks
down with resignation from the wall behind them

Again anonymous and critical verses appeared on the palace gates:

> Here lives a man of fifty-four
> Whose royal father's will he tore
> And thrust his children out of door
> Then killed his wife and took a whore.[25]

Amalie was soon allocated lodgings at both St James's and
Kensington Palaces, and none other than Molly Hervey was asked
to recommend English servants to pad out her entourage.[26] The
housekeeper at Kensington, Mrs Jane Keen, was still in harness
but by now made immobile by gout. She prepared for Amalie the

spacious but damp apartment formerly occupied by Henrietta. Amalie did at least insist upon having it smartened up with expensive wallpaper.[27]

Since the queen's death, Kensington Palace had no longer been bustling with busy courtiers, and people wondered why Amalie was placed in Henrietta's 'unwholesome apartment' when other, drier, nicer ones were available. She herself was philosophical on the subject: there may well have been better apartments, she said, *'mais pas pour moi'*.[28] It was another example of George II's extreme devotion to precedent and routine, and also an indication of Amalie's calm, soothing character. Wisely, she never wearied the king with 'solicitations either for herself, her relations, her creatures or dependents'.[29] She was biddable, not formidable.

Now Amalie began to appear in the palace drawing room of an evening, 'like one that has been used to the courts of Princes'.[30] The warmth of her reception caused a stir, and it was considered 'quite new; for, though all kings have had mistresses, they were attended at their own lodgings, and not in so public a manner'.[31] And, in 1740, all the other potential mistresses received a sad setback when Amalie, newly divorced by her German husband, was naturalised as a British citizen and given the title of Countess of Yarmouth. (There was once an embarrassing incident at a dinner when a gentleman unfamiliar with the court proposed a toast to the 'Count of Yarmouth', failing to realise that he didn't exist.[32])

Despite her strong position, though, Amalie suffered from various disadvantages. She was Hanoverian, a nationality less than popular with the British. Her English was poor; at thirty-six she had lost her youth; and she was pretty much friendless at court. Germans in general, and Amalie in particular, were thought to be poor lovers, the most 'inert bedfellows in the world'.[33] She never made jokes, and never burst into 'immoderate fits of mirth' at anybody else's.[34]

Even her writing was monotonously neat and sloped like a schoolgirl's, her prose heavy as German dumplings.[35]

'Inoffensive, and attentive only to pleasing' was Horace

Walpole's conclusion on Amalie von Wallmoden: not the perfect qualities to engage for long the attention of the man who had loved the feisty Caroline.[36]

So much for Amalie von Wallmoden. She was a sound candidate for the job of chief mistress, but she faced a formidable adversary: the solidly British Mary Howard, dowager Countess of Deloraine. Mary Deloraine had the advantages of being pretty, English and completely unscrupulous.

Born in Hampshire to a naval family, Mary made her court debut in about 1723 as yet another of the Maids of Honour appointed to attend Caroline as Princess of Wales. Three years later she resigned from her post upon her marriage to Henry Scott, first Earl of Deloraine. They'd met through work, as Henry was a Gentleman of the Bedchamber to George Augustus, then Prince of Wales. Henry Scott and Prince George Augustus were hand in glove. Together they trawled London incognito on nights out: once they visited Bartholomew Fair in Smithfield, dined at the Red Lion Tavern and came home at 4 o'clock the next morning.[37] Henry also held a post in the army, and after his marriage took Mary to live in his house in Leicester Fields.

On Christmas Day 1730, he was climbing into his coach when he was suddenly 'taken with a fit of an apoplexy' and died.[38] Although he'd been twenty-seven years older than her, Mary took her husband's death very badly and mourned him deeply. But she also rather liked the idea of herself as a tragic, widowed countess.

She'd had two daughters with Henry, and now she miscarried a third child, a boy, who'd been conceived before his death. After all the upset, she made something of a recovery and returned to royal service. In 1733, she, Henrietta Howard and Queen Caroline all went out together on a shopping expedition, with the aim of seeing 'several fine curiosities in china' lately arrived from India.[39]

Mary's new job at court was as governess to the youngest princesses, Mary and Louisa. At first she struggled severely with her responsibilities. She was still seen to be 'often in tears for the loss of her Lord, which sometimes leaves marks of grief in her eyes'.[40] This spoof advice to a governess sums up her rather giddy and emotional approach to her duties: 'make the Misses read *French* and *English* novels, and *French* romances . . . to soften their nature, and make them tender-hearted'.[41]

But Mary would now prove herself to be an idealistic if slightly unstable romantic, falling in love easily, dusting herself down and beginning again after each failure. She appeared to advantage as a 'Sea-Goddess' in a court masque, and despite her grief she quickly acquired a new suitor. Court etiquette decreed that she should have vacated her post again on her second marriage, to William Wyndham, in April 1734 (the year that Henrietta left court). When he first proposed, the town talk had it that

> Lady Deloraine had asked the Queen's leave to marry Mr Wyndham, and that the Queen told her she had no objection to her marrying, though she had an insurmountable one to any married woman being Governess to her daughters. Upon which my Lady has prudently resolved to keep her own employment, and give Mr Wyndham no new one.[42]

'I am sorry for her,' wrote one court insider, 'for I believe she has a mind to it, and it would certainly be a great advantage to her.'[43] It was another romance made on the job, for Mr Wyndham was a tutor to Prince William Augustus. Mary Deloraine remained for some time 'undetermined which is best, a husband, or a court employment'.[44]

Somehow Mary eventually talked Caroline round into allowing her to continue as governess, even as a married woman. So she and Mr Wyndham wed, and the king and queen did 'the new married couple the honour to sup with them, at their apartment in St James's House'.[45]

But she continued to be unlucky. It may be remembered that her miscarriage of Mr Wyndham's child interrupted preparations for Prince William Augustus's birthday ball for children in 1735. Her labour had lasted four dreadful days, during which the drums and music for the changing of the guard at St James's Palace were cancelled to avoid disturbing her.[46]

'Poor dear thing . . . so beautiful a creature,' Mary said, telling everybody who'd listen all about her stillborn baby, until theatrical 'tears stopped her voice'.[47]

Although Mary was now Mrs Wyndham, everyone continued to call her Lady Deloraine from her first and grander marriage. She can be seen hard at work once again, accompanying her royal charges to a private theatrical performance in William Hogarth's painting *A Performance of 'The Indian Emperor, or, The Conquest of Mexico by the Spaniards'*. Instead of enjoying the show, she is busily castigating one of the children. She looks a little harassed, though cruelly and elegantly corseted into slenderness.

While people were slightly equivocal about Amalie von Wallmoden's appearance, Mary Deloraine was decidedly pretty, and pretty in the English fashion. One foreigner visiting London decided that if he were ever to hang himself for love, 'it should be for an *English* woman'. 'They have the finest hair in the world,' he judged, 'and are only obliged to pure Nature for the beauty of their complexions. It is a pleasure to see them blush.'[48] Mary retained into her thirties the wonderful 'bloom' of a fifteen-year-old, and even the pernickety John Hervey found her face extraordinarily charming. The only feature he could find to criticise 'was something remarkably awkward about her arms which were long and bony, with a pair of ugly white hands at the end of them'.[49]

Good skin, awkward posture: Mary Deloraine was the archetypal English rose.

But Mary Deloraine had two important disadvantages. The first was her tendency to be as tipsy as she was pretty: she was addicted to alcohol. The king complained that she 'stank of Spanish wine', and Horace Walpole said she had 'most of the vices of her own sex, and the additional one of ours, drinking'.[50]

Secondly, as their former governess, she was heartily disliked by George II's daughters the princesses, and they would do all they could to damage her chances. In fact, her long and tangled relationship with the royal family meant that the courtiers treated her with familiarity but also a touch of contempt. Far from being a favourite at court, as Henrietta had been, she was considered 'very dangerous . . . a weak head, a pretty face, a lying tongue, and a false heart'.[51]

During her years at court, Mary had developed an unenviable reputation for silliness and arrogance: people said that she 'really works miracles in idiocy'.[52] While she may have been rather shallow and self-absorbed, though, she also had the serious misfortune to make an enemy of John Hervey, and much of the vitriol that corroded her reputation dripped from his malevolent but influential pen. In 1731, he wrote ironically to Ste Fox that

> your beauty, friend and passion, Lady Deloraine, came to me the other day, and complained that she was not in fashion this year, and asked me if I could conceive the reason of it. She said everybody seemed to neglect and avoid her. I told her I thought it was easy to be accounted for; that envy kept the women at a distance, and despair the men; to which she only answered, 'Pshaw', turned to the glass, reflected on her conduct, and believed me.[53]

In his letters he often called Mary Deloraine by her court nickname of 'La Mouche', 'La Moscula' or 'The Fly', and revelled in her misfortunes.[54]

'The Fly' tried to buy the popularity that seemed always just beyond her grasp with extravagant parties. Many were happy to take advantage, including the 120 'Ladies and Gentleman' who came to a very elegant breakfast that she hosted in hired rooms for Princess Mary's birthday in 1739.[55]

And even her enemies were forced to admire Mary's unwavering and indomitable spirit and ambition. It was said that she would stop at nothing in order to get what she wanted, and she had already seen off a number of other potential royal mistresses.

In 1731, John Hervey reported his disappointment that nice Northumbrian Lady Tankerville was leaving court; he liked her better than 'all those fine ladies put together'. Straightforward Camilla Bennett, Countess of Tankerville, was a butcher's daughter from Tyneside; her husband was in Prince Frederick's household. For a few months she was another, earlier and particularly good-natured rival of Mary Deloraine's for the king's affections. Mary was said to be 'grown lean with hearing her commended, and I believe has never slept since Lady Tankerville has taken her place at the King's commerce-table'.[56] But Lady Tankerville's departure cheered her up immeasurably.

Mary also saw off a challenge from the warm-hearted Maid of Honour Anna Maria Mordaunt, 'as good as she was silly', who had likewise taken the king's fancy with her handsome face and the buxom big 'breasts of an overgrown wet nurse'. Yet the supposedly 'silly' Miss Mordaunt was sensible enough to turn down the proffered post of royal mistress. Refusing to become a royal playmate, she remained 'a Maid of Honour in the literal sense, and not in the usual [sexually licentious] acceptation of that word' until she married and became the respectable Mrs Poyntz.[57]

Mary gained another victory over the youthful and bashful Miss MacKenzie. The 'prettiest creature that ever was looked on', she was clearly cut out to become a great favourite at court. She was appointed as a dresser to Princess Louisa, but unfortunately her immediate superior in the royal household was Louisa's governess, Mary Deloraine. According to John Hervey at least, Mary was so envious of Miss MacKenzie's beauty that she made 'her cry regularly once or twice a day, by putting her out of countenance and telling her of her Scotch Highland awkwardness'.

During one embarrassing dinner for the members of the household then in waiting, Miss MacKenzie found herself being manhandled. Intending to demonstrate her theory that the girl had thin hair, Mary yanked off Miss MacKenzie's headdress 'crying, "Look at her, do you see how bald she is?" The poor girl coloured like scarlet', John Hervey continued. 'Her Ladyship is so good to treat the court with such farces.'[58]

Humiliating her helpless subordinates may have been cruel, but rumour claimed that Mary Deloraine could be even crueller.

When Miss MacKenzie fell ill, everyone at court assumed that Mary had administered poison.[59]

George II was well accustomed to the self-dramatisation, the histrionic storms and sunshine which were unavoidable when keeping company with his daughters' governess. He often spent the evening playing cards in the princesses' apartments, 'constraining them, tiring himself, and talking a little bawdy to Lady Deloraine'.[60] Over time, bawdy talk led on to other things.

According to Mary herself, she put up quite a fight against George II's advances, and surrendered only in the summer of 1737. Then she was heard bragging that 'the King had been very importunate these two years, telling her that it was mere unkindness and crossness that made her refuse him'. Surely her husband Mr Wyndham wouldn't mind, George II had wheedled.

In 1737, it became generally known that Mary Deloraine had become his mistress. She showed off about it so much that 'the most incredulous now began to cease doubting of His Majesty's tasting all the pleasures with Lady Deloraine which she was capable of bestowing'. All the courtiers – John Hervey among them – were forced to admit that, unlikely though it seemed, the king had made 'the governess of his two youngest daughters his whore'.

Now Mary joked with Sir Robert Walpole that her next child might very well have a father who was not Mr Wyndham. Walpole was not impressed: he was overheard saying that 'he was not sorry the King had got a new plaything' but 'wished His Majesty had taken somebody that was less mischievous than that lying bitch'.[61]

Yet another spoof letter written as a court joke pretended an unlikely total disinterest in another, minor, rivalry with a visiting Frenchwoman:

> For court intrigues I ne'er enquire
> Nor who blows oftenest George's Fire,
> Valmot or Deloraine.[62]

And there were certainly heady moments, immediately after Caroline's death, when Mary Deloraine – 'that pretty idiot' – was clearly the first mistress, despite her having 'the silliest head, and the most vicious heart that ever were created'.[63]

Her former charges the princesses were very much chagrined by this turn of events. They did their best to oust their governess from pole position, trying 'to divert their father's melancholy by bringing women about him, and in scarce covert terms persuaded them to bawd for him'.

In his usual brutal way, Walpole advised the princesses to let Mary Deloraine reign supreme for the time being, as 'people must wear old gloves till they could get new ones'.

So George II, after Caroline's death, and in Amalie's absence, sent 'for this old acquaintance to his apartment from just the same motives that people send casually for a new one to a tavern'.[64]

With all this high-profile coming and going of mistresses, it was no wonder that a pamphleteer could indulge in the 'melancholy reflection' that 'infidelities are much more frequent among people of elevated rank, than those of less exalted station'.[65]

By 1742, though, Mary Deloraine was on a downward trajectory, and deserved more than a little pity.

Her entire court career had been defined by her marriages and her role as mistress. Unlike Henrietta before her, though, she seemed to lack both the inner stability that led to social success and the ability to see that success for the shallow thing it was. Mary was beginning to feel that she'd failed.

She was not satisfied to be thought of as a mere interim mistress, and the arrival of Amalie von Wallmoden – a more whole-hearted passion of the king's – made her own slice of his attention seem remarkably meagre. So she talked it up. As Horace Walpole put it, 'this thing of convenience, on the arrival of [Amalie], put on all that dignity of passion'.[66]

On the night of the conclusive conflict in the drawing room at Kensington Palace, the vulnerable and slightly jaded countess was just about to turn forty. Mary was also putting on weight. In another discomforting drawing-room incident, she had been complaining about the food at court to a gentleman, who responded that it would do her good to have a minimal meal for a change. The demeaning result was that 'she cried, and the Princesses, who were near, were very much diverted, and laughed mightily'.[67]

Under the circumstances, the courtiers would be well advised to back Amalie von Wallmoden rather than Mary Deloraine. John Hervey stood corrected when he made the mistake of assuming otherwise. On being told that the king had bought some lottery tickets for 'his favourite', he'd said he supposed that Mary was the recipient.

'No, I mean the Hanover woman,' Sir Robert Walpole put him right. 'He does not go so deep to his lying fool here.'[68]

But maybe Mary could a produce surprise comeback. Unlike the passive Amalie, she certainly had plenty of courage, both natural and Dutch.

And the courtiers knew better than to express surprise at 'any sudden change of favour'. They'd all seen those 'who lean'd against the throne yesterday, beneath the footstool today'.[69]

What did Amalie and Mary hope to win in this battle of the mistresses? Was their dispute just a storm in a drawing-room tea cup, something unworthy of our attention?

While the subjects of court disputes often seem unbearably trivial to our eyes, eighteenth-century Britain was fascinated by titbits of gossip about who was in and who was out. The more sophisticated might justify themselves by claiming that this was 'not so much for the sake of the royal favour in itself, as for the value which the foolish ... set upon it'.[70]

So contemporaries did indeed think it well worth following the squalls among the mistresses, and women in the early Georgian court could potentially play a very powerful role.

People tended to make a lot of false assumptions about what

the job of royal mistress actually involved. It did not necessarily result in vast wealth, as Henrietta Howard's experience had shown. Nor was it merely a physical role: a patient listening ear was at least as important to George II. What a mistress could hope to win (although Henrietta had also failed in this area) was a measure of influence over people and events. The other chances for eighteenth-century women to gain these things, except through a good marriage, were very limited indeed.

The status of the female sex was still not high: Lord Chesterfield agreed with Dryden that women 'are only children of larger growth; they have an entertaining tattle, and sometimes wit; but for solid, reasoning good sense, I never in my life knew one that had it'.[71] (Molly Hervey characteristically subverted this aphorism to claim that both women *and men too* were merely 'children of larger growth'.[72])

Despite his denigration of women, Chesterfield went straight on to claim that they could be hugely influential in palace life:

> They have, from the weakness of men, more or less influence in all Courts . . . It is, therefore, absolutely necessary to manage, please, and flatter them; and never to discover the least marks of contempt, which is what they never forgive . . . Remember, therefore, most carefully to conceal your contempt, however just, where you would not make an implacable enemy.[73]

The Duchess of Marlborough was also ambivalent about the role of females at court, considering that 'women signify nothing, unless they are the mistress of a Prince'.[74]

And Amalie and Mary had other role models to emulate beyond the retiring, honest and surprisingly un-mistress-like Henrietta. Like any intimate of the king's, a mistress could win the power that was expressed through pensions, peerages or the patronage of posts. Lady Mary Wortley Montagu painted a fantastical, barbed picture of George I's earlier court as a royal menagerie, the king 'surrounded by all his German ministers and playfellows male and female', while politicians on the make won a 'share in the King's councils by bribing his women'.[75] Chief among them had been Melusine, George I's partner-in-life but never his queen (although some people claimed he had married her unofficially, 'with the left hand').

She, the former 'May Pole', was still just about alive as her successors jostled for position in 1742. The courtiers admitted that in Melusine's heyday, 'her interest did everything' and that she had been 'in effect, as much Queen of England as ever any was'.[76] She was now living a leisured life of retirement at Kendal House, her villa by the Thames at Isleworth.

Two of her three daughters had made prestigious marriages: one to Lord Chesterfield, the other to a German count. Melusine's children were still referred to as her nieces, though in fact everyone knew that she was their mother and George I had been their father.

Melusine's long-held and semi-respectable role as George I's unofficial consort had even won her admiration and affection from his son and daughter-in-law, and after George I's death she'd been allowed to mourn like a wife. 'My first thought, my dear Duchess,' Caroline had written to her at the time, 'has been of you ... I know well your devotion and love for the late King ... I hope you realise that I am your friend.'[77]

And Melusine seems to have grieved quite genuinely. George I had promised her that he'd return to her even 'after his death', and Horace Walpole recounted the visits of a black raven to the household at Isleworth. Melusine believed that this 'was the soul of her departed monarch' and intended to treat it tenderly 'till the royal bird or she took their last flight'.[78] In October 1742, that last flight was not long away, for she had only six months left to live.

This strange suburban afterlife was becoming quite normal for retired mistresses. Isleworth was not far from Twickenham, where Henrietta (now Berkeley) was also living in her own riverside villa. An early drawing-room occasion during George I's reign had witnessed a remarkable gathering of three more apparently respectable old ladies: Lady Dorchester, formerly mistress of James II; the Duchess of Portsmouth, retired mistress of Charles

II; and Lady Orkney, once mistress of William III. 'God! who would have thought that we three royal whores should meet here!' quipped the latter.[79]

But obviously these formidable females were not just bimbos, and together they brought to the court an impressive platoon of wit and experience.

George I and George II both liked to pass the hours in their mistresses' apartments quietly having supper and reflecting on events, and this provided necessary relief from the constant harassment that they endured at work. 'I may well look ill,' George I once said, 'for I have had a world of blood drawn from me to-day.'[80] Fifty people seeking an audience daily, with their fifty separate requests for a favour, were hard to bear. The mistress provided some much-needed royal down time and discussion time. However much their power was debated and despised, they deserved at least some of it for the arduous claims their job made on their skills.

Their role and influence in later courts would be much reduced, not least because of the bourgeois sensibilities of George III. George II's grandson and successor was wary of what he perceived to have been the malign influence of the women at his grandfather's court. He wrote that princes fallen into female hands 'make miserable figures'. His grandfather's lifestyle, he thought, was proof of this.

George III preferred women in a more domestic role, as mothers and submissive daughters. His rejection of women like Melusine and Henrietta, Mary and Amalie, as political advisors and entertainers would be a bland and boring triumph of respectability over female firepower.[81]

The two contestants for the title of chief mistress in 1742 were fighting over a man well past his prime.

George II, now aged fifty-nine, suffered from angina. After meals, he 'always took off his cloaths, and reposed himself for an hour in bed', and Sir Robert Walpole would come in for a chat.[82]

When dressed, the king's aging figure remained imposing: at a wedding he wore gold with diamond buttons on his coat; in mourning, he appeared in purple with knots of black crape and a silver waistcoat.[83] However, he did begin to be concerned in his advancing years that 'a very handsome suit' he had ordered should not 'make a boy or a fop of him'.[84]

By now the king's habits, character, capacity – and to some extent his reputation – were fully formed and firmly fixed.

A picture of this rather comical, red-faced, apoplectic figure, with Sir Robert Walpole kneeling by his bedside, was painted in the numerous and slightly jeering contemporary assessments of his reign. There was certainly something of a sense, by the mid-eighteenth century, that the monarchy was just another branch of London's tourist industry. The city's 'fine sights', said the satirists, included 'the tombs, the lions, the king, the royal family, the fine plays and operas'.[85]

Some might have said that the prize for which Amalie and Mary were playing, staking their bodies and futures on the outcome, was not worth the candle.

The wily old Walpole's opinion of George II – and he had many opportunities of forming it – was that the king lacked political courage. 'He thinks he is devilish stout,' the minister used to say, but in truth he was 'as great a political coward as ever wore a crown, and as much afraid to lose it'.[86] Walpole created a lasting image: George II as a king who always gave in to his politicians' demands, albeit reluctantly and with bad grace.

'I want very much to know', wrote Molly Hervey, 'what he can think (if he thinks at all) of those people who call themselves his friends, and are his servants.'[87]

In the privacy of his closet, George II certainly grumped and groaned his way through his daily audiences with his ministers. 'Now I see, I am to be wheedled, sometimes forced . . . to bring about, what you want,' he complained to them. 'I see it very plainly, I am nothing, & wish to be gone.'[88] When his ministers urged him to come back from his lengthy holidays in Hanover, he would moan that there were already 'Kings enough in England. I am nothing there. I am old and want rest, and should go only to be plagued and teased there about that damned House of Commons.'[89]

Certainly the ministers and the politicians and the king's constitutionally limited position intensified the trouble within his family, setting father against son with such hideous results. George II's eldest son was still alienated (and still the focus for trouble-making Opposition politicians), while his daughters were now scattered to the foreign marriages dictated by international politics.

While the king's power as a constitutional monarch may not have been unlimited, power it still was, and in reality it was very considerable in quantity. The twentieth-century historian Aubrey Newman established that George II's political influence has been underestimated because of the way he dealt with his paperwork.

On one occasion when he was instructed to search the king's desk, George II's Lord Chamberlain made a strange discovery: 'what is extraordinary, scarce any papers'. 'The King never loved to keep any papers,' he was told.[90] In fact, George II had the habit, when he received a letter, of scribbling notes and instructions in the margins *of the letter itself* and returning it to the sender. That's why – unlike George III, for example – he amassed no great archive of correspondence. Most of his political interventions are scattered widely throughout the archives of his ministers and correspondents, often unrecognised by historians as royal letters at all.[91]

Eighteenth-century commentators more kindly disposed towards the king noted that after a long apprenticeship, he was in fact getting better at business, and that 'his observations, and replies to the notes of his ministers . . . prove good sense, judgement, and rectitude of intentions'.[92]

After Caroline's death he became increasingly hard-working. This was partly because his continued distance from his children and the loss of the social life that Caroline had organised left paperwork as 'almost his only amusement'.[93]

It was certainly a diligent king who was involved in one trans-
action tracked down by Aubrey Newman. An urgent letter was
sent to the king by his Secretary of State:

> I beg Your Majesty's pardon for presuming to send the enclosed so
> blotted and interlined, but as Lord Chesterfield presses for an answer
> ... I chose rather to send it in this condition than to lose time in hav-
> ing it written over.

George II, though, was well ahead of the game, answering
gruffly that he had dealt with the matter the previous day. The
implication was that his secretary should try harder to keep up to
speed.[94]

The king also retained more power over Parliament than one
might think from his constant complaints. He could make the
lives of his ministers miserable if they crossed him. As one of them
complained, 'no man can bear long, what I go through, every day,
in our joint audiences in the closet'.[95] But then again, it has to be
admitted that George II was simply not the brightest button in
the box: he could comment 'sensibly and justly on single propos-
itions; but to analyse, separate, combine, and reduce to a point,
complicated ones, was above his faculties'.[96]

Despite his carefully cultivated attention to detail, he was
trapped in a role that did not really suit him.

George II's devotion to Hanover – and not just to the person of
Amalie – remained strong and brought with it all kinds of trouble
for Britain. The British found their position in European politics
constantly compromised by Hanover's needs. John Hervey
thought it was dreadfully wrong that George II often made decisions as Elector of Hanover, when 'his interest as King of England
ought only to have been weighed'.[97] He would secretly negotiate,
for example, to extricate the German state from continental con-
flicts without the knowledge of his British ministers.[98]

As he grew older, the king still longed for the soldierly days of
his youth. His sole pleasure as age came fast upon him was to
dream nostalgic dreams of war and action. Battle, after all, had

been the only activity in which he'd excelled. Childlike, he still liked to dress in the hat and coat that he'd worn at the tremendous victory of Oudenarde in 1708 (his courtiers found it hard not to laugh at this).[99]

He was often heard to say that he could hardly bear 'the thought of growing old in peace, and rusting in the cabinet, while other princes were busied in war and shining in the field'.[100]

This longing for action manifested itself in his keeping an encyclopaedic knowledge of all the officers in the army and participating enthusiastically in endless military reviews.[101] On one memorable, if deafening, occasion the king was saluted by 'three running fires of the whole army from right to left'.[102] These great army set-piece occasions were fast losing any real relationship they may once have had with tactics upon the battlefield, but they were still an important display of military might, besides being good fun for everyone.

George II also had a thwarted soldier's obsession with uniforms, and insisted that his colonels consult him upon their proposed designs for each regiment. And, in paying minute attention to matters of clothing, the king was acting as a true barometer of his age.

Out on the streets of London in 1742, the year of the battle of the mistresses, there was much evidence of an accelerating obsession with the stuff of fashion, with fabric and with furnishings.

The men and women strolling through St James's Park were becoming ever more extravagantly dressed, 'embroidered and bedawb'd as much as the *French*'.[103] A town lady sent a country cousin a bonnet with the warning: 'don't be frightened at its bigness, 'tis all the fashion . . . and what now every creature wears'.[104]

The day dress for a young blade about town might by now have consisted of the frock coat, described as 'a close body'd coat . . . with strait sleeves'.[105] He could choose from a cornucopia of euphoniously named wig styles: 'Pidgeon's wing, Comet, Cauliflower, Royal Bird, Staircase, Wild Boar's Back, She-dragon, Rose, Negligent, Cut Bob, Drop-wig, Snail Back, and Spinnage Seed'.[106]

One extreme manifestation of 1740s fashion came in the form of the new 'hoop-petticoats, narrow at the top, and monstrously wide at the bottom'.[107] Richard Campbell, author of *The London Tradesman*, was quick to see their dual advantage: when they tipped up, they revealed the 'secrets of the ladies' legs, which we might have been ignorant of to eternity without their help'. Of more practical benefit, the demand they created for 'whale bone renders them truly beneficial to our allies the *Dutch*'.[108] An enormous 20 per cent of London's labour force was employed in the clothing industry.

At court, the archaic, other-worldly mantua was still the formal female dress, remaining obligatory for drawing-room evenings, coronations and royal weddings. The ordeal of wearing a mantua was more than familiar to Amalie von Wallmoden and Mary

A court mantua. The dress itself weighed ten pounds (it was made of silver thread), while the whalebone hoops burdened the wearer with the same again in weight. No wonder ladies complained about the agony of wearing them

Deloraine, although people outside the palace walls had abandoned them long ago.

The immense cost of a mantua appropriate for George II's drawing room lay in its expensive materials: silk and silver lace sold by weight. The cutting out and sewing of a gown cost less than 2 per cent of the total bill, and discarded dresses would sometimes be melted down to recover the precious metal. The dress Lady Huntingdon wore to Prince Frederick's birthday celebration in 1738 nearly killed her with its metallic weight: she became 'a mere shadow that tottered under every step she took under the load'.[109]

While court fashions were antiquated and awkward, there was one new development: the mantua was gradually being ousted from pride of place by the hyper-elegant French alternative, which nevertheless went by the inelegant name of the 'sacque', or 'sack'. Cut from just one piece of cloth, the sack featured the so-called 'Watteau pleat', a cascading pleat falling from the shoulders to the floor at the back. Seen on Jean-Antoine Watteau's delicate painted ladies, it is ravishingly weird.

An obsession with fashion was a well-recognised eighteenth-century affliction. It was mocked by Alexander Pope in his poem about the small-minded 'Chloe' and her preference for things rather than people:

> She, while her lover pants upon her breast,
> Can mark the figures on an Indian chest;
> And when she sees her friend in deep despair,
> Observes how much a chintz exceeds mohair.[110]

The model that Pope had in mind when writing about Chloe was said to be Henrietta Berkeley. She was now happily occupied with her husband and with decorating and redecorating her house at Marble Hill. This was at the expense of maintaining the sympathetic correspondence that her friends had received from her during her miserable court servitude. Her happy home life meant that her former friendship with Alexander Pope had soured on his part to jealous disgust.

Elsewhere in London, Molly Hervey, returned from France, had also been seduced by the new mania for decorating. She commissioned the architect Henry Flitcroft to design a house in St James's Place. She mocked both it and her gout: 'the one my amusement (for old people must not pretend to pleasures), and the other my torment'.[III]

Now well used to her independence, her husband long gone and her eight children grown up, she enjoyed choosing her surroundings to please herself. She described herself as 'deeply' rooted in her garden, and wished that her plants would 'flourish half as well' as she did.

The formerly sylph-like Molly was growing comfortably fat in middle age: 'though I can't say I have run up in height, yet I have *spread* most luxuriantly'.[112]

Not far from Molly's chic London residence, William Kent in 1742 was working on a similar house in Berkeley Square for one of Princess Amelia's ladies.[113] But he was about to fall worryingly and 'suddenly ill of his eyes'.[114]

Kent was now living in his own little house nearly next door to his old friend the Earl of Burlington at Burlington House. His eye strain should have been a warning that his health needed more attention, but he still hadn't discarded his feckless, pleasure-seeking lifestyle. In one of his letters Kent presents an amusing vignette of himself, the grumpy artist, being cured of a hangover by looking at pictures. In his customary telegraphese, Kent told a friend that one morning Alexander Pope had come round to his house 'before I was up, it had rained all night & rained when he came I would not get up & sent him away to disturb somebody else – he came back & said could meet with nobody'.

So Kent reluctantly got 'drest & went with him'. Off they strolled to an art dealer's, where they looked at pictures '& had great diversion'.[115] Yet Kent and his chums were clearly over-indulging their middle-aged bodies: one of Lord Burlington's daughters would write archly in 1743 that Mr Kent 'took all the

A life of 'high feeding and much inaction' took
its toll on the rosy-cheeked Signior

potted hare with him so I can't tell his opinion of it yet, but I dare
say he will like it wondrously'.[116]

Kent's actress mistress, Elizabeth Butler, had by now abandoned the former royal haunt of Leicester Fields and moved to
the suitably theatrical parish of Covent Garden. Like Kent, she
was a self-made woman, and perhaps they were both too independent to share a single home. Elizabeth had two children,
George and Elizabeth, and the supposition is that William Kent
was their father.

Elizabeth had become quite entrepreneurial, leasing part of her
theatre, thereby receiving part of its profits, and renting a reasonably grand house in King Street. Her finances remained a little
wobbly, though, and once she was locked out of her new home for
six weeks because of unpaid bills.[117]

Although Kent had 'long lived' with Elizabeth on these
friendly, if semi-detached, terms, he was still half searching for
something better.[118] As he wrote to Lady Burlington, 'I wonder
when the time will come that I shall be in love?'[119]

Kent's latest professional accolade was to have been made

portrait-painter to the king, although capturing likenesses had never been the strongest of his skills. It seems that even the inartistic George II found the idea of being painted by Kent too much to bear, and 'declared he would never sit to him for his picture'.[120]

And Peter Wentworth would never serve the king again either. Without Caroline to jolly him out of his shyness and his drinking, he had died in alcoholic penury. In one rare and beseeching letter written shortly before his death, his otherwise silent wife Juliana begged a rich contact for financial help. She explained that she was writing behind her husband's back because if Peter were given money directly, he would immediately squander it rather than pay off their numerous creditors. 'Therefore I desire this may be a secret from him,' she begged, 'tho' what I am doing I think wholly for his service.'[121]

In 1738, Wentworth had written what was probably his last-ever letter to his brother, recounting new difficulties at court: 'I can't imagine who puts it into your head that I fall out with people, there are many people that have unaccountably fallen out with me.' He griped about the 'spite and malice of the world'. Writing almost indecipherably (and presumably under the influence), he rightly predicted that he would be 'falling soon off this terestable Glob [terrestrial Globe]'.[122]

At least his death was painless. He died very suddenly in his lodgings in the Royal Mews, halfway through a hand of quadrille.[123]

Peter Wentworth's addictive illness had been so horrible, and his estate so squalidly indebted, that his relatives were almost relieved by his passing. His eldest son William was advised to try to stave off the many creditors pressing for payment by making 'a voluntary declaration' that he would 'have nothing to do with any of his late father's effects'.

The bereaved young man had mixed emotions: sure, 'he had a natural feeling for the loss of a father', but 'own'd he lived in such daily agony of something even worse than death befalling him ... 'twas a mercy it pleased God to take him'.[124]

[285]

Wentworth did bequeath his son one very valuable possession: the belief that a court life was not a good life. William Wentworth declared instead that 'the summit of my ambition is to be easy & quiet from a long attendance as my father has had at court'.[125]

The court – the very worst environment for an uncertain, unsuccessful, oversensitive soul – had chewed up Peter Wentworth and spat him out. Only Caroline, had she lived, could have kept him going.

By October 1742, the court had also lost the presence of Sir Robert Walpole, though this was greatly against the wishes of the aging king. George II had tried desperately hard to retain Walpole in office as First Lord of the Treasury, but Walpole's political enemies had at long last grown too strong to resist. In February 1742, a major upheaval had seen 'the grand Corrupter' depart from power after losing a general election because of the unpopular Spanish war.

This election had been the occasion of another spat between king and prince: George II had attempted to buy Prince Frederick's support for Walpole's precarious position by offering to add an extra £50,000 a year to the much-disputed allowance. Frederick's refusal to bargain saw the king behaving like a caricature of himself, stirred by 'great passions' and 'flinging off his wig'.[126]

The cash-strapped prince eventually accepted the offer of the additional annuity. In an echo of the unwilling reconciliation of 1720, he managed to appear at a levee at St James's, and his father managed to ask him, not too impolitely, if Princess Augusta was well.[127] This brief and stilted conversation was, in fact, a triumph of goodwill for this particular father and son.

Sir Robert Walpole's departure from power meant a major alteration in the galaxy of political alliances. In the wake of his departure, his political acolyte John Hervey also flounced out of the royal circle in disgust. Hervey resigned from his relatively recent appointment to the government office of Privy Seal and refused the proffered royal pension in order to demonstrate his chagrin at the loss of his boss.

Cast outside the inner circle, his health began to fail, although his vituperation against George II remained very venomous.

Despite the temporary turbulence caused by the departure of such significant characters, life at court from day to day chugged on monotonously. The remaining palace servants longed for a little excitement. 'All I can say of Kensington', wrote one weary courtier, 'is that it is just the same as it was.'[128]

Its habitués complained that a drawing-room evening was 'a perpetual round of hearing the same scandal, and seeing the same follies acted over and over'.[129] The institutionalised courtier turned into a kind of machine, 'little superior to the court clock', telling you 'now it is *levée*, now dinner, now supper time, &c'.[130] Everybody was ready for some new outrage to liven things up, and they were not to be disappointed.

On the evening in the October of 1742 when matters came to a head between Amalie and Mary, card games were in progress, fans were fluttering, the silver in the ladies' dresses was sparkling, the room was crowded with conversing courtiers and the two rival mistresses were glaring daggers at each other. At first everything seemed just as usual, but this would turn out to be a most memorable occasion.

It was later described as the night of the 'great fracas at Kensington'.[131]

The '*virtuous*, and *sober*, and *wise* Deloraine' (who was really none of these things) was sitting playing cards as usual. She had the habit of playing a nightly game with the old-time German courtier Augustus Schutz, known by his circle as the 'court booby'.[132] Winning money at cards was the highest hope of pleasure during many a dreary evening in the drawing room. George II's favourite pastime was commerce, a game which 'must surely have played its cards excellently well, to have kept its ground so long'.[133] But Amalie preferred quadrille: her court nickname was

'Madame Vole', from the term *'sans-prendre-vole'* that was called out during the game.[134]

Mary Deloraine was probably not entirely sober on the evening of the 'fracas', and she was certainly vulnerable to pranksters. Now one of the princesses sought their revenge on their governess and old enemy. It was probably the audacious Amelia, who was still trapped in the role of unmarried daughter and required daily to decorate the drawing room.

When Mary rose for a moment from the card table, a royal hand silently pulled the chair out from beneath her. As she sat, she lost her seat. Her fall to the floor was ignominious, horribly public . . . and much to the amusement of the king.

This was the moment in which Mary realised that even the king himself was treating her with the contempt that she received from everybody else, and her self-control failed her. 'Being provoked that her Monarch was diverted with her disgrace,' rage boiled up in her, and she maliciously pulled the king's seat out from under him in return.

But this was a terrible error, which compounded her humiliation. George II was famously 'mortal in the part which touched the ground'. His haemorrhoids made his fall even more painful than hers, both to his posterior and to his dignity. It was a matter beyond joking. Now, as Horace Walpole said, George II was 'so hurt and so angry' that Mary Deloraine was conclusively disgraced.[135]

This small but significant incident was the sorry end of Mary's ambition: long of waning power, her former lover now cast her out. Yes, he had taken 'a taste of her', but he 'did not like that taste well enough to take any more'.[136]

In Walpole's words, 'her German rival remains in the sole and quiet possession of her royal Master's other side'.[137]

Amalie would henceforth be recognised as the king's unofficial partner, even to the extent of appearing alongside him, in miniature, on top of a dessert served by the Countess of Northumber -

An unusually intelligent princess, Amelia had 'her ears shut to
flattery, and her heart open to honesty'

land. (This unusual compliment – a 'clumsy apotheosis of her con-
cubinage' – in fact embarrassed her.[138])

The newspapers now fell silent upon the subject of Mary
Deloraine's court appearances and parties, previously so frequently
chronicled, and she embarked upon a quick and quiet decline. In
1743, her and Mr Wyndham's only son died, and a couple of
months later it was reported that Mary herself lay 'dangerously ill'
in her apartments at St James's Palace.[139] She was exiled to
Twickenham, on the Thames, the resting place of so many discarded mistresses, 'by the advice of the physicians, for the recovery
of her health'.[140]

But the spell in rehab failed, and Mary expired on 9 November
1744, only two years after her drawing-room defeat.[141] It was
almost as if she died of humiliation.

And yet, and yet, there could be no real winner in this battle of the
mistresses.

The king kept the promise he made to Caroline on her
deathbed: he would never replace her. Despite his promiscuity, he

longed to be faithful; despite his predatory behaviour with women, he only really wanted the one he couldn't have.

Amalie could never quite measure up to the lost Caroline, and her triumph seemed unlikely to last for long. If the king required sex – which he did – there would always be younger, prettier women than her.

Dying when she did, in November 1744, Mary Deloraine lived just long enough to experience the opening skirmishes of the next battle of the mistresses. In a satirical pamphlet published that year, John Hervey suggested that Amalie had been once more threatened in her position as chief mistress by Viola, a dancer from France. The king had hopes that Viola would prove herself to be a 'more vivacious companion' than Amalie, who could 'never pretend to excel' in '*les Engagements de l'Amour*'.

So the German Amalie lost to a French dancer the power over the king that she'd possessed for 'so many years', despite 'the rival beauty of the *British* ladies' and their efforts to snatch it from her.[142]

Had she lived long enough to see it, Mary Deloraine would have been filled with spite and delight.

TEN

The Circle Breaks

'I now behold only a withering King.'
(Horace Walpole)

On Friday 24 October 1760, a seventy-six-year-old George II was dining at Kensington Palace, his residence for the entire summer. What would prove to be his final meal consisted of soup, salmon, mutton, ham, sweetbreads, 'ravioles', prawns and jelly.[2] Later that night he passed the hours between nine and eleven quietly playing cards, as usual, with his daughter Princess Amelia and his mistress Amalie. Although there'd been many contenders for her title, Amalie had so far seen off her challengers and was once again the king's paramount paramour.

During this evening of mild domestic activity, something unusual was happening to George II's heart. Over the years, its muscles had been starved of oxygen by the layers of fat narrowing their feeder arteries. (This had caused his long-familiar chest pains.) The weakened right ventricle of his heart was now pumping under immense pressure and was on the point of losing the battle to bludgeon blood round his body.

While the physical organ was wearing out and its beat softening, the king's heart in the metaphysical sense, too, had never been softer.

This was visible in his surprisingly sympathetic recent behaviour towards those he loved.

Kensington in 1760 was very different from the animated, vibrant community which Henrietta had relinquished in 1734. Caroline's illness had seen the beginning of the end of the high life there. After her death, the king had 'locked up half the palace', and during these later years there was 'scarce enough company to pay for lighting the candles'.[3] Time no longer mattered, and even the

The aged king, seen for once with a smile on his lips.
His heart softened towards the end of his life

clocks were 'very foul and out of repair'.[4] Horace Walpole gives an evocative description of the geriatric court at Kensington: its members were 'seldom young: they sun themselves in a window, like flies in autumn, past even buzzing', all ready 'to be swept away in the first hurricane of a new reign'.[5]

The king had now reached a greater age than any of his predecessors upon the throne. The only people he still wanted to see were his old friends and, even among them, he preferred the ones who had been 'beauties in his younger days'.[6]

A visiting Frenchman vividly conjures up a former femme fatale of the court as she tries to maintain former standards in an increasingly grotesque parody of glamour. She travels in her sedan chair to an evening drawing room, her face 'painted up to the eyes . . . the glasses of the vehicle are drawn up that the winds of Heaven may not visit the powder and paint too roughly'.

Encased in glass like a natural-history specimen, she 'does not ill resemble the foetus of a hippopotamus in a brandy bottle'.[7]

Kensington and the courtiers had changed; so had the world outside the palace gates. Britain's support of Austria against the

Prussians and the French had looked likely to embroil her in continental warfare at the time of the battle of the mistresses in 1742. Matters came to a head the following year, and George II's military enthusiasm got the better of concerns for his safety and senility. His second great personal military triumph took place at the advanced age of fifty-nine.

The location was the battlefield of Dettingen, in what is now south-west Germany; the enemies were the French, and the engagement was part of the War of the Austrian Succession. This was a gallant cause: the defence of the right of Maria Theresa of Austria to inherit her father's throne despite her gender. A soldier present saw cannonballs fly 'within half a yard' of George II's head. When it was suggested that he should leave the field, he answered, '*Don't tell me of danger*, I'll be even with them!' 'He is certainly the boldest man I ever saw,' one eyewitness gushed. George II was undoubtedly bold, and inspiring too, as he yelled: '*Now, boys, – Now for the honour of* England, *fire, and behave brave, and the* French *will soon run.*'[8]

After the success of the 1743 campaign that included the king's own victory at Dettingen, 'female loyalty was brilliantly displayed' in Kensington Gardens. A company of ladies raised subscriptions to pay for a 'gala, and rural illumination, that darkened the stars'. In a last burst of splendour, Kensington Palace was illuminated with wax lights and 'the trees at a distance, in front of every angle, were equally resplendent'.[9]

But the advantage gained at Dettingen was not followed up, and war weariness set in during the latter part of 1743. British troops were pulled out of the continent in 1745 and brought home to deal with the second major uprising of the Jacobites. The outlook was distinctly dicey: Charles Edward Stuart, the Young Pretender (or 'Bonnie Prince Charlie'), had landed in Scotland; he and his rebel forces had achieved early successes against the British army and now they were heading south towards London.

During the weeks of the rebel advance, the tension in the drawing room mounted inexorably. Yet George II kept up an impressive show of sangfroid: 'void of the least appearance of fear . . . with cheerfulness enough to give spirit to others'. One person present acknowledged the enormous strain the king must have endured to maintain this display: 'I never saw him I think show so much of true greatness as he then did.'[10]

When they reached Derby, though, the Jacobite forces lost heart and turned back. George II was triumphant over the Young Pretender, just as George I had vanquished his father the Old Pretender in 1715. The British were extremely affronted that an enemy had dared to invade so deeply into their realm, and they exhibited a great surge of patriotic pride in their country and king. Having survived this crisis, the Hanoverians seemed at last to be safe and secure upon the throne. A visitor to a crowded, celebratory court reported that 'I never saw anybody in such glee as the King.'[11]

In George II's extreme old age, though, a new, protracted and more global conflict had broken out: the Seven Years' War (known in North America as the French and Indian War). It all began in the Ohio valley, where British and French colonists came to blows with the Native Americans. This local dust-up escalated in due course into the first-ever 'World War', and the competition between France and England flared up as far afield as the Philippines and Canada.

In 1756, there was major political upheaval in Europe when Britain abandoned its old ally Austria in favour of Prussia and once again declared war against France. Suddenly, though, there was a string of ignominious military defeats on both sides of the Atlantic – the loss of Minorca, defeat in Carolina, an unsuccessful attack on Ticonderoga – a series of disasters which brought the government into contempt and 'much diminished the national affection borne towards the Sovereign'.[12] More dissatisfaction was caused by the creeping taxes – now newly applied to coaches and servants, for example – which were needed to pay for all this bellicosity.

In his old age George II was still to be seen reviewing the

troops from the ramparts of the garden wall at Kensington, and he remained a soldier at heart. In 1759, the recklessly aggressive James Wolfe was appointed general of the fighting forces in Canada. When complaints were made on the grounds that Wolfe was mad, the sparky old king famously retorted: 'Mad, is he? I wish he would bite some of my other generals.'[13]

And something of Wolfe's mad fighting spirit did rub off on the rest of the army and navy. George II had been forced by the 'misfortunes and disgraces' of 1756 to invite William Pitt to take over the government and conduct of national affairs. Despite the king's dislike of Pitt and his 'utmost reluctance' to work with him, the new 'Prime Minister' performed magnificently as a war leader.

His strategy was 'to win North America on the plains of Europe', forcing the French to fight there as well as in the further theatre of India. By 1759, Britain's army and navy contained record numbers of troops: 71,000 in the fleet and 52,000 available to fight on land.[14]

And they won her the upper hand at last. In the final eighteen months before George II's quiet last supper at Kensington, he and Pitt had achieved huge success upon the world stage. The French had been driven from Canada; Britain's great empire had expanded rapidly. In a sharp contrast with earlier years, the king by 1760 'certainly enjoyed great and universal popularity'.

It was to Mr Pitt that he owed 'this gratifying distinction at the close of life, when Victory was said to have erected her altar between his aged knees'.[15]

Despite these military triumphs, nothing could rejuvenate the court. It was a long time since guests had found 'the square full of coaches; the rooms full of company, everything gay and laughing'.[16]

The sedan chairs that did manage to totter towards the sparse drawing rooms of the reign's closing years came through a London much better built than that of 1720. An architect wrote that George II's period in power had seen bare boards (stained brown 'with soot and small beer to hide the dirt') give way to carpeted floors, stone hearths replaced by marble, the woven rush seats of chairs superseded by damask upholstery.[17] But despite these improvements in living standards, the city was still incommoded with dirt and disease. In August 1760, there'd been a cull of rabid dogs, with two shillings promised for every canine corpse.

Meanwhile, at Kensington Palace, Jane Keen, the old housekeeper, was distracted by a messy and ridiculous legal dispute with the neighbouring parish over a footpath: 'if they will send me to jail I promise you I am ready to go'.[18] Damp seeped into the bones of the surviving residents of this palace built over a running stream, and many of the courtiers once familiar to us had already passed over the Styx.

Horace Walpole's father, Sir Robert, was long dead. He had been ushered out of life in 1745 by none other than the Dr John Ranby who had also supervised Queen Caroline's departure.

Like Walpole senior, John Hervey had never really recovered his spirits after they both left government office in 1742. Only a year after the battle of the rival mistresses he too was dying, of 'disappointment, rage and a distempered condition'.[19]

In one of his final letters, written in June 1743, Hervey celebrated the only one of his significant relationships to survive: that with his tireless correspondent Lady Mary Wortley Montagu. 'The last stages of an infirm life are filthy roads,' he wrote in his final farewell to her. 'May all your ways . . . be ways of pleasantness, and all your paths peace . . . Adieu.'[20]

John Hervey wrote an epitaph for himself that summed up all the warped but in some ways laudable integrity that led to his unhappy, fruitless and isolated later years:

> Few men he lik'd, and fewer still believ'd,
> Fewest of all he trust'd, none deceiv'd;
> But as from temper, principle or pride,
> To gain whom he dislik'd he never try'd.
> And this the pride of others disapprov'd,
> So lik'd by many, few by he was lov'd.[21]

It had been a long time since he had loved and been loved by his wife and the mother of his children, the marvellous Molly. He treated her with extraordinary harshness in his will, leaving her the bare legal minimum: 'Whatever I am obliged to leave my wife by the writing signed at our marriage she must have. I leave her nothing more.'[22] The will caused a scandal, and it was said that John Hervey had 'finished his charming character by it'.[23]

Molly, with fine diplomacy, found her late husband 'no more to be mistaken, or forgot, than to be imitated, being indeed inimitable'.[24]

She, like so many others, had given her heart unwisely to a courtier. Yet, by leaving the court behind, she managed to survive, and indeed, for many years, to thrive.

Hopefully Molly was past caring about old injuries by 1760, when her own failing health began to cause her trouble. Of course, she made light of her 'great weakness' with flashes of the wit of the scintillating seventeen-year-old Mistress Lepell: 'I . . . slide once or twice up and down my room, with the help of a cane on one side, and a strong servant on the other; but I cannot call it walking.'[25] Her difficulties were caused by gout, even though she wore on her feet warm 'bootikins' intended to 'keep up the perspiration, which everybody knows is the only thing that can be done' for the disorder.[26]

Some people still remembered verses written about Molly in her twenties; their author had been in love with her, 'as everybody was then'. A friend asked her one day if she recollected this particular poem and its reference to her queue of fifty suitors. 'Do you think', Molly asked in return, 'that we women ever forget flattery?'[27]

It was as well that Molly did not take herself too seriously, for the children who should have been the consolations of her old age had brought nothing but trouble. Her favourite son Augustus had married one Elizabeth Chudleigh, who notoriously went on to become a bigamist (or so it was claimed) when she also married the Duke of Kingston.

And Molly's daughter-in-law Elizabeth Chudleigh would vigorously challenge Amalie von Wallmoden (now Yarmouth) as a late pretender to the title of royal mistress.

Elizabeth Chudleigh first entered court circles when she was appointed as a Maid of Honour to 'Princess Prudence', Augusta, who was married to 'poor' Frederick, Prince of Wales. Soon afterwards she met Augustus Hervey, Molly's sailor son. In a strange echo of Molly's own story, in 1744 Augustus and Elizabeth entered into a rushed and passionate marriage, a 'scrambling shabby business' that was kept secret from both of their families because it was a form of financial suicide for both of them. Just like Molly, Elizabeth would have lost her job as Maid of Honour if she were known to be married.[28]

In September 1747, Elizabeth obtained a short leave of absence from her post in order to give birth secretly to a short-lived son. Augustus was now spending long periods at sea. By New Year 1749, he and Elizabeth had decided to split. He recorded in his journal that he had 'carried it very cool with Miss Chudleigh' and decided to go abroad, 'never having any more to do in that affair'.[29]

Later the couple would deny that they had ever been married, but a few witnesses insisted otherwise. Another prudish Victorian Hervey descendant tantalisingly wielded the scissors once again, cutting out and destroying some further and possibly illuminating passages about Elizabeth from Augustus's diary. This diary might otherwise have definitively cleared up the still unanswered question of whether or not they had been legally wed.[30]

The year 1749, and the rowdy celebrations of the Peace of Aix-la-Chapelle, brought Molly's daughter-in-law (or daughter-in-sin) to prominence. Still claiming to be an unmarried Maid of Honour, Elizabeth created a sensation at a masquerade at Somerset House by appearing in a vestigial costume as Iphigenia, ready (un)dressed for the sacrifice at Aulis.

The masqueraders included an old man who asked if she would be kind enough to let him give her a squeeze. The king's disguise failed to conceal his identity, so Elizabeth took advantage of the situation for a piece of charming cheek. Grabbing his hand, 'she replied that she would put it to a still softer place, and immediately raised it to his royal forehead'.[31]

Inevitably George II was smitten, and with this a new claimant to the title of chief mistress entered the running. The insolent Elizabeth was overheard declaring that Amalie was dismissed and that she was delighted to belong 'to a King who turns off an old mistress when he has got a new one' rather than keeping both of them on the go simultaneously.[32] The German faction at court panicked because 'their Countess [Amalie] is on the wane'.

Elizabeth's mother was awarded the lucrative position of housekeeper at Windsor Castle, and Elizabeth herself was distinguished in the drawing-room circle, 'against all precedent', with a kiss from the king. Marvellous vistas of possible power opened up: 'why should not experience and a charming face on her side, and near seventy years on his, produce a title?'[33]

But Mistress Chudleigh had overreached herself. Amalie was not permanently dismissed, George II tired of his liaison – if indeed it really was one – and Elizabeth had to console herself with the second string to her bow, the Duke of Kingston, whom she now persuaded to marry her. And she enjoyed life as a duchess, at least until the unresolved matter of her possible previous marriage to Augustus Hervey came to light. London was thrilled by Elizabeth's subsequent trial for bigamy.

Fortunately Molly remained on speaking terms with the foolish but lively Augustus. After various rows, her dull and decorous son Frederick and daughter Lepell had cut themselves off from her completely. Molly claimed that 'there is no difficulty I cannot surmount to please those I love,' but her pride meant that this was not quite true.[34] She was hurt by the long-running quarrels she had with her children over what they saw as her embarrassing, unconventional behaviour.

Since her estrangement from the Hanoverian court, Molly had been a fairly open Jacobite. Her friends noticed that she always wore white roses on 10 June to commemorate the birthday of the Pretender and described 'how angry she used to grow if anybody, to teaze her, brought up the story of the warming-pan'.[35] During her spells of living in France, Molly had even flirted with Roman Catholicism. Well-wishers worried that 'she has changed her principles in politics, and her religious ones I have heard were in danger'.[36]

But her sense of self and her sense of humour were safe.

Molly's late husband, with typical bitterness, had called William Kent 'a man much in fashion as a gardener, an architect, a painter, and about fifty other things, with a very bad taste and little understanding'.[37] But his many friends were sorry to have lost Kent's effervescent company when his unhealthy lifestyle – 'high feeding and much inaction' – led to his death in 1748.[38]

Grown plump upon his royal patronage, Kent had become the bustling and successful creator of country houses and gardens throughout Britain. In later years, 'The Signior' (as he was still called) 'often gave his orders when he was full of Claret', leading to poor decisions and his workmen's time and money being wasted.[39] He still had his detractors, who continued to mock his conceits:

> Rare Architect, in whose exotick school
> Our English connoisseurs may learn by rule
> To spoil their Houses and to play the fool.[40]

Even in later life Kent had preferred to spend more time with Lord Burlington than with his mistress Elizabeth Butler, and during his last illness he was attended for more than a fortnight 'with great care at Burlington House'. He died on 12 April of 'a mortification in his bowels & feet especially inflamed' and was carried from Lord Burlington's house in 'a hearse & 9 mourning coaches to Chiswick'. There his coffin was laid to rest in the vault of the Burlingtons, so that in due course he would lie beside his near lifelong patron and friend.[41] An inscription on his coffin gave him sixty-four years of age.

Despite his closeness to his old benefactor in these final days, William Kent had not forgotten Elizabeth Butler. His will revealed that she was still living in the thespian parish of Saint Paul, Covent Garden.[42] He left £600 to her and £300 to each of their two children, George and Elizabeth. These two were to become orphans only five months later when Elizabeth Butler followed Kent, her on-and-off partner of a lifetime, to the grave.[43]

She was described as a 'widow' in these closing stages of her life, so perhaps her lover, despite his fear of commitment, had finally married her.[44]

Although Kent may have died, the style he created would live on for ever. '*Kentissime*' is the word that Horace Walpole used to describe the best work of the Earl of Burlington's beloved 'Kentino'.

Unlike John Hervey, George II in his old age had begun to lose something of his sting. 'I am sick to death of all this foolish stuff,' he could still be heard to bellow. 'The devil take the Parliament, and the devil take the whole island, provided I can get out of it and go to Hanover.'[45] While he remained full of bluster, it was growing increasingly impotent.

He could now be neutralised by something sorely lacking earlier on: humour. One courtier, who needed the king's signature on a form to validate the awarding of an honour, found him unwilling to approve the candidate proposed. 'Give it the devil, if you will,' the king bawled in his customary curt manner.

The quick-witted courtier filled in the form and then read out: 'George II, by the grace of God, &c. to his trusty and well-beloved friend *the devil*, greeting.' This put the king into a mood good enough to sign as asked.[46]

As he entered his eighth decade, George II's way of life became startlingly secluded, almost like his father's had been. A visitor to Kensington Palace in 1756 reported that he 'goes to bed alone, rises, lights his fire and mends it himself . . . and is up several hours before he calls anybody'.[47] His most riotous social occasions were the summer Saturdays when he travelled, 'regularly as clock-work', down to Richmond to dine with Amalie and a few of 'the late queen's ladies'. They went 'in the middle of the day, with the heavy horse-guards kicking up the dust before them, dined, walked an hour in the garden, returned'.[48] The king liked a sermon to be less than fifteen minutes long as twenty would send him off to sleep.[49] 'He'll have no more night drawing rooms', Molly Hervey heard, 'owing to his eyes being too bad.'[50]

In years gone by the reclusive habits of George I had brought him endless bad publicity, but the elderly George II did not suffer in the same way. This was partly because ideas about monarchy were changing by the 1750s. Respectability and economy were becoming expected of a king, perhaps even more so than cere-mony and show. 'The King's manner of living would not diminish my idea of a King,' remarked one visitor to the shrouded Kensington Palace, because it looked like he diligently 'applied to business' and submitted only reluctantly 'to the pageantry' of monarchy.[51]

It remained the case that trivial matters riled the king most. When he was in his very worst temper, 'and the devil to everybody that comes near him, it is always because one of his pages has powdered his periwig ill, or a housemaid set a chair where it does not use to stand, or something of that kind'.[52] The kinder and more indulgent courtiers suggested that 'some allowance must be made for the infirmities of great old age'.[53] Behind his back, they now giggled rather than trembled and called him 'Old Square - toes'.[54]

Rather than simply writing him off as an crude and ignorant boor, as so many historians have done, we might likewise take a more charitable view that sums up George II's image problem: an essential lack of subtlety. He may have been bad-tempered, but he was always sincere; 'he might offend, but he never deceived'.[55]

Although he'd long had Amalie to comfort him, George II still missed his wife. With sentimental resolution, he had 'never suf-fered the Queen's room to be touched since she died'. For more than twenty years, its fireplace had still contained the same wood that had been laid but not lit during her last days.[56] The king also cherished Caroline's old servants. John Teed, the queen's former chocolate-maker, remained on the books as a part-time 'Extra-ordinary Page of the Backstairs', doubtless with light duties.[57] And in his private rooms the king kept a portrait of Peter the Wild Boy.[58]

A rather moving painting of George II depicts him as he was in 1759. He stands at the top of William Kent's Grand Staircase at Kensington Palace; Yeomen of the Guard are glimpsed in the background. The king was by now deaf and blind in one eye. He found that time now dragged heavily: his affairs insufficient 'to fill up the day; his amusements are without variety, & have lost their relish; he becomes fretful and uneasy merely for want of employ-ment'.[59] Yet this portrait, based on a lightning sketch taken of the king unawares, makes him look tranquil, relaxed, half-smiling at a courtier just out of view. He looks kindly, capable of compassion, very human.

When someone close to him lost a child, the king had always been deeply and movingly sympathetic. One of those who wit-nessed this tenderness thought it was 'his real disposition and way of thinking', while his famed temper tantrums were temporary: 'a fit, or a storm'.[60]

His own children, on the other hand, had often found him hor-ribly hard of heart. He had never been slow to have them whipped.[61] One of his grandsons developed a lifelong loathing of Hampton Court Palace, for example, associating it with harsh beatings administered by the king himself. George II had forever acted the king with his children, treating them with 'all the reserve and majesty of his rank'.

In Horace Walpole's opinion this was a fatal flaw: he could have had a happy life if only 'he had never hated his father, or had ever loved his son'.[62] But the king's own parents had taught him that royal fathers and mothers could not afford to grow fond of their offspring and that political considerations took precedence.

This was a lesson in enduring loss that it took many years for him to unlearn. Only in his dotage did George II's feelings of paternal pride start slowly to sprout once more. One by one, his children began to predecease him, and he began to realise what he had lost.

'I know I did not love my children when they were young,' he freely admitted. 'I hated to have them running into my room.' But now, as he said, he loved them 'as well as most fathers'.[63]

As it was with his wife, so it proved with his children: love grew strongest in the hour of parting. 'He is in very low spirits,' murmured the courtiers.[64]

Unlike the king, Prince Frederick had managed to overcome the difficulties of his own upbringing in order to become a wonderful father to his own family. 'My dear children,' he would write to them, 'you have giv'n me too much joy to-day.'[65] (These children included a much-loved, physically disabled daughter, described as a 'dwarf' and named Elizabeth.[66]) At Leicester House there was 'all the freedom of private life, all the festivity of wit', in contrast to Kensington Palace, where there was 'little but the gloomy pomp of state and court etiquette'.[67]

Frederick's relationship with his father never really recovered from the intense quarrels of the 1730s. In 1747, George II announced that 'his son, for whom he did not care a louse, was to succeed him, and would live long enough to ruin us all'.[68]

Surprisingly, though, the expected reign of a kind King Frederick would never arrive. On 20 March 1751, the prince died. Some people said that an accidental blow to the head from a cricket ball had finished him off, but an account of his final moments shows that the immediate cause of death was a pulmonary embolism, or a clot of blood in the lungs, which stopped him from breathing. Prince Frederick had been complaining of pleurisy pains in his chest since catching a cold in Kew Gardens three weeks previously.[69]

The courtiers observed the king closely, hoping for further

deplorable evidence of his hard-hearted hatred for his son. And they thought they had found it in the events of that evening, when the news arrived at St James's Palace:

> His Majesty had just sat down to play, and was engaged at cards, when a page, dispatched from Leicester House, arrived, bringing information that the Prince was no more. He received the intelligence without testifying either emotion or surprise. Then rising, he crossed the room to Lady Yarmouth's table, who was likewise occupied at play; and leaning over her chair, said to her in a low tone of voice, in German, 'Fritz is dode'. (Freddy is dead).[70]

But it wasn't a lack of emotion that made the king maintain such tight control. It was just his rigid, royal training: 'the guarded conduct of kings must not always be tried by the rules of common life'.[71]

This muted reaction disguised much warmer feelings. A few days later George II went to see Prince Frederick's bereaved wife Princess Augusta, 'sat by her on the couch, embraced, and wept with her'. Crying and hugging, he told his grandsons that 'they must be brave boys, obedient to their mother, and deserve the fortune to which they were born'.[72]

The widowed Princess Augusta enraged Prince Frederick's ever-troublesome political supporters by gratefully 'falling at old George's feet'. They thought she'd 'betrayed the whole party' with this belated family reconciliation.[73] Frederick's death devastated the ranks of his erstwhile political friends, the members of the 'reversionary interest'. Now 'all who had flattered themselves with rising in his reign' were extremely disappointed: 'some peerages were still-born, more first-ministerships, and sundry regiments'.[74] Prince Frederick's funeral was marred by disorganisation, a lack of catering and heavy rain, and was read by his former friends as a final insult from father to son.[75]

And now, of course, the 'reversionary interest' transferred itself instead to Prince Frederick's eldest son, shy little Prince George, the future King George III.

Each year his birthday would be celebrated at Leicester House, that traditional hotbed of opposition, with the customary huge party. Cramped and crowded, Leicester House proved far too small 'for the worship of the rising Sun, of whose future influence every single idolater expects a particular portion'.[76]

The old king may have had something of a rapprochement with his daughter-in-law, Princess Augusta, but he remained a frightening and forbidding figure to his grandson. Little George claimed that 'whilst this Old Man lives; I will rather undergo anything ever so disagreeable than put my trust in him'. George III rejected everything his grandfather stood for. His own reign as king would be a lifelong reaction against the splendour, warped morals and German focus of the early Georgian court and its lavish summer sprees at Kensington Palace.

It is clear that this family had paid an enormous emotional price in return for the role of royalty and had been placed under terrible pressure by the reversionary problem.

In the very last months of his life, though, George II seems to have made an effort to reach out to his grandson. 'The reception at St James was very different from what I expected,' little George wrote after one visit, 'the old man was in as good humour as ever I saw him.'[77] And, while he condemned his grandfather for giving himself up into the hands of his mistresses, little George was not slow to use Amalie as an intermediary to pass on requests to the king.

George II failed to make similar efforts to re-establish good relations with his only surviving son, William Augustus, Duke of Cumberland. Once his parents' favourite, William Augustus was last seen by us dancing at the ball for his fourteenth birthday. Since then he'd tasted life at sea, but the most exciting action that he experienced on board HMS *Victory* was the occasion upon which his ship was accidentally rammed by another. Abandoning his naval aspirations, William Augustus turned instead to the army and became a rather successful soldier. In 1743, he was shot in the leg on the battlefield of Dettingen while helping his father

and 'riding about animating the men with great bravery and resolution'.[78]

He was treated by none other than his mother's and Sir Robert
Walpole's old surgeon, John Ranby, but he would never be able to
walk easily again, and grew immensely fat as a result.[79]

When Charles Edward Stuart, the Young Pretender, arrived in
Scotland in 1745, the British Establishment was taken by surprise
at his success in rousing an army of Jacobites and heading south.
So William Augustus was hurriedly brought back from the continent to face the threat, and the British troops 'leaped and skipped
about like wild things that the Duke was to command them'.[80]
They were certainly correct to show confidence in his ability to
lead them in battle, although the renowned victory at Culloden in
April 1746 was achieved by overwhelming technological superior-
ity (bayonets trumping broadswords), a suspicion of dirty tactics
and a remorseless determination to kill rather than give quarter to
the defeated. Cumberland was appropriately rewarded with the
epithet 'Butcher', and a powerful legacy of pity was born for the
slain Jacobites and the ending of the Highland way of life.

After Prince Frederick's death in 1751, George II wanted
William Augustus to be designated as regent in the event that his
grandson should come to the throne before coming of age. But
'Butcher Cumberland's' reputation for bloody violence was just
too deep for this to wash. Prince Frederick's death was greeted on
the streets with cries of 'Oh! that it was but his brother!'[81] As he'd
maintained only poor relations with Princess Augusta, the future
king's mother, William Augustus found himself gradually eased
out of influence.

He also resigned all his military commissions in a fit of pique
when his father brutally failed to support his decision to make
peace with the French in 1757 during the opening stages of the
Seven Years' War. George II's temper had not quite left him in his
old age, and William Augustus felt the wrath of an inconsiderate
father just as his elder brother had done so frequently. His son had
'ruined me and disgraced himself', the king decreed.[82]

Through long habit, Amalie Yarmouth had become a kind of stepmother to the royal family. So, when William Augustus decided to leave the army, he asked Amalie to break the news. She stood up for her pseudo-stepson, attempting to the calm the king, saying that 'it was to no purpose to be always blaming what was passed'.

Typically, George II 'grew angry with her' and 'told her *he* knew better . . . how to act towards his own children'. So William Augustus remained estranged.[83]

In 1739, Amalie had moved into the damp apartment previously occupied at Kensington Palace by Henrietta, and she remained in these central but uncongenial quarters for the next twenty-one years. She kept fires burning continually to aid her 'ague' and to disperse the 'damps' that invaded the rooms.[84] (Once the flames got out of hand and damaged the apartment.) Amalie still remained a slightly disappointing mistress to those who expected more glamour: she was a 'quiet, orderly, well-behaved, honest German, well past her youth'. She 'did no mischief, made no enemies', and lived with the king just like a 'stiff old gentleman and his respectable housekeeper'.[85]

Some people thought that a little more 'destructive luxury, or a spirit of dissipation' would have been in order from a royal mistress.[86] But the closest Amalie came to scandal was the occasion upon which another lady at court wrote a 'very fond' letter to her husband in France. It was also 'mightly improper as to politicks'. She'd had the sense not to sign it in case it was opened – which of course it was – but unfortunately she'd directed that an answer should be sent to Amalie's lodgings. This led people to think that Amalie had been the author, and she had to explain away a 'very disagreeable mistake'.[87] She nevertheless managed to recover her reputation. Like Caroline, Amalie had discovered that sympathy, rather than sex, was the secret of success as George II's consort.

The king had always been quick to deny that Amalie had any

political influence. Whenever he detected that his ministers were trying to manipulate him through his mistress, he would explode. 'Why do you plague her?' he'd bark. 'What has she to do with these things? The only comfortable two hours I have in the whole day, are those I pass [with Amalie]; and you are always teazing her.'[88]

In consequence, a visiting Frenchman wrote home to France with the view that 'whereas Madame de Pompadour shares the absolute power of Louis XV, Lady Yarmouth shares the absolute impotence of George II'.[89]

But this was not entirely true. We've already seen that George II was not completely powerless, and neither was Amalie. When Mr Pitt came to the palace during a political crisis, for example, 'the pages of the backstairs were seen hurrying about, and crying, "Mr Pitt wants my Lady Yarmouth."'[90] And Amalie's measure of influence with the ministers was not entirely of her own making, because the king was only too glad to burden her with the duties of a secretary.[91]

She'd also become known as the person to visit, cash in hand, if you wanted a peerage, 'including among her customers, the grandson of a footman and the son of a Barbados pedlar'.[92] She certainly wasn't cheap: it was said that she had 'touched twelve thousand' for one particular coronet, and 'sixteen thousand pounds' for a viscountcy.[93] Horace Walpole thought that she was obsessed with 'selling peerages whenever she had an opportunity', although, having had to put up with so much bad temper over so many years, she did deserve some financial compensation.[94]

Meanwhile, George II and Caroline's daughters the princesses had undergone many vicissitudes. The pock-marked and harpsichord-loving Princess Anne had been so desperate to get married that she'd accepted the horrifically ugly Prince William of Orange. But her new life in the Netherlands was miserable and she took every opportunity to come running back to her parents.

Her father gave her only a cold welcome. George II thought

that having made her marital bed she must lie in it. Anne also struggled to have babies: it was nearly ten years before she produced the requisite son and heir for Prince William. She outlived her husband but failed to reverse the steady decline of his state. On 12 January 1759, her death (from dropsy) took place in The Hague. She'd been fifty years old, far from the land of her birth and missed by few.[95]

Anne's younger sister Princess Louisa had been packed off to marry the king of Denmark. She'd died in the same year as her brother Frederick, after a bungled operation just like her mother's. Louisa's first pregnancy had given her 'a slight rupture which she concealed', and 'her death . . . was terrible'.[96]

In 1737, when Queen Caroline had died, her modest, mild and favourite daughter Princess Caroline had suffered a nervous breakdown. The younger Caroline had confidently expected to follow her mother to the grave, but somehow she managed to limp on through life, in poor health, for another twenty years. She lived as a recluse, shut up 'in two chambers in the inner part of St James's', all other possibilities 'now dead to her'.[97] Here she received no visitors except close family and John Hervey, for whom she had cherished a long-lived but hopeless passion.[98] She finally died in 1757.

At seventeen Princess Mary had been married off to the hereditary Prince of Hesse-Cassel, but found her husband 'a brutal German, obstinate, of no genius'.[99] He treated her with 'the greatest inhumanity' until they parted in 1755. His conversion to Catholicism gave Mary the excuse she needed to leave. Her sister Princess Amelia remarked with relief that it was for Mary the final 'fifth Act of the Tragedy, which will make it soon over'.[100] After a recuperative spell in England, Mary returned to Hesse-Cassel to look after the interests of her sons.[101]

Princess Amelia was by 1760 the only child to remain with her father. No prince had ever emerged as a possible husband for her, and marriage to a commoner was unthinkable. She had lost her old squire, 'Booby' Grafton, the former Lord Chamberlain, to a fatal hunting fall in 1757.[102] Still outspoken, still well-informed, it was unfortunate that Amelia clashed with her father's favourite, the meeker, more malleable Amalie Yarmouth. Her talents were wasted in her role as an aging spinster princess, though she constantly shocked her prudent sister-in-law, Princess Augusta, with 'highly improper' but successful spells at the gaming table during trips to Bath.[103]

Princess Amelia's friends thought that she 'knew more of the world than princes usually do; partly from native sagacity, partly from keeping better company and having a mind above that jealous fear of the superior in understanding'.[104]

While the sparks still sometimes flew at Kensington, George II had recently begun to give Princess Amelia more of the appreciation that she deserved. He could not help noticing that she was now the only one left of his and Caroline's eight merry children: Mary was gone back abroad; her brother William Augustus was hostile; the rest were dead.

While the king had always had mistresses, and while politics had complicated his relationships with his children, he had always really wished to place his family first.

Yet, by 1760, a succession of desperately unfortunate quarrels and accidents had seen his family fizzle away. As a child, George II had lost his own mother when she was imprisoned for adultery. Then he lost contact with his eldest son through the move to Britain in 1714. Next he effectively lost his own father through the quarrel that also saw his three eldest daughters taken from him. His second son was snatched and died in George I's care, cementing the enmity between them. After a few short years of peaceful life with what was left of his family, George II lost his richly, truly, deeply beloved Caroline. His grandchildren were turned against him, and he lost his eldest son to a premature death. Death took three more daughters, Louisa, Anne and Caroline, while an ill-considered, snarling slight saw his only remaining son sink into silent enmity.

Bearing in mind all these losses, it was no wonder that the king was bitter, disappointed, enraged. The British Empire was no consolation, and 'his eyes were now constantly full of tears'.[105]

Meanwhile, outside the court, Henrietta Berkeley's beloved George had died, after a painfully brief eleven years of happy married life, on 29 October 1746.

She could not have failed to mourn him, and their surviving letters reveal how greatly they had loved each other. He'd used to beg her: 'for my sake take more than usual care of yourself', while she herself was accustomed to sign off with 'God bless you . . . I do with all my heart and soul nor do I yet repent that I am H. Berkeley.'[106]

Bereft of George, Henrietta continued to live quietly at their country house at Marble Hill and their town house at 15 Savile Row. She amused herself by taking a kindly interest in young relatives. But her health was poor, and she must have regretted the years of her youth given to her first husband and to the king. Regret must have almost overwhelmed her when she thought about her only son, Henry, turned against her by his father and altogether lost to her, although he led a successful life and became a Member of Parliament.[107]

Down at Marble Hill, Henrietta passed the time entertaining her friend and neighbour Horace Walpole with stories of the court of old. Sir Robert Walpole's son was described as 'long and slender to excess; his complexion, and particularly his hands, of a most unhealthy paleness'. He had a very characteristic walk, in a 'style of affected delicacy', which made it look like he was 'afraid of a wet floor'.[108] An indefatigable collector of snippets of history from court dowagers, his letters and memoirs are an entertaining if inaccurate guide to the Georgian court of his youth. His favourite activity of an evening was to sit gossiping about old times with aged royal mistresses, namely Henrietta Berkeley or Amalie Yarmouth.

He found life in his house at Strawberry Hill, as Henrietta's near neighbour, most satisfactory to his macabre taste: 'dowagers as plenty as flounders inhabit all around, and Pope's ghost is just now skimming under my window by a most poetical moonlight'.[109]

Henrietta brushed with the court one last time just before George II's death, the occasion a final, chance encounter with her former lover. Her friend Horace reports how 'oddly' it happened. Two days before the king died, she went to make a visit to Kensington Palace. She didn't know that one of the regular reviews of the troops was taking place in Hyde Park and 'found herself hemmed in by coaches' in the resultant road chaos. Here, stuck in the jammed traffic, Henrietta's vehicle came close to the coach of the king, 'whom she had not seen for so many years, and to my Lady Yarmouth'. She recognised them immediately.

But, despite their proximity, 'they did not know her. It struck her.'[110]

George II may have erased her from his memory. Just as she'd promised, though, when she'd left court so long ago, Henrietta had never forgotten him.

In the old days Henrietta had often heard George II saying that Kensington Palace's reputation for dampness was undeserved. Certainly it didn't affect him personally, because 'incessant fires' were kept blazing in his rooms to ensure that there was 'no possibility of His Majesty's catching cold'.[111] He'd frequently boasted that he 'would never die' at Kensington.[112] On 25 October 1760, he was to be proved wrong.

The events of George II's last morning unfolded in the first-floor private apartments at Kensington Palace that overlooked the gardens to the south-east. The king's simple bedroom contained his 'small bed' with its hair mattress, his single candle and a wicker basket standing on the table to hold his nightcap during the day.[113]

That Saturday morning, George II rose at six as usual. Schröder, his valet, later remarked that the king had 'never looked better than when he gave him his chocolate at seven'.[114] After drinking, the king 'threw up his window and said it was a fine morning, he would go into the garden'.[115]

Horace Walpole's diary contains the most entertaining account of what happened over the next few minutes, before the king had the chance to leave.

> A little after seven he went into the water-closet – the German valet de chambre heard a noise, louder than the royal wind, listened, heard something like a groan, ran in, and found the hero of Oudenarde and Dettingen on the floor, with a gash on his right temple, by falling against the bureau.[116]

Walpole painted the scene with his customary relish for the bizarre. A less sensational account records Schröder's small but painful dilemma: hearing an 'unusual noise in the room', he had to think very hard before he 'ventured to open the door, which he had never done before'.[117]

There was the king, lying on the floor, his head hurt by his fall, obviously dying. His heart had given out at last. The valet lifted the king onto the bed. While Horace Walpole claimed that 'he tried to speak, could not, and expired', there were other, rival accounts that recorded a few final muttered words, and the last words of kings were always a matter of much moment.[118]

It has been said that the dying king called out for Amalie, his mistress, and certainly the noise he produced sounded like her name.[119] This fact has been taken to confirm the king's unpleasant nature: unfaithful to his wife to the last. (It is also certain that his faithful mistress Amalie would have fulfilled the bargain between them and been a steadfast companion to the very end.)

In fact, though, the king's inability to speak clearly caused a good deal of confusion. It was his daughter, not his mistress, for whom he called.

Princess Amelia, known to the English as Princess Emily, was the child of a polyglot family. She signed her letters as 'Amalie', and so she was known by her father.[120] The king wanted to die in the presence of the only person still living who'd been present at Caroline's death.

So it was Princess Amelia who was summoned, though with

the misunderstanding there was too much delay. Because she was now a little deaf, she did not catch the servants' muffled words and only discovered for herself that her father was dead when she touched his lifeless body laid out on the bed.[121]

And it was a terrible experience for her. Amelia had been forcibly parted from her father in her youth, and there is no doubt that she at times had cordially hated him, griping 'Jesus! How tiresome he is!'; complaining about him; doing her best to avoid him.[122] Unlike her seven siblings, though, she had also come to feel something like sympathy for him towards the end, and now found herself subject to strange emotions.

She was hurled 'into an agony' by her father's death, 'this shock so sudden, so unexpected, and so violent'.[123] Now Amelia and Amalie were probably the only people who genuinely grieved for George II.

So sudden was the king's death that an investigation was needed, and his body was opened up. The right ventricle of his heart was found to have 'burst, and the pericardium filled with a great quantity of coagulated blood'. The left ventricle was empty, and the 'coats of all the vessels were worn away extremely thin'. No wonder the king 'had been frequently out of order of late'.[124]

Nevertheless, the heart of the palace beat on, and, after heading his blank page 'this morning his most gracious Majesty departed this life', the kitchen clerk stolidly enumerated the supplies the kitchen would still require for the day: five ducks, two dozen larks, two quarts of shrimps, two barrels of oysters, two pecks of French beans and twelve dozen peaches.[125] Hungry mouths still waited to be fed.

The Lord Chamberlain now ordered the same court mourning as had been decreed for George I back in 1727: black bombazines, black crape hoods, gloves and crape fans; the whole palace of St James's was to be hung with black.[126] At another royal death, that of Princess Caroline three years previously, 'everybody that think themselves anybody' wore deep mourning, and ladies who'd worn even black flounces on their skirts had been told to remove them.[127]

Now, once again, the many who considered themselves intimate enough with the royal family to wear mourning made an assault upon the shops, and over 1,500 yards of crape were sold by one retailer in Bath on the Sunday night.[128] Those unrecognised by the shopkeepers as regular customers, or those with a 'Right Honourable' before their name, had to pay a shilling more than others for the same stuff.[129]

By Saturday night London was completely empty of hackney horses, as so many messengers had been sent to take the news to 'persons of distinction' all over the kingdom; and every hour brought new arrivals to London as the nobility began to gather for the funeral that would follow.[130]

The change of monarch meant that the court was once again full of 'hopes and fears', and that even the most potent of George II's 'great lords look[ed] as if they dreaded wanting bread'.[131]

The king's funeral ceremonies began at 7 p.m. on 9 November, when his bowels were carried from Kensington to the royal vault in Henry VII's chapel, Westminster Abbey. The bowels led the way because they'd been removed from the corpse during the process of embalming it and needed to be disposed of first. The rest of his body followed the next day, carried to its hearse by twelve faithful Yeomen of the Guard. On 11 November, they carried it from the Prince's Chamber at Westminster, where it had rested overnight, into the vault itself.[132] The king had given instructions that he wanted his and Caroline's dust to mingle in a joint coffin.[133]

He now rejoined his wife, the love of his life.

So, at length, George II was buried, a king who had never perhaps quite lived or loved well enough, but who had done his best to live up to his idea of his job under trying circumstances. At his birth nobody could have predicted the chain of coincidences that would lead to his becoming king of Great Britain, and many of his hopes of personal happiness had been crushed by the unlucky crown.

Now he was respectfully mourned, and sermons were preached on the text: 'he died in a good old age, full of days, riches, and honour'.[134] 'Posterity will celebrate him as a good Prince,' mused one of his courtiers, 'tho' many of the present age knew him not to have been an amiable man.'[135]

Only a month later, though, one of George II's former subjects could write that 'he seems already to be almost forgotten'.[136] This was partly because there was now a vigorous young king to excite people. Luckily George III felt himself more equal than his grandfather to the task of ruling, more British than Hanoverian. He famously declared that, unlike his predecessors, he'd been born and educated in the country, and gloried 'in the name of Britain'.[137]

He was resolved, too, 'to introduce a new custom': that all his 'family should live well together', because he was 'very sorry for the misunderstandings that there had formerly been'.[138]

Soon Henrietta was once again required, for she was one of the few people who could teach the court about the ceremonies now to be followed. At the coronation of Queen Charlotte, George III's new young wife, which took place in September 1761, it was Henrietta who best remembered the jewels and rules that Queen Caroline had worn and obeyed in 1727, and her advice was sought.[139]

So who were the winners and losers of the second Georgian age, which ended so ignominiously in the water closet on 25 October 1760?

Two days after the king's death, Horace Walpole paid a visit to Kensington Palace, the scene of so many triumphs and disasters for our courtiers. He was on his way to see Lady Yarmouth, the former Amalie von Wallmoden, who'd managed to hold off all her rivals until the very end of the battle of the mistresses.

Much had changed since Horace Walpole had last tripped into the porter's lodge of the palace. Although he and his father had been so closely associated with the old court, he was not even recognised on that autumn morning. 'No one knew me', he wrote. 'They asked my name – when they heard it, they did not seem ever to have heard it before, even in that house. I waited half an hour in a lodge with a footman of Lady Yarmouth's.'

Yet he took his loss of prestige with his customary dry philosophy: 'I smiled to myself.'[140]

When he finally breached the palace's new defences, Walpole found that his old friend Amalie was emotionally, but not financially, distressed. There would now be little to detain her in Britain, except the '£9,000 in bank bills and 11 bags with a 100 gold sovereigns in each' that the king had left for her in his bureau. Alongside the money he gave her his '2 gold snuff boxes', each containing a cherished miniature picture of Amalie herself.[141] It was a reasonable, but not astronomical, compensation for the mistress who'd never really possessed her lover's heart. (Jane Keen, the palace's old housekeeper, would also die a fairly wealthy woman: the estate she left included £3,500 and a portrait of herself wearing diamond earrings.[142])

Amalie soon returned to her birthplace in Hanover, and died there of 'a cancer in her breast' only five years later, aged sixty-one.[143] At her death, a rather wild report claimed that she'd made so much money out of George II that she'd been able to leave her two sons 'a million of crowns'.[144] This vast sum was probably plucked from the air by the sort of people who thought, wrongly, that a German royal mistress was bound to have made enormous profit from her position. Her son Johann Ludwig, who was George II's final if unacknowledged child, built a mansion near Herrenhausen, entered the Hanoverian army, served in the French revolutionary war and died in 1811.[145] His house is now a museum of cartoons.

Amalie's ties with her unofficial step-family, George II's children, were obviously not strong enough to long survive his death. William Augustus, the fat Duke of Cumberland, had suffered a stroke just two months before his father's final heart attack. From this he recovered the power of speech but not of full movement, and he was not popular with the new courtiers now surrounding his nephew George III. Butcher-like to the end, he talked about 'the vermin the court is now full of' under the new regime; 'vermin' was a term he had also used when flushing out and killing the Jacobites in 1745.[146] He died in 1765.

Meanwhile, Molly Hervey's daughter-in-law, Elizabeth Chudleigh, was reported to have been deeply upset by the demise of George II, her quondam lover, although her grief was not taken entirely seriously. One person thought her weeping was caused by a bad oyster rather than the death of a close attachment.[147] Perhaps she was regretting the time when she'd been so close to the prize of becoming chief mistress, or perhaps she was mourning the loss of a youth not to be regained by 'sticking roses and sweet peas in one's hair, as Miss Chudleigh still does!'[148]

Whether or not she was legitimately married to the Duke of Kingston, and whether or not she was truly a duchess, no one will ever know. If her first marriage to Augustus Hervey was in fact valid, she became a legitimate countess at least, because his elder brother died before him and he inherited the family title.

'The court's a golden, but a fatal circle' reads the inscription to *Court tales: or, a History of the Amours of the Present Nobility*, and the real winners were those who had escaped from the gilded cage.[149]

Molly Hervey was left tranquil by the king's death. She looked forward enthusiastically to the reign of George III and continued to enjoy the company of Horace Walpole and her other witty friends. She 'gave dinners, and was always at home in an evening to a select company: men of letters and *beaux esprits*', preserving into old age the 'uncommon remains' of her beauty.[150] Walpole's devotion to her was all the stronger because – and we would expect no less from Molly – she combined 'great goodness with great severity' towards him, and was always glad to take him down a peg or two.[151]

Henrietta had likewise proved herself to be, as Lord Peterborough put it, a

> wonderful creature! a woman of reason!
> Never grave out of pride, never gay out of season.[152]

George II's death brought with it the end of her court pension, but at the age of seventy-one she retained 'spirits and cleverness and imagination'. Horace Walpole worshipped her for her conversation and her 'old court-knowledge'.[153] At nearly eighty she still had 'all her senses as perfect as ever', except, of course, for her long-lost hearing.[154] Walpole, addicted to her anecdotes, lamented their life in Twickenham when he was detained in London, and longed for its 'roses, strawberries, & banks of the river'.[155] 'Pray keep a little summer for me,' he begged her, and 'I will give you a bushel of politics, when I come to Marblehill, for a teacup of strawberries & cream.'[156]

When she'd left court in 1734, a friend rightly commended Henrietta on her wise choice of pleasures: 'old wine to drink, old friends to converse with, and old books to read; you may be sure of enjoying all these . . . in a more perfect degree than *his majesty or his queen*'.[157]

Apart from the devoted Walpole, Henrietta's life was now lived among the recollected characters of times long gone. One of her few surviving friends thought of her as a sage, a wise woman well left to herself, 'to think of what is past, so as to be able to judge of what is to come'.[158] We leave Henrietta and Horace talking together happily about the gory, glory days of the 1730s, celebrating the fulfilment of a wish so often expressed when she was in court bondage and put into the words of her former friend Alexander Pope:

> . . . quickly bear me hence
> To wholesome solitude, the nurse of sense:
> Here contemplation prunes her ruffled wings,
> And the free soul looks down to pity kings.[159]

Princess Amelia was another of Horace Walpole's friends, although they had frequent fallings-out. After losing her palace apartments following her father's death, the princess became another of the formidable retired court ladies of west London, buying Gunnersbury House in Ealing, Middlesex.[160] She spent the rest of her life criticising her nephew, George III, who ignored her, and left her estate to her unlucky sister Mary's children.

Molly, Henrietta and Princess Amelia all endured vicious attacks from their contemporaries: Molly for her status-consciousness and shyness; Henrietta for her bland conversation and lack of exceptional looks; Amelia for her bluntness and rudeness. But this was really because all three women had dared to be different. They could not help discomfiting the world by giving it a glimpse of what women were not supposed to have: wit, humour and inner resources.

The other survivor among the courtiers was Peter the Wild Boy. In 1760, he was still living on a farm in Berkhamsted, the little market town just north-west of London. It sits in a shallow valley, in low, rolling country, with neat fields, wooded hills and snug timber-framed buildings along a high street larded with coaching inns. In and about this town Peter enjoyed a life of quiet enjoyment and wore an iron collar marked with his name and address so that people could bring him home again when he wandered off.

Peter in later years looked 'just like busts of Socrates'.
No one knew how old he really was

Lodged with Farmer Fenn at Broadway Farm, he would exasperate his master by helpfully loading a cart with dung, then unloading it again for pleasure. He remained 'exceedingly timid and gentle in his nature' and 'would suffer himself to be governed by a child'. He was fond of gin, and of onions, which he would eat raw like apples. In spring he would sing all day long, and if music were played he would dance and caper about 'till he was almost quite exhausted with fatigue'. In the autumn he would still show 'a strange fondness for stealing away into the woods, where he would feed eagerly' upon acorns.

Only when bad weather approached would Peter begin 'growling and howling, and showing great disorder'. He loved to watch a fire and sometimes stood with his face turned to the sun; he liked 'to be out on a starry night'.[161]

Nothing could have been further from life in the gloomy, glittering world of the Georgian court.

ELEVEN

The Survivors

'I had lost all taste for courts and princes and power.'[1]
(Horace Walpole)

My search for the stories of the people who lived and worked in the Georgian royal palaces began on William Kent's staircase at Kensington. The more I learnt about their lives, the more convinced I became that the whole sumptuous and luxurious cocoon of court life was in many ways a prison.

This was as true for kings and queens as it was for their servants. The first two Georges were rather successful in smoothing over the religious and social cracks in the realm that they had accidentally inherited. They worked hard at the job of being king. But there's something sad and stunted about their lives off duty. In personal terms they paid a high price for their royal role.

History has not been kind to either of them. George I has been marginalised within the story of Britain, his German 'otherness' made less threatening by transposing him into a minor key and making him into a quaint buffoon. (According to one widely read Victorian historian, he and Melusine – his 'antiquated Sultana' – liked nothing better than to spend the evening cutting paper into various shapes.[2])

And George II has an even less enviable reputation than his 'dull and dreary' father. Sandwiched in royal history between his father (founder of a new dynasty) and George III (the 'mad' king who lost America), George II has been practically forgotten. If he ever appears in pub quizzes, it's merely as the last monarch to lead his troops in person on the battlefield.

Few people today could name his other achievements or the great events of his reign, which was marked by growing peace and prosperity, an emerging sense of nationhood and the successful seizure of all of France's power in North America. All these things helped to define and promote a new sense of what it meant to be 'British'.

Yet ironically they were achieved by foreign rulers whom the British themselves promptly forgot.

Despite the strenuous efforts of historians to 'rescue' George II from his embattled reputation as a slightly useless king, a 'king in toils' as one biographer put it, they have largely failed.[3]

Caroline's reputation has survived far better than her husband's. Thanks to John Hervey's efforts, she has long been feted as a cultured and clever woman who was sorely tried by her German-accented husband's well-known hatred for all of her 'boets and bainters'. She is something of a celebrity among eighteenth-century queens: generous, enlightened, a very human ray of light illuminating the murky world of the court.

Contemporaries Horace Walpole and John Hervey have done more than anyone to shape perceptions of George II and his court. Both are much-loved, much-loathed figures whose texts are treacherously opinionated as well as deliciously quotable. 'Nothing can be more cheery than Horace's letters,' wrote William Thackeray in the nineteenth century. 'Fiddles sing all through them: wax-lights, fine dresses, fine jokes, fine plate, fine equipages, glitter and sparkle there: never was such a brilliant, jigging, smirking Vanity Fair as that through which he leads us.' Flicking through either writer, the court seems like a sparkling, amusing, playful place. But Thackeray could also see the dark side of Hervey's memoirs: he found certain passages frightful, like wandering through a 'city of the dead . . . through those godless intrigues and feasts, through crowds, pushing, and eager, and struggling – rouged, and lying, and fawning'.[4]

With George II's death, the palace at Kensington fell from favour. To the new young king, 'ceremony seems to have been always unpleasant; so that all the common splendour of a court was totally laid aside', and his drawing-room gatherings were less frequent.[5] George III's young and lively court clearly brought with it a renewal of court life, but it was a little less focused upon the court set piece, the ball and the levee, and never again did the full court return to Kensington.

George III's accession brought change to the personnel of the royal household, although some old-timers like John Teed, his grandmother's chocolate-maker, were still employed.[6] There were also changes of style and tone. While his grandfather had been widely promiscuous, George III was faithful to his wife. While George II had spent his latter days in dark and stately private apartments with his mistress, George III presented his devoted wife and their numerous children as a model of family life for the nation to emulate. And while George II lived in lavish style, George III is best known for the periods in his life when he lived in modest domesticity at tiny Kew Palace. Like Kensington, Hampton Court Palace was also left deserted. Buckingham Palace (then known as The Queen's House) and Windsor Castle became the favoured residences instead. The drawing room at Kensington quietly became a museum, and would in due course echo with the shuffling footsteps of curious tourists.

'All this is now so changed that I seem to be speaking of the world before the flood,' wrote one ex-courtier in her memoirs.[7]

While everything else was changed, though, one thing would remain the same in the next reign. George III had been scarred by the rows he had experienced between the earlier generations of his family. In due course the 'reversionary interest' worked its mischief once more, and, despite his best intentions, he too ended up at war with his own eldest son, the future George IV.

George III nevertheless went on to become one of the most popular kings ever, placing the monarchy on the track of pleasant respectability that Queen Victoria maintained with such success. She herself had a prudish distaste for her predecessors, George I and George II, and thought that 'the morals of the ladies surrounding these sovereigns left much to be desired'.[8]

The decline of the drawing room was no bad thing. Despite its surface glamour, the life of a Georgian courtier – sought so earnestly by so many – was not a life to be longed for. Lord

Chesterfield felt he could never laugh; Molly Hervey took great trouble to disguise her intelligence; Georgian princesses knew that 'at Court, one learns deceit'.[9] All the avenues leading to the court, it was said, 'are gay, smiling, agreeable to the sight, and all end in one and the same point, honour, and self-interest'.[10]

George II's generation certainly did not regret the regular trauma of being 'curled, powdered, dressed' for court, always in 'hurry and confusion', and arriving only to be 'touz'd and hunched', 'hot and dispirited', 'very pleasing to the sight, but perhaps not altogether so refreshing to the smell'.[11]

Until her death in 1786, Princess Amelia complained about the toxic trial of court attendance and pretended to be too deaf to go. (This was much to her nephew's relief, for George III was 'afraid of her frankness'.[12]) Amelia herself was delighted to neglect the biweekly routine and revelled in the freedom to 'stay them days comfortably at home & rest'.[13]

Henrietta finally died in 1767, and was visited on her life's penultimate evening by the faithful Horace Walpole. He would sharply regret his 'sincere and unalterable friend' who had, in her long life, 'seen, known and remembered so much'.[14] Her final decade had been marred by penury, for her outgoings at Marble Hill exceeded her income. This once again brought a certain 'anguish' to 'the last years of her life, though concealed'.[15]

Henrietta asked to be 'buried as Mr Berkeley's widow very privately as he was and with the Earl of Berkeley's leave near him'.[16] And so she ended up lying with her beloved second husband in his family mausoleum at Berkeley Castle.

Molly Hervey soon followed her, only a year later, and faced her death (from diarrhoea) bravely: 'It is not *that* I fear, but 'tis the way to it; 'tis the struggles, the last convulsions that I dread; for once they are over, I don't question but to rise to a new and better life.'[17] These words formed part of the last letter she is known to have written. She died on 2 September 1768 and was buried a week later in the parish church at Ickworth.

She was not forgotten. The young daughter of a friend found

that Molly's loving attention and lavish gifts of books had 'fixed her so strongly in my memory that I see and hear her still'.[18] And Horace Walpole, missing her dreadfully, recollected how her terrible 'suffering with the gout' could 'never affect her patience or divert her attention to her friends'.[19]

Molly nevertheless went to the grave retaining something, still, of her intriguing air of mystery: 'what her inside was my Lord only knew, and he I believe but partly'.[20]

The last survivor of all, Peter the Wild Boy, lived on quietly in Berkhamsted until the 1780s. He was constantly visited by the curious, including the novelist Maria Edgeworth, who commented that he looked in old age just like busts of Socrates. When sightseers gave him money, Peter meekly handed it over to the wife of the farmer who looked after him.[21] He paid a last visit to court in 1767, at the request of George III, who wanted his family to see his grandmother's pet.[22]

Then it was back to Berkhamsted. After his initial splashy arrival in London, he had lived a quiet and blameless life, largely forgotten, misunderstood but in some measure loved by the farming families who looked after him.

And Peter ended up deeply attached to his carers, the last of whom was Farmer Brill of Berkhamsted. Discovering the aged Farmer Brill dead in his bed one day, Peter 'tried to awaken him, but finding his efforts unavailing, refused food, pined away, and died in a few days, without apparently any illness'.[23] It was 22 February 1785.

Peter's gravestone still lies by the south porch of the flinted church of St Mary at Northchurch, Berkhamsted, under a wild rose bush, surrounded by speedwell, wild parsley and marguerites. The lettering on his grave is painted and the plot is carefully tended. To this day a mysterious person regularly but discreetly places flowers on his grave, a person who has no connection with the church's official Flower Guild.

One of the Guild's members guesses that the flowers must be left by 'someone who thinks he should be remembered'.[24]

At George II's abandoned palace, Kensington, life went quietly on. The palace was gradually filled up by minor members of the royal family requiring lodgings, including the Duchess of Kent and her daughter Princess Victoria.

Victoria was the unlikely winner of the 'baby race' that took place between George III's numerous sons to provide a legitimate heir to the throne. Although George III and his wife Charlotte churned out fifteen offspring, they had only one legitimate grandchild, named Charlotte. When she died in childbirth in 1817, the king's younger sons were forced to abandon their various mistresses, marry princesses and set to work at the business of procreation.

The satirical poet Peter Pindar described how 'Hot and hard each Royal pair/ are at it hunting for the heir'. George III's fourth son, Edward, Duke of Kent, married a German princess and won the race by producing Victoria in 1819; he and his young family moved into the rooms which had formerly been George II's private apartments at Kensington.

After the Duke of Kent's early death, his widow, her household and his daughter crept discreetly upwards and began to colonise the state apartments at the top of the King's Grand Staircase (the duchess's brother-in-law, King William IV, was extremely annoyed when he found out). It was in the grand but by now slightly ramshackle environment of William Kent's rooms for George I that Princess Victoria grew up. It was at Kensington Palace that the sixteen-year-old Victoria first met Albert; it was there that she woke up on the morning in 1837 that she became queen.

Although she promptly moved to Buckingham Palace upon her accession, Victoria retained a certain fondness for her childhood home. In 1897, she decided to open the palace to the public. There was a period of restoration and refurbishment, including a (misguided) application of varnish to William Kent's King's Grand Staircase. Then, in 1899, the doors were unlocked and the crowds surged in.

Nineteenth-century visitors climb the King's Grand Staircase
at Kensington Palace. You can see William Kent's portraits of
Peter the Wild Boy and Doctor Arbuthnot on the
landing just ahead of them

In 1911, tourists climbing the King's Grand Staircase found a novel sight in the State Apartments: the 'London Museum' was in residence, and the rooms were full of display cases. Throughout the twentieth century, Kent's paintings continued to be tweaked and refreshed by professional conservators. Then, in the 1980s, the State Apartments were restored to the appearance that William Kent himself would have recognised. The project, the work of the Historic Royal Palaces Agency, employed historical detective work, conservation techniques and artefacts from the Royal Collection.

After the death of the palace's most celebrated resident, Diana, Princess of Wales, in 1997, the State Apartments at Kensington became flooded with more curious visitors than ever before. Nevertheless, George II's ghost is still said to haunt the tower in Clock Court, and can be seen on stormy nights 'shaking his fist at cruel fate'.[25]

And you too, if you like, can still visit Kensington Palace today and climb the King's Grand Staircase, meeting the eyes of Peter the Wild Boy, Mustapha, Elizabeth Butler, Mohammed, Dr Arbuthnot, William Kent . . . You'll almost hear them whispering about you and wondering who you are. They remain at their posts, watching over and welcoming the very latest arrivals to their lost world.

Acknowledgements

Firstly, I would like to single out a group of eighteenth-century historians – Jeremy Black, Tracy Borman, John Brewer, Bob Bucholz, Clarissa Campbell Orr, Isobel Grundy, Joanna Marschner, Lucy Moore and Stella Tillyard – whose books have given me so much information and inspiration. Above all, Hannah Smith's *Georgian Monarchy* seems to me to be the most rigorous and refreshing re-examination of early Georgian court life of recent years.

Documents from the Royal Archives are quoted by the kind permission of Her Majesty Queen Elizabeth II. Miss Allison Derrett, Assistant Registrar, was exceptionally helpful, as was my friend Lucy Whitaker of the Royal Collection.

My fellow curators at Historic Royal Palaces are inspiring, often infuriating, but incomparable colleagues. Many of them are named below. Additionally, I could not have completed this project without the support – both now and over the last ten years – of my director, John Barnes. I'd also like to say hurrah for Alison Heald, the cheerful and competent person who really runs Apartment 25 at Hampton Court. She makes going to work a pleasure.

Other kind people who have provided me with encouragement or information include: Nigel Arch, Beatrice Behlen, Brett Dolman, Olivia Fryman, Esther Godfrey (whose research into slavery for Historic Royal Palaces was invaluable), John Harris, Maurice Howard, Alison Knowles (the present resident of Broadway Farm), Angelika Marks, Dr Randle McRoberts (my medical guru), Konrad Ottenheym, Julia Parker, David Pearce (editor of the *Old Berkhamstedian*), Lee Prosser (who first suggested that 'The Mysterious Quaker' could be Dr Arbuthnot), Robert Sackville-West, Jane Spooner, Tina Graham and the Georgian Group. I owe special thanks to Andrew Thompson, Stephen Taylor, Robin Eagles, Matthew Kilburn, Hannah Smith and the History of Parliament Trust for their seminar on Frederick and subsequent help. I have been honoured with stalwart draft readers including: David Adshead, Stephen Clarke, Clair Corbey, Lynne Darwood, Susanne Groom, Holger Hoock, Katherine Ibbett, Joanna Marschner, Harvey Murray Smith, Michael Turner, Kate Retford and Stephen Taylor. Sincere thanks to every single one of them.

I owe a huge debt to the irrepressible Felicity Bryan in the UK, as well as to Zoe Pagnamenta in the US, to Rebecca Pearson, Susan Holmes, Anne Owen, Ian Bahrami and all the nice people at Faber, and to George Gibson and Margaret Maloney at Bloomsbury USA. Regarding my editor Julian Loose, I would gladly gnaw off my own foot to win a word of his praise.

Lastly, I dedicate my work to Mark Hines, my very own kind and handsome prince.

A NOTE ON DATES

In 1752, Britain's calendar changed from the Julian to the Gregorian system and the start of the New Year was moved to 1 January, instead of 25 March. (Our tax years still follow the old system.) Unless otherwise stated, dates in this book have been silently corrected so that the months of January, February and March pre-1752 are given the year that we would use today.

PICTURE CREDITS

Plate Section

Page 1: (top) *The View of Kensington House from the South*, c.1713–14 © The Royal Borough of Kensington and Chelsea Library Service; (bottom) *Tea Party at Lord Harrington's House, St James's*

by Charles Phillips, Yale Center for British Art reference 147965 ©
Bridgeman/Yale Center for British Art. Pages 2–3: Chris
Puddephatt. Page 4: (top left) *King George I*, studio of Sir Godfrey
Kneller, NPG 544 © National Portrait Gallery, London; (top
right) *Self-Portrait of Sir James Thornhill*, James Thornhill © The
Dean and Chapter of St Paul's Cathedral; (bottom left) The
Cupola Room, Kensington Palace, photographed by Chris
Puddephatt; (bottom right) Chris Puddephatt. Page 5: (top left
and right, bottom left) Lucy Worsley; (bottom right) Detail from
The Royal Hunting Party at Göhrde, 1725 © Her Majesty Queen
Elizabeth II. Page 6: (top left and right) *King George II, when
Prince of Wales* and *Caroline of Anspach, when Princess of Wales* by
Sir Godfrey Kneller, 1716 © Her Majesty Queen Elizabeth II;
(bottom) *Frederick Prince of Wales and His Sisters* by Philip
Mercier, NPG 1556 © The National Portrait Gallery, London.
Page 7: (top) *A Performance of 'The Indian Emperor' or 'The
Conquest of Mexico by the Spaniards'*, William Hogarth, 1732–5,
Private Collection; (bottom left) *John, Lord Hervey, Holding Purse
of Office as Lord Privy Seal*, by J. B. Van Loo, 1741, Ickworth House
(The National Trust) © NTPL/Angelo Hornak; (centre right)
SRO 941/47/4, showing how the first thirteen pages have been
removed. © Suffolk Record Office, Bury St Edmund's; (bottom
right) Berkhamsted School/photo Lucy Worsley. Page 8: (top left)
Queen Caroline of Ansbach by Joseph Highmore, c.1735 © Her
Majesty Queen Elizabeth II; (top right) *Henrietta Howard,
Countess of Suffolk*, c.1724, by Charles Jervas © English Heritage;
(bottom left) *George II* by Robert Edge Pine, 1759 © English
Heritage.

Illustrations in the Text

Pages xviii–xx, 9, 11, 14, 16, 28, 77, 79, 83, 88, 100, 107, 115, 148, 189, 284,
289: Mark Hines. Pages 18, 65, 156: Lucy Worsley. Pages 30, 95, 323:
© All Rights Reserved. The British Library Board. Licence
Number: PRIIND17 (shelfmarks: p. 30, Maps.*3518.(9); p. 95,
1201.a.30; p. 323, 10602 h.15). Pages 48, 73, 281: Historic Royal

Palaces (p. 48, print of court occasion at St James's Palace; p. 73, William Kent's design for drawing room ceiling at Kensington Palace; p. 281, the Rockingham mantua from the Royal Ceremonial Dress Collection). Pages 58, 250: Devonshire Collection, Chatsworth. Reproduced by permission of the Chatsworth Settlement Trustees; photograph, the Courtauld Institute of Art (sketches of William Kent, p. 58, and Queen Caroline, p. 250, by Lady Burlington). Page 74: © www.CartoonStock.com (detail from William Hogarth, 'The Bad Taste of the Town ('Masquerades and Operas') 1724'). Pages 96, 199, 333: private collection. Page 118: The Royal Borough of Kensington and Chelsea Libraries Service (print of Kensington Palace from the east, 1736). Pages 151, 153, 232, 264: copyright The British Museum (p. 151, British Museum reference number 1868,0808,3588; p. 153, Crace IX; p. 232, William Hunter, an unborn child (1750s); p. 264, satirical print of 'Solomon in his Glory'). Page 157: © V&A Images/Victoria and Albert Museum, London (V&A item reference E.903-1928). Pages 223, 224: by courtesy of the Trustees of Sir John Soane's Museum (William Kent's design for Queen Caroline's library at St James's Palace, Sir John Soane's Museum Vol. 147/197). Page 294: © National Portrait Gallery, London (George II sketched by George Townshend, NPG 4855(2)).

Sources

ARCHIVES

The Bodleian Library, Oxford
The British Library (referred to in the Notes as 'BL')
Hertfordshire Archives
Historic Royal Palaces, Kensington Palace, curators' archives. (Especially useful was
    Peter Gaunt and Caroline Knight's compendious unpublished history of the
    palace [1988–9].)
Kensington Public Library. (Especially useful were the two 'Extra illustrated' edi-
    tions of Thomas Faulkner, *History and Antiquities of Kensington*, 2 vols [London,
    1820]. One is bound into two volumes and one in three. Each volume contains
    different pictures and documents.)
The National Archives (referred to in the Notes as 'TNA')
The Royal Archives (referred to in the Notes as 'RA')
Suffolk Record Office, Bury St Edmunds (referred to in the Notes as 'SRO')

BOOKS AND ARTICLES

L'Abbé, Anthony, *A New Collection of Dances*, Ed. Carol Marsh (London, 1991).
Anon., *To a Thing They Call Prince of Wales* (n.p., 1718?).
– *The Grand Exemplar Set forth, in an Impartial Character Of His Sacred Majesty
    King George* (London, 1715).
– *Court tales: or, a History of the Amours of the Present Nobility* (London, 1717).
– *The Criticks. Being papers upon the times* (London, 1719).
– *The Present State of the British Court* (London, 1720).
– (attributed to Daniel Defoe), *Mere Nature Delineated: or, a Body without a Soul.
    Being Observations upon the Young Forester Lately brought to Town from Germany*
    (London, 1726).
– *The Most Wonderful Wonder That ever appear'd to the Wonder of the British Nation*
    (London, 1726).
– *A New Guide to London* (1726).
– (attributed to Dr Arbuthnot or Jonathan Swift) *It cannot Rain but it Pours: Or,
    London strow'd with Rarities*, parts one and two (London, 1726).
– *An Enquiry How the Wild Youth, Lately taken in the Woods near Hanover, (and now
    brought over to England) could be there left, and by what Creature he could be suckled,
    nursed and brought up* (London, 1726).
– *Some Memoirs of the life of Lewis Maximilian Mahomet, Gent. Late Servant to his
    Majesty* (London, 1727).

– *The Ceremonial of the Coronation Of His most Sacred Majesty King George II And of His Royal Consort Queen Caroline* (Dublin, 1727).
– *Plain Reasons for the Growth of Sodomy in England* (London, 1728).
– (attributed to William Pulteney) *A Proper Reply to a Late Scurrilous Libel* (London, 1731).
– *The Contest: being poetical essays on the Queen's grotto: wrote in consequence of an invitation in the Gentlemen's Magazine for April, 1733* (London, 1734).
– *The Ladies Physical Directory* ('the eighth edition, with some very material additions', London, 1742).
– *A representation of the Cloathing of His Majesty's Household* (London, 1742).
– *A Book to Help the Young and Gay* (London, 1750).
– *By several hands, sketches and characters of the most Eminent and most Singular Persons Now Living* (London, 1770).
– *The Character of George the First, Queen Caroline, Sir Robert Walpole . . . Reviewed. With Royal and Noble Anecdotes* (London, 1777).
– *The New Foundling Hospital for Wit, Being a Collection of Fugitive Pieces, in Prose and Verse* (London, 1784).
– *The annual register, or a view of the history, politics, and literature for the years 1784 and 1785* (London, 1787).
– *A collection of ordinances and regulations for the government of the Royal Household* (Society of Antiquaries, London, 1790).
– *George the Third, His Court and Family* (London, 1820).
Appleby, John H., 'Rowley, John (*c.*1668–1728)', *Oxford Dictionary of National Biography* (Oxford, 2004).
Arbuthnot, John, *Mr Maitland's Account of Inoculating the Small Pox* (London, 1722).
– *Miscellanies* (Dublin, 1746).
Arch, Nigel, and Joanna Marschner, *Splendour at Court: Dressing for Royal Occasions since 1700* (London, 1987).
Arciszewska, Barbara, *The Hanoverian Court and the Triumph of Palladio* (Warsaw, 2002).
Arkell, R. L., *Caroline of Ansbach, George the Second's Queen* (London, 1939).
Ashton, John, *Social Life in the Reign of Queen Anne* (London, 1882).
Aston, Nigel, 'The Court of George II: Lord Berkeley of Stratton's perspective', *The Court Historian*, Vol. 13.2 (December, 2008), pp. 171–93.
Ault, Norman, and John Butt (Eds), *Alexander Pope, Minor Poems* (London and New York, 1964).
Barber, Tabitha, 'Thornhill, Sir James (1675/6–1734)', *Oxford Dictionary of National Biography* (Oxford, 2004).
Bateson, F. W. (Ed.), *Alexander Pope, Epistles to Several Persons* (London and New Haven, 1961).
Bathoe, W., *Catalogue of the Pictures at Kensington* (London, 1758).
Beard, Geoffrey, *Craftsmen and Interior Decoration in England, 1660–1820* (London, 1981).
Beattie, J. M., *The English Court in the Reign of George I* (Cambridge, 1967).
– *Crime and the Courts in England, 1660–1800* (Princeton, 1986).
Beckett, William, *A Collection of Chirurgical Tracts* (London, 1740).
Bickham, George, *Apelles Britannicus* (London, 1741).

Bielfeld, Jacob Friedrich, *Letters of Baron Bielfeld*, trans. William Hooper, 4 vols (London, 1768–70).

Bingley, William, *Correspondence between Frances, Countess of Hertford, and Henrietta Louisa, Countess of Pomfret, between the years 1738 and 1741*, 3 vols (London, 1805).

Black, Jeremy, '"George II and All That Stuff": On the Value of the Neglected', *Albion*, Vol. 36.4 (winter 2004a).

– *The Hanoverians, The History of a Dynasty* (London, 2004b).

– *George II, Puppet of the Politicians?* (Exeter, 2007).

Borman, Tracy, *Henrietta Howard, King's Mistress, Queen's Servant* (London, 2007).

Bowen, Marjorie, *The Third Mary Stuart* (London, 1929).

Bowers, Toni, *The Politics of Motherhood* (Cambridge, 1996).

Boyle, John, fifth Earl of Orrery, *Remarks on the Life and Writings of Dr Jonathan Swift* (London, 1752).

Brooke, John (Ed.), *The Yale Edition of Horace Walpole's Memoirs* (New Haven and London, 1985).

Brown, Thomas, *Amusements Serious and Comical, Calculated for the Meridian of London* (London, 1700).

Bucholz, R. O., *The Augustan Court, Queen Anne and the Decline of Court Culture* (Stanford, California, 1993).

– 'Going to Court in 1700: a visitor's guide', *The Court Historian*, Vol. 4.3 (December 2000), pp. 181–215.

Burnet, James, Lord Monboddo, *Antient Metaphysics: or, the Science of Universals*, 6 vols (Edinburgh and London, 1779–99).

Burney, Fanny, *Diary and Letters of Madame D'Arblay*, edited by her niece (London, 1842).

Burrows, Donald, 'Handel, George Frideric (1685–1759)', *Oxford Dictionary of National Biography* (Oxford, 2004).

Campbell, Richard, *The London tradesman. Being a compendious view of all the trades, professions, arts, both liberal and mechanic, now practised* (London, 1747).

Campbell Orr, Clarissa (Ed.), *Queenship in Britain, 1660–1837: Royal Patronage, Court Culture, and Dynastic Politics* (Manchester, 2002).

– (Ed.), *Queenship in Europe, 1660–1815: The Role of the Consort* (Cambridge, 2004).

Cannon, John, 'George II (1683–1760)', *Oxford Dictionary of National Biography* (Oxford, 2004).

Carswell, John and Lewis Arnold Dralle (Eds), *The Political Journal of George Bubb Dodington* (Oxford, 1965).

Cartwright, J. J. (Ed.), *The Wentworth Papers 1705–1739, selected from the private and family correspondence of Thomas Wentworth, Lord Raby, created in 1711 Earl of Strafford* (London, 1883).

Caudle, J. J., 'Mohammed von Königstreu, (Georg) Ludwig Maximilian (c.1660–1726)', *Oxford Dictionary of National Biography* (Oxford, 2004).

– 'Mustapha, Ernst August (d.1738)', *Oxford Dictionary of National Biography* (Oxford, 2004).

Cavendish, William, fourth Duke of Devonshire, *Memoranda on the State of Affairs, 1759–1762*, Eds P. D. Brown and K. W. Schweizer, Camden Society, fourth series, Vol. 27 (London, 1982).

Chalus, E. H., 'Amelia, Princess (1711–1786)', *Oxford Dictionary of National Biography* (Oxford, 2004).

Chandler, Samuel, *The character of a great and good king* (London, 1760).

Clark, J. C. D. (Ed.), *The Memoirs and Speeches of James, 2nd Earl Waldegrave* (Cambridge, 1988).

Clarke, Dr Alured, *An Essay towards the Character of Her late Majesty Caroline, Queen-Consort of Great Britain* (London, 1738).

Cleland, John, *Fanny Hill or Memoirs of a Woman of Pleasure* (London, 1748–9; Harmondsworth, 1985).

Clerk, Sir John, *Memoirs of Sir John Clerk*, Ed. John M. Gray (London, 1895).

Linda Colley, *Britons* (London and New Haven, 1992).

Colvin, Howard (Ed.), *The History of the King's Works*, Vol. V (1660–1782) (London, 1976).

– *A Biographical Dictionary of British Architects* (New Haven and London, 1995) .

Cooper, Anthony Ashley, Earl of Shaftesbury, *Letters of the Earl of Shaftesbury* (n.p., 1746).

Cowper, Mary, *Diary of Mary, Countess Cowper* (London, 1864).

Coxe, William (Ed.), *Fables by John Gay, illustrated with notes and the life of the author* (Salisbury, 1798a).

– *Memoirs of Sir Robert Walpole*, 3 vols (London, 1798b; 1816).

– *Memoirs of John Duke of Marlborough*, 3 vols (London, 1819).

Croker, J. W. (Ed.), *Letters to and from Henrietta, Countess of Suffolk and her second husband the Hon. George Berkeley from 1712 to 1767*, 2 vols (London, 1824).

Cunningham, Andrew, and Roger French (eds.) *The Medical Enlightenment of the Eighteenth Century* (Cambridge, 1990).

Cunningham, Peter (Ed.), *The Letters of Horace Walpole*, 9 vols (London, 1857).

Cussans, John Edwin, *History of Hertfordshire*, 3 vols (London, 1879–1881).

Dann, Uriel, *Hanover and Great Britain 1740–1760* (Leicester, 1991).

Davies, J. D. Griffith, *A King in Toils* (London, 1938).

Defoe, Daniel, *Reasons against the Succession of the House of Hanover* (London, 1713).

– *Mere Nature Delineated: or, a Body Without a Soul* (London, 1726).

Dobree, B., and V. Webb, *The Complete Works of Sir John Vanbrugh*, 4 vols (London, 1927–8).

Dutton, Ralph, *English Court Life* (London, 1963).

Eagles, Robin, '"No more to be said"? Reactions to the death of Frederick Lewis, prince of Wales', *Historical Journal*, Vol. 80, No. 209.

Edgeworth, Maria, *Practical Education* (London, 1798).

Edwards, Averyl, *Frederick Lewis, Prince of Wales* (London, 1947).

Entick, John, *A New and Accurate History and Survey of London, Westminster and Southwark* (London, 1766).

Faulkner, Thomas, *History and Antiquities of Kensington*, 2 vols (London, 1820).

Fergusson, Alexander (Ed.), *Letters and Journals of Mrs Calderwood of Polton from England, Holland and the Low Countries in 1756* (Edinburgh, 1884).

Field, Ophelia, *The Favourite: Sarah, Duchess of Marlborough* (London, 2002).

Fielding, Henry, *The Modern Husband, a Comedy* (Dublin, 1732).

– *Tom Jones* (London, 1749; 1991).

Fitzgerald, Brian (Ed.), *Correspondence of Emily, Duchess of Leinster*, 3 vols (Dublin, 1949–57).

Fleming, J., *Robert Adam and his Circle* (London, 1962).

Franklin, Colin, *Lord Chesterfield, His Character and Characters* (Aldershot, 1993).

Fraser, Flora, *Princesses, the Six Daughters of George III* (London, 2004).

Fritz, Paul S., 'From "Public" to "Private": The Royal Funerals in England, 1500–1830' in Joachim Whaley (Ed.), *Mirrors of Mortality, Studies in the Social History of Death* (London, 1981), pp. 61–79.

Furnivall, Frederick J. (Ed.), *The Babees Book, etc.*, Early English Text Society (London, 1868).

Gaunt, Peter, and Caroline Knight (1988–9), see under 'Archives'.

Gay, John, *A panegyrical epistle to Mr Thomas Snow* (London, 1721).

– *Poems on Several Occasions* (London, 1720; 1731; 1775).

– *The poetical works of John Gay, from the royal quarto edition of 1720* (London, 1797).

Gerrard, C., 'Queens-in-waiting: Caroline of Anspach and Augusta of Saxe-Gotha as princesses of Wales', *Queenship in Britain, 1660–1837: Royal Patronage, Court Culture, and Dynastic Politics*, Ed. C. Campbell Orr (Manchester, 2002), pp. 143–61.

Glasheen, Joan, *The Secret People of the Palaces* (London, 1998).

Glendinning, Victoria, *Jonathan Swift* (London, 1998).

Glover, Richard, *Memoirs of a Celebrated Literary Character* (London, 1813).

Goff, Moira, '"The Art of Dancing, Demonstrated by Characters and Figures": French and English sources for court and theatre dance, 1700–50', *British Library Journal*, Vol. 21, No. 2 (autumn 1995), pp. 202–31.

Grace, Sheffield (Ed.), *A Letter from the Countess of Nithsdale* (London, 1828).

Graham, John Murray (Ed.), *Annals and Correspondence of the Viscount and the First and Second Earls of Stair*, 2 vols (Edinburgh and London, 1875).

Greenwood, Alice Drayton, *Lives of the Hanoverian Queens of England*, 2 vols (London, 1909).

Greig, Hannah, and Giorgio Riello, 'Eighteenth-Century Interiors – Redesigning the Georgian: Introduction', *Journal of Design History*, Vol. 20, No. 4 (2007), pp. 273–89.

Grenville, George, *The Grenville Papers*, Ed. W. J. Smith (London, 1852).

Grieser, Rudolf (Ed.), *Die Memoiren des Kammerherrn Friedrick Ernst von Fabrice (1683–1750)* (Hildesheim, 1956).

Grundy, Isobel, *Lady Mary Wortley Montagu, Comet of the Enlightenment* (Oxford, 1999).

Guilding, Ruth, 'Sculpture at Holkham', *Country Life* (6 March 2008).

Haile, Martin, *Queen Mary of Modena, her life and letters* (London, 1905).

Hailes, Lord (Ed.), *The Opinions of Sarah Duchess-Dowager of Marlborough* (London, 1788).

Hallett, Mark, *The Spectacle of Difference* (New Haven and London, 1999).

Halsband, Robert (Ed.), *The Complete Letters of Lady Mary Wortley Montagu* (Oxford, 1965–7).

– *Lord Hervey, Eighteenth-Century Courtier* (Oxford, 1973).

– and Isobel Grundy (Eds), *Mary Wortley Montagu, Essays and Poems and 'Simplicity', a Comedy* (Oxford, 1977).

Hamilton, A., *Memoirs of Count Grammont*, Ed. W. Scott (London, 1905).

Hanham, Andrew, 'Caroline of Brandenburg-Ansbach and the "Anglicisation" of the House of Hanover', in Clarissa Campbell Orr (Ed.), *Queenship in Europe, 1660–1815: The Role of the Consort* (Cambridge, 2004), pp. 276–99.

Hardy, Alan, *The Kings' Mistresses* (London, 1980).

Harley, R. D., *Artists' Pigments, c.1660–1835* (London, 1982).

Harris, James Howard, third Earl of Malmesbury (Ed.), *Letters of the First Earl of Malmesbury*, 2 vols (London, 1870).

Harris, John, 'Kent, William (*bap.* 1686, *d.*1748)', *Oxford Dictionary of National Biography* (Oxford, 2004).

Harvey, A. D., *Sex in Georgian England* (London, 1994; 2001).

Hastings Wheler, George (Ed.), *Hastings Wheler Family Letters 1704–1739* (West Yorkshire, 1935).

Hatton, Ragnhild, *George I, Elector and King* (London, 1978).

– *The Anglo-Hanoverian Connection 1714–1760* (Creighton Trust Lecture, 1982).

Haynes, John, *Kensington Palace* (London, 1995).

Hennell, Colonel Sir Reginald, *The History of the King's Body Guard of the Yeomen of the Guard* (London, 1904).

Hervey, Augustus, *Augustus Hervey's Journal*, Ed. David Erskine (Rochester, 2002).

Hervey, John, first Earl of Bristol, *Letter-Books of John Hervey, first Earl of Bristol, 1651–1750*, 3 vols (Wells, 1894).

Hervey, John, Baron Hervey of Ickworth, *The Court-Spy; Or, Memoirs of St J–m–es's* (London, 1744).

– *Some Materials towards Memoirs of the Reign of George II*, Ed. Romney Sedgwick, 3 vols (London, 1931).

Hervey, Mary, *Letters of Mary Lepel, Lady Hervey* (London, 1821).

Hervey, Sydenham, *Journals of the Hon. William Hervey* (Bury St Edmunds, 1906).

Hibbert, Christopher, *George III, A Personal History* (London, 1998).

Highfill, Philip H., Kalman A. Burnim and Edward A. Langhams, *A Biographical Dictionary of Actors, Actresses, Musicians & Other Stage Personnel in London 1660–1800* (Carbondale, 1973).

Hilton, Lisa, *Mistress Peachum's Pleasure, The Life of Lavinia, Duchess of Bolton* (London, 2005).

HMC 11th Report, *The Manuscripts of the Marquess Townsend* (London, 1887).

HMC 12th Report, appendix, Part III, *The Manuscripts of Earl Cowper* (London, 1889).

HMC 12th Report, appendix III, *Manuscripts of the Coke Family of Melbourne Hall, Derbyshire, belonging to the Earl Cowper* (London, 1898).

HMC 12th Report, appendix, Part X, *The Manuscripts and Correspondence of James, first earl of Charlemont*, 2 vols (London, 1891–4).

HMC 14, *Report on Manuscripts in Various Collections* (London, 1895).

HMC 15th Report, *Manuscripts of the Earl of Carlisle*, appendix, part 6 (London, 1897).

HMC, *Report on Manuscripts in Various Collections*, Vol. 8 (London, 1913).

HMC, *Report on the Manuscripts of his Grace the Duke of Portland*, Vol. 5 (London, 1899).

HMC, *Report on the Manuscripts of Lord Polwarth*, Vol. 1 (London, 1911).

HMC, *Calendar of the Stuart Papers belonging to His Majesty the King* (London, 1912).

HMC, *Manuscripts of the Earl of Egmont*, diary of the first Earl of Egmont, 3 vols (London, 1920–3).

HMC 67, *Report on the Manuscripts of the Right Honourable Lord Polwarth* (London, 1961).

Holland, John, *The History, Antiquities, and Description of the Town and Parish of Worksop* (Sheffield, 1826).

Holland, Lord (Ed.), *Horace Walpole's Memoirs of the Reign of King George the Second*, 3 vols (London, 1846).

Home, J. A. (Ed.), *The letters and journals of Lady Mary Coke*, 4 vols (Edinburgh, 1889–96).

Hone, William, *The Table Book*, Vol. 1 (London, 1827; Detroit, 1966).

Hunt, Lynn, *The Family Romance of the French Revolution* (London, 1992).

Hutchins, John, *The history and antiquities of the county of Dorset*, 2 vols (London, 1774), third edn revised by William Shipp and James Whitworth Hodson, 4 vols (London, 1868).

Ilchester, Earl of (Giles Stephen Holland Fox-Strangways) (Ed.), *Lord Hervey and his Friends, 1726–38, based on letters from Holland House, Melbury, and Ickworth* (London, 1950).

Impey, Edward, *Kensington Palace, The Official Illustrated History* (London, 2003).

James, Charles Warburton, *Chief Justice Coke, his family and descendants at Holkham* (London, 1929).

Jesse, John Heneage, *Memoirs of the Court of England*, 3 vols (London, 1843).

Johnson, Samuel, *The Lives of the most Eminent English Poets, with Critical Observations on their Works* (London, 1781).

Jones, M. G., *Hannah More* (Cambridge, 1952).

Jourdain, Margaret, *The Work of William Kent* (Country Life, 1948), p. 72.

Kilburn, Matthew, 'Hervey (neé Lepell), Mary, Lady Hervey of Ickworth (1699/1700–1768)', *Oxford Dictionary of National Biography* (Oxford, 2004).

– 'Frederick Lewis, prince of Wales (1707–1751)', *Oxford Dictionary of National Biography* (Oxford, 2004).

– 'Howard, Henrietta, countess of Suffolk (c.1688–1767)', *Oxford Dictionary of National Biography* (Oxford, 2004).

– 'Wallmoden, Amalie Sophie Marianne von, suo jure countess of Yarmouth (1704–1765)', *Oxford Dictionary of National Biography* (Oxford, 2004).

Klopp, Onno (Ed.), *Correspondence de Leibniz* (Hanover, 1874).

Knight, Caroline, and Peter Gaunt (1988–89), see under 'Archives'.

Kroll, Maria (Ed.), *Letters from Liselotte* (London, 1970, 1998).

Kugler, Anne, *Errant Plagiary: The Life and Writing of Lady Sarah Cowper, 1644–1720* (Stanford, California, 2002).

Langford, Paul, *A Polite and Commercial People, England 1727–1783* (Oxford, 1989; 1998).

Laprade, William Thomas, *Public Opinion and Politics in Eighteenth Century England* (New York, 1936).

Laqueur, Thomas, *Making Sex, Body and Gender from the Greeks to Freud* (Cambridge, Massachusetts, and London, 1990).

Law, Ernest, *The History of Hampton Court Palace* (London, 1891).

Lawson, Cecil C., *A History of the Uniforms of the British Army*, 5 vols (London, 1940–1).

Lewis, W. S. (Ed.), *The Yale Edition of Horace Walpole's Correspondence*, 48 vols (Oxford, 1937–83).

Llanover, Lady (Ed.), *The Autobiography and Correspondence of Mary Granville, Mrs Delaney*, 3 vols (London, 1861).

Louis, George, and R. L. Arkell, 'George I's letters to his daughter', *The English Historical Review*, Vol. 52, No. 207 (July 1938), pp. 492–9.

McKendrick, Neil, John Brewer and J. H. Plumb, *The Birth of a Consumer Society: The Commercialization of Eighteenth-Century England* (London, 1982).

McLynn, Frank, *1759, The Year Britain Became Master of the World* (London, 2004).

McParland, E., 'Sir Thomas Hewett and the new junta for architecture', in *The Role of the Amateur Architect*, Ed. Giles Worsley (The Georgian Group, 1994), pp. 21–6.

Mahon, Lord (Ed.), *Letters of the Earl of Chesterfield* (London, 1845).

– *History of England from the Peace of Utrecht to the Peace of Versailles, 1713–83*, 7 vols (London, 1858).

Mandeville, Bernard, *The Fable of the Bees: or, private vices publick benefits* (London, 1714) .

Manning, F. J. (Ed.), *The Williamson Letters, 1748–1765*, publications of the Bedfordshire Historical Record Society, Vol. XXXIV (Luton, 1954).

Mansel, Philip, *Pillars of Monarchy: An Outline of the Political and Social History of Royal Guards 1400–1984* (London, 1984).

March, Earl of, *A Duke and his Friends. The Life and Letters of the Second Duke of Richmond*, 2 vols (London, 1911).

Marie Louise, Princess, *My Memories of Six Reigns* (London, 1956).

Marlow, Joyce, *The Life and Times of George I* (London, 1973).

Marples, Morris, *Poor Fred and the Butcher, Sons of George II* (London, 1970).

Marschner, Joanna, 'Queen Caroline of Ansbach: attitudes to clothes and cleanliness, 1727–1737', *Costume*, No. 31 (1997).

– 'Caroline of Ansbach: The Queen, Collecting and Connoisseurship at the Early Georgian Court', PhD thesis, University College (London, 2007).

Matthews, William (Ed.), *The Diary of Dudley Ryder, 1715–1716* (London, 1939).

Mavor, Elizabeth, *The Virgin Duchess, A Study in Survival: The Life of the Duchess of Kingston* (London, 1964).

Meli, D. Bertoloni, 'Caroline, Leibniz and Clarke', *Journal of the History of Ideas*, Vol. 60, No. 3 (1999), pp. 469–86.

Melville, Lewis, *Life and Letters of John Gay (1685–1732)* (London, 1921).

Michael, Wolfgang, *England under George I: The Quadruple Alliance*, trans. Annemarie MacGregor and George E. MacGregor (London, 1939).

Millar, Oliver, *Pictures in the Royal Collection, Tudor, Stuart and Early Georgian Pictures* (London, 1963).

Misson, Henri, *M. Misson's memoirs and observations in his travels over England*, trans. Mr Ozell (London, 1719).

Montagu, William Drogo, seventh duke of Manchester, *Court and Society from Elizabeth to Anne, edited from the papers at Kimbolton*, 2 vols (London, 1864).

SOURCES

Moore, Andrew, *Houghton Hall, The Prime Minister, The Empress and The Heritage* (London, 1996).

Moore, Lucy, *Amphibious Thing, the Life of Lord Hervey* (London, 2000).

Morrell, Philip (Ed.), *Leaves from the Greville Diary* (London, 1929).

Morton, Andrew, *Inside Kensington Palace* (London, 1987).

Mowl, Timothy, *William Kent, Architect, Designer, Opportunist* (London, 2006).

Newman, A. L., 'The Political Patronage of Frederick Louis, Prince of Wales', *Historical Journal*, Vol. 1, No. 1 (1958).

Newman, Aubrey, *The Stanhopes of Chevening* (London, 1969).

– *The World Turned Inside Out: New Views on George II* (inaugural lecture, Leicester University, 1988).

Newton, Isaac, *The chronology of ancient kingdoms amended* (London, 1728).

Newton, Michael, 'Bodies Without Souls: The Case of Peter the Wild Boy', *At the Borders of the Human*, Eds E. Fudge, R. Gilbert and S. Wiseman (Basingstoke, 1999).

– *Savage Girls and Wild Boys, a History of Feral Children* (London, 2002).

O'Connell, Sheila, *London 1753* (London, 2003).

Osborn, E. F. D. (Ed.), *Political and Social Letters of a Lady of the Eighteenth Century* (London, 1890).

Owen, J. B., 'George II Reconsidered' in A. Whiteman, S. J. Bromley and P. G. M. Dickson (Eds), *Statesmen, Scholars and Merchants: Essays in Eighteenth-Century History* (Oxford, 1973), pp. 113–34.

Page, William (Ed.), *The Victoria History of the Counties of England, A History of Hertfordshire* (London, 1908).

Paglia, Camille, 'Lord Hervey and Pope', *Eighteenth-Century Studies*, Vol. 6, No. 3 (spring 1973), pp. 348–71.

Pegge, Samuel, *Curialia: or an Historical Account of Some Branches of the Royal Household* (London, 1791).

Phillimore, Robert Joseph (Ed.), *Memoirs and Correspondence of George, Lord Lyttelton, from 1734 to 1773*, 2 vols (London, 1845).

Picard, Liza, *Dr Johnson's London* (London, 2000).

Plumb, J. H., *Sir Robert Walpole*, 2 vols (1956, 1961).

– *The Growth of Political Stability in England, 1675–1725* (1967).

Pöllnitz, Karl Ludwig, *The Memoirs of Charles-Lewis, Baron de Pollnitz* (London, 1737 and 1738).

– *Memoirs of Charles-Lewis, Baron de Pollnitz* (second edition, with additions, London, 1739).

Pope, Alexander, *Miscellaneous poems and translations* (London, 1722).

– *&c., Court Poems* (London, 1726).

– *The Impertinent, or a Visit to the Court* (London, 1733).

– *Ethic epistles, satires, &c.* (London, 1735).

– *Bounce to Fop. An Heroick Epistle from a Dog at Twickenham to a Dog at Court* (London, 1736).

– *Epistles to Several Persons* (London, 1744).

– *The Works Of Alexander Pope Esq.* (London, 1751).

Porter, Roy, *Enlightenment* (London, 2000).

Pottle, Frederick A., *Boswell's London Journal* (London, 1950).

Power, D'A., 'Ranby, John (1703-1773)', rev. Michael Bevan, *Oxford Dictionary of National Biography* (Oxford, 2004).

Prior, Matthew, *The history of his own time*, Ed. Adrian Drift (London, 1740).

Prüser, Jürgen, *Die Göhrde* (Hildesheim, 1969).

Pulteney, William, *A Proper Reply to a Late Scurrilous Libel* (London, 1731).

– *An Answer to One Part of a Late Infamous Libel* (London, 1731).

Pyne, W. H., *The History of the Royal Residences* (London, 1819).

Ralph, James, *A Critical Review of the Public Buildings . . . in and about London and Westminster* (London, 1734).

Ribeiro, Aileen, *Dress in Eighteenth Century Europe* (London, 1984).

Rose, G. H. (Ed.), *A Selection from the papers of the Earls of Marchmont*, 3 vols (London, 1831).

Rosenthal, Norman (Ed.), *The Misfortunate Margravine, the Early Memoirs of Wilhelmina, Margravine of Bayreuth* (London, 1970).

Ross, Angus (Ed.), *The Correspondence of Dr John Arbuthnot* (Münster, 2006).

Rumbold, Valerie, *Women's Place in Pope's World* (Cambridge, 1989).

Russell, Rachel, *Letters of Lady Rachel Russell; from the manuscript in the library at Wooburn Abbey* (London, 1792).

Sainty, J. C., and R. O. Bucholz, *Officials of the Royal Household, 1660–1837* (Institute of Historical Research, 1997).

Saussure, César de, *A Foreign View of England in the Reigns of George I and George II*, trans. Madame van Muyden (London, 1902).

Schaer, Friedrich-Wilhelm (Ed.), *Briefe der Gräfin Johanna Sophie zu Schaumburg-Lippe* (Rinteln, 1968).

Sedgwick, Romney (Ed.), *Letters from George III to Lord Bute, 1756–1766* (London, 1939).

– *The House of Commons, 1715–54*, 2 vols (London, 1970).

Sherburn, George (Ed.), *The Correspondence of Alexander Pope* (Oxford, 1956).

Simms, Brendan, and Torsten Riotte, *The Hanoverian Dimension in British History, 1714–1837* (Cambridge, 2007).

Simond, Louis, *Journal of a Tour and Residence in Great Britain*, 2 vols (Edinburgh, 1815).

Smith, David Nichol (Ed.), *The Letters of Thomas Burnet to George Duckett, 1712–1722* (Oxford, 1914).

Smith, Hannah, *Georgian Monarchy, Politics and Culture, 1714–1760* (Cambridge, 2006).

– and Stephen Taylor, 'Hephaestion and Alexander: Lord Hervey, Frederick, Prince of Wales, and the Royal Favourite in England in the 1730s', *The English Historical Review*, Vol. CXXIV, No. 507 (2009), pp. 283–312.

Smith, John, *The Art of Painting in Oyl* (London, 1701 edn).

Smollett, Tobias, *The History of England from the Revolution to the Death of George the Second*, 4 vols (London, 1848 edn).

Somerset, Anne, *Ladies in Waiting* (London, 1984).

Speck, W. A., 'William Augustus, Prince, duke of Cumberland (1721–1765)', *Oxford Dictionary of National Biography* (Oxford, 2004).

Stanhope, Philip, Earl of Chesterfield, *Letters written by the late right honourable Philip Dormer Stanhope, Earl of Chesterfield, to his son Philip Stanhope, esq.* published by Mrs Eugenia Stanhope, 2 vols (London, 1774).

– *Lord Chesterfield's witticisms* (London, 1775).

– *Miscellaneous Works*, 3 vols (n.p., 1777).

– *Characters of Eminent Personages* (London, 1778).

Starkey, David, 'Representation through Intimacy: A Study in the Symbolism of Monarchy and Court Office in Early-Modern England', in *Symbols and Sentiments: Cross-cultural Studies in Symbolism*, Ed. I. Lewis (London, New York and San Francisco, 1977).

Steffensen, James L., 'Lillo, George (1691/1693–1739)', *Oxford Dictionary of National Biography* (Oxford, 2004).

Stuart, Dorothy Margaret, *Molly Lepell, Lady Harvey* (London, 1936).

Styles, John and Amanda Vickery (Eds), *Gender, Taste, and Material Culture in Britain and North America, 1700–1830* (New Haven and London, 2006).

Swift, Jonathan, *The lady's dressing room* (London, 1732).

– *A Beautiful Young Nymph Going to Bed* (London, 1734).

– *Directions to Servants* (London, 1745).

– *Letters, written by the late Jonathan Swift*, 6 vols (London, 1766–68).

– *The Beauties of Swift: or, the favourite offspring of wit & genius* (London, 1782).

Taylor, Stephen, Richard Connors and Clyve Jones, *Hanoverian Britain and Empire* (Woodbridge, 1998).

Taylor, Stephen, 'Walpole, Robert, first earl of Orford (1676–1745)', *Oxford Dictionary of National Biography* (Oxford, 2004).

Taylor, W. D., *Jonathan Swift: a Critical Essay* (London, 1933).

Tennant, C. M., *Peter the Wild Boy* (London, 1938).

Thackeray, William, *The Four Georges* (London, 1848).

Thomas, Keith, 'The Double Standard', *Journal of the History of Ideas*, Vol. 20, No. 2 (April 1959), pp. 195–216.

Thomas, W. Moy (Ed.), *The letters and works of Lady Mary Wortley Montagu*, 2 vols (London, 1887).

Thomson, A. T. (Ed.), *Memoirs of Viscountess Sundon, Mistress of the Robes to Queen Caroline*, 2 vols (London, 1847).

Thomson, Gladys Scott (Ed.), *Letters of a Grandmother, 1732–35, being the correspondence of Sarah, Duchess of Marlborough with her granddaughter Diana, Duchess of Bedford* (London, 1943).

Thomson, Peter, 'Cuyler [*married name* Rice], Margaret (1758–1814)', *Oxford Dictionary of National Biography* (Oxford, 2004).

Tickell, Thomas, *Kensington Garden* (London, 1722).

Tillyard, Stella, *A Royal Affair, George III and his Troublesome Siblings* (London, 2006).

Tindal, Nicolas, *The continuation of Mr Rapin's History of England; from the revolution to the present times* (London, fourth edn 1758).

Towle, Matthew, *The Young Gentleman and Lady's Private Tutor* (London, 1771).

Trench, Charles Chenevix, *George II* (London, 1973).

Trumbach, Ralph, 'Modern Sodomy: The Origins of Homosexuality, 1700–1800', in Matt Cock (Ed.), *A Gay History of Britain* (Oxford, 2007), pp. 77–105.

Turnor, Edmund, *Collections for the history of the town and soke of Grantham* (London, 1806).

Uffenbach, Zacharias Conrad von, *London in 1710, from the travels of Zacharias*

Conrad von Uffenbach, trans. and edited by W. H. Quarrell and M. Mare (London, 1934).

Van Der Kiste, John, *King George II and Queen Caroline* (Stroud, 1997).

Van Koughnet, Lady Jane, *A History of Tyttenhanger* (London, 1895).

Verney, Margaret Maria (Ed.), *Verney Letters of the Eighteenth Century from the MSS. at Claydon House*, 2 vols (London, 1930).

Wade, John, *The Extraordinary Black Book* (London, 1931).

Wagstaffe, William, *A Letter to Dr Freind, Shewing The Danger and Uncertainty of Inoculating the Small Pox* (London, 1722).

Waller, Maureen, *1700, Scenes from London Life* (London, 2000).

– *Ungrateful Daughters* (London, 2002).

Walpole, Horace, *Anecdotes of painting in England* (second edn, Strawberry Hill, 1771).

– *Reminiscences, written in 1788, for the amusement of Miss Mary and Miss Agnes B***y* (London, 1818 edn).

Walters, John, *The Royal Griffin: Frederick, Prince of Wales, 1707–1751* (London, 1972).

Ward, Ned, *The London Spy* (fourth edition, London, 1709), Ed. Paul Hyland (East Lansing, Michigan, 1993).

Warner, Jessica, *Craze, Gin and Debauchery in an Age of Reason* (London, 2003).

Wharncliffe, Lord (Ed.), *The Letters and Works of Lady Mary Wortley Montagu* (London, 1837, 1861).

White, T. H., *The Age of Scandal* (London, 1950).

Whitworth, Rex, *William Augustus, Duke of Cumberland: A Life* (London, 1992).

Wildeblood, Joan, *The Polite World: A Guide to the Deportment of the English in Former Times* (London, 1973).

Wilkins, W. H., *Caroline the Illustrious*, 2 vols (London, 1901).

Williams, Charles Hanbury, *The odes of Sir Charles Hanbury Williams* (London, 1775).

Williams, Harold (Ed.), *The Correspondence of Jonathan Swift*, 5 vols (Oxford, 1963–5).

Williamson, David, 'Mary, Princess (1723–1772)', *Oxford Dictionary of National Biography* (Oxford, 2004).

Wilson, Adrian, 'The Politics of Medical Improvement in Early Hanoverian London', in Andrew Cunningham and Roger French (Eds), *The Medical Enlightenment of the Eighteenth Century* (Cambridge, 1990), pp. 4–39.

Wilson, Henry, *Wonderful Characters* (London, 1821).

Wilson, Kathleen, *The Sense of the People: Politics, Culture and Imperialism in England, 1715–1785* (Cambridge, 1995).

Wilson, Michael I., *William Kent* (London, 1984).

Wood, John, *An Essay towards a Description of Bath*, 2 vols (London, 1749).

Woodfin, Maude H. (Ed.), *Another Secret Diary of William Byrd of Westover, 1739–1741, with letters and literary exercises 1696–1726* (Richmond, Virginia, 1942).

Worsley, Giles, 'Hewett, Sir Thomas (1656–1726)', *Oxford Dictionary of National Biography* (Oxford, 2004).

Wraxall, Sir N. William, Bart., *Historical Memoirs of my own time* (London, 1904).

Wright, L. S., and M. Tinling (Eds), *William Byrd, The London Diary, 1717–21* (New York, 1958).

Wright, Thomas, *England under the House of Hanover*, 2 vols (London, 1848).

Yorke, Philip, Earl of Hardwicke, *Walpoliana* (London, 1783).

– *The Life and Correspondence of Philip Yorke, Earl of Hardwicke*, 3 vols (Cambridge, 1913).

Young, Sir George, *Poor Fred, the People's Prince* (London, 1937).

Notes

EPIGRAPH (p. v)

1. John Hervey, *Some Materials towards Memoirs of the Reign of King George II*, Ed. Romney Sedgwick, Vol. 2 (London, 1931), p. 347.

PREFACE

1. Philip Stanhope, Earl of Chesterfield, *Letters written by the late right honourable Philip Dormer Stanhope, Earl of Chesterfield, to his son Philip Stanhope, esq.*, published by Mrs Eugenia Stanhope, Vol. 1 (London, 1774), p. 442.
2. W. S. Lewis (Ed.), *The Yale Edition of Horace Walpole's Correspondence* (Oxford, 1937–83) Vol. 9, p. 202.
3. William A. Shaw (Ed.), *Calendar of Treasury Books* (January–December 1716) (London, 1957) pp. 321–2.
4. Hervey (1931), Vol. 2, p. 625.

CHAPTER I: TO THE PALACE

1. Frederick A. Pottle, *Boswell's London Journal* (London, 1950), p. 148.
2. César de Saussure, *A Foreign View of England in the Reigns of George I and George II*, trans. Madame van Muyden (London, 1902), pp. 45–6.
3. William Coxe, *Memoirs of Sir Robert Walpole*, Vol. 1 (London, 1798), p. 271.
4. *Ibid.*; Saussure (1902), p. 46.
5. Coxe (1798), Vol. 1, p. 271; Norman Rosenthal (Ed.), *The Misfortunate Margravine, the Early Memoirs of Wilhelmina, Margravine of Bayreuth* (London, 1970), p. 84.
6. TNA SP 84/161, p. 595, Poley to Harley (Hanover, 28 July 1705).
7. HMC *Manuscripts of the Earl of Egmont*, diary of the first Earl of Egmont, Vol. 2, 1734–38. p. 320 (London, 1923).
8. Coxe (1798b), Vol. 1, pp. 272–3.
9. Mrs Modern to her maid in Henry Fielding, *The Modern Husband, a Comedy*, p. 9 (Dublin, 1732).
10. Fanny Burney, *Diary and Letters of Madame D'Arblay*, edited by her niece (London, 1842) Vol. 2, p. 191.
11. Jonathan Swift, *Letters, written by the late Jonathan Swift* (London, 1768) Vol. 5, p. 132 (10 November 1711).
12. *Ibid.*, p. 181.

13. Robert Halsband (Ed.), *The Complete Letters of Lady Mary Wortley Montagu* (Oxford, 1965–7), Vol. 1, p. 288, Lady Mary Wortley Montagu to the Lady Rich, Hanover (1 December 1716).

14. Stanhope (1774), Vol. 1, p. 183.

15. Horace Walpole, *Reminiscences, written in 1788, for the amusement of Miss Mary and Miss Agnes B***y* (London, 1818 edn), p. 80.

16. *Ibid.*

17. Colin Franklin, *Lord Chesterfield, His Character and Characters* (Aldershot, 1993) p. 96; BL Add MS 22627, f. 87v.

18. George Sherburn (Ed.), *The Correspondence of Alexander Pope* (Oxford, 1956), Vol. 2, pp. 201–2, Pope to Judith Cowper (26 September 1723).

19. SRO, 941/21/2(ii), 'A Character of Lady Mary Hervey', f. 3.

20. Duchess of Marlborough to James Dalrymple, second Earl of Stair (3 December 1737), quoted in Peter Cunningham (Ed.), *The Letters of Horace Walpole* (London, 1857), Vol. 1, p. clii.

21. Stanhope (1774), Vol. 2, p. 44.

22. Anson MS quoted in M.G. Jones, *Hannah More* (Cambridge, 1952), p. 50.

23. Sir Charles Hanbury Williams, quoted in Hervey (1931), Vol. 1, p. xvii.

24. Duchess of Marlborough to James Dalrymple, second Earl of Stair (3 December 1737), quoted in Cunningham (1857) Vol. 1, p. clii.

25. SRO 941/21/2(ii), 'A Character of Lady Mary Hervey', f. 2.

26. SRO 941/48/1, p. 272, Mary Hervey to the Reverend Edmund Morris (5 April 1750).

27. Karl Ludwig Pöllnitz, *The Memoirs of Charles Lewis, Baron de Pollnitz* (the second edition, with additions) (London, 1739), Vol. 2, p. 437.

28. Louis Simond, *Journal of a Tour and Residence in Great Britain* (Edinburgh, 1815) Vol. 1, p. 162.

29. James Ralph, *A Critical Review of the Public Buildings, Statues and Ornaments, in and about London and Westminster* (London, 1734) p. 179; Jacob Friedrich Bielfeld, *Letters of Baron Bielfeld*, trans. William Hooper (London, 1768–70), Vol. 4, pp. 57–60.

30. David Nichol Smith (Ed.), *The Letters of Thomas Burnet to George Duckett, 1712–1722* (Oxford, 1914), p. 63, Thomas Burnet to George Duckett (April 1714).

31. Philip Frowde (1728), quoted in Hannah Smith, *Georgian Monarchy* (Cambridge, 2006) p. 226.

32. Quoted in Lewis Melville, *Maids of Honour* (London, 1927), p. 57.

33. Saussure (1902), p. 40; Ward (1709), p. 135.

34. TNA LS 13/176, p. 12 (17 January 1715).

35. William Matthews (Ed.), *The Diary of Dudley Ryder, 1715–1716* (London, 1939), p. 76 (15 August 1715).

36. Matthews (1939), p. 356 (30 October 1716).

37. Pöllnitz (1739), Vol. 2, p. 450; Saussure (1902) p. 44.

38. Anon., *A New Guide to London* (1726), p. 4.

39. William Coxe (Ed.), *Fables by John Gay, illustrated with notes and the life of the author* (Salisbury, 1798), p. 12.

40. SRO 941/47/4, p. 100, John Hervey to Ste Fox (25 November 1729).

41. Quoted in Wilkins (1901), Vol. 2, p. 108.

42. Halsband (1965–7) Vol. 2, pp. 98–9 (30 October 1734).
43. BL Add MS 31144, f. 525r, Peter Wentworth to Lord Strafford (12 October 1714).
44. Pöllnitz (1739), Vol. 2, p. 465.
45. Lady Llanover (Ed.), *The Autobiography and Correspondence of Mary Granville, Mrs Delaney* (London, 1861), Vol. 1, p. 593 (3 March 1737); Wilkins (1901) Vol. 1, pp. 173–4.
46. Lady Mary Wortley Montagu, 'An Account of the Court of George I', in Lord Wharncliffe (Ed.), *The Letters and Works of Lady Mary Wortley Montagu* (London, 1861), Vol. 1, p. 133.
47. Sir N. William Wraxall, Bart., *Historical Memoirs of my own time* (London, 1904), pp. 256–7.
48. Wraxall (1904), p. 75.
49. Coxe (1798b), Vol. 1, p. 270.
50. SRO 941/47/4, p. 100, John Hervey to Ste Fox (25 November 1729).
51. Mary Cowper, *Diary of Mary, Countess Cowper* (London, 1864), p. 152.

CHAPTER 2: THE PETULANT PRINCE

1. Robert Halsband and Isobel Grundy (Eds), *Mary Wortley Montagu, Essays and Poems and 'Simplicity', a Comedy* (Oxford, 1977), p. 261.
2. Lady Mary Wortley Montagu, 'An Account of the Court of George I', in Wharncliffe (1861), Vol. 1, p. 134.
3. Maria Kroll (Ed.), *Letters from Liselotte* (London, 1970), pp. 171–2 (23 April 1715).
4. Cowper (1864), p. 108.
5. Stanhope (1774), Vol. 1, p. 123.
6. BL Add MS 47028, f. 7v, John Percival (26 January 1715).
7. Coxe (1798b), Vol. 2, p. 60.
8. Hervey (1931), Vol. 3, p. 702.
9. Coxe (1798b), Vol. 2, p. 59.
10. Walpole, *Reminiscences* (1818 edn), p. 38.
11. Cowper (1864), p. 161.
12. BL Add MS 61426, f. 68r, memoirs of Sarah, Duchess of Marlborough (n.d.).
13. Daniel Defoe, *Reasons against the Succession of the House of Hanover* (London, 1713), p. 3.
14. Saussure (1902), p. 45.
15. Franklin (1993), p. 92.
16. Saussure (1902), pp. 43–4.
17. *Ibid.*, p. 45; Coxe (1798b), Vol. 1, p. 56.
18. Coxe (1798b), Vol. 1, p. 56.
19. BL Stowe 308, f. 3r, Lord Chesterfield's character of George I.
20. Sheffield Grace (Ed.), *A Letter from the Countess of Nithsdale* (London, 1828), p. 36.
21. Duchess of Orléans, quoted in Ralph Dutton, *English Court Life* (London, 1963), p. 193.
22. Lady Mary Wortley Montagu, 'Account of the Court of George I', in Wharncliffe (1861), Vol. 1, p. 126.

23. Kroll (1998), p. 181.

24. J. W. Croker (Ed.), *Letters to and from Henrietta, Countess of Suffolk and her second husband the Hon. George Berkeley from 1712 to 1767* (London, 1824), Vol. 1, p. 18, Henry Pelham to George Berkeley (3 November 1717).

25. Thomas Pennant, *Some Account of London*, second edn (London, 1791), p. 114.

26. HMC *Report on the Manuscripts of his Grace the Duke of Portland*, Vol. 5 (London, 1899), p. 536.

27. Walpole, *Reminiscences* (1818 edn), p. 45.

28. Cowper (1864), p. 102.

29. Coxe (1798b), Vol. 1, p. 57.

30. BL Add MS 31144, f. 523r, Peter Wentworth to his brother (8 October 1714).

31. Hatton (1978), p. 131.

32. *La Correspondence Secrète du Comte Broglie*, quoted in Wilkins (1901), Vol. 1, p. 201.

33. Cowper (1864), p. 99.

34. Pöllnitz (1739), Vol. 3, p. 253.

35. Walpole, *Reminiscences* (1818 edn), p. 87.

36. BL Add MS 61492, ff. 205r-v.

37. *Ibid.*

38. Walpole, *Reminiscences* (1818 edn), p. 46.

39. RA, GEO/MAIN/53037.

40. Kroll (1998), p. 207.

41. Lord Berkeley of Stratton, quoted in Nigel Aston, 'The Court of George II: Lord Berkeley of Stratton's perspective', *The Court Historian*, Vol. 13.2 (December 2008), p. 183.

42. HMC *Portland*, Vol. 5, p. 544.

43. Anon., *The Criticks. Being papers upon the times* (London, 1719), Vol. 1, p. 10.

44. BL Egerton MS 1717, f. 66, 'An Excellent new Ballad, To the Tune of Chivy Chace', sometimes attributed to John Arbuthnot.

45. Nicolas Tindal, *The continuation of Mr Rapin's History of England; from the revolution to the present times* (London, fourth edn, 1758), Vol. 7, p. 169.

46. *The Historical Register containing An Impartial Relation of all Transactions, Foreign and Domestick*, Vol. 3 (London, 1718), pp. 30–1.

47. Anonymous reviewer of Lord Chesterfield's *Characters*, *The Character of George the First, Queen Caroline, Sir Robert Walpole [. . .] Reviewed. With Royal and Noble Anecdotes* (London, 1777), pp. 9-10.

48. *Weekly Journal* (11 August 1716), p. 495, transcript in Historic Royal Palaces curators' files.

49. HMC *Portland*, Vol. 5, p. 546.

50. Sundon Forster MS 503, f. 15, Lady Cowper writing on Caroline's behalf to Mrs Clayton ('about the time of the quarrell'), transcript in Historic Royal Palaces curators' files.

51. Halsband (1965–7), Vol. 2, p. 31.

52. HMC *Stuart Papers*, Vol. 5, p. 381 (30 December 1717).

53. Coxe (1798b), Vol. 1, p. 274.

54. Hervey (1931), Vol. 1, p. 261.

55. Lord Wharncliffe quoted in W. Moy Thomas (Ed.), *The letters and works of Lady Mary Wortley Montagu* (London, 1887), Vol. 1, p. 394, note.

56. Quoted in Wolfgang Michael, *England under George I: The Quadruple Alliance*, trans. Annemarie MacGregor and George E. MacGregor (London, 1939), p. 28.

57. Duchess of Orléans to the Raugravine Louise (10 February 1718), quoted in Wilkins (1901), Vol. 1, p. 284.

58. Ralph (1734), p. 188.

59. *London Gazette* (8 February 1718), issue 5615.

60. TNA T 56/18, Lord Chamberlain's warrants, p. 90 (3 April 1718).

61. TNA LC 5/157, p. 81 (12 February 1718).

62. BL Stowe MS 231, ff. 54–55 (February 1718).

63. *Ibid.*, f. 53.

64. Kroll (1998), p. 209.

65. Hatton (1978), p. 327.

66. Frances Vivian, *A Life of Frederick, Prince of Wales, 1707–1751*, Ed. Roger White (Lewiston, 2006), p. 10.

67. John Brooke (Ed.), *The Yale Edition of Horace Walpole's Memoirs* (New Haven and London, 1985), Vol. 3, p. 313.

68. Kroll (1998), p. 186.

69. Walpole, *Reminiscences* (1818 edn), p. 32.

70. *Weekly Journal or Saturday's Post*, issue 130 (27 May 1721).

71. 'An Account of the Court of George I', in Wharncliffe (1861), Vol. 1, p. 127; Walpole, *Reminiscences* (1818 edn) p. 31.

72. Franklin (1993), p. 92.

73. TNA LS 13/176, p. 57 (31 August 1716).

74. 'An Account of the Court of George I', in Wharncliffe (1861), Vol. 1, p. 132.

75. *The Criticks: Being papers upon the times*, London (10 February 1718), quoted in Wilkins (1901), Vol. 1, p. 319.

76. Pöllnitz (1739), Vol. 2, p. 451.

77. Stephen Taylor, 'Walpole, Robert, first earl of Orford (1676–1745)', *Oxford Dictionary of National Biography* (Oxford, 2004).

78. Quoted in Taylor (2004); Pöllnitz (1739), Vol. 2, p. 451.

79. Cowper (1864), pp. 133, 130, 141.

80. *Ibid.*, p. 142.

81. Hervey (1931), Vol. 3, p. 918.

82. Cowper (1864), pp. 141–4.

83. William Coxe, *Memoirs of John Duke of Marlborough* (London, 1819), Vol. 3, pp. 646–7.

84. William Thomas Laprade, *Public Opinion and Politics in Eighteenth Century England* (New York, 1936), p. 230.

85. Cowper (1864), p. 143.

86. BL Add MS 22629, ff. 8v–9r, E. Molesworth to Henrietta Howard (31 April 1720).

87. Cowper (1864), p. 149.

88. *Ibid.*, p. 161.

89. *Ibid.*, pp. 135–9.

90. George Louis and R. L. Arkell, 'George I's letters to his daughter', *The English Historical Review*, Vol. 52, No. 207 (July 1938), p. 497; Cowper (1864), p. 137.

91. Cowper (1864), pp. 129–32.

92. Mary II to William III (5 September 1690), quoted in Marjorie Bowen, *The Third Mary Stuart* (London, 1929), p. 222.

93. Westmorland MS, 13.417, quoted in Cannon (2004).

94. BL Add MS 61492, ff. 232v–233r.

95. Halsband (1965–7), Vol. 2, p. 17.

96. Walpole, *Reminiscences* (1818 edn), p. 73; BL Add MS 20104, ff. 153r-v, Lady Pomfret to Lady Sundon, from Bath (19 May 1728).

97. BL Egerton MS 1717, f. 66.

98. John Gay, *Poems on Several Occasions* (London, 1775), p. 142.

99. SRO 941/47/4, p. 346, John Hervey to the Dean of Norwich (14 November 1732).

100. John Hervey, first Earl of Bristol, *Letter-Books of John Hervey, first Earl of Bristol, 1651–1750* (Wells, 1894), Vol. 2, p. 143, Lord Bristol to Molly Lepell (2 October 1720).

CHAPTER 3: THE PUSHY PAINTER

1. Stanhope (1774), Vol. 2, p. 159.

2. Jourdain (1948), p. 37.

3. Stanhope (1774), Vol. 1, p. 476 (17 October 1749).

4. *The Walpole Society*, Vol. 24 (1935–6) (Vertue IV), p. 163.

5. BL Add MS 75358, William Kent to Lord Burlington (27 January 1739).

6. BL Add MS 75358, Lady Burlington (4 November 1731); Sherburn (1956), Vol. 4, p. 140, Alexander Pope to Countess of Burlington (29 October 1739).

7. Chatsworth MS, William Kent to Lady Burlington (14 December 1738), quoted in Jourdain (1948), p. 86.

8. Sherburn (1956), Vol. 4, p. 125, Alexander Pope to the Countess of Burlington (*c.*8 September 1738).

9. Tabitha Barber, 'Thornhill, Sir James (1675/6–1734)', *Oxford Dictionary of National Biography* (Oxford, 2004).

10. Letter from Queen Caroline to Princess Anne quoted in R. L. Arkell, *Caroline of Ansbach* (London, 1939), p. 297.

11. *The Walpole Society*, Vol. 18 (1930) (Vertue I), p. 45.

12. John Hutchins, *The history and antiquities of the county of Dorset* (London, 1774), Vol. 1, p. 410; third edn revised by William Shipp and James Whitworth Hodson (London, 1868), Vol. 3, p. 675.

13. Franklin (1993), p. 92.

14. *Weekly Journal or Saturday's Post*, issue 130 (27 May 1721).

15. HMC *Portland*, Vol. 5, p. 602 (23 August 1720).

16. Thomas Tickell, *Kensington Garden* (London, 1722), p. 1.

17. John Haynes, *Kensington Palace* (London, 1995), p. 2.

18. Rizzini to the Duke of Modena (20 January 1695), quoted in Martin Haile, *Queen Mary of Modena, her life and letters* (London, 1905), p. 310.

19. TNA Work 4/1 (13 June 1716).

20. HMC *Report on the Manuscripts of Lord Polwarth*, Vol. 1 (London, 1911), p. 176.

21. L. S. Wright and M. Tinling (Eds), *William Byrd, The London Diary, 1717–21* (New York, 1958), p. 127.

22. J. M. Beattie, *The English Court in the Reign of George I* (Cambridge, 1967), p. 274.
23. TNA Work 6/11, p. 2 (1715); TNA T 56/18, Lord Chamberlain's warrants, p. 34 (2 July 1717).
24. TNA Work 6/7, p. 148 (19 December 1719).
25. *Ibid.*, p. 68 (19 June 1718).
26. Peter Gaunt and Caroline Knight, an unpublished history of Kensington Palace, Historic Royal Palaces (1988–9), Vol. 2, p. 304.
27. John Holland, *The History, Antiquities, and Description of the Town and Parish of Worksop* (Sheffield, 1826), p. 176.
28. TNA Work 6/7, p. 153.
29. Kroll (1998), p. 231.
30. BL Add MS 22227, ff. 98–100, Peter Wentworth to Lord Strafford (25 July 1729).
31. HMC, 15th Report, *Manuscripts of the Earl of Carlisle*, appendix, part 6 (London, 1897), p. 35 (19 August 1721).
32. John Arbuthnot, *Mr Maitland's Account of Inoculating the Small Pox* (London, 1722), p. 3.
33. Romney Sedgwick, *The House of Commons, 1715–54* (London, 1970), Vol. 2, p. 115.
34. *The Walpole Society*, Vol. 18 (1929–30) (Vertue I), p. 100.
35. TNA T 1/243, No. 70 (14 February 1723).
36. *The Walpole Society*, Vol. 18 (1929–30) (Vertue I), p. 100.
37. *The Walpole Society*, Vol. 17 (1933–34) (Vertue III), p. 139.
38. William Kent to Burrell Massingberd (26 June 1713), quoted in Jourdain (1948), pp. 27–8.
39. Michael I. Wilson, *William Kent* (London, 1984), p. 16; HMC 12th Report, appendix, Part III, *The Manuscripts of Earl Cowper* (London, 1889), Vol. 3, p. 122.
40. William Kent (1719), quoted in Jourdain (1948), p. 46.
41. Barbara Arciszewska, *The Hanoverian Court and the Triumph of Palladio* (Warsaw, 2002), p. 279.
42. TNA Works 6/7, p. 272, '*la proposition de Monsr. Kent pour peindre la Voute de la Grande Chambre*'.
43. *The Walpole Society*, Vol. 22 (1933–34) (Vertue III), p. 139.
44. *The Walpole Society*, Vol. 18 (1929–30) (Vertue I), p. 100.
45. *The Walpole Society*, Vol. 22 (1933–4) (Vertue III), p. 55.
46. *The Walpole Society*, Vol. 18 (1929–30) (Vertue I), p. 101.
47. John Gay, 'Epistle IV', *Poems* (1720), p. 306.
48. TNA Work 6/7, pp. 272–4.
49. Beard (1981), p. 25.
50. *Ibid.*, pp. 90–2.
51. TNA Work 6/7, pp. 273–4 (22 May 1722).
52. R. D. Harley, *Artists' Pigments, c.1660–1835* (London, 1982) p. 44.
53. *Ibid.*, p. 152.
54. *Ibid.*, p. 71.
55. HMC, *Report on Manuscripts in Various Collections*, Vol. 8 (London, 1913), p. 368 (12 December 1723).

56. HMC *Carlisle*, appendix, part 6, p. 42, Sir John Vanbrugh to Lord Carlisle (19 July 1722).

57. BL Add MS 78514 B, 'Journal of Sir John Evelyn Baronet', f. 64v (1 July 1722).

58. TNA Work 4/2, f. 80r (15 August 1722).

59. *Ibid.*, f. 81v (22 August 1722).

60. TNA Work 6/7, p. 277 (22 August 1722).

61. *The Walpole Society*, Vol. 22 (1933–4) (Vertue III), p. 140.

62. Horace Walpole, *Anecdotes of painting in England* (second edn, Strawberry Hill, 1771), Vol. 4, p. 137.

63. *The Walpole Society*, Vol. 22 (1933–4) (Vertue III), p. 19.

64. TNA T 56/18, p. 232 (5 October 1726); Edward Impey, *Kensington Palace, The Official Illustrated History* (London, 2003), p. 69.

65. John Murray Graham (Ed.), *Annals and Correspondence of the Viscount and the First and Second Earls of Stair* (Edinburgh and London, 1875), Vol. 2, p. 94.

66. *The Walpole Society*, Vol. 22 (1933–4) (Vertue III), pp. 35–6.

67. *Ibid.*, p. 68.

68. William Aikman to Sir John Clerk (15 July 1725), quoted in John Fleming, *Robert Adam and his Circle* (London, 1962), p. 39.

69. Haynes (1995), p. 22.

70. BL Add MS 20101, f. 30r (12 May 1735).

71. Ruth Guilding, 'Sculpture at Holkham', *Country Life* (6 March 2008), p. 85.

72. Stanhope (1774), Vol. 1, p. 444.

73. Beattie (1967), pp. 48, 174.

74. Anon., *The Present State of the British Court* (London, 1720).

75. BL 1890c.1 (Miscellaneous Tracts), Book II; George Bickham, *Apelles Britannicus* (London, 1741), p. 28.

76. Rudolf Grieser (Ed.), *Die Memoiren des Kammerherrn Friedrick Ernst von Fabrice (1683–1750)* (Hildesheim, 1956), p. 126; BL Add MS 40843, f. 9r.

77. Anon, attributed to Dr Arbuthnot or Jonathan Swift, *It cannot Rain but it Pours*, part two (London, 1726), p. 4.

78. Grieser (1956), p. 126.

79. The painting is in the Royal Collection. Oliver Millar, *Pictures in the Royal Collection, Tudor, Stuart and Early Georgian Pictures* (London, 1963), No. 616; Jürgen Prüser, *Die Göhrde* (Hildesheim, 1969), pp. 68–70.

80. BL Add MS 47028, f. 7v, John Percival (26 January 1715); Anon., *Some Memoirs of the life of Lewis Maximilian Mahomet, Gent. Late Servant to his Majesty* (London, 1727) (copy kindly provided by Esther Godfrey).

81. BL Stowe MS 563, William III's bedchamber orders, which were still presumably at least officially in force in the reign of George I (11 June 1689, a copy made in 1736).

82. TNA SP 1/47, f. 55; Frederick J. Furnivall (Ed.), *The Babees Book, etc.*, Early English Text Society (London, 1868), p. 180.

83. Hatton (1978), p. 206.

84. J. J. Caudle, 'Mohammed von Königstreu, (Georg) Ludwig Maximilian (*c.*1660–1726)', *Oxford Dictionary of National Biography* (Oxford, 2004).

85. *Ibid.*

86. TNA LC 5/89 f. 4v (29 May 1717; 24 January 1720).

87. TNA LC 5/89 f. 5v (25 September 1718).

88. TNA LS 13/115 f. 121v (2 August 1722).

89. Anon., *Lewis Maximilian Mahomet* (1727), pp. 11, 15.

90. Early nineteenth-century editor's note in Croker (1824), Vol. 1, p. 269 (spotted by Joanna Marschner); 'E. Tempest, Milliner' is mentioned in RA GEO/ADD17/75/71 (1733).

91. E. Tempest supplied Caroline with three yards of 'Black frinch Lace' in 1733, RA GEO/ADD 17/75/78.

92. Samuel Pegge, *Curialia: or an Historical Account of Some Branches of the Royal Household* (London, 1791), Vol. 1, p. 84.

93. Colonel Sir Reginald Hennell, *The History of the King's Body Guard of the Yeomen of the Guard* (London, 1904), p. 23.

94. Saussure (1902), p. 40.

95. Cosmo, Grand Duke of Tuscany, quoted in Hennell (1904), p. 29.

96. W. H. Pyne, 'The History of Kensington Palace', in *The History of the Royal Residences* (London, 1819), Vol. 2, pp. 29–30.

97. Alexander Pope, *Bounce to Fop. An Heroick Epistle from a Dog at Twickenham to a Dog at Court* (London, 1736), p. 6.

98. Pyne (1819), Vol. 2, p. 30.

99. Philip H. Highfill, Kalman A. Burnim and Edward A. Langhams, *A Biographical Dictionary of Actors, Actresses, Musicians & Other Stage Personnel in London 1660–1800* (Carbondale, 1973) Vol. 2, p. 450.

100. Walpole (1771), Vol. 4, p. 116.

101. James L. Steffensen, 'Lillo, George (1691/1693–1739)', *Oxford Dictionary of National Biography* (Oxford, 2004).

102. HMC *Cowper*, Vol. 3, p. 187 (n.d.).

103. *Brice's Weekly Journal* (8 April 1726), p. 3.

CHAPTER 4: THE WILD BOY

1. Lord Berkeley of Stratton quoted in Aston (2008), p. 189.

2. Stanhope (1774), Vol. 2, p. 171.

3. Llanover (1861), Vol. 1, p. 175 (1728).

4. Saussure (1902), p. 149.

5. Anon., *An Enquiry How the Wild Youth, Lately taken in the Woods near Hanover, (and now brought over the England) could be there left, and by what Creature he could be suckled, nursed and brought up* (London, 1726), p. 3.

6. *Brice's Weekly Journal* (8 April 1726), p. 3.

7. *Ibid.*; Saussure (1902) p. 149.

8. Plaque at the gate of Herrenhausen Garden, Hanover.

9. The forest is named as Hertswold in the brass plaque in Northchurch Church. See John Edwin Cussans, *History of Hertfordshire* (London, 1879–1881), Vol. 3, p. 90.

10. Anon., *An Enquiry* (1726), p. 2.

11. *The St James's Evening Post* (14 December 1725), quoted in James Burnet, Lord Monboddo, *Antient Metaphysics* (1779–99), Vol. 3 (London and Edinburgh, 1784), p. 58.

12. Anon., *An Enquiry* (1726), p. 2.

13. *Brice's Weekly Journal* (8 April 1726), p. 3.
14. Anon., *An Enquiry* (1726), p. 4.
15. *Brice's Weekly Journal* (8 April 1726), p. 3.
16. *The St James's Evening Post* (14 December 1725), quoted in Burnet, Vol. 3 (1784), p. 58.
17. *The Gentleman's Magazine*, Vol. 20 (November, 1751), p. 522.
18. Burnet, Vol. 3 (1784), p. 370.
19. *Brice's Weekly Journal* (8 April 1726), p. 3.
20. Anon., *An Enquiry* (1726), p. 3.
21. Harold Williams (Ed.), *The Correspondence of Jonathan Swift*, 5 vols (Oxford, 1963–5), Vol. 4, p. 98, Swift to Lady Elizabeth Germain (8 January 1733).
22. *Ibid.*, Vol. 3, p. 128, Swift to Thomas Tickell (16 April 1726).
23. Walpole, *Reminiscences* (1818 edn), pp. 7–8.
24. *Ibid.*
25. BL Egerton MS 1717, f. 79 (1726).
26. Rosenthal (1970), p. 93.
27. Quoted in Coxe (1798b), Vol. 1, p. 267.
28. Wraxall (1904), pp. 450–1.
29. Coxe (1798b), Vol. 1, p. 57.
30. Anon., *The Character of George the First* (1777), p. 2.
31. Anon., *The Grand Exemplar Set forth, in an Impartial Character Of His Sacred Majesty King George* (London, 1715), pp. 1–2.
32. BL Add MS 75358, Richard Arundell to Lord Burlington (14 April 1726).
33. *The Country Gentleman*, No. 10 (11 April 1726), quoted in Burnet, Vol. 3 (1784), p. 60.
34. Williams (1963–5), Vol. 3, p. 128, Swift to Thomas Tickell (16 April 1726); Anon. (attributed to Daniel Defoe), *Mere Nature Delineated* (1726), p. 31.
35. *The Gentleman's Magazine*, Vol. 55 (March, 1785), p. 236; Joanna Marschner, 'Caroline of Ansbach: The Queen, Collecting and Connoisseurship at the Early Georgian Court', PhD thesis, University College (London, 2007), p. 52.
36. Zacharias Conrad von Uffenbach, *London in 1710, from the travels of Zacharias Conrad von Uffenbach* (London, 1934), p. 118.
37. Smith (2006), p. 80.
38. Kathleen Wilson, *The Sense of the People: Politics, Culture and Imperialism in England, 1715–1785* (Cambridge, 1995), p. 37.
39. Anon. (attributed to Daniel Defoe), *Mere Nature Delineated* (1726), p. iii.
40. Newton (2002), p. 35.
41. Anon. (attributed to Daniel Defoe), *Mere Nature Delineated* (1726), pp. 22, iv.
42. SRO 941/47/4, p. 111, John Hervey to Ste Fox (13 June 1730).
43. Stanhope (1774), Vol. 1, p. 146.
44. *London Magazine* (London, 1774), p. 213, quoted in Ribeiro (1984), p. 120.
45. Anon., *An Enquiry* (1726), p. 4.
46. Saussure (1902), p. 43; Cowper (1864), p. 21.
47. Anon., *A collection of ordinances and regulations for the government of the Royal Household* (Society of Antiquaries, London, 1790), p. 367; R. O. Bucholz, 'Going to Court in 1700: a visitor's guide', *The Court Historian*, Vol. 4.3 (December 2000), p. 200.
48. Saussure (1902), pp. 40–1.

49. BL Add MS 61474, f. 16v, Mrs South to Sarah, Countess of Marlborough (15 March ?1694).
50. BL Add MS 22627, ff. 90v–91r.
51. Anne Somerset, *Ladies in Waiting* (London, 1984), p. 203.
52. Bucholz (2000), p. 185.
53. Stanhope (1774), Vol. 2, p. 165.
54. *Ibid.*, Vol. 1, pp. 268–9.
55. Anon., *It cannot Rain* (London, 1726), p. 9.
56. *Brice's Weekly Journal* (8 April 1726), p. 3; *Edinburgh Evening Courant* (12 April 1726), quoted in Burnet, Vol. 3 (1784), p. 60.
57. *Brice's Weekly Journal* (8 April 1726), p. 3.
58. Anon. (attributed to Daniel Defoe), *Mere Nature Delineated* (1726), p. 24.
59. Anon., *An Enquiry* (1726), p. 4.
60. Burnet, Vol. 3 (1784), p. 369.
61. Anon., *An Enquiry* (1726), p. 3.
62. Anon., *It cannot Rain* (1726), p. 5.
63. Anon., *An Enquiry* (1726), p. 3.
64. *Ibid.*, p. 4.
65. Burnet, Vol. 3 (1784), p. 58.
66. *Brice's Weekly Journal* (8 April 1726), p. 3.
67. John Boyle, fifth Earl of Orrery, *Remarks on the Life and Writings of Dr Jonathan Swift* (London, 1752), p. 164.
68. George Berkeley quoted in George Aitken, *The Life and Works of John Arbuthnot* (Oxford, 1892), p. 55.
69. Lord Chesterfield quoted in Aitken (1892), p. 134.
70. Sherburn (1956), Vol. 2, p. 253; Angus Ross (Ed.), *The Correspondence of Dr John Arbuthnot* (Münster, 2006), p. 259 (Swift to Pope, 29 September 1725).
71. Anon., *The Most Wonderful Wonder That ever appear'd to the Wonder of the British Nation* (London, 1726), p. 7.
72. Anon., *An Enquiry* (1726), p. 3.
73. Franklin (1993), p. 106.
74. Anon., *The Most Wonderful Wonder* (1726), p. 7.
75. Anon., *An Enquiry* (1726), p. 4.
76. *Edinburgh Evening Courant* (14 November 1726), quoted in Burnet, Vol. 3 (1784) p. 61.
77. *Edinburgh Evening Courant* (5 July 1726), quoted in Burnet, Vol. 3 (1784), p. 60.
78. Coxe (1798b), Vol. 1, p. 275.
79. Margaret Maria Verney (Ed.), *Verney Letters of the Eighteenth Century from the MSS. at Claydon House* (London, 1930), Vol. 2, p. 22.
80. Williams (1963–5), Vol. 4, p. 98, Swift to Lady Elizabeth Germain (8 January 1733).
81. Onno Klopp (Ed.), *Correspondence de Leibniz* (Hanover, 1874), p. 105 (25 October 1704).
82. *Ibid.*, p. 108 (1 November 1704).
83. John Gay, *The poetical works of John Gay, from the royal quarto edition of 1720* (London, 1797), 'Epistles', p. 9.
84. TNA SP 84/161, p. 594, Poley to Harley (Hanover, 28 July 1705).
85. Hervey (1931), Vol. 2, p. 514.

86. RA GEO/ADD28/52, transcript by Mrs Clayton of a letter from Caroline to Mrs Clayton (n.d.).

87. Letter from Queen Caroline to Princess Anne quoted in Arkell (1939), pp. 297–8.

88. Kroll (1970), p. 214 (27 August 1719).

89. Edmund Turnor, *Collections for the history of the town and soke of Grantham* (London, 1806), p. 164, 'Memoirs of Sir Isaac Newton, sent by Mr Conduitt to Monsieur Fontenelle' (1727).

90. *By several hands, Sketches and Characters of the most Eminent and most Singular Persons Now Living* (London, 1770), p. 10.

91. Smith (2006), p. 206.

92. Account given by Frederick the Great, quoted in Wilkins (1901), Vol. 1, p. 34.

93. Ross (2006), p. 274 (John Arbuthnot to Jonathan Swift, 30 November 1726).

94. Walpole, *Reminiscences* (1818 edn), p. 73.

95. A. Hamilton, *Memoirs of Count Grammont*, Ed. W. Scott (London, 1905), p. 225.

96. BL Add MS 31144, f. 524v, Peter Wentworth to Lord Strafford (12 October 1714).

97. Jonathan Swift and Alexander Pope in John Arbuthnot, *Miscellanies* (Dublin, 1746), p. 254, 'A true and faithful narrative of what pass'd in *London*'.

98. BL Add MS 22628, f. 21r, Molly Hervey to Henrietta Howard (7 July 1729).

99. Wilkins (1901), Vol. 1, pp. 166–7.

100. Lewis (1937–83) Vol. 34, p. 257.

101. BL Add MS 22629, ff. 4r, 7r, Sophy Howe to Henrietta Howard (1719?).

102. Thomson (1847), Vol. 2, pp. 320–1.

103. SRO 941/48/1, p. 1, Mary Hervey to Reverend Edmund Morris (20 September 1742).

104. Sherburn (1956), Vol. 1, p. 427, Pope to Teresa and Martha Blount (13 September 1717).

105. *Ibid.*, Vol. 2, p. 41, Pope to Mary Hervey (1720).

106. Halsband (1965–7), Vol. 2, p. 8 (*c.*15 July 1721), p. 48 (*c.*20 March 1725).

107. Hervey (1894), Vol. 3, p. 244, Lord Bristol to Lord Hervey (17 May 1740).

108. Halsband (1965–7), Vol. 2, p. 45 (February 1725).

109. 'Introductory Anecdotes', probably using information from Lady Bute, in Wharncliffe (1837), p. 66.

110. Quoted in Melville (1927), p. 176.

111. Charles Hanbury Williams quoted in Hervey (1931), Vol. 1, p. xvii.

112. SRO 941/21/2(ii), 'A Character of Lady Mary Hervey', f. 1; Sir Charles Hanbury Williams quoted in Hervey (1931), Vol. 1, p. xvii.

113. Duchess of Marlborough to the second Earl of Stair (3 December 1737), quoted in Melville (1927), p. 178.

114. Halsband (1965–7), Vol. 2, pp. 58–9, Lady Mary Wortley Montagu to Lady Mar (*c.*3 February 1726).

115. SRO 941/53/1, p. 219, William Hervey's commonplace book, 'Ballad of Molly Le Pell', 1726'.

116. Ross (2006), p. 269 (John Arbuthnot to Jonathan Swift, 5 November 1726).

117. RA EB/EB 48 (unpaginated).

118. Anon. (attributed to Daniel Defoe), *Mere Nature Delineated* (1726), p. 22.

CHAPTER 5: THE NEGLECTED EQUERRY

1. BL Add MS 22227, f. 27r, Peter Wentworth to his brother (1 November 1718).

2. BL Add MS 31144, f. 488r, Peter Wentworth to his brother (30 July 1714).

3. BL Add MS 22227, f. 101, Peter Wentworth to his brother (22 October 1729).

4. *Ibid.*, f. 28 (1 November 1718).

5. *London Daily Post and General Advertiser*, issue 493 (31 May 1736).

6. BL Add MS 31144, f. 570r, Peter Wentworth to his brother (21 September 1714).

7. *Ibid.*, f. 480r, Peter Wentworth to his brother (3 August 1714).

8. *Ibid.*, f. 493r, Peter Wentworth to his brother (6 August 1714).

9. Halsband (1965–7), Vol. 1, pp. 226–9.

10. Sherburn (1956), Vol. 2, p. 395.

11. John Gay, *Poems* (1720) pp. 279, 276.

12. Sherburn (1956), Vol. 1, p. 379, Alexander Pope to Martha Blount (December 1716).

13. *Ibid.*, p. 512, Pope to Martha and Teresa Blount (17 September 1718).

14. BL Add MS 22626, ff. 60r-v, Henrietta Howard to John Gay (n.d.).

15. Halsband (1965–7), Vol. 1, pp. 226–9.

16. BL Add MS 31144, f. 532r, Peter Wentworth to his brother (2 November 1714).

17. Smith (1914), p. 135, Thomas Burnet to George Duckett (6 September 1717).

18. *Ibid.*, p. 144, Thomas Burnet to George Duckett (5 March 1718).

19. *Ibid.*, p. 170, Thomas Burnet to George Duckett (2 May 1719).

20. Williams (1963–5), Vol. 3, p. 294, Swift to Alexander Pope (16 July 1728).

21. Thomas Brown, *Amusements Serious and Comical, Calculated for the Meridian of London* (London, 1700), p. 15.

22. J. J. Cartwright (Ed.), *The Wentworth Papers 1705–1739, selected from the private and family correspondence of Thomas Wentworth, Lord Raby, created in 1711 Earl of Strafford* (London, 1883), p. 3.

23. BL Add MS 31144, f.516v, Peter Wentworth to his brother (1 October 1714).

24. BL Add MS 22227, f. 31r, Peter Wentworth to his brother (16 November 1718).

25. Gaunt and Knight (1988–9), Vol. 2, Chap. 4, p. 489.

26. Saussure (1902), pp. 39–48.

27. Cowper (1864), p. 140.

28. *Ibid.*, p. 38.

29. Thomson (1847), Vol. 2, p. 287.

30. RA GEO/ADD28/3, GEO/ADD28/12, GEO/ADD28/18, GEO/ADD28/20, transcripts by Mrs Clayton of letters from Caroline to Mrs Clayton (n.d.).

31. Saussure (1902), pp. 39–48; Hervey (1931), Vol. 1, p. 275.

32. Lewis (1937–83), Vol. 37, p. 341 (23 June 1752).

33. Hervey (1931), Vol. 1, pp. 275–6.

34. Thomson (1847), Vol. 1, p. 146 (22 April 1728).

35. Saussure (1902), pp. 39–48.

36. Walpole, *Reminiscences* (1818 edn), p. 101.

37. Lynn Hunt, *The Family Romance of the French Revolution* (London, 1992).

38. Duchess of Orléans to the Raugravine Louise, St Cloud (30 June 1718), quoted in Wilkins (1901), Vol. 1, p. 317.

39. BL Egerton MS 1710, f. 18r, Princess Amalie to the Countess of Portland (1733).

40. Hertfordshire Archives, MS DE/P/F134, f. 26r.
41. BL Egerton MS 1710, f. 1r, Princess Amalie to the Countess of Portland (August 1728).
42. RA GEO/MAIN/53038, p. 52.
43. Quoted in Alice Drayton Greenwood, *Lives of the Hanoverian Queens of England* (London, 1909), Vol. 1, p. 357 (N.B. Greenwood's reference, BL MS Egerton MS 1700, is incorrect).
44. Hertfordshire Archives, Panshanger MS, Letterbooks, Vol. 5, pp. 24–5, Mrs Allanson to Lady Cowper (29 May 1718), quoted in Beattie (1967), p. 274.
45. Wright and Tinling (1958), p. 127.
46. BL Add MS 22629, f. 117.
47. *Ibid.*, ff. 117–8.
48. Hervey (1931), Vol. 2, p. 406.
49. Paymasters' Accounts for 1717, 1718, 1721 and 1723, quoted by Colvin (1976), p. 201.
50. HMC 12th Report, appendix, Part III, *Cowper*, pp. 115–6, Madame de Kielmensegge to Vice Chamberlain Coke (15 December 1716); Gaunt and Knight (1988–9), Vol. 2, p. 482; Count de Broglie to the King of France (10 July 1724), quoted in Wilkins (1901), Vol. 1, p. 376.
51. TNA LS 13/115 f. 127 (17 June 1724).
52. Count de Broglie to the King of France (10 July 1724), quoted in Wilkins (1901), Vol. 1, p. 376.
53. Isobel Grundy, *Lady Mary Wortley Montagu, Comet of the Enlightenment* (Oxford, 1999), p. 191.
54. HMC *Polwarth*, Vol. 1, p. 176 (7 February 1717).
55. HMC *Calendar of the Manuscripts of the Marquis of Bath*, Vol. 1 (London, 1904), p. 201, Shrewsbury to Robert Harley (25 April 1711).
56. BL Add MS 63764, f. 5r, Henry Savile to Lord Preston (London, 10 May 1682).
57. Bucholz (2000), pp. 209–10.
58. Jonathan Swift, *Directions to Servants* (London, 1745) p. 88.
59. The Hon. Peter Wentworth to the Earl of Strafford (10 August 1730), quoted in Wilkins (1901), Vol. 2, pp. 109–10.
60. Hervey (1931), Vol. 2, p. 345.
61. Stanhope (1774), Vol. 2, p. 214.
62. SRO 941/47/4, p. 337, John Hervey to Ste Fox (30 December 1731).
63. Anon., *It cannot Rain* (1726), p. 7.
64. Stanhope (1774), Vol. 1, pp. 89–90.
65. Quoted in Neil McKendrick, John Brewer and J. H. Plumb, *The Birth of a Consumer Society: The Commercialization of Eighteenth-Century England* (London, 1982), p. 59.
66. Fielding (1732), p. 16.
67. BL Add MS 22626, f. 116r, Thomas Allen to Henrietta Howard (17 December 1766).
68. TNA LC 5/158, p. 151 (2 May 1723).
69. Lord Berkeley of Stratton, quoted in Aston (2008), p. 185.
70. BL Add MS 31144, f. 516v, Peter Wentworth to his brother (1 October 1714).
71. TNA LS 13/173, p. 106, 'Order for keeping the Court and Parke &c cleare from Beggars' (2 May 1687).

72. HMC *Egmont* (1923), Vol. 2, p. 61 (wedding of Princess Anne to William of Orange).

73. Peter Wentworth to Lord Strafford (25 July 1729), quoted in Wilkins (1901), Vol. 2, pp. 123–4.

74. Thomson (1847), Vol. 2, pp. 39–40.

75. Beattie (1967), pp. 78–9.

76. TNA LS 13/115, f. 126v (2 June 1724).

77. The Earl of March, *A Duke and his Friends. The Life and Letters of the Second Duke of Richmond* (London, 1911), Vol. 1, p. 89; TNA LS 13/115, f. 126v (2 June 1724); references kindly provided by Esther Godfrey.

78. TNA LS 13/115, f. 126v (3 June 1724); March (1911), Vol. 1, p. 89.

79. *Ibid.*, f. 126v (3 June 1724).

80. *Ibid.*; March (1911), Vol. 1, p. 89.

81. HMC 12th Report, appendix, Part III, *Cowper* (1889), p. 117.

82. www.oldbaileyonline.org, 'The proceedings of the Old Bailey', ref. t17310428-28.

83. *Ibid.*, ref. t17311208-58.

84. Gaunt and Knight (1988–9), Vol. 2, p. 512; TNA LS 13/84 (unpaginated); 'The proceedings of the Old Bailey', ref. t17361208-42.

85. Anon., *Lewis Maximilian Mahomet* (1727), p. 9.

86. Caudle (2004).

87. Anon., *Lewis Maximilian Mahomet* (1727), pp. 10, 13.

88. Hanover Archives, Cal. Br. 15 Nr. 2684, George II to Geheime Räte, St James's, 28/1.8/2/1729, information kindly provided by Andrew Thompson.

89. From the king's private accounts, quoted by Caudle (2004).

90. J. D. Griffith Davies, *A King in Toils* (London, 1938), p. 80.

91. Wilkins (1901), Vol. 1, p. 380.

92. Brooke (1985), Vol. 3, p. 121.

93. HMC, 12th Report, appendix III, *Manuscripts of the Coke Family of Melbourne Hall, Derbyshire, belonging to the Earl Cowper* (London, 1898), p. 187.

94. SRO 941/47/4, p. 45, John Hervey to Ste Fox (30 May 1727).

95. Wilkins (1901), Vol. 1, p. 381.

96. Coxe (1798b), Vol. 1, p. 266; Grieser (1956), p. 147.

97. Grieser (1956), p. 148.

98. HMC *Polwarth*, Vol. 5, p. 5, Arthur Villette to the Earl of Marchmont (June 1727).

99. Coxe (1798b), Vol. 1, p. 266.

100. *The Historical Register*, quoted in C. Gibbs, 'George I (1660–1727)', *Oxford Dictionary of National Biography* (Oxford, 2004).

101. Coxe (1798b), Vol. 1, pp. 265–6.

102. Quoted in Marlow (1973), p. 212.

103. Hanover Archives, Cal. Br. 15 Nr. 2684, George II to Geheime Räte, St James's, 28/1.8/2/1729, information kindly provided by Andrew Thompson.

104. BL Add MS 31144, f. 527v, Peter Wentworth to his brother (15 October 1714).

105. BL Add MS 47032, f. 346, Daniel Dering to Lord Egmont (June 1730).

106. Hervey (1931), Vol. 2, p. 495.

107. Thomson (1847), Vol. 1, p. 317.

108. BL Add MS 78465, f. 45r, Mrs Boscawen to Lady Evelyn (21 February 1716).

109. Cowper (1864), p. 21 (21 November 1714).

110. BL Add MS 22227, ff. 121–2, Peter Wentworth to his brother (3 August 1731).

111. *Ibid.*, f. 8r, Peter Wentworth to his brother (2 September 1729); f. 101, Peter Wentworth to his brother (22 October 1729).

CHAPTER 6: THE WOMAN OF THE BEDCHAMBER

1. Lord Berkeley of Stratton, quoted in Aston (2008), p. 188.

2. BL Add MS 22625, f. 4r, Jonathan Swift, 'Character of the Honorable Mrs [Howard]'.

3. *Ibid.*, ff. 4v, 5r, Jonathan Swift, 'Character of the Honorable Mrs [Howard]'.

4. Tracy Borman, *Henrietta Howard, King's Mistress, Queen's Servant* (London, 2007), p. 3.

5. Hervey (1931), Vol. 1, p. 40.

6. Franklin (1993), p. 93.

7. BL Add MS 22627, f. 41r.

8. *Ibid.*, f. 41v.

9. Stanhope (1774), Vol. 2, p. 177.

10. Walpole, *Reminiscences* (1818 edn), p. 76.

11. Kroll (1998), p. 214 (St Cloud, 30 June 1718).

12. Keith Thomas, 'The Double Standard', *Journal of the History of Ideas*, Vol. 20, No. 2 (April 1959), pp. 195–216.

13. John Kelyng, Lord Chief Justice, quoted in J. M. Beattie, *Crime and the Courts in England, 1660–1800* (Princeton, 1986), p. 95.

14. Quoted in A. D. Harvey, *Sex in Georgian England* (London, 1994; 2001), p. 57.

15. Valerie Rumbold, *Women's Place in Pope's World* (Cambridge, 1989), p. 212.

16. BL Add MS 22627, f. 42f.

17. *Ibid.*, f. 13r.

18. Halsband and Grundy (1977), p. 231.

19. BL Add MS 22627, f. 70r, Lady Lansdowne to Mrs Howard.

20. BL Add MS 22628, f. 30r, Molly Hervey to Henrietta Howard (10 July 1731).

21. Coxe (1798b), Vol. 1, p. 277.

22. BL Add MS 22627, f. 94r.

23. Ambrose Phillips, epilogue to *The Distrest Mother* (London, 1712).

24. Coxe (1798b), Vol. 1, p. 272.

25. Franklin (1993), p. 95.

26. Philip Yorke, Earl of Hardwick, *Walpoliana* (London, 1783), p. 6.

27. BL Add MS 22627, f. 94.

28. Walpole, *Reminiscences* (1818 edn), p. 22.

29. Coxe, *Robert Walpole* (1816 edn), Vol. 3, pp. 261–2.

30. Black (2004b), p. 77.

31. Hervey (1931), Vol. 3, p. 917.

32. *The Historical Register containing an Impartial Relation of all Transactions, Foreign and Domestick*, Vol. 12 (London, 1727), p. 17.

33. Coxe (1798b), Vol. 2, p. 519.

34. BL Add MS 69285, f. 95r, Harriet Pitt to her mother (27 June 1727).

35. Earl of Strafford to James the Pretender (21 June 1727), quoted in Lord Mahon,

History of England from the Peace of Utrecht to the Peace of Versailles, 1713–83 (London, 1858), Vol. 2, p. 119.

36. Thomas Prince (1727), quoted in Smith (2006), p. 19.
37. Halsband (1965–7), Vol. 2, p. 85 (October 1727).
38. Llanover (1861), Vol. 1, p. 138 (1727).
39. *The Walpole Society*, Vol. 17 (1933–4) (Vertue III), pp. 73, 140.
40. Bodleian Library, MS Rawlinson D.540, f. 111, Kent's notes in the back of 'Breve Compendio delle Metamorfosi di Ovidio, Istoricamente spiegate e descritte da Guglielmo Kent'.
41. *The Walpole Society*, Vol. 22 (1933–4) (Vertue III), p. 55.
42. The Earl of Ilchester (Ed.), *Lord Hervey and his Friends, 1726–38, based on letters from Holland House, Melbury, and Ickworth* (London, 1950), p. 116.
43. Sir Thomas Coke to the Earl of Burlington (26 November 1736), quoted in Charles Warburton James, *Chief Justice Coke* (1929), pp. 228–9.
44. 'An Epistle from Ld. Lovel to Lord Chesterfield at Bath, Wrote by Mr Poulteney', quoted in James (1929), p. 230.
45. Halsband (1965–7), Vol. 2, pp. 98–9 (30 October[?] 1734).
46. BL Add MS 31144, f. 454v, Peter Wentworth to his brother (23 April 1714).
47. Halsband (1965–7), Vol. 3, p. 22.
48. Coxe (1798b), Vol. 1, p. 277.
49. Henrietta's words provided by Horace Walpole, quoted in Coxe (1798b), Vol. 1, p. 272.
50. HMC *Polwarth*, Vol. 5, p. 6, Arthur Villette to the Earl of Marchmont (June 1727).
51. Halsband (1965–7), Vol. 2, p. 86, Lady Mary Wortley Montagu to Lady Mar (October 1727).
52. Hervey (1931), Vol. 1, p. xiv.
53. *Ibid.*, Vol. 2, p. 347.
54. Hannah Smith and Stephen Taylor, 'Lord Hervey's Frederick', paper given at *Politics and Patronage: a tercentenary colloquium for Frederick Lewis, Prince of Wales*, The History of Parliament Trust, London (14 April 2007) and subsequently published. I gratefully acknowledge their work on Hervey.
55. Hervey (1931), Vol. 2, p. 349.
56. Hervey (1894), Vol. 3, p. 64, Earl of Bristol to Molly (7 October 1730).
57. SRO 941/21/2(ii), 'A Character of Lady Mary Hervey', f. 3.
58. Hervey (1931), Vol. 1, pp. 103–4.
59. Horace Walpole commenting on Lord Chesterfield's character of Queen Caroline, BL Stowe MS 308, f. 1v; Franklin (1993), p. 96.
60. Coxe (1798b), Vol. 1, p. 280.
61. Walpole, *Reminiscences* (1818 edn), p. 64.
62. Wraxall (1904), p. 257.
63. Hervey (1931), Vol. 1, p. 153.
64. Quoted in Wilkins (1901), Vol. 2, p. 44.
65. Hervey (1931), Vol. 2, p. 361.
66. *Ibid.*, Vol. 1, p. 93; Vol. 2, p. 473.
67. *Ibid.*, p. 94.
68. Fielding (1732), p. 29.
69. Croker (1824), Vol. 1, p. 335, Lady Hervey to Mrs Howard (7 July 1729).

70. BL Add MS 22627, f. 5v (n.d., *c.*1728).

71. Kilburn (2004).

72. BL Add MS 22628, f. 100r, George Berkeley to unknown (1735); Lewis (1937–83), Vol. 20, p. 88 (17 August 1749).

73. Bielfeld (1770), Vol. 4, p. 41, translator's note; Smith (2006), p. 59.

74. Pöllnitz (1739), Vol. 2, p. 431.

75. Jonathan Swift, *Dean Swift's Literary Correspondence* (London, 1741), p. 133.

76. Saussure (1902), pp. 139, 136.

77. Quoted in Impey (2003), p. 81.

78. Pottle (1950), p. 265; Thomas Faulkner, *History and Antiquities of Kensington* (London, 1820), Vol. 2, p. 411.

79. Cartwright (1883), pp. 459, 470 (26 July 1731).

80. BL Add MS 22227, Peter Wentworth to his brother (21 August 1729).

81. SRO 941/47/4, p. 119, John Hervey to Ste Fox (21 August 1730).

82. Kensington Public Library, 'Extra illustrated' edition of Thomas Faulkner, *History and Antiquities of Kensington* (London, 1820) (3-volume version), Vol. 3, item 326, representation of Jane Kien.

83. BL Add MS 22227, f. 79r, Peter Wentworth to his brother (31 July 1729).

84. *Daily Advertiser*, issue 91 (19 May 1731); Cartwright (1883), p. 469.

85. Kensington Public Library, 'Extra illustrated' edition of Thomas Faulkner, *History and Antiquities of Kensington* (London, 1820) (3-volume version), Vol. 3, item 335, 'Chimneys Swept at Kensington Palace'.

86. BL Add MS 20101, f. 6r.

87. BL Add MS 78514 E, 'Journal of Sir John Evelyn Baronet', f. 33r (2 November 1729).

88. Impey (2003), p. 38.

89. TNA Work 6/7, p. 154.

90. John H. Appleby, 'Rowley, John (*c.*1668–1728)', *Oxford Dictionary of National Biography* (Oxford, 2004).

91. TNA LS 13/82, f. 7r.

92. Gaunt and Knight (1988–9), Vol. 2, Chap. 4, p. 506.

93. Matthew Kilburn, 'Hervey (neé Lepell), Mary, Lady Hervey of Ickworth (1699/1700–1768)', *Oxford Dictionary of National Biography* (Oxford, 2004).

94. RA EB/EB 31, p. 15.

95. HMC 12th Report, Appendix, Part III, *Cowper*, pp. 118–20, 'the memorial of Henry Wise and Joseph Carpenter' (1717).

96. BL Add MS 22227, f. 162r, Peter Wentworth to his brother (3 June 1735).

97. 'The Basset-Table, an Ecologue', in Mr Pope, &c., *Court Poems* (London, 1726), p. 9.

98. Hervey (1894), Vol. 3, p. 68, Lord Bristol to Lord Hervey (5 August 1731).

99. Pöllnitz (1739), Vol. 2, p. 463.

100. BL Add MS 22227, ff. 98–100, Peter Wentworth to Lord Strafford (25 July 1729).

101. *London Evening Post*, issue 392 (13 June 1730); Cartwright (1883), p. 468; pp. 471–2; BL 22227, f. 94r, Peter Wentworth to his brother (2 October 1729), f. 161, Peter Wentworth to his brother (3 June 1735).

102. *The Gentleman's Magazine*, Vol. 13 (December 1743), p. 629.

103. For example, *Weekly Journal or Saturday's Post* (29 October 1720), issue 100.

104. Stanhope (1774), Vol. 1, p. 211.

105. Thomson (1847), p. 240.

106. Stanhope (1774), Vol. 2, p. 263.

107. Kroll (1998), p. 216.

108. William Hone, *The Table Book*, Vol. 1 (London, 1827; Detroit, 1966), p. 378.

109. Anon. (1721), quoted in Black (2004b), p. 64.

110. Pöllnitz (1739), Vol. 2, p. 464.

111. Henri Misson, *M. Misson's memoirs and observations in his travels over England*, trans. Mr Ozell (London, 1719), p. 315.

112. BL Add MS 61463, f. 88v, Mary Cowper to Sarah, Duchess of Marlborough, Hampton Court (20 August 1716).

113. Pöllnitz (1739), Vol. 2, p. 449.

114. TNA LC 5/3, p. 81 (9 December 1728).

115. BL Add MS 78514 E, 'Journal of Sir John Evelyn Baronet', f. 3r (19 July 1728).

116. Hervey (1894), Vol. 3, p. 37, Lady Bristol to Lord Bristol (16 January 1729).

117. Gaunt and Knight (1988–9), Vol. 2, Chap. 4, p. 507.

118. Ross (2006), p. 281 (John Arbuthnot to Henrietta Howard, 30 May 1728).

119. Hervey (1931), Vol. 2, p. 552.

120. HMC *Egmont*, Vol. 1, p. 426 (1920).

121. *Stamford Mercury*, Vol. 32, No. 3 (25 July 1728).

122. *London Gazette/The Post Boy* No. 3040 (2 November 1714).

123. Saussure (1902), p. 265.

124. Black (2004b), p. x.

125. BL Add MS 22626, f. 91r, Lord Chesterfield to Henrietta Howard (13 July n.y.).

126. BL Add MS 22628, f. 19, Molly Hervey to Henrietta Howard (31 August 1728).

127. Pöllnitz (1739), Vol. 2, p. 449.

128. Lord Berkeley of Stratton, quoted in Aston (2008), pp. 171–93, 182.

129. Matthews (1939), p. 66 (1 August 1715).

130. Pöllnitz (1739), Vol. 2, p. 450.

131. BL Add MS 78514 E, 'Journal of Sir John Evelyn Baronet', f. 16r (2 March 1729).

132. Donald Burrows, 'Handel, George Frideric (1685–1759)', *Oxford Dictionary of National Biography* (Oxford, 2004).

133. BL Add MS 20102, William Burnet, Governor of New England, to Mrs Clayton (Boston, 7 July 1729).

134. Thomson (1847), Vol. 1, pp. 264–5, Dr Alured Clarke to Mrs Clayton (Kensington Square, 3 August 1734).

135. Saussure (1902), p. 44.

136. Thomson (1847), Vol. 1, pp. 264–6.

137. Matthews (1939), p. 356 (30 October 1716).

138. Gladys Scott Thomson (Ed.), *Letters of a Grandmother, 1732–35* (London, 1943), p. 74, Sarah, Duchess of Marlborough to Diana, Duchess of Bedford (23 September 1732).

139. Quoted in Wilkins (1901), Vol. 2, p. 103.

140. BL Add MS 22229, f. 61, Lord Wentworth to his father the Earl of Strafford (15 April 1735).

141. Quoted in Wilkins (1901), Vol. 2, p. 104.

142. *The Walpole Society*, Vol. 22 (1933–4) (Vertue III), p. 68.

143. Halsband and Grundy (1977), pp. 93–4.

144. Hervey (1931), Vol. 2, pp. 485, 610.

145. Stanhope (1774), Vol. 2, p. 266; Coxe (1798b) Vol. 1, pp. 271–2; Lord Hervey to H. Walpole (31 October 1735), quoted in Coxe (1798b), Vol. 1, p. 272.

146. BL Add MS 20104, ff. 6–7, Lord Hervey to Mrs Clayton (Hampton Court, 31 July 1733).

147. BL Add MS 75358, Lady Burlington (1730).

148. Brooke (1985), Vol. 1, p. 117.

149. Hervey (1931), Vol. 1, p. 42; Vol. 2, p. 380.

150. BL Add MS 4805, f. 160v, Henrietta Howard to Jonathan Swift (16 August 1727).

151. Hervey (1931), Vol. 2, p. 490.

152. Lord Holland (Ed.), *Horace Walpole's Memoirs of the Reign of King George the Second*, 3 vols (London, 1846), Vol. 1, p. 140.

153. HMC *Egmont* (1923), Vol. 2, p. 53.

154. Hervey (1931), Vol. 2, p. 496.

155. Coxe (1798b), Vol. 1, p. 275.

156. BL Add MS 20101, ff. 60r, 64v, 'The Inventory of the Curiositys & Medals in the Cabinets in His Maj^ties Librairy of wch Mrs Purcell had the Original'.

157. Matthews (1939), p. 62 (25 July 1715).

158. Hervey (1931), Vol. 2, p. 501.

159. Anon., *The Contest: being poetical essays on the Queen's grotto: wrote in consequence of an invitation in the Gentlemen's Magazine for April, 1733* (London, 1734), p. 6, 'Essay V, On the Royal Grotto'.

160. Thomson (1847), Vol. 1, p. 205.

161. Kensington Public Library, 'Extra illustrated' edition of Thomas Faulkner, *History and Antiquities of Kensington* (London, 1820) (2-volume version) part 2, accounts for Richmond property ending Lady Day 1747, following p. 358.

162. Hervey (1931), Vol. 2, p. 504; BL Stowe MS 308, f. 4.

163. BL Add 78468, f. 73v, Mrs Godolphin to Lady Evelyn (13 November 1716); Smith (2006), p. 228.

164. Sherburn (1956), Vol. 1, Pope to Teresa and Martha Blount (13 September 1717).

165. David Starkey, 'Representation through Intimacy: A Study in the Symbolism of Monarchy and Court Office in Early-Modern England', in *Symbols and Sentiments: Cross-cultural Studies in Symbolism*, Ed. I. Lewis (London, New York and San Francisco, 1977), p. 219.

166. John Wade, *The Extraordinary Black Book* (London, 1931), p. 497.

167. *The Times* (24 November 1837), p. 3.

168. Hervey (1931), Vol. 1, p. 140.

169. TNA LC 5/158 p. 243 (1 April 1724).

170. Quoted in E. J. Burford, *Royal St James's, Being a Story of Kings, Clubmen and Courtesans* (London, 1988), p. 29.

171. Stanhope (1774), Vol. 2, p. 59.

172. Jonathan Swift, *The Lady's Dressing Room* (London, 1732), p. 6.

173. Hervey (1931), Vol. 1, p. 194.

174. Quoted in Burford (1988), p. 30; SRO 941/47/4, p. 75, John Hervey to Ste Fox (9 January 1728).

175. Marschner (1997), pp. 34–5.

176. Stanhope (1774), Vol. 2, p. 59.

177. BL Add MS 22227, ff.98–100, Peter Wentworth to Lord Strafford (25 July 1729).

178. Brooke (1985), Vol. 1, p. 117.

179. Coxe (1798b), Vol. 1, pp. 278–9.

180. Hervey (1931), Vol. 1, p. 43.

181. Sherburn (1956), Vol. 2, p. 182, Alexander Pope to John Gay (13 July 1723).

182. Hervey (1931), Vol. 2, p. 474.

183. Brooke (1985), Vol. 1, p. 117.

184. Cowper (1864), p. 19 (19 November 1714).

185. BL Add MS 22625, f. 27r, John Arbuthnot to Henrietta Howard (30 May 1728).

186. RA GEO/ADD17/75/46 (1733).

187. Marschner (1997), p. 31.

188. BL Add MS 22625, f. 27r, John Arbuthnot to Henrietta Howard (30 May 1728).

189. RA GEO/ADD17/75/4 (July–September 1730); Joanna Marschner, 'Queen Caroline of Ansbach: attitudes to clothes and cleanliness, 1727–1737', *Costume*, No. 31 (1997), p. 32.

190. RA GEO/ADD 17/75/44 (1732); RA GEO/ADD 17/75/20 (1730); Thomson (1943), p. 147, Sarah, Duchess of Marlborough to Diana, Duchess of Bedford (21 October 1734).

191. Jonathan Swift, *The Lady's Dressing Room* (London, 1732), p. 5.

192. RA GEO/ADD 17/75/72 (1733); Marschner (1997), p. 33.

193. Brooke (1985), Vol.1, p. 117.

194. Lady Mary Wortley Montagu, 'An Account of the Court of George I', in Wharncliffe (1861), Vol. 1, p. 122.

195. Marschner (1997), p. 33.

196. BL Add MS 22625, f. 27r, John Arbuthnot to Henrietta Howard (30 May 1728).

197. Hervey (1931) Vol. 2, p. 474.

198. *Ibid.*, Vol. 1, p. 107.

199. 'Song, by the Earl of Peterborough', quoted in Croker (1824), Vol. 1, p. xlvii.

200. Sherburn (1956), Vol. 2, p. 401, Pope to Swift (*c.*20 September 1726); BL Add MS 22628, f. 20r, Henrietta Howard to Molly Hervey (September 1728).

201. BL Add MS 22626, f. 58v, Henrietta Howard to John Gay (5 September 1731).

202. Thomson (1847), Vol. 1, p. 243.

203. BL Add MS 22626, f. 53r, Henrietta Howard to John Gay (29 June 1731).

204. Thomson (1847), Vol. 1, pp. 242–3.

205. BL Add MS 22626, ff. 53r–v, Henrietta Howard to John Gay (29 June 1731).

206. BL Add MS 27777, f. 107v, Peter Wentworth to his brother (1 July 1731).

207. BL Add MS 22628, f. 100r, George Berkeley to unknown (1735).

208. Hervey (1931), Vol. 2, p. 381.

209. *Ibid.*, p. 383.

210. BL Add MS 22627, ff. 8r, 9r (1734).

211. *Ibid.*, ff. 9r–v (1734).

212. Hervey (1931), Vol. 2, p. 601.

213. Walpole, *Reminiscences* (1818 edn), p. 82.

214. BL Add MS 22627, f. 6v.

215. The Duke of Newcastle to Sir Robert Walpole (13 November, 1734), quoted in Wilkins (1901), Vol. 2, p. 259.

216. Halsband (1965–7), Vol. 2, p. 57.

217. Holland (1846), Vol. 1, p. 75; BL Add MS 22627, f.107v, Margaret Bradshaw to Henrietta Howard (n.d.).

218. BL Add MS 22627, f. 113r, Margaret Bradshaw to Henrietta Howard (n.d.).

219. Burford (1988), pp. 31–2; Peter Thomson, 'Cuyler [*married name* Rice], Margaret (1758–1814)', *Oxford Dictionary of National Biography* (Oxford, 2004).

220. Undated letter (Ickworth MSS) from Molly to Dr Arbuthnot, quoted in Stuart (1936), p. 38.

221. Henrietta Jannsen to Lady Denbigh, quoted in Melville (1927), p. 210; Lewis (1937–83), Vol. 34, p. 256.

222. Charles Hanbury Williams, *The odes of Sir Charles Hanbury Williams* (London, 1775), p. 11.

223. Croker (1824), Vol. 1, p. 49, Mrs Bradshaw to Mrs Howard (April 1720).

224. Hervey (1931), Vol. 2, p. 385.

225. Ross (2006), p. 277, John Arbuthnot to the Editor of the *London Journal* (March 1727).

226. *Ibid.*, p. 364, John Arbuthnot to Jonathan Swift (5 December 1732).

227. Hervey (1931), Vol. 2, pp. 477, 389.

228. 'Introductory Anecdotes', probably using information from Lady Bute, in Wharncliffe (1837), p. 69.

229. SRO 941/47/15, f. 13, John Lord Hervey Maxims.

230. BL Add MS 22628, f. 23v, Molly Hervey to Henrietta Howard (7 October 1728).

231. Quoted in Lucy Moore, *Amphibious Thing, the Life of Lord Hervey* (London, 2000), p. 54.

232. BL Add MS 22628, f. 28r, Molly Hervey to Henrietta Howard (19 June 1731).

233. Quoted in Borman (2007), p. 211.

234. Hervey (1931), Vol. 2, p. 472.

235. Quoted in Borman (2007), p. 211.

236. Williams (1963–5), Vol. 4, p. 294, Lady Elizabeth Germain to Swift (13 February 1735).

237. SRO 941/47/4, p. 486, John Hervey (13 January 1735).

238. BL Add MS 22626, f. 19, Lord Bathurst to Henrietta (26 November 1734).

239. BL Add MS 22625, ff. 4–5, Jonathan Swift, 'Character of the Honorable Mrs [Howard]'.

240. BL Add MS 22626, f. 19v, Lord Bathurst to Henrietta (26 November 1734).

241. Williams (1963–5), Vol. 4, p. 362, Lady Elizabeth Germain to Swift (12 July 1735).

242. Hervey (1931), Vol. 2, p. 471.

243. Quoted in Borman (2007), p. 220.

244. BL Add MS 22629, f. 40r, Henrietta to George Berkeley (1735?).

245. Croker (1824), Vol. 2, p. 125, Thomas Coke to George Berkeley (23 July 1735).

246. Hervey (1931), Vol. 2, p. 471.

247. Sherburn (1956), Vol. 3, p. 479, Alexander Pope to Fortescue (2 August 1735).

CHAPTER 7: THE FAVOURITE AND HIS FOE

1. Halsband (1965–7), Vol. 2, p. 476, Lady Mary Wortley Montagu to her husband (2 March 1751).
2. Brooke (1985), Vol. 1, p. 51.
3. Hervey (1931), Vol. 2, p. 37.
4. Duchess of Marlborough to the second Earl of Stair (17 August 1737), quoted in Cunningham (1857), Vol. 1, p. cxlix.
5. Robert Halsband, *Lord Hervey, Eighteenth-Century Courtier* (Oxford, 1973), p. 28.
6. Hervey (1894), Vol. 2, p. 41, his father to John Hervey (14 December 1716).
7. Hervey (1931), Vol. 2, p. 874.
8. Halsband (1965–7), Vol. 1, pp. 286–7, Lady Mary Wortley Montagu to the Countess of Bristol, Hanover (25 November 1716).
9. Hervey (1894), Vol. 3, p. 29, Lady Bristol to Lord Bristol (7 January 1729).
10. Holland (1846), Vol. 1, p. 77.
11. Wilkins (1901), Vol. 1, p. 90.
12. 'The Griff . . . was a nickname the King had long ago given the Prince', Hervey (1931), Vol. 3, p. 804; see Sir George Young, *Poor Fred, the People's Prince* (London, 1937), pp. 8–9; but for a refutation of Young see also Frances Vivian, *A Life of Frederick, Prince of Wales (1707–1751)*, Ed. Roger White (Lewiston, 2006), pp. 14–15.
13. Matthew Kilburn, 'Frederick Lewis, prince of Wales (1707–1751)', *Oxford Dictionary of National Biography* (Oxford, 2004).
14. Hervey (1931), Vol. 2, p. 559.
15. RA GEO/MAIN/54227, Frederick, Prince of Wales, 'Instructions for my Son George'.
16. Coxe (1798b), Vol. 1, p. 522.
17. Thomson (1943), p. 86, Sarah, Duchess of Marlborough to Diana, Duchess of Bedford (3 January 1733).
18. SRO 941/48/1, p. 49, Mary Hervey to the Reverend Edmund Morris (24 March 1744).
19. BL Sloane MS 4076, f. 98r.
20. Tobias Smollett, *The History of England from the Revolution to the Death of George the Second* (London, 1848 edn), Vol. 3, p. 62.
21. Rosenthal (1970), p. 135.
22. Hervey (1931), Vol. 1, p. 306.
23. *Ibid.*, Vol. 2, p. 504.
24. George Hastings Wheler (Ed.), *Hastings Wheler Family Letters 1704–1739* (West Yorkshire, 1935), p. 153, Lady Catherine Jones (24 December 1737).
25. Hervey (1931), Vol. 2, p. 371.
26. Pöllnitz (1737), Vol. 1, p. 64.
27. Romney Sedgwick (Ed.), *Letters from George III to Lord Bute, 1756–1766* (London, 1939), p. 259.
28. Brooke (1985), Vol. 1, p. 116.
29. *Ibid.*, Vol. 3, p. 121.
30. RA GEO/MAIN/53039.
31. Cannon (2004).

32. HMC *Polwarth*, Vol. 1 (London, 1911), p. 112 (19 October 1716).
33. Quoted in Greenwood (1909), Vol. 1, p. 228.
34. *Daily Post*, No. 2873 (5 December 1728).
35. Verney (1930), Vol. 2, p. 139 (April 1736).
36. Hervey (1931), Vol. 2, pp. 550–1.
37. Cartwright (1883), p. 522.
38. Stella Tillyard, *A Royal Affair, George III and his Troublesome Siblings* (London, 2006), p. 7.
39. Hervey (1931), Vol. 2, p. 493.
40. *The Gentleman's Magazine*, Vol. 5.6 (April 1736), p. 230.
41. Hervey (1931), Vol. 2, p. 550.
42. HMC *Carlisle*, appendix, part 6, p. 167, Lady A. Irwin to Lord Carlisle (April 1736).
43. Cartwright (1883), p. 522.
44. *The Gentleman's Magazine*, Vol. 5.6 (April 1736), p. 231.
45. Hervey (1931), Vol. 2, p. 553.
46. *Read's Weekly Journal Or British Intelligencer* (8 May 1736), issue 609.
47. *The Gentleman's Magazine*, Vol. 8 (November 1738), p. 603.
48. Duchess of Marlborough quoted in Averyl Edwards, *Frederick Lewis, Prince of Wales* (London, 1947), p. 60.
49. Hervey (1931), Vol. 2, p. 564.
50. *Ibid.*, p. 613.
51. Ilchester (1950), pp. 258–9.
52. Gaunt and Knight (1988–9), Vol. 2, p. 488.
53. Hervey (1931), Vol. 3, pp. 868–9.
54. Morris Marples, *Poor Fred and the Butcher, Sons of George II* (London, 1970), p. 18.
55. BL Add MS 24407, 'Kew Book' containing accounts of Frederick, Prince of Wales for Kew; Vivian (2006), pp. 134–5.
56. Mowl (2006), p. 109.
57. Hervey (1931), Vol. 2, p. 628.
58. *The Daily Gazetteer* (2 October 1736), quoted in Wilkins (1901), Vol. 2, pp. 305–6.
59. HMC *Egmont* (1923), Vol. 2, p. 325.
60. Hervey (1931), Vol. 2, p. 628.
61. HMC *Egmont* (1923), Vol. 2, p. 10.
62. Hervey (1931), Vol. 3, pp. 662, 670, 681.
63. *Ibid.*, Vol. 2, p. 615.
64. *Ibid.*, pp. 615, 617–18.
65. Halsband (1973), p. 138.
66. Halsband and Grundy (1977), p. 261.
67. HMC *Egmont* (1920), Vol. 1, p. 208 (1731).
68. Ralph Trumbach, 'Modern Sodomy: The Origins of Homosexuality, 1700–1800', in Matt Cock (Ed.), *A Gay History of Britain* (Oxford, 2007), pp. 77–105.
69. Misson (1719), p. 24.
70. Anon., *Plain Reasons for the Growth of Sodomy in England* (London, 1728).
71. SRO 941/47/4, p. 295, John Hervey to Ste Fox (26 August 1731).

72. *Ibid.*, p. 53, John Hervey to Ste Fox (1 June 1727).

73. Anon., *Plain Reasons* (1728), p. 14.

74. SRO 941/47/4, p. 98, John Hervey to Ste Fox (22 November 1729).

75. *Ibid.*, the first thirteen pages have been cut out.

76. Lewis (1937–83), Vol. 33, p. 156 (3 January 1780).

77. SRO 941/47/1, Frederick, Prince of Wales to John Hervey (n.d.); SRO 941/47/4, p. 207, John Hervey to Frederick, Prince of Wales (16 July 1731); Hannah Smith and Stephen Taylor, 'Hephaestion and Alexander: Lord Hervey, Frederick, Prince of Wales, and the Royal Favourite in England in the 1730s', *The English Historical Review*, Vol. CXXIV, No. 507 (2009), pp. 283–312.

78. Hervey (1931), Vol. 3, p. 671.

79. SRO 941/47/4, p. 320, John Hervey to Ste Fox (14 December 1731).

80. *Ibid.*, p. 165, John Hervey to Ste Fox (31 August 1731).

81. Quoted in Moore (2000), p. 53.

82. 'Introductory Anecdotes', probably using information from Lady Bute, in Wharncliffe (1837), p. 69.

83. Thomson (1847), Vol. 2, p. 374, Countess of Pomfret to Lady Sundon (23 September 1735); BL Add MS 75358, Lady Burlington (23 September 1735).

84. SRO 941/21/2(ii), 'A Character of Lady Mary Hervey', f. 1.

85. Sir Charles Hanbury Williams, quoted in Hervey (1931), Vol. 1, p. xvii.

86. 'Introductory anecdotes', probably based on information from Lady Bute, in Wharncliffe (1837), Vol. 1, p. 69; Stuart (1936), p. 127.

87. Harvey (1994; 2001), p. 134.

88. William Pulteney, *A Proper Reply to a Late Scurrilous Libel* (London, 1731), pp. 6–7.

89. Alexander Pope, *Ethic epistles, satires, &c.* (London, 1735), p. 108.

90. Hervey (1931), Vol. 2, p. 562.

91. *Ibid.*, Vol. 3, p. 757.

92. Quoted in Grundy (1999), p. 368.

93. *Weekly Miscellany*, issue CCXLI (5 August 1737), 'Domestic Occurences'.

94. BL Add MS 20104, ff. 6–7, Lord Hervey to Mrs Clayton, Hampton Court (31 July 1733).

95. Hervey (1931), Vol. 2, p. 528.

96. *Ibid.*, Vol. 3, p. 758.

97. BL Add MS 75358, Lady Burlington ('Thursday eight o'clock', 1737); HMC *Egmont* (1923), Vol. 2, p. 426.

98. G. H. Rose (Ed.), *A Selection from the papers of the Earls of Marchmont* (London, 1831), Vol. 2, p. 88, Alexander, Earl of Marchmont (13 October 1737).

99. HMC *Egmont* (1923), Vol. 2, p. 426; BL Add MS 75358, Lady Burlington ('Thursday 8 o'clock', 1737).

100. HMC *Egmont* (1923) Vol. 2, p. 425.

101. *Ibid.*, pp. 425–6; Hervey (1931), Vol. 3, p. 758.

102. Hervey (1931), Vol. 3, p. 759.

103. Walpole, *Reminiscences* (1818 edn), p. 95.

104. HMC *Egmont* (1923), Vol. 2, p. 425.

105. BL Add MS 75358, Lady Burlington ('Thursday eight o'clock', 1737).

106. Holland (1846), Vol. 1, p. 74.

107. Hervey (1931), Vol. 3, p. 758.

108. *Ibid.*, p. 759.

109. Holland (1846), Vol. 1, p. 74.

110. Hervey (1931), Vol. 3, p. 759.

111. HMC *Egmont* (1923), Vol. 2, p. 425.

112. Hervey (1931), Vol. 3, p. 761.

113. HMC *Egmont* (1923), Vol. 2, p. 425.

114. BL Add MS 75358, Lady Burlington ('Thursday 8 o'clock', 1737); Duchess of Marlborough to the second Earl of Stair (17 August 1737), quoted in Cunningham (1857), Vol. 1, p. cli.

115. The Earl of Bolingbroke quoted in Walter Sichel, *Bolingbroke and his Times*, 2 vols, (London, 1901), Vol. 2, p. 357.

116. Holland (1846), Vol. 1, p. 74.

117. Hervey (1931), Vol. 3, pp. 767, 793.

118. *Ibid.*, pp. 760, 763.

119. SRO 941/47/4, p. 610, John Hervey to Count Algarotti (17/28 September 1737).

120. Ilchester (1950), p. 267.

121. TNA LC 5/202, p. 436 (11 September 1737).

122. Brooke (1985), Vol. 1, p. 52.

123. Philip Yorke, *The Life and Correspondence of Philip Yorke, Earl of Hardwicke* (Cambridge, 1913), Vol. 1, p. 171.

124. Hailes (1788), p. 92.

125. Tillyard (2006), p. 18.

126. HMC *Egmont*, Vol. 2 (1923), p. 436.

127. Cambridge University Library SPCK MS D4/43, f. 26, quoted in Smith (2006), p. 219.

128. Pennant (1791), p. 119.

CHAPTER 8: THE QUEEN'S SECRET

1. Jonathan Swift, 'Directions for making a BIRTH-DAY SONG, Written in the Year 1729', in *The Beauties of Swift: or, the favourite offspring of wit & genius* (London, 1782), p. 211.

2. Pöllnitz (1739), Vol. 2, p. 435; Colvin (1976), p. 244.

3. HMC *Egmont*, Vol. 2 (1923), p. 325.

4. Sir John Soane's Museum, Vol. 147/192–198; Marschner (2007), p. 271.

5. Ross (2006), p. 269 (John Arbuthnot to Jonathan Swift, 5 November 1726); Hervey (1894), Vol. 3, p. 37; Cowper (1864), p. 13.

6. Ilchester (1950), p. 269.

7. Quoted in Smith (2006), p. 36; Hastings Wheler (1935), p. 152, Lady Catherine Jones (24 December 1737).

8. HMC *Egmont*, Vol. 2 (1923), p. 446.

9. Clarke (1738), p. 25.

10. Hervey (1931), Vol. 2, pp. 372–3.

11. TNA SP 36/111, Ryder to Newcastle (16 October 1749).

12. Hervey (1931), Vol. 2, p. 485.

13. *Ibid.*, Vol. 3, pp. 656–7.

14. *Ibid.*, Vol. 2, pp. 372–3.

15. BL Add MS 22227, f. 157, Peter Wentworth to his brother (10 December 1734).

16. HMC *Egmont*, Vol. 2 (1923), p. 442.

17. Hervey (1931), Vol. 2, pp. 373, 374.

18. William Byrd, 'A discourse concerning the plague', in Maude H. Woodfin (Ed.), *Another Secret Diary of William Byrd of Westover, 1739–1741, with letters and literary exercises 1696–1726* (Richmond, Virginia, 1942), p. 430.

19. Grundy (1999), pp. 99–100.

20. Coxe (1798b), Vol. 1, p. 274.

21. Woodfin (1942), p. 429.

22. Smith (2006), pp. 93–4.

23. *Brice's Weekly Journal* (8 April 1726), p. 3.

24. Grundy (1999), p. 218.

25. E. F. D. Osborn (Ed.), *Political and Social Letters of a Lady of the Eighteenth Century* (London, 1890), p. 25 (the 'Lady' is Sarah Osborn, née Byng).

26. Kroll (1998), p. 260.

27. Osborn (1890), p. 25.

28. BL Sloane MS 4076, f. 99r.

29. William Wagstaffe, *A Letter To Dr Freind, Shewing The Danger and Uncertainty of Inoculating the Small Pox* (London, 1722), pp. 5–6.

30. Grundy (1999), p. 217.

31. Adrian Wilson, 'The Politics of Medical Improvement in Early Hanoverian London', in Andrew Cunningham and Roger French (Eds), *The Medical Enlightenment of the Eighteenth Century* (Cambridge, 1990), pp. 4–39.

32. Andrew Stone to the elder Horace Walpole (11 November 1737), quoted in John Heneage Jesse, *Memoirs of the Court of England* (London, 1843), Vol. 3, p. 105.

33. HMC *Egmont*, Vol. 2 (1923), p. 443.

34. BL Add MS 7075, f. 1v (7 January 1706).

35. TNA SP 81/162, f. 258r, Howe to Harley (Hanover, 1/5 February 1707).

36. Preussisches Staatsarchiv, Hanover, MS Y. 46c, XI, ff. 114–5, quoted in Arkell (1939), p. 46.

37. BL Add MS 61463, f. 88v, Mary Cowper to Sarah, Duchess of Marlborough, Hampton Court (20 August 1716); BL MS Lansdowne 1013, f. 203, Dr White Kennet to Rev. Samuel Blackwell (9 November 1716).

38. BL Add 78465, f. 79v, Mrs Boscawen to Lady Evelyn (8 November 1716).

39. Cowper (1864), p. 126; Friedrich-Wilhelm Schaer (Ed.), *Briefe der Gräfin Johanna Sophie zu Schaumburg-Lippe* (Rinteln, 1968), pp. 46–8.

40. BL MS Lansdowne 1013, f. 203, Dr White Kennet to Rev. Samuel Blackwell (9 November 1716).

41. Cowper (1864), p. 127; BL Add 78465, f. 79v, Mrs Boscawen to Lady Evelyn (8 November 1716).

42. Cowper (1864), p. 127.

43. Kroll (1998), p. 201 (1 December 1716).

44. *The London Gazette* No. 5587 (5 November 1717).

45. Thomson (1847), p. 333, Countess Cowper to Mrs Clayton (undated but about the time that the Duke of Cumberland was born).

46. BL Add MS 20102, f. 24, Lady Carteret to Mrs Clayton (19 December 1724).

47. Ilchester (1950), p. 257.

48. RA GEO/ADD 17/75/85 (1733); Marschner (1997), p. 31.

49. Medical information kindly provided by Dr Randle McRoberts.

50. HMC *Egmont*, Vol. 2 (1923), p. 443.

51. Walpole, *Reminiscences* (1818 edn), pp. 89, 90.

52. Duchess of Marlborough to the second Earl of Stair (1 December 1737), quoted in Cunningham (1857), Vol. 1, p. cxlviii.

53. Hervey (1931), Vol. 3, p. 890.

54. Wraxall (1904), p. 257.

55. Sir Robert Walpole to his brother Horace Walpole (15 November 1737), quoted in Jesse (1843), Vol. 3, pp. 106–7.

56. Saussure (1902), p. 46.

57. Ilchester (1950), p. 182.

58. HMC *Egmont*, Vol. 2 (1923), p. 319.

59. Burford (1988), p. 42.

60. Pottle (1950), p. 227.

61. Hervey (1931), Vol. 3, p. 891.

62. Franklin (1993), p. 95.

63. Hervey (1931), Vol. 2, p. 490.

64. Nicolas Venette, *Conjugal Love Reveal'd* (seventh, English edn of 1720), pp. 161, 118.

65. Anon., *The Ladies Physical Directory* ('the eighth edition, with some very material additions', London, 1742), p. 70.

66. Harvey (1994; 2001), pp. 40–1.

67. 'Prostitution' in *The Westminster and Foreign Quarterly Review*, Vol. 53 (April–July 1850), p. 457.

68. Thomas Laqueur, *Making Sex, Body and Gender from the Greeks to Freud* (Cambridge, Massachusetts, and London, 1990).

69. Hervey (1931), Vol. 2, p. 609.

70. Verney (1930), Vol. 2, p. 129 (10 August 1738).

71. HMC *Egmont*, Vol. 2 (1923), pp. 424, 299.

72. Hervey (1931), Vol. 2, pp. 457, 502, 503.

73. BL Add MS 23728, f. 15, Countess of Hertford to Lady Luxborough (8 November 1745).

74. Coxe (1798b), Vol. 1, p. 272.

75. HMC *Egmont*, Vol. 2 (1923), p. 445.

76. TNA SP 84/161, p. 543, Poley to Harley (Hanover, 9 June 1705).

77. The Elector of Hanover to Privy Councillor von Eltz, Hanover (17 June 1705), quoted in Wilkins (1901), Vol. 1, p. 44.

78. Documents in the Royal Archives at Hanover, quoted in Wilkins (1901), Vol. 1, pp. 48–54.

79. TNA SP 84/161, p. 594, Poley to Harley (Hanover, 28 July 1705).

80. Preussisches Staatsarchiv, Hanover, MS Y. 46c, XI, ff. 106–111, quoted in Arkell (1939), pp. 23–4.

81. Hervey (1931), Vol. 2, pp. 641–2.

82. Advertised in the back of William Beckett, *A Collection of Chirurgical Tracts* (London, 1740).

83. Walpole, *Reminiscences* (1818 edn), p. 28.

84. Lewis (1937–83), Vol. 38, p. 456 (1 November 1764).

85. Cartwright (1883), p. 533.

86. Hervey (1931), Vol. 3, p. 906; Cartwright (1883), p. 533.

87. 'Some curious Observations made (by my Friend John Ranby, Esq; Surgeon to his Majesty's Household, and F.R.S.) in the Dissection of Three Subjects, 1728', in Beckett (1740), pp. 77–9.

88. Henry Fielding, *Tom Jones* (London, 1749; 1991), p. 302.

89. HMC *Egmont*, Vol. 2 (1923), pp. 444–6.

90. Hastings Wheler (1935), p. 153, Lady Catherine Jones (24 December 1737).

91. Brown (1700), p. 93.

92. John Ashton, *Social Life in the Reign of Queen Anne* (London, 1882), p. 8.

93. Hervey (1931), Vol. 3, p. 881.

94. *Ibid.*, p. 889.

95. Burford (1988), p. 31.

96. Hervey (1931), Vol. 2, pp. 580–2.

97. Brooke (1985), Vol. 1, pp. 151–2.

98. Hervey (1931), Vol. 3, pp. 885, 889.

99. HMC *Egmont*, Vol. 2 (1923), pp. 443–4.

100. *Ibid.*, pp. 445–6.

101. Lady Jane van Koughnet, *A History of Tyttenhanger* (London, 1895), p. 78, 'Copy'd from a Letter of Mrs. Purcel (a Dresser to ye late Queen) to a Lady at Bath'; another copy is at RA GEO/MAIN/52824, catalogued as 'copy of a letter from Mrs Selwyn to Mrs Lowther' (soon after 29 November 1737).

102. HMC *Egmont*, Vol. 2 (1923), p. 444.

103. BL 22227, f. 185, Peter Wentworth to his brother (19 November 1737).

104. Hervey (1931), Vol. 3, pp. 905–6.

105. Alexander Pope, 'On Queen *Caroline's* Death-bed', in Norman Ault and John Butt (Eds), *Alexander Pope, Minor Poems* (London and New York, 1964), p. 390.

106. HMC *Egmont*, Vol. 2 (1923), p. 445.

107. Hervey (1894), Vol. 3, p. 177, Lady Bristol to Lord Bristol (19 November 1737).

108. Koughnet (1895), pp. 77–8.

109. Hervey (1931), Vol. 3, p. 896.

110. Koughnet (1895), pp. 77–8.

111. HMC *Egmont*, Vol. 2 (1923), pp. 445–6.

112. Hastings Wheler (1935), p. 153, Lady Catherine Jones (24 December 1737).

113. HMC *Report on the Manuscripts of the Earl of Denbigh*, part V (London, 1911), p. 225, J. Stanhope to Lady Denbigh (16 December 1737).

114. Clarke (1738), p. 35.

115. Hailes (1788), p. 13.

116. Jesse (1843), Vol. 3, p. 83.

117. Williams (1963–5), Vol. 5, p. 75, Charles Ford to Jonathan Swift (22 November 1737).

118. Hastings Wheler (1935), p. 153, Lady Catherine Jones (24 December 1737).

119. Clarke (1738), p. 8.

120. Koughnet (1895), pp. 77–8.

121. *Ibid.*, p. 78.

122. Cartwright (1883), p. 532.

123. Hennell (1904), pp. 194–5.

124. *The Gentleman's Magazine*, Vol. 7 (December 1737), p. 765.

125. Hastings Wheler (1935), p. 153, Lady Catherine Jones (24 December 1737).

126. Hailes (1788), p. 37.

127. BL Add MS 74005, f. 21, 'Sketch of Mr Walpole's conduct'.

128. Hailes (1788), p. 40.

129. Coxe (1798b), Vol. 2, pp. 547–8.

130. Cartwright (1883), p. 538.

131. Ilchester (1950), p. 275.

132. Hervey (1894), Vol. 3, p. 188, Lady Bristol to Lord Bristol (13 December 1737).

133. Hervey (1931), Vol. 2, p. 577.

134. *Ibid.*, p. 579; Cowper (1864), p. 11.

135. Hervey (1931), Vol. 2, p. 581; Vol. 3, p. 922.

136. *Ibid.*, Vol. 2, p. 580.

137. BL Add MS 27735, f. 123r, Lord Gower (25 March 1736).

138. Cartwright (1883), p. 532.

139. BL Add MS 22227, f. 162v, Peter Wentworth to his brother (3 June 1735).

140. *Ibid.*, f. 94r, Peter Wentworth to his brother (2 October 1729).

141. *Ibid.*, f. 85r, Peter Wentworth to his brother (21 August 1729).

142. *Ibid.*, f. 163, Peter Wentworth to his brother (9 August 1735).

143. BL Add MS 22229, ff. 216–17, Captain William Wentworth to Earl of Strafford (26 November 1737).

144. Hervey (1894), Vol. 3, pp. 192–3, Lady Bristol to Lord Bristol (22 December 1737).

145. Koughnet (1895), p. 77.

146. Quoted in Trench, p. 203.

147. Halsband and Grundy (1977), pp. 105–6.

148. HMC *Egmont*, Vol. 2 (1923), p. 459.

149. Halsband and Grundy (1977), pp. 105–6.

150. Anon., *The annual register, or a view of the history, politics, and literature for the years 1784 and 1785* (London, 1787), p. 44, 'a particular Account of Peter the Wild Boy; extracted from the Parish Register of North Church, in the County of Hertford'.

151. Sherburn (1956), Vol. 3, p. 58, Pope to Swift (9 October 1729); John Boyle, fifth Earl of Orrery, *Remarks on the life and writings of Dr Jonathan Swift* (London, 1752), p. 164.

152. Anon., *It cannot Rain*, part 2 (London, 1726), p. 7.

153. Robert Joseph Phillimore (Ed.), *Memoirs and Correspondence of George, Lord Lyttelton, from 1734 to 1773* (London, 1845), Vol. 1, p. 89, Lord Chesterfield (15 November 1737).

154. Hervey (1931), Vol. 3, p. 904.

CHAPTER 9: THE RIVAL MISTRESSES

1. Hervey (1931), Vol. 2, p. 609.

2. Hailes (1788), p. 39.

3. Hervey (1931), Vol. 3, p. 904.

4. *Ibid.*, Vol. 2, p. 609.

5. Hervey (1744), p. 16.

6. Hervey (1931), Vol. 3, p. 918.

7. Matthew Kilburn, 'Wallmoden, Amalie Sophie Marianne von, suo jure count-ess of Yarmouth (1704–1765)', *Oxford Dictionary of National Biography* (Oxford, 2004).

8. Hervey (1931), Vol. 2, p. 609.

9. Brooke (1985), Vol. 1, p. 117.

10. Hervey (1931), Vol. 2, p. 603; translation by Katherine Ibbett.

11. HMC 11th Report, Appendix, Part IV, *The Manuscripts of the Marquess Townshend* (London, 1887), p. 356, Ashe Windham to [Charles, third Viscount Townshend?] (22 June 1738).

12. *General Evening Post*, issue 5674 (22 February 1770), Baron Bielfield, 'A Character of the celebrated Countess of Yarmouth'; Hervey (1931), Vol. 2, p. 457.

13. *General Evening Post, ibid.*

14. Hervey (1931), Vol. 2, p. 484.

15. *Ibid.*, p. 486.

16. HMC *Egmont*, Vol. 2 (1923), pp. 369–70.

17. Hervey (1931), Vol. 2, pp. 507–8.

18. *Ibid.*, p. 539.

19. *Ibid.*, p. 610.

20. *Ibid.*, p. 604.

21. HMC *Egmont*, Vol. 2 (1923), p. 307.

22. Hervey (1931), Vol. 2, pp. 604–5; Brooke (1985), Vol. 1, p. 117.

23. HMC *Egmont*, Vol. 2 (1923), p. 304.

24. Duchess of Marlborough to the second Earl of Stair (20 June 1738), quoted in Cunningham (1857), Vol. 1, p. clii.

25. HMC *Egmont*, Vol. 2 (1923), p. 503.

26. Grundy (1999), p. 383.

27. Kensington Public Library, 'Extra illustrated' edition of Thomas Faulkner, *History and Antiquities of Kensington* (London, 1820) (3-volume version), Vol. 3, item 258; Gaunt and Knight (1988–9), Vol. 2, p. 487.

28. Lewis (1937–83), Vol. 20, p. 88 (17 August 1749).

29. *General Evening Post*, issue 5674 (22 February 1770), Baron Bielfield, 'A Character of the celebrated Countess of Yarmouth'.

30. HMC 11th Report, p. 356, Ashe Windham to [Charles, third Viscount Townshend?] (22 June 1738).

31. Duchess of Marlborough to the second Earl of Stair (20 June 1738), quoted in Cunningham (1857), Vol. 1, p. clii.

32. *General Evening Post*, issue 5674 (22 February 1770), Baron Bielfield, 'A Character of the celebrated Countess of Yarmouth'.

33. Hervey (1744), pp. 16–17.

34. *General Evening Post*, issue 5674 (22 February 1770), Baron Bielfield, 'A Character of the celebrated Countess of Yarmouth'.

35. BL Add MS 6856, ff. 1–5.

36. Brooke (1985), Vol. 1, pp. 118–19.

37. *Daily Journal*, issue 1442, p. 2 (30 August 1725).

38. *Daily Post*, issue 3516 (25 December 1730); BL Add MS 22229, f. 49, Lord

Wentworth to his father the Earl of Strafford (26 December 1730).

39. *Daily Courant*, issue 5525 (21 December 1733).

40. Thomson (1847), Countess of Pomfret to Mrs Clayton (7 August 1731), Vol. 2, p. 49.

41. Jonathan Swift, *Directions to Servants* (London, 1745), p. 93.

42. Ilchester (1950), p. 149.

43. Thomson (1847), Countess of Pembroke to Mrs Clayton (n.d.) Vol. 1, p. 227.

44. BL Add MS 27732, f. 57v, Henrietta Howard to Lord Essex (19 November n.y.).

45. *London Evening Post*, issue 995 (4 April 1734).

46. *General Evening Post*, issue 241 (15 April 1735).

47. SRO 941/47/4, p. 226, John Hervey to Stephen Fox (30 September 1731).

48. Pöllnitz (1739), Vol. 2, p. 460.

49. Hervey (1931), Vol. 3, p. 745.

50. *Ibid.*, p. 919; Brooke (1985), Vol. 1, p. 118.

51. *Ibid.*, Vol. 2, p. 491.

52. SRO 941/47/4, p. 225, John Hervey to Stephen Fox (30 September 1731).

53. *Ibid.*, p. 323, John Hervey to Ste Fox (21 December 1732).

54. Ilchester (1950), pp. 101, 109.

55. *London Evening Post*, issue 1761 (24 February 1739).

56. SRO 941/47/4, pp. 169–70, John Hervey to Ste Fox (4 September 1731).

57. Franklin (1993), p. 97.

58. SRO 941/47/4, p. 226, John Hervey to Ste Fox (30 September 1731).

59. William Drogo Montagu, seventh duke of Manchester, *Court and Society from Elizabeth to Anne, edited from the papers at Kimbolton* (London, 1864), Vol. 2, p. 330.

60. Hervey (1931), Vol. 2, p. 498.

61. *Ibid.*, Vol. 3, pp. 744–8.

62. 'An Epistle from Ld. Lovel to Lord Chesterfield at Bath, Wrote by Mr Poulteney', quoted in James (1929), p. 230.

63. SRO 941/47/4, p. 337, John Hervey to Ste Fox (30 December 1731); Franklin (1993), p. 97.

64. Hervey (1931), Vol. 3, pp. 919–20.

65. Quoted in Harvey (1994; 2001), p. 57.

66. Brooke (1985), Vol. 1, p. 118.

67. Thomson (1847), Vol. 1, p. 240, Countess of Pembroke to Mrs Clayton (n.d.).

68. Hervey (1931), Vol. 3, p. 853.

69. Quoted in Borman (2007), p. 95.

70. Brian Fitzgerald (Ed.), *Correspondence of Emily, Duchess of Leinster* (Dublin, 1949–57), Vol. 1, p. 67 (26 April 1759).

71. Stanhope (1774), Vol. 1, pp. 330–1.

72. SRO 941/48/1, p. 58, Mary Hervey to the Reverend Edmund Morris (20 July 1744).

73. Stanhope (1774), Vol. 1, pp. 330–2.

74. Hailes (1788), p. 120.

75. 'Account of the court of George the First' in Wharncliffe (1861), Vol. 1, p. 125.

76. Cowper (1864), p. 132.

77. Caroline to Melusine (5 June 1727), quoted in Wilkins (1901), Vol. 2, pp. 26–7.

78. Walpole, *Reminiscences* (1818 edn), pp. 28–9.

79. Lewis (1937–83), Vol. 33, p. 529 (28 September 1786).

80. Wilkins (1901), Vol. 1, p. 251.

81. Sedgwick (1939), p. 37, George III to Bute (?winter 1759–60).

82. Wraxall (1904), p. 255.

83. *The Gentleman's Magazine*, Vol. 5.6 (April, 1736), p. 230.

84. James Howard Harris, third Earl of Malmesbury (Ed.), *Letters of the First Earl of Malmesbury* (London, 1870), Vol. 1, p. 80 (3 December 1754).

85. John Cleland, *Fanny Hill or Memoirs of a Woman of Pleasure* (London, 1748–9; Harmondsworth, 1985), p. 41.

86. Hervey (1931), Vol. 2, p. 507.

87. SRO 941/48/1, p. 40, Mary Hervey to the Reverend Edmund Morris (2 March 1744).

88. BL Add MS 32896, f. 140v, Newcastle to Lord Hardwicke (copy) (28 September 1759).

89. Quoted in Edwards (1947), p. 7.

90. William Cavendish, fourth duke of Devonshire, *Memoranda on the State of Affairs, 1759–1762*, Eds P. D. Brown and K. W. Schweizer, Camden Society, fourth series, Vol. 27 (London, 1982), p. 50 (30 October 1760).

91. Aubrey Newman, *The World Turned Inside Out: New Views on George II*, inaugural lecture, Leicester University (1988), p. 6.

92. Coxe (1798b), Vol. 1, p. 271.

93. J. C. D. Clark (Ed.), *The Memoirs and Speeches of James, 2nd Earl Waldegrave* (Cambridge, 1988), p. 147 (1758).

94. BL Add MS 38507, f. 248, Lord Townshend to the king (24 September 1728).

95. BL Add MS 32703, f. 282r (26 August 1744).

96. BL Stowe MS 308, f. 4r.

97. Hervey (1931), Vol. 2, p. 340.

98. Owen (1973), p. 123.

99. Anon., *George the Third, His Court and Family* (London, 1820), p. 88.

100. Hervey (1931), Vol. 2, p. 341.

101. BL Add MS 9176, f. 34r, old Horace Walpole to Robert Trevor (22 February 1740).

102. BL Add MS 23814, f. 597 (12/23 June 1743).

103. Pöllnitz (1739), Vol. 2, p. 436.

104. F. J. Manning (Ed.), *The Williamson Letters, 1748–1765*, publications of the Bedfordshire Historical Record Society, Vol. XXXIV (Luton, 1954), p. 43, Tidy Williamson to Edmund Williamson (5 June 1759).

105. Pöllnitz (1739), Vol. 2, p. 462.

106. Joan Glasheen, *The Secret People of the Palaces* (London, 1998), p. 112.

107. Pöllnitz (1739), Vol. 2, p. 460.

108. Richard Campbell, *The London tradesman. Being a compendious view of all the trades, professions, arts, both liberal and mechanic, now practised* (London, 1747), p. 212.

109. Llanover (1861), Vol. 2, p. 28.

110. Alexander Pope, 'Epistle to a Lady', in F. W. Bateson (Ed.), *Alexander Pope, Epistles to Several Persons* (London and New Haven, 1961), p. 64.

111. SRO 941/48/1, p. 367, Mary Hervey to the Reverend Edmund Morris (25 September 1759).

112. *Ibid.*, p. 206, Mary Hervey to the Reverend Edmund Morris (24 October 1747).
113. Mowl (2006), p. 230.
114. *The Walpole Society*, Vol. 22 (Oxford, 1933–4) (Vertue III), p. 115.
115. BL Add MS 75358, William Kent to the Earl of Burlington (28 November 1738).
116. Quoted in Wilson (1984), p. 85.
117. Highfill, Burnim and Langhams (1973), Vol. 2, p. 451.
118. Walpole (1771), Vol. 4, p. 116.
119. Chatsworth MS, William Kent to Lady Burlington (7 October 1738), quoted in Wilson (1984), p. 87.
120. *The Walpole Society,* Vol. 22 (Oxford, 1933–4) (Vertue III), p. 140.
121. BL Add MS 22227, f. 103, Juliana Wentworth (Peter's wife) to Lord Strafford (8 December 1729).
122. Cartwright (1883), pp. 533–4.
123. *London Evening Post*, issue 1742 (11 January 1739).
124. Cartwright (1883), pp. 533–4.
125. BL Add 22229, f. 217v (1737).
126. HMC *Egmont*, Vol. 3 (1923), p. 240; Cannon (2004).
127. Lewis (1937–83), Vol. 17, p. 337 (18 February 1741/2); Cannon (2004).
128. Thomson (1847), Vol. 2, p. 349.
129. Sherburn (1956), Vol. 1, p. 412, Lady Mary Wortley Montagu to Alexander Pope (17 June 1717).
130. Stanhope (1774), Vol. 1, p. 287.
131. Horace Walpole writes on 8 October 1742 of events that had clearly taken place very recently. Lewis (1937–83), Vol. 18, p. 71 (8 October 1742).
132. John Hervey quoted in Lewis (1937–83), Vol. 18, p. 82 (16 October 1742 OS).
133. Croker (1824), Vol. 2, p. 65, Lord Chesterfield to Lady Suffolk (17 August 1733).
134. Lewis (1937–83) Vol. 17, p. 188 (2 November 1741 OS).
135. *Ibid.*, Vol. 18, p. 71 (8 October 1742 OS).
136. Franklin (1993), p. 97.
137. Lewis (1937–83), Vol. 18, p. 71 (8 October 1742 OS).
138. *Ibid.*, Vol. 21, p. 191 (14 April 1758).
139. *Daily Advertiser*, issue 3992 (3 November 1743).
140. *Daily Advertiser*, issue 3998 (10 November 1743).
141. *London Evening Post*, issue 2655 (10 November 1744).
142. Hervey (1744), pp. 16–17, 12.

CHAPTER 10: THE CIRCLE BREAKS

1. Brooke (1985), Vol. 2, p. 3.
2. TNA LS 9/177 (24 October 1760).
3. Lewis (1937–83), Vol. 20, p. 88 (17 August 1749 OS); p. 89 (12 September 1749 OS).
4. BL Add MS 20101, f. 49r (29 January 1759).
5. Lewis (1937–83), Vol. 20, p. 438 (5 July 1754).
6. Clark (1988), p. 147 (1758).
7. Simond (1815), Vol. 1, p. 162.

8. Mr Kendal of Lord Ashburnham's Troop, writing in *The Gentleman's Magazine*, Vol. 13 (July 1743), p. 387.

9. Kensington Public Library, 'Extra illustrated' edition of Thomas Faulkner, *History and Antiquities of Kensington* (London, 1820) (3-volume version), Vol. 3, item 205b (17 August 1743).

10. HMC, *14th Report*, appendix 9, p. 523, 'note on the rebellion of 1745'.

11. Quoted in Black (2007), p. 197.

12. Wraxall (1904), p. 257.

13. Cannon (2004).

14. Frank McLynn, *1759, The Year Britain Became Master of the World* (London, 2004), p. 233.

15. Wraxall (1904), pp. 257–8.

16. Cowper (1864), p. 143.

17. John Wood, *An Essay towards a Description of Bath* (London, 1749), Vol. 2, preface.

18. BL Add MS 20101, f. 36v (4 December, n.y.).

19. Walpole, *Reminiscences* (1818 edn), p. 101.

20. Halsband (1965–7), Vol. 2, p. 306 (29/18 June 1743).

21. SRO 941/53/1, p. 210, William Hervey's commonplace book.

22. Quoted in Stuart (1936), p. 119.

23. Mrs Russell to Lieutenant-Colonel Charles Russell (August 1743), quoted in Sydenham Hervey, *Journals of the Hon. William Hervey* (Bury St Edmunds, 1906), introduction, p. xxxix.

24. SRO 941/48/1, p. 191, Mary Hervey to the Reverend Edmund Morris (18 November 1743).

25. *Ibid.*, p. 377, Mary Hervey to the Reverend Edmund Morris (15 December 1760).

26. Lewis (1937–83), Vol. 23, p. 78 (2 December 1768).

27. *Ibid.*, Vol. 33, p. 37 (7 August 1778).

28. Elizabeth Mavor, *The Virgin Duchess, A Study in Survival: The Life of the Duchess of Kingston* (London, 1964), pp. 38–9.

29. Augustus Hervey, *Augustus Hervey's Journal*, Ed. David Erskine (Rochester, 2002), p. 77.

30. *Ibid.*, p. xxx.

31. Thomas Wright, *England under the House of Hanover* (London, 1848), Vol. 1, p. 343, note.

32. Quoted in Mavor (1964), p. 57.

33. Lewis (1937–83), Vol. 20, pp. 212–13 (22 December 1750 OS).

34. SRO 941/21/2(ii), 'A Character of Lady Mary Hervey', f. 3.

35. Lady Louisa Stuart to Lord Wharncliffe, quoted in Stuart (1936), p. 145.

36. Lewis (1937–83), Vol. 37, p. 308 (14 July 1751).

37. Hervey (1931), Vol. 2, p. 581.

38. *The Walpole Society*, Vol. 22 (1933–4) (Vertue III), p. 140.

39. Sir Thomas Robinson quoted in Jourdain (1948), p. 41.

40. Anonymous satirical poem at Chatsworth, quoted in Wilson (1984), p. 250.

41. *The Walpole Society*, Vol. 22 (1933–4) (Vertue III), p. 140.

42. Will of William Kent (April 1748), quoted in Jourdain (1948), p. 89.

43. Highfill, Burnim and Langhams (1973), Vol. 2, p. 451.

44. I'm grateful to John Harris for suggesting this.

45. Hervey (1931), Vol. 2, p. 539.

46. Philip Stanhope, Earl of Chesterfield, *Lord Chesterfield's witticisms* (London, 1775), p. 37.

47. Alexander Fergusson (Ed.), *Letters and Journals of Mrs Calderwood of Polton from England, Holland and the Low Countries in 1756* (Edinburgh, 1884), pp. 31–2.

48. Walpole, *Reminiscences* (1818 edn), p. 97.

49. Anon., *George the Third* (1820), p. 100.

50. SRO 941/48/1, p. 353, Mary Hervey to the Reverend Edmund Morris (21 November 1758).

51. Fergusson (1884), p. 32.

52. Hervey (1931), Vol. 1, p. 278.

53. Yorke (1913), Vol. 3, pp. 110–11.

54. J. A. Home (Ed.), *The letters and journals of Lady Mary Coke* (Edinburgh, 1889–96), Vol. 1, 'Memoir by Lady Louisa Stuart', p. lxxx.

55. HMC, 12th Report, appendix, Part X, *The Manuscripts and Correspondence of James, first earl of Charlemont* (London, 1891–4), Vol. 1, p. 14.

56. Horace Walpole, 'Horace Walpole's Journals of Visits to Country Seats', Ed. Paget Toynbee, *The Walpole Society*, Vol. 16 (Oxford, 1927–8), p. 16.

57. Burford (1988), p. 31.

58. Horace Walpole, 'Horace Walpole's Journals of Visits to Country Seats', Ed. Paget Toynbee, *The Walpole Society*, Vol. 16 (Oxford, 1927–8), p. 16.

59. Clark (1988), pp. 147–8 (1758).

60. Yorke (1913), Vol. 3, p. 111.

61. 'Introductory anecdotes', probably based on information from Lady Bute, in Wharncliffe (1837), p. 77.

62. Brooke (1985), Vol. 1, p. 120.

63. *Ibid.*, p. 152.

64. Fergusson (1884), p. 31.

65. Royal Archives, quoted in Edwards (1947), p. 164.

66. Lord Berkeley of Stratton quoted in Aston (2008), p. 188.

67. Anon., *George the Third* (1820), p. 119.

68. Rose (1831), Vol. 1, p. 187, diary of Hugh, Earl of Marchmont (1747).

69. *The Gentleman's Magazine*, Vol. 21 (March 1751), p. 140.

70. Wraxall (1904), pp. 251–2.

71. Anon., *George the Third* (1820), p. 128.

72. Holland (1846), Vol. 1, p. 83.

73. Lady Firebrace to Lady Denbigh, quoted in Young (1937), p. 218.

74. Holland (1846), Vol. 1, p. 87.

75. John Carswell and Lewis Arnold Dralle (Eds), *The Political Journal of George Bubb Dodington* (Oxford, 1965), pp. 112–13 (13 April 1751).

76. Aston (2008), p. 187.

77. Sedgwick (1939), pp. 40–1, the future George III to Lord Bute (winter 1759–60).

78. Frankland-Russell-Astley MSS, 253, quoted in W. A. Speck, 'William Augustus, Prince, duke of Cumberland (1721–1765)', *Oxford Dictionary of National Biography* (Oxford, 2004).

79. Speck (2004).
80. Staffordshire Record Office MS D/798/3/1/1, F. O. Eld to J. Eld (23 November 1745), quoted in Speck (2004).
81. Brooke (1985), Vol. 1, p. 55.
82. *Ibid.*, Vol. 2, p. 282.
83. Yorke (1913), Vol. 3, p. 184.
84. Lewis (1937–83) Vol. 20, p. 88 (17 August 1749 OS).
85. Home, Vol. 1 (1889), 'Memoir by Lady Louisa Stuart', p. lxxix.
86. *General Evening Post*, issue 5674 (22 February 1770), Baron Bielfield, 'A Character of the celebrated Countess of Yarmouth'.
87. BL Add MS 22629, f. 82v, A. Pitt to Henrietta Berkeley (10 November 1758).
88. BL Add MS 32896, f. 136v, Newcastle to Lord Hardwicke (copy) (27 September 1759).
89. Quoted in Alan Hardy, *The Kings' Mistresses* (London, 1980), p. 91.
90. Brooke (1985), Vol. 2, p. 183.
91. BL Add MS 32904, f. 428, Lady Yarmouth to Newcastle (18 April 1760).
92. HMC *Egmont*, Vol. 2 (1923), p. 459.
93. Lewis (1937–83), Vol. 9, p. 51 (2 July 1747); *Public Advertiser*, issue 11715 (30 September 1772).
94. Brooke (1985), Vol. 1, p. 119.
95. *Ibid.*, Vol. 3, p. 49.
96. *Ibid.*, Vol. 1, pp. 151–2.
97. *Ibid.*, Vol. 2, p. 295; Hastings Wheler (1935), p. 153 Lady Catherine Jones (24 December 1737).
98. Brooke (1985), Vol. 2, p. 295.
99. *Ibid.*, p. 23.
100. BL Egerton MS 1710, f. 271, Princess Amelia to Princess Anne (19 July 1757).
101. David Williamson, 'Mary, Princess (1723–1772)', *Oxford Dictionary of National Biography* (Oxford, 2004).
102. Montagu (1864), Vol. 2, p. 335.
103. Tillyard (2006), p. 31.
104. Home, Vol. 1 (1889), 'Memoir by Lady Louisa Stuart', p. lxxxi.
105. Yorke (1913), Vol. 3, p. 170.
106. BL Add MS 22629, f. 39v, George Berkeley to Henrietta (1735?), f. 40v, Henrietta to George Berkeley (1735?).
107. Borman (2007), p. 179.
108. Miss Mary Laetitia Hawkins on Horace Walpole, quoted in Stuart (1936), p. 187.
109. Lewis (1937–83), Vol. 33, p. 270 (8 June 1747).
110. *Ibid.*, Vol. 9, p. 318 (4 November 1760).
111. Kensington Public Library, 'Extra illustrated' edition of Thomas Faulkner, *History and Antiquities of Kensington* (London, 1820), 3-volume version, Vol. 3, item 328 (2 April 1759).
112. Lewis (1937–83), Vol. 9, p. 312 (25 October 1760).
113. Fergusson (1884), p. 31.
114. Yorke (1913), Vol. 3, p. 253.
115. Manning (1954), p. 63, Talbot Williamson to Edmund Williamson (28 October 1760).
116. Lewis (1937–83), Vol. 9, p. 311 (25 October 1760).

117. Yorke (1913), Vol. 3, p. 253.

118. Lewis (1937–83), Vol. 9, p. 311 (25 October 1760).

119. Borman (2007), p. 268.

120. See, for example, BL Egerton 1710, f. 1v.

121. *The Gentleman's Magazine*, Vol. 30 (October 1760), p. 486.

122. Hervey (1931), Vol. 3, p. 913.

123. *The Gentleman's Magazine*, Vol. 30 (October 1760), p. 486.

124. *Ibid.*, p. 487.

125. TNA LS 9/48 (25 October 1760).

126. Lord Chamberlain's Office (28 October 1760), *The Gentleman's Magazine*, Vol. 30 (October 1760), p. 488; *The London Chronicle* (25–28 October 1760), Vol. 8, No. 599, p. 410.

127. Manning (1954), p. 28, Talbot Williamson to Edmund Williamson (26 January 1758).

128. Llanover (1861), Vol. 3, pp. 606–7.

129. Manning (1954), pp. 63–4, Talbot Williamson to Edmund Williamson (30 October 1760).

130. *The London Chronicle* (25–28 October 1760), Vol. 8, No. 599, p. 410.

131. Lewis (1937–83), Vol. 9, p. 314 (28 October 1760).

132. Hennell (1904), p. 194.

133. HMC *Egmont*, Vol. 2 (1923), p. 454.

134. Samuel Chandler, *The character of a great and good king* (London, 1760), p. 1.

135. Lord Berkeley of Stratton quoted in Aston (2008), p. 183.

136. Sarah Stanley (7 December 1760), quoted in Black (2007), p. 254.

137. Quoted in Christopher Hibbert, *George III, A Personal History* (London, 1998), p. 77.

138. Cavendish, William (1982), p. 41 (27 October 1760).

139. BL Add MS 22627, ff. 10–11.

140. Lewis (1937–83), Vol. 9, p. 314–15 (28 October 1760).

141. Cavendish, William (1982), p. 49 (30 October 1760).

142. Gaunt and Knight (1988–9), Vol. 2, chapter 4, p. 521.

143. BL Add MS 33069, f. 295, J. Twells to the duke of Newcastle (31 October 1765).

144. *The Gentleman's Magazine*, Vol. 35 (November, 1765), p. 534.

145. Kilburn, 'Wallmoden' (2004).

146. Chatsworth MS 332/20, Cumberland to Devonshire (31 October 1762), quoted in Rex Whitworth, *William Augustus, Duke of Cumberland: A Life* (London, 1992), p. 218.

147. Lewis (1937–83), Vol. 9, p. 318 (4 November 1760).

148. *Ibid.*, Vol. 10, p. 245 (31 July 1767).

149. Anon., *Court tales: or, a History of the Amours of the Present Nobility* (London, 1717), title page.

150. Lewis (1937–83), Vol. 31, pp. 416, 417.

151. Lewis (1937–83), Vol. 31, p. 16, Horace Walpole to Molly Hervey (12 January 1760); p. ix, introduction.

152. 'Song, by the Earl of Peterborough', quoted in Croker (1824), Vol. 1, p. xlvii.

153. Lewis (1937–83), Vol. 10, p. 118 (11 January 1764).

154. *Ibid.*, Vol. 22, p. 324 (12 August 1765).

155. BL Add MS 22626, f. 121v, Horace Walpole to Henrietta (3 July 1765).

156. *Ibid.*, f. 122v, Horace Walpole to Henrietta (20 September 1765).

157. Croker (1824), Vol. 2, p. 122, Lord Bathurst to Lady Suffolk (26 November 1734).

158. BL Add MS 22629, f. 127r, M. Vere to Henrietta (16 August n.y.).

159. Alexander Pope, *The Impertinent, or a Visit to the Court* (London, 1733), p. 12.

160. E. H. Chalus, 'Amelia, Princess (1711–1786)', *Oxford Dictionary of National Biography* (Oxford, 2004).

161. Anon., *The annual register, or a view of the history, politics, and literature for the years 1784 and 1785* (London, 1787), p. 44, 'a particular Account of Peter the Wild Boy; extracted from the Parish Register of North Church, in the County of Hertford'; Burnet (1779–99), Vol. 3 (London and Edinburgh, 1784), p. 371.

CHAPTER II: THE SURVIVORS

1. Walpole, *Reminiscences* (1818 edn), p. 9.

2. Jesse (1843), Vol. 2, p. 327.

3. Davies (1938); Owen (1973), pp. 113–34; Newman (1988); Black (2007).

4. William Thackeray, *The Four Georges* (London, 1848), p. 48; Smith (2006), p. 7.

5. Anon., *George the Third* (1820), p. 3.

6. Burford (1988), p. 31.

7. Home, Vol. 1 (1889), 'Memoir by Lady Louisa Stuart', p. lxxxvii.

8. Princess Marie Louise, writing about her grandmother, in *My Memories of Six Reigns* (London, 1956), p. 142.

9. Harcourt MSS, Princess Elizabeth to Elizabeth, Lady Harcourt (8 July 1793), quoted in Flora Fraser, *Princesses, the Six Daughters of George III* (London, 2004), p. 147.

10. Brown (1700), p. 11.

11. Matthews (1939), p. 76 (15 August 1715); Llanover (1861), Vol. 1, p. 556 (1736); Lord Berkeley of Stratton quoted in Aston (2008), p. 188.

12. Brooke (1985), Vol. 1, p. 122.

13. BL Egerton MS 1710, f. 7, Princess Amelia to Countess of Portland (4 October n.y.).

14. Lewis (1937–83), Vol. 22, p. 544 (31 July 1767).

15. *Ibid.*, Vol. 35, p. 321 (29 July 1767).

16. Quoted in Borman (2007), p. 285.

17. SRO 941/48/1, p. 437, Mary Hervey to the Reverend Edmund Morris (22 June 1768).

18. Lady Louisa Stuart quoted in Stuart (1936), p. 182.

19. Lewis (1937–83), Vol. 23, p. 59 (22 September 1768).

20. Sir Charles Hanbury Williams, quoted in Hervey (1931), Vol. 1, p. xviii.

21. Maria Edgeworth, *Practical Education* (London, 1798), p. 64.

22. *Gazetteer and New Daily Advertiser*, issue 11, 808 (8 January 1767).

23. *Notes and Queries*, sixth series (11 October 1884), p. 294; Anon., *The annual register, or a view of the history, politics, and literature for the years 1784 and 1785* (London, 1787), p. 45, 'a particular Account of Peter the Wild Boy; extracted from the Parish Register of North Church, in the County of Hertford'.

24. Conversation with parishioners at St Mary, Northchurch (25 May 2007).

25. Andrew Morton, *Inside Kensington Palace* (London, 1987), p. 8.

Index

A NOTE ON THE TYPE

The text of this book is set in Adobe Caslon, named after the
English punch-cutter and type-founder William Caslon I
(1692–1766). Caslon's rather old-fashioned types were
modelled on seventeenth-century Dutch designs, but found
wide acceptance throughout the English-speaking world for
much of the eighteenth century until being replaced by newer
types towards the end of the century. Used in 1776 to print
the Declaration of Independence, they were revived in the
nineteenth century, and have been popular ever since,
particularly amongst fine printers. There are several digital
versions, of which Carol Twombly's Adobe Caslon is one.